Land Rover
Series II, IIA and III
Restoration Manual

Land Rover Series II, IIA and III Restoration Manual

Emrys Kirby

THE CROWOOD PRESS

First published in 2023 by
The Crowood Press Ltd
Ramsbury, Marlborough
Wiltshire SN8 2HR

enquiries@crowood.com

www.crowood.com

© Emrys Kirby 2023

All rights reserved. No part of this publication may be reproduced or transmitted in any form or by any means, electronic or mechanical, including photocopy, recording, or any information storage and retrieval system, without permission in writing from the publishers.

British Library Cataloguing-in-Publication Data
A catalogue record for this book is available from the British Library.

ISBN 978 0 7198 4185 9

Cover design by Blue Sunflower Creative

Typeset and designed by D & N Publishing, Baydon, Wiltshire

Printed and bound in India by Parksons Graphics

Contents

	Preface and Acknowledgements	6
1	Introduction to Land Rover Series II, IIA and III Restoration	7
2	Land Rover History, 1948–85: The 'Series' Years	12
3	Identifying a Series II, IIA and III Land Rover	16
4	Assessing the Viability of a Project Land Rover	30
5	Engine Restoration and Conversions	40
6	Fuel and Exhaust Systems	71
7	Ignition System	85
8	Cooling System	92
9	Clutch	100
10	Gearbox	110
11	Transfer Box	130
12	Axles and Propshafts	144
13	Steering	162
14	Wheels and Tyres	173
15	Suspension	180
16	Braking System	189
17	Wiring	203
18	Chassis Replacement and Restoration	213
19	Bulkhead Restoration	228
20	Bodywork Fitting, Repairs and Finish	238
21	Lighting	260
22	Internal Trim, Fixings and Glazing	266
23	Vehicle Details and Rivet Counting	277
	Index	286

Preface and Acknowledgements

Welcome to the wonderful world of classic Land Rover restoration and maintenance. Whether you're a newbie to the scene or an old hand at spannering on leaf sprung motors, I trust you will find this book helpful. Many of the images used and techniques described in this book have been gathered over eighteen months of diverse restoration and maintenance work at LSL 4×4 Ltd based on the Fylde Coast in Lancashire. Overseen by the experienced Jim Gardner, LSL 4×4 specialises in classic Land Rovers, from basic maintenance and servicing, through to concourse and resto-mod special builds. Most work is done in-house and this makes it the ideal environment to compile a manual on the subject.

While the official 'Green Bible' Workshop Manuals are invaluable and essential reading for a variety of technical details, they were written for experienced professional mechanics to repair the vehicles when they were fairly new and unmodified. Most workshop manuals are rather dull, light on photographs and short on useful vernacular tips and tricks. The world moves on, parts availability changes, new products come on the market and the Land Rover community finds new ways to solve problems. In addition, we were all new to it once and what can seem a simple task needing no explanation to one person can be remarkably complex to another. This manual was written to assist amateur owners to understand and solve many of the problems that they are likely to encounter when restoring old Land Rovers decades after they were built. It is designed to be photo-heavy, understanding that many practical people benefit from visual references as well as the written word.

Restoring a classic Land Rover is simple enough and can be tackled by fairly inexperienced home mechanics. However, Land Rovers are also very easy to bodge and given that even the youngest leaf sprung motor is now almost forty years old, most will have had their fair share of poor-quality repairs and modifications. The interchangeability of many major components between different eras of Land Rovers means that identifying exactly what parts are required can be something of a minefield. I include a range of historical and technical information that will assist with this and I thoroughly recommend having a parts manual to hand.

Whether you're about to undertake a full restoration, carrying out significant repairs, looking for a workshop reference resource or simply maintaining your Series II, IIA or III, this manual is designed to be simple to navigate and guide you through.

Emrys Kirby
July 2022

ACKNOWLEDGEMENTS

Special thanks go to the following people:

Lucinda Kirby
The team at LSL 4×4: Jim Gardner, Dave Gardner, Graham Briers and William Hearn-Moore
Wayne Taylor at Taylor's Paintworks
All the team at *Classic Land Rover Magazine*, in particular to John Carroll
Tom Benson
Barney Netherwood
Nick Dimbleby

1
Introduction to Land Rover Series II, IIA and III Restoration

So you've bought a Series Land Rover: congratulations and welcome to the amazing world of rivet counting and dirty hands! The buzz of excitement as you bag your dream vehicle can soon be tempered with the reality that it's likely to require more work than initially expected. It will break down, it will cause you headaches and it will be better suited for leisure driving than for everyday motoring. However, Series Land Rovers are easy to repair and one of the best hobby vehicles for you to cut your teeth on. Some jobs can be tackled by a beginner with no experience, others may well benefit from experienced fellow owners and professional input. Every day is a school day, even for the most experienced Land Rover mechanic.

RESTORATION – TO WHAT END?

At some point in your vehicle's life it is very likely to require significant overhaul. You might be able to carry out a 'rolling restoration', keeping it fairly complete while you work your way through those essential jobs. However, it might have reached the point where the only option is to strip it down to the bare bones and start from scratch. Mission creep is pretty much inevitable and before long you're in a position where once you've got so far, you might as well go the whole hog – but where do you stop?

The following general categories of restoration might help to decide what you want from your classic Land Rover. None of these are mutually exclusive, but may well be useful when it comes to inspiration and aspiration.

Concourse Restoration

The zenith in some people's eyes, the concourse standard is building your vehicle to 'as new' (possibly better than new) condition using genuine new, OEM, remanufactured or fully refurbished components. Attention to detail will include the correct factory finish on all components, the correct fixtures and fittings, right down to the shape and size of the rivets. Vast amounts of historical research may be required and, unless you are a very skilled restorer, you are likely to have to rely on external specialists to achieve some elements of this. This will be expensive – potentially very expensive – but you will be rewarded with an outstanding vehicle you are likely to be very proud of.

The author's own Series III was restored to a high standard in 2020 with a desire to make it as authentic to the original factory specification as possible.

A concourse vehicle built to 'as new' standard is the ultimate level of restoration, but it can create a vehicle that is almost unusable for fear of damaging it. This vehicle seldom goes out in the wet.

Introduction to Land Rover Series II, IIA and III Restoration

Pristine paint, highly polished and show ready is the aim of undertaking a concourse restoration, but it takes significant time, money and skill to get it to a high standard. It's very satisfying, but you're really just creating a museum piece.

the potential to create a vehicle that is somewhat clinical or over-restored in its appearance. Remember that Land Rovers were built quickly on a production line to a price. The correct orientation of screwheads is great for personal satisfaction but would never have crossed the mind of a worker on the production line.

Resto/Retro Mod

Resto/retro mod can be a broad category but generally it involves building a vehicle that has been restored to a high standard but with a range of styling or performance-enhancing modifications.

The downside of a concourse restoration is you might then be afraid to use the vehicle. This is no problem if the enjoyment is the process of restoration and attending shows, but it is worth bearing in mind. There is also

Bespoke paint finishes, plush interiors, retro-style stereo systems, brushed stainless or plated fixtures and fittings are all very common in the styling department. Beyond the visual appear-

This special 6×6 Series IIA was built by LSL 4×4 Ltd as a resto-mod breakdown truck, reflecting old period modifications but with a modern twist, some clever engineering and a 300Tdi engine.

Resto-mod vehicles typically have chrome detailing, bespoke paintwork and engine upgrades, such as this 3.9 Rover V8 fitted with a performance carburettor.

Wood lining reminiscent of luxury yachts is a trend from luxury Defenders that has found its way into the classic resto-mod scene and gives a 'Sunshine State' look.

Introduction to Land Rover Series II, IIA and III Restoration

Yellow passivated plating is the 'in' thing at the moment on resto-mod restorations: it protects and enhances the look of functional items. It was actually used on some brackets on Series Land Rovers from the late 1960s onwards, so it's not new.

ance, performance modifications might include engine and transmission upgrades: Rover V8s with fabulously detailed ancillaries are not uncommon. Classic Land Rovers have become fashionable and aspirational way beyond the traditional fan base and the growing resto-mod market reflects this. Some of these vehicles can be considered automotive art as much as they are functional items.

Equally well, a resto/retro mod can simply be a vehicle that has been restored for a specific purpose or to be easier to use on an everyday basis with simple improvements like a modern, economical diesel engine and power steering. It is common to see a modern twist on fashions such as aftermarket wheels, wider tyres and retro/resto styling.

Patina Restoration

A patina vehicle can broadly be described as one that is largely original in appearance and has age-related marks, surface rust and paintwork that illustrates its age and history. There is a large amount of personal opinion when it comes to patina: one person's patina is another person's scruffy, but this should perhaps revolve round the question whether a vehicle component is worn in or worn out. Again, there is a certain amount of personal preference, but original paint with age-appropriate wear is high on the list of celebrated characteristics. Patina vehicles have become very much in vogue recently and indeed, original, patina-rich vehicles are not only rare but desirable and can command premium prices. After all, a vehicle can only be original once and to a certain extent you are buying exclusivity.

A patina restoration seeks to preserve many viable original components whilst ensuring the vehicle is safe and reliable. There is sometimes a perception that a patina restoration is a lazy one, a misunderstanding that can be a long way from the truth. A barn-find vehicle that gives the impression of being able to be dusted off and driven is a dream to many people, but the reality is that a sympathetic restoration is something of an art form. The aim of a patina restoration is to restore the vehicle to look like it has never been repaired and this can take considerable time and skill. A common approach is to remove the bodywork, restore all the underpinnings and put the unrestored body back on. Aluminium panels with original paint can be unpicked and fitted to new frames, light surface rust can be treated and enhanced.

The aim of a patina restoration or recommission is to preserve the original bodywork to reflect the age of the vehicle and retain some of the history – done correctly, it's not a cheap job but a labour of love.

Every little ding and every spot weld is visible on the author's survivor 1968 Series IIA and very few restored vehicles can replicate this original paint finish.

Factory-applied paint that has thinned through to the aluminium is in vogue at the moment. This skin was removed, the frame repaired and the skin refitted with appropriate corrosion protection.

Factory process markings can be preserved or reinstated and good-quality original parts can be made to go again. It takes considerable skill to match old paintwork and replacing a component like a door is far quicker and indeed often cheaper than repairing an old one.

Functional Rebuild/Everyday Restoration

This again can be a broad category but may involve getting your vehicle to a good, everyday usable standard. Not everybody needs, wants or can afford a top-level restoration and vehicles in this category probably provide the best value for money. This is the category that most tidy, everyday Land Rovers fall into. We need them to be dependable, safe and durable, but not necessarily pristine. Originality might not be top of the priority list and engine changes and engineering upgrades might make the vehicle more enjoyable or usable. Very likely the vehicle will have to be built outside or stored in a makeshift shelter, with jobs done when the weather allows. Panels might be hand painted with a brush or roller and the rivets might not be quite correct, but who cares? Being proud of what you've built and enjoying the process of bringing a vehicle back to life is surely what it's all about. This is also the easiest level for the amateur mechanic to achieve and keeps our hobby accessible for younger generations and new enthusiasts. Everyday motors are the lifeblood of our hobby and should never be looked down on.

SUPPORT NETWORKS

You're not alone! There are a range of local, national and international clubs that cater for Series II, IIA and III ownership. The Series 2 Club in particular is widely respected and is also recognised by the DVLA in the UK for vehicle verification and registration purposes. It also has local representatives and local area meetings as well as a forum for sharing information. In the UK (available worldwide), there are Land Rover enthusiast magazines such as *Classic Land Rover Magazine*, *Land Rover Monthly* and *Land Rover Owner International*, all of which have significant Series Land Rover content for your inspiration and information.

Beyond the formal clubs and physical publications, there is a range of social media platforms with groups and pages. It is worth noting that if a question is asked, there is likely to be a broad range of answers – possibly saying the same thing many times over – or conflicting. Many groups have trusted group experts so choose your advice wisely. Also, we all make mistakes and explaining a practical process can be challenging from behind a keyboard. While there are 'keyboard warriors', most owners are happy to help fellow Series Land Rover enthusiasts.

Attending shows and getting into the social scene will greatly enhance your Series Land Rover ownership. On an author's personal note, I have made some real friends for life through Series Land Rovers and am lucky enough to have made my hobby into a profession, driving, restoring and writing about Land Rovers.

The author's own early Series III was assembled outside at the old family home in Scotland when spare time and the weather allowed, a real contrast to the pristine one pictured here.

Introduction to Land Rover Series II, IIA and III Restoration

An everyday rebuild is the most common and most accessible to anyone thinking about getting into the Land Rover scene. It's as much about the fun and challenge of the build as it is about the finished product and can be a great family-bonding project.

It might have been hand painted and built with cast-off spare parts, but the author's old family Series III still looks tidy and presentable. Do not be ashamed of a budget build, just make sure it's safe and reliable and put it to work!

This Series II 109in was rebuilt as an everyday usable vehicle with a 200Tdi engine, Series III gearbox and a high-ratio transfer box. It offers power, economy, reliability and working on one is well within the capabilities of the amateur mechanic. Vehicles like this are the grassroots of the scene and represent a lot of fun for relatively little investment.

2

Land Rover History, 1948–85: The 'Series' Years

The Land Rover is something of a worldwide success story, occasionally against the odds, and was born out of the postwar recovery period. The concept of a light utility 4×4 gained momentum with the expediency of World War II and the Willys MB/Ford GPW military Jeep became the first mass-produced model in 1941. At the end of the war the Willys company launched the CJ-2A, a civilian version of the wartime model. In addition, many surplus MB Jeeps were sold off into private hands. It was clear that there was a worldwide market for such a vehicle that could perform a variety of practical, land-based tasks and yet could be driven at higher speeds on paved roads.

The Rover Car Company, which had specialised in middle-class semi-luxury cars in the 1930s, had ceased production during the war and the new Solihull factory sequestered for the war effort. At the end of the war the company had to quickly recommence the production of vehicles. There was significant rationing of steel, however, and allocation was given to companies that could export a large percentage of their products. In response, the Rover company decided it could build a light 4×4 that utilised a predominantly aluminium body based on a steel chassis and using the basic engineering components of the pre-war Rover car models.

THE SERIES I: ORIGINS

Brothers Spencer and Maurice Wilks were Managing Director and Chief Engineer at Rover and tradition has it that they conceived the idea of the Land Rover when using an MB Jeep to access the beach on Red Wharf Bay while on holiday on Anglesey in Easter 1947. Working with the basic 80in wheelbase of the Jeep, the Rover company developed a new steel box-section chassis and used the base engineering of the Rover P3, including the 1595cc IOE engine and basic gearbox and axle designs. The majority of the bodywork was fabricated out of flat aluminium alloy, reducing the dependence on steel and complicated press tools. By April 1948 the new vehicle was ready to be launched at the Amsterdam Motor Show and, as production ramped up, it was clear that it was going to be a worldwide success.

While not originally designed as a military vehicle, it was soon realised that the Land Rover was perfect for a variety of military applications. The first military contract with the Ministry of Supply started in 1949 and would mark the beginning of a long and successful relationship between Land Rover and Armed Forces worldwide. Indeed, the stipulations of the first military contract called for the colour to be changed from the original light green to the now traditional Deep Bronze Green that is so often associated with classic Land Rovers.

As the uses for 'Britain's Most Versatile Vehicle' expanded, customers were soon asking for more power and the basic engine was bored out to 1997cc for the 1952 year model. Customers also requested more load-carrying capacity and by 1953 the company launched the 86in and 107in models. By 1957 a 2052cc ohv diesel engine became available and at the same time the chassis was modified at the front. This moved the axle 2 inches forward to accommodate the longer engine, so creating the 88in and 109in wheelbase models.

The Land Rover was launched in April 1948 and it shared the 80in wheelbase of the MB Jeep by which it was inspired. This is an early 1950 model and was photographed on one of the unofficial testing grounds on the Island of Islay where the Wilks family had an estate.

Land Rover History, 1948–85: The 'Series' Years

By 1957 the Land Rover had been sold to governments and armed forces worldwide. This vehicle was built under a contract for the Ministry of Supply and used as an auxiliary fire service vehicle.

The Series II model was launched in 1958 and saw the arrival of the barrel side profile that continued throughout utility Land Rover production.

The Series IIA was initially little more than a Series II with a new chassis numbering system, although there would be a raft of engineering changes from 1961 to 1971.

THE SERIES II: THE STYLISH ERA

By 1958 more than 200,000 units had been built and more than 70 per cent had been exported. To celebrate the tenth anniversary, the company launched the Series II model with the same 88in and 109in wheelbase options: all preceding vehicles collectively became known as Series I models. The new Series II reflected changing times and styles; instead of the slightly austere post-war slab sides, the Series II exterior was penned by Rover's designer David Bache. The Series II had the now iconic barrel sides, a design feature that would continue throughout to the end of classic utility Land Rover production in 2016. The Series II saw the arrival of the ubiquitous 2286cc petrol engine (commonly known as the 2.25 or 'two and a quarter'). The diesel option continued to be the 2052cc diesel introduced in 1957 for the 88in and 109in Series I models. This basic engine design would actually continue throughout Series Land Rover production and indeed provide the basic engineering for 4-cylinder engines until 1998.

THE SERIES IIA: THE GOLDEN ERA

In 1961 the company launched the Series IIA model, which marked the arrival of a new chassis numbering system with different suffix letters denoting subsequent engineering changes. The Series IIA also saw improvements to the 2286cc petrol and the arrival of the 2286cc diesel engine with which it shared a common block casting.

The year 1962 saw the arrival of a heavy-duty 109in Forward Control model, which offered a huge 3,380lb load capacity but was somewhat underpowered with the 4-cylinder options. By 1966 it had been re-engineered to 110in wheelbase and was fitted with the 2625cc version of the 6-cylinder engine from the Rover P4.

In 1966 the Rover Company celebrated the building of 500,000 Land Rover units. By 1967 the 2625cc engine became an option in standard bonneted control 109in models, offering a welcome, though modest, power improvement. The following year also saw a dramatic change in the structure of the Rover Car Company, as it was subsumed into the leviathan British Leyland.

Land Rover History, 1948–85: The 'Series' Years

This is a 1970 1-Ton model, a significantly upgraded version of the standard 109in 6-cylinder model. Note it has headlights in the wings and a wire mesh grille, two of the most obvious identifying features of a Late Series IIA.

The military-only Half-Ton GS Air-Portable 88in Land Rover, commonly referred to as the Lightweight, with flat body panels and boxy wings, arrived in 1968. In the same year came the launch of the 1-Ton 109in model with wider wheels, taller tyres and a greater carrying capacity. The most noticeable styling change to standard Series IIA models came in 1969 with the headlamps moving from the recess of the grille panel to the wings, primarily to comply with new lighting regulations in the USA and Benelux countries. In 1971, just before the end of Series IIA production, the 750,000th rolled off the production line.

THE SERIES III: THE REFINEMENT ERA

September 1971 saw the launch of the Series III, which is considered by some as little more than an update of the Series IIA. This is slightly unfair as the Series III feels significantly more car-like to drive, with more in the way of internal trim. A new bulkhead, a padded vinyl-covered dash, integral fresh air heater and plastic grille were the main visual differences, but under the skin there was a new all-synchromesh gearbox. The small refinements did make a significant difference to the feel of the vehicle, adding comfort and gradual improvements. Other than that, it was a period of evolution not revolution, with small upgrades to streamline production and comply with increasing legislation. The Series III continued to be a good seller, even though there was increasing competition from Japanese manufacturers, but it was clear that it was based on ageing technology with more innovative vehicles available.

In 1976, the 1,000,000th Land Rover rolled off the production line, a striking 88in Station Wagon finished in metallic green. In the mid-1970s, British Leyland was struggling from a toxic combination of worldwide recession, poor management, outdated products and industrial unrest and had to be bailed out with government backing. The Land Rover and Range Rover products had always been a viable part of an otherwise struggling parent company so in 1978 Land Rover Ltd became a separate operation within the troubled British Leyland group.

In 1979 the Company launched the Land Rover 109 V8, commonly known as the Stage 1. This was a necessary move to offer a Land Rover product with more power, initially to export markets then to the home market in 1980. It involved re-engineering the basic 109in chassis to accommodate the engine and gearbox from the Range Rover, which had been launched in 1970. The Stage 1 is easily identifiable by its flush front panel, extended bonnet and wire grille. While commonly referred to as the Stage 1 (named after the first round of Government financial backing), its correct name is simply the Land Rover V8. By 1980 the Stage 1 had replaced the 109in 6-cylinder models.

The year 1981 saw the arrival of a 5-bearing variant of the 2286cc petrol and diesel engines, making the already tried and tested engine smoother, stronger and easier to work on. In 1982

The Series III was launched in 1971 and was an evolution of the Series IIA with a plastic grille and a few creature comforts, such as a soft dashboard and a full synchromesh gearbox.

Land Rover History, 1948–85: The 'Series' Years

The Stage 1 V8 model was launched in 1979 to address the common complaint that the Land Rover was underpowered. It is immediately identifiable by its flush front and wire grille. This is one of the earliest prototypes and was registered in 1976.

the company launched the 109in High Capacity Pick Up (HCPU) model with a larger rear cargo body in direct response to the Toyota FJ45, which had a wide body, full-width tailgate and an integrated ladder rack. The same year also saw the launch of the County Station Wagon, a plush version of the existing Station Wagon models in both 88in and 109in form. This model featured improved internal trim, Sundym tinted glass, new cloth seats and side decals.

The Series III 109in model was replaced with the launch of the coil sprung One Ten model in March 1983 and the 88in was replaced by the launch of the Ninety model in April 1984, although run-out fleet orders meant production continued for a little longer. 'Land Rover's New Land Rover' may have been a completely new model but was in line with the 'evolution, not revolution' ethos. It was by no means working from a clean slate, being based on an evolution of the chassis design, axles and running gear of the Range Rover, which had been launched in 1970 and utilised significant elements of the Series III bodywork profile and silhouette. Indeed the very first prototypes were based on cut-down Range Rover and Series III 109in components.

The Series III 109in model was replaced by the new coil-spring One Ten model in 1983 and the 88in was replaced by the Ninety in 1984. The silhouette is still obviously based on the Series III. This Ninety is from the first year of production and still has Series-style galvanised body cappings.

3

Identifying a Series II, IIA and III Land Rover

Series Land Rovers are the ultimate kit car. Throughout Series II, IIA and III production there was gradual evolution but no revolution, and many parts are interchangeable across the different models and generations. Many vehicles have been kept on the road by the simple expedient that components from different eras can be bolted together. All-original vehicles are something of a rarity and it is very common to see 'bitsa' vehicles – bits of this and bits of that. This is not always a reason to reject a vehicle but something to bear in mind with regards to originality, future value, personal preference and what parts you can and can't use together. We own Series Land Rovers for a variety of reasons: nostalgia, practicality, simplicity of repair or investment in a little bit of history. Engineering upgrades can make for an easier driving experience and knowing what parts are interchangeable can be invaluable.

TAX EXEMPTION RULES, IDENTITY AND HISTORICAL VEHICLE STATUS

Vehicle taxation laws in the UK changed in 1997, meaning vehicles over twenty-five years old became tax exempt and categorised as an Historic Vehicle. The original policy was to make this a rolling twenty-five years, but the plan was abandoned the following year meaning that any vehicle built after 1973 still attracted tax. Unfortunately this U-turn resulted in later vehicles being driven on earlier tax-exempt identities. While this was illegal, it was fairly common and something to be aware of when considering a potential purchase. Generally speaking, it is uncommon for these to be stolen vehicles: it was just a case of owning one vehicle in reasonable condition with tax liabilities and another in poor condition but with tax-free status.

On the other hand, because Land Rover components are so interchangeable, many perfectly legitimate vehicles have evolved over time to appear either newer or older than they are. There is nothing wrong with a 'bitsa' vehicle if you simply want a classic Land Rover to use and enjoy, but if you are interested in originality and history, you want to understand fully what you're buying.

Furthermore to the tax exempt status story, the Historic Vehicle rules changed in May 2018 to a forty-year rolling policy, making the vehicles not only tax exempt but also MOT exempt, as long as the vehicle remains substantially unmodified. This actually means that, at the time of writing, most Series Land Rovers fall into this category.

This chapter focuses on identifying vehicles, either with a view to confirming identity, age of components or working out what parts you need to buy for repair and restoration. Headlight position, grille types and bulkhead/dash types are some of the main visual clues to identify a vehicle, but further information may well be required.

CHASSIS NUMBERING

The chassis number of your vehicle is the starting point for identifying what you have. The number contains year codes, model details and a unique serial number. It should always match the documentation with the vehicle. *See the table at the end of this chapter for a list of common Home Market chassis number codes.*

On most Series II, IIA and III models, the chassis number was originally stamped on the right-hand front spring hanger (commonly known as the dumb iron). This would have been stamped by hand on the assembly line and is often quite uneven, so can look somewhat amateurish. It can be difficult to read: rubbing chalk into the numbers can help to reveal it, as can taking a photo on a mobile phone or taking a pencil rubbing. It is also common for the number to be missing, either due to a chassis replacement or previous repairs.

The chassis number should also be stamped on a plate on the bodywork. The original plates were accurately stamped and a replacement should

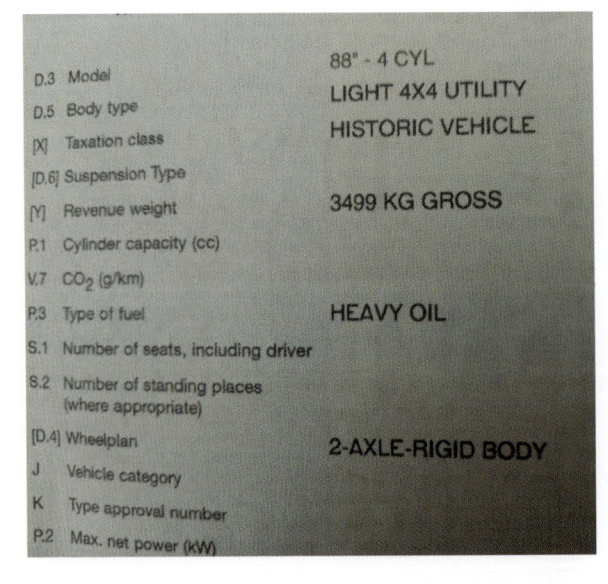

This V5 correctly shows the taxation class as Historic. Unfortunately many newer vehicles were run on older log books to avoid paying VED.

Identifying a Series II, IIA and III Land Rover

ABOVE LEFT: *The vehicle chassis number, the official identity of the vehicle, was originally stamped on the RHS dumb iron.*

ABOVE RIGHT: *Closer shot of the stamping on the dumb iron cleaned up to read the digits. Expect them to be uneven as they were stamped by hand on the production line.*

be obvious. The presence of a replacement plate is not necessarily a cause for concern as long as other features check out on the vehicle. The plates and their location vary over the years: the following is a résumé, but there were variations and of course if a vehicle has been legitimately rebuilt, the position may have changed:

- 1958–1968 models: Screwed to centre panel of the bulkhead.
- 1968–1971 models: Screwed to parcel shelf on the bulkhead to accommodate the square Smiths heater.
- 1971–1976 models: Screwed to centre panel of the bulkhead.
- 1976–1979 models: Riveted to flap on front panel above the horn.
- 1979–1984 models: Now called VIN plate with international manufacturer identifier. Riveted on engine side of bulkhead below rain channel.

Military vehicles are likely to have data plates in other places, such as in the seat box or on the dashboard shelf panel.

CHASSIS DETAILS

The backbone of any Land Rover is the chassis and it is also where the identity of the vehicle lies. Made of box-section mild steel and only protected by a coat of paint (original chassis were not normally galvanised), corrosion is all too common. Given that the last Series vehicles were built in 1984, most chassis will have been repaired or replaced over the years. There were a number of small design changes over the years, but the basic engineering of a standard Land Rover chassis remained pretty much the same with little more than changes to brackets, fixings and strengthening gussets. If originality is important, then it is worth being able to tell the difference between a Series II, IIA and Series III chassis, but they are pretty much interchangeable on a practical level with some minor modifications.

Series II/IIA Chassis Details

The Series II and IIA chassis evolved slightly over the years. There was some extra bracketry left over from the Series I era on very early models. Broadly we can identify two basic II/IIA chassis eras:

- Series II and IIA to suffix C (1958 to 1967): Predominantly identifiable by a bolt-on handbrake relay and tapped plates for the rear axle straps.
- Series IIA suffix D to H: Changes included simplified handbrake and handbrake relay brackets, and braces on the bulkhead outriggers.

Series II and IIA chassis had front brake pipe brackets that routed the fixed pipes along the top of the chassis and the flexible pipes screwed directly into the wheel cylinders.

ABOVE LEFT: *Chassis plate on a Series II screwed to the centre of the bulkhead.*

ABOVE RIGHT: *Chassis plate on a Series IIA, also screwed to the bulkhead; note the different design.*

Identifying a Series II, IIA and III Land Rover

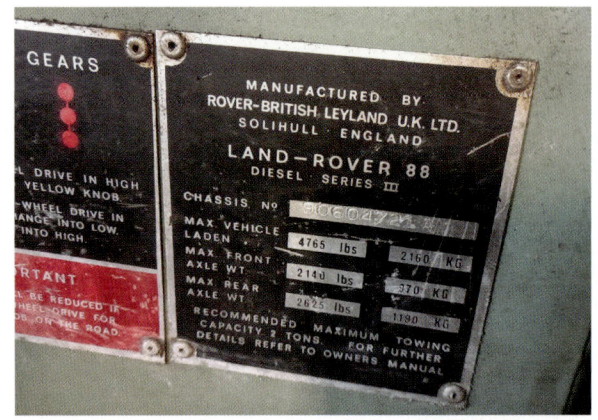

ABOVE LEFT: *Chassis plate on a late Series IIA was moved to the parcel shelf to accommodate the large centrally mounted Smiths heater.*

ABOVE RIGHT: *Series III chassis plate with extra weight information back on the centre of the bulkhead from about 1971 to 1976.*

ABOVE LEFT: *Series III chassis plate moved to the front panel by the horn on 1976–79 models.*

ABOVE RIGHT: *1979 saw the introduction of VIN numbers, an internationally recognised system for all vehicle manufacturers. The plate moved to the bulkhead below the drain channel.*

RIGHT: *Two 88in chassis side by side: the closer one is a Series III, the one further away an early Series IIA. They are geometrically the same but there are detail differences.*

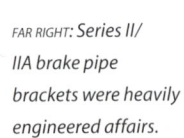

FAR RIGHT: *Series II/IIA brake pipe brackets were heavily engineered affairs.*

LEFT: *This is a late Series I 88in: some of the extra unused brackets continued on to the early Series II.*

FAR LEFT: *Series II and IIA to suffix C had tapped holes in the chassis to hold the rear axle straps in place.*

Identifying a Series II, IIA and III Land Rover

ABOVE LEFT: *Series III had much simpler brake pipe brackets and bump stop strengtheners.*

ABOVE RIGHT: *The late Series III chassis was universal left- and right-hand drive. This design became the generic replacement chassis for all previous models.*

ABOVE LEFT: *Late Series IIIs had uprated dumb irons, introduced for the Stage 1 V8 model.*

ABOVE RIGHT: *Series IIA suffix D onwards and Series III had simple plates welded to the side of the chassis for the axle retaining strap.*

Series III Chassis Details

The Series III saw the introduction of a different engine crossmember to accommodate the bulge in the bellhousing for the new clutch release mechanism. The Series III had simplified brake pipe brackets and bump stop gussets.

From approximately 1977 the 109in chassis was constructed from two C-section rails welded together instead of a four-sided box section. The 88in chassis remained as a four-sided box section.

The Stage 1 V8 chassis available from 1979 had a different front crossmember mounted further forward on the dumb irons and brackets for left- and right-hand steering relay on the inside face of the chassis leg. It also had a different (bolt-on) engine crossmember.

From approximately 1981 the Series III chassis became a 'universal' design with steering relay holes on both sides and uprated dumb iron gussets.

CHASSIS REPLACEMENT

A Land Rover chassis can be considered a replaceable component in the UK and the law allows for an original chassis to be replaced with a new one of the same specification. Until the rules were tightened up, it was common for a second-hand chassis to be used to rebuild a vehicle and this was not really frowned upon back in the day. Now it is legal to use parts from another chassis, but the use of a complete used chassis on another vehicle is technically against the rules.

There are various companies manufacturing replacement chassis as the classic Land Rover restoration market has boomed. Some companies offer a 'generic' chassis, usually based on the late Series III universal design. Other companies offer an age/suffix specific chassis or even a replica chassis, matching as many of the original details as possible. It is worth noting that when available from the factory, even a new Genuine Parts replacement chassis would have been supplied as a universal part to the latest specification and with left- and right-hand drive bracketry, further adding to the complexity of the chassis replacement story.

Depending on what you want from your vehicle, you need to do your research and find out exactly what you're dealing with. A new chassis, especially a galvanised one, can add value and longevity to your vehicle. Equally well, an original chassis in good condition or

Identifying a Series II, IIA and III Land Rover

repaired to a high standard maintains authenticity and provenance and is sought after by many collectors.

BODYWORK AND KEY VISUAL DESIGN FEATURES

Series II, 1958–1961: 88in (Regular) and 109in (Long)

Model variants: Soft top, hard top, truck cab, station wagon, chassis cab for specialist conversions

The Series II was launched in April 1958 and was an evolution of the outgoing Series I 88in and 109in models. The bodywork was totally redesigned although the basic design of the chassis was very close to the old model, with little more than different bulkhead outriggers and a different rear crossmember. In terms of main identifiable visual features, the Series II model introduced the famous barrel sides, a feature and profile that continued all the way through to the end of traditional utility Land Rover production. Series II models can usually (though not exclusively) be quickly distinguished from later vehicles by a square-profile front valance panel and headlamps proud of the front grille panel, usually with chrome bezels. They had bolt-on bulkhead vent flaps that opened with Bakelite turn-knobs.

Series IIA, 1961–1971: 88in (Regular) and 109in (Long)

Model variants: As Series II but with the introduction of Forward Control, 1-Ton and Air Portable (Lightweight) models

The change to the Series IIA in 1961 was little more than a change in chassis numbering to identify engineering changes and upgrades. Any significant change introduced a different suffix (A to H). In terms of visual differences, the first suffix A Series IIA models were very similar to the outgoing Series II, but the body design did gradually change over time.

Very soon after the launch of the IIA the headlight panel changed with a pressing for the headlamps and recessed fixings and adjustors, removing the need for a chrome bezel. The square profile (there were actually two different versions) was soon replaced with a rounded front valance.

From 1967 the 'black dash' model was launched (prior to that the dash was body coloured). The dash was redesigned to include a key start (as opposed to a push-button start) as well as different switch gear for lights

Series II headlamps were finished with a chrome bezel.

LEFT: *The Series II (and very early IIA) had a square profile valance panel and surface-mounted headlights.*

ABOVE LEFT: *Bakelite screw-type vent flaps as fitted to a Series II.*

ABOVE RIGHT: *Bolt/screw-on vent flaps are one of the other features on the Series II and very early IIA model.*

Identifying a Series II, IIA and III Land Rover

ABOVE LEFT: *Body colour dash as fitted to Series II and IIA until 1967.*

ABOVE RIGHT: *Bulkhead/windscreen brackets as fitted to all Series II and IIA models.*

Series IIA headlights sit behind the panel and have external adjustors.

LEFT: *Series IIA from 1962 to 1968 had headlight pressings in the front panel and a rounded front valance panel.*

and heater controls. This also saw the introduction of the single wiper bulkhead-mounted motor as opposed to two individual Lucas FW2 wiper motors mounted on the windscreen.

Shallow door sills were brought in during 1968 and in the same year the headlights were moved to the wings with corresponding changes to the grille panel and a 'Maltese Cross' wire grille. The late model Series IIA with lights in the wings is often confused with the Series III and, to add to the confusion, it was common to update a IIA with a Series III plastic grille. In more recent times it is more common to see Series IIIs made to look older with Series IIA grilles.

Other changes included different heaters, small bulkhead design changes, handbrakes and wiring and lighting changes. Some changes were in response to changing legislation such as lighting and seatbelts, others were about improving comfort and rationalising parts.

There were a number of small changes to the bulkhead from 1958 to 1971, the most notable being the change from the twin wipers mounted in the screen to the single type mounted on

Black dash as fitted to Series IIA from 1967 to 1971.

21

Identifying a Series II, IIA and III Land Rover

Headlights were moved to the wings on late Series IIA models to comply with new lighting regulations: do not confuse with the Series III.

the bulkhead. These are not directly interchangeable unless the windscreen is also changed.

Series III, 1971–1984/5: 88in (Regular) and 109in (Long)

Model Variants: Soft top, hard top, truck cab, station wagon, V8, chassis cab for specialist conversions, Military Air Portable (Lightweight), 1-Ton

In many ways the Series III model was an updated version of the Series IIA and the changes were again mostly in response to improved comfort and increasing safety legislation. The clocks and main dash controls were moved from the centre of the bulkhead to in front of the driver; a full-width soft dash

ABOVE LEFT: *Series III saw a whole new dashboard with crash protection and clocks in front of the driver.*

ABOVE RIGHT: *The Series III is immediately identifiable by the ABS plastic grille. Note that owners sometimes fit Series IIA grilles to Series IIIs, or vice versa, so look closer for other clues to confirm identity.*

RIGHT: *Very late Series III models had rear lights in top and bottom positions, like the recently introduced coil spring One Ten.*

FAR RIGHT: *All Series III models had this design of bulkhead/ windscreen mount.*

22

Identifying a Series II, IIA and III Land Rover

ABOVE LEFT: Early Series IIIs (from about 1971 to 1973) had twin small gutters on the bulkhead. Later models had a full-length gutter.

ABOVE RIGHT: Early Series IIIs had a 'blank' internal vent panel.

Flush front panel and wire mesh grille as fitted to Stage 1 V8 models.

with the option for an integral heater also improved crash protection. New flush hinges improved pedestrian safety, although the earliest examples still had the proud Series II/IIA type hinge.

Externally, the most obvious visual change was the introduction of an ABS plastic grille as well as a round vent hole in the passenger wing for the new fresh-air heater. In addition, the lower windscreen mounting brackets were redesigned with an upright box profile welded to the front face instead of brackets welded to the side, as on the Series II/IIA.

Later models (about 1980) had silver headlamp bezels (body colour prior to that) and latterly different rear lighting orientation with top and bottom tail-light and indicator positions, matching the new One Ten model. Stage 1 V8 models tended to have black headlamp surrounds although there seems to be inconsistency with this styling feature.

The bulkhead went through a number of small changes. Vehicles to 1973 had small twin rain gutters and a 'blank' internal vent flap panel. Later vehicles had a single long gutter and square holes cut in the vent flap panel to improve fresh air flow. From approximately 1981 the design of the transmission tunnel changed to include a screw-on diaphragm.

An upmarket version, the County Station Wagon, arrived in 1982 with cloth seats, improved interior trim, side stripes and tinted glass. A V8 engine option became available for 109in models from 1979 and these vehicles can be identified by a flush front grille panel, a wire mesh grille and a long-nose bonnet.

ORIGINAL ENGINE OPTIONS

The very first Series II 88in models still had the 1997cc IOE (inlet over exhaust) design engine from the outgoing Series I, but the 109in model and most 88in models were fitted with the new ohv (overhead valve) 2286cc petrol engine.

The diesel option remained the 2052cc ohv engine introduced for the Series I in 1957. The diesel engine was re-engineered to 2286cc displacement for the arrival of the Series IIA and shared the same block as the corresponding petrol model.

A 2625cc 6-cylinder option was available for 109in, 1-Ton and Forward Control models. This engine was based on the old IOE engine design from the Series I and offered slightly improved power and torque over the 2286cc option.

The 2625cc 6-cylinder engine was replaced by the 3528cc V8 engine and LT95 gearbox from the Range Rover from 1979. The front of the vehicle had to be redesigned to accommodate the extra length of the engine and drivetrain package. This model was technically known simply as the Land Rover V8, but is commonly known as the Stage 1 V8. Note that fitment of a V8 engine was a common owner modification, but this was usually connected to a standard LT76 Series gearbox via a conversion plate, meaning the grille panel usually remained in the original recessed position.

The 2286cc engine continued with slight engineering upgrades to the very end of Series Land Rover production in 1984/85. A five-bearing variant was launched in 1981 and can be identified by a terracotta red block,

Identifying a Series II, IIA and III Land Rover

ABOVE LEFT: Series II saw the launch of the ubiquitous 2286cc petrol engine, which remained the most common option throughout Series II/IIA and III production.

ABOVE RIGHT: The 2286cc version of the diesel engine was launched in 1961.

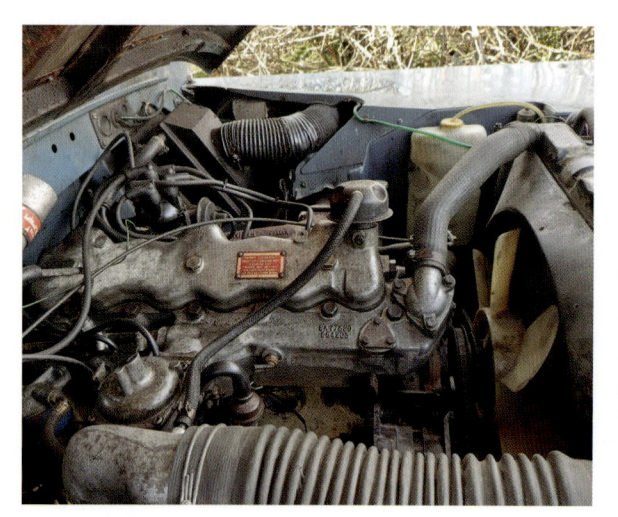

ABOVE LEFT: The 2625cc 6-cylinder engine was introduced for 109in models in 1967.

ABOVE RIGHT: A five-bearing variant of the 2286cc engine was launched in 1981. It can be identified by the terracotta block with strengthening ribs.

black cylinder head and cross-webbing in the lower casting. (Note that military versions of these engines are likely to have been painted light blue/green all over.)

Many Land Rovers will have had engine changes over the years, either as a service exchange, an expedient second-hand replacement or as a performance or economy upgrade. The engine number will confirm what is under the bonnet and this can be found on the front left-hand side of the block beside exhaust port number 1. (*See* Chapter 5 for information on common engine conversions and the table at the end of that chapter for a list of engine identification numbers.)

KEY COMPONENT SERIAL NUMBERS

Engines

As above, the 2286cc and 2625cc engine number is normally stamped on the front left-hand side of the block near exhaust port no.1. The first three (type prefix) numbers would normally match the chassis number but the rest of the serial number will not be the same as the chassis number. Note that this number connection does not apply to late Series models with a VIN type chassis number. If a later engine of Land Rover origin has been fitted,

The engine number on all variants is stamped on the block near exhaust port 1.

24

Identifying a Series II, IIA and III Land Rover

the number is usually stamped on the block above the rear camshaft cover plate/fuel pump mounting plate.

Gearboxes

The gearbox number is normally stamped on the rear right on the top cover; the prefix would usually have matched the engine prefix. Note that most Series III gearbox numbers were stamped on the transfer box. Again, a replacement gearbox is very common (more gearbox identification pointers can be found in Chapter 10).

Axles

Axle numbers were stamped on the upper side of the casing beside the axle breather. Although it is possible to identify a Series II, IIA and III axle case via the numbers, there is no direct connection to the chassis or engine type.

Suffix Connections

Note that vehicle specifications, gearboxes and axles underwent various modifications over the years and were designated with a component update suffix letter. The original chassis, engine, gearbox and axle suffixes may not be the same. For example, the author's own original 1967 Series IIA has a 271 suffix E chassis number with 241 suffix B axles. If further information is required, the Land Rover Series 2 Club has compiled a comprehensive database.

DATABLE ANCILLARY COMPONENTS

Beyond the identity of the main components that have serial numbers, such as the chassis, engine, gearbox and axles, many ancillaries have date markings. Very often these will have a month/date code format, for example 1/61 would be January 1961. Other formats could be a letter code for a month or quarter, such as c/65. This is particularly relevant on a vehicle with significant provenance or when attempting to date a vehicle for registration purposes. It also appeals to the 'rivet counter' who thrives on details. However, one should be wary of being a detail snob – remember we all get pleasure out of different aspects of Land Rover ownership.

ABOVE LEFT: Gearbox number is usually stamped on the top cover, but note that on most Series IIIs it is on the transfer box.

ABOVE RIGHT: Axle number is stamped near the axle case vent (this axle has a modern extended breather pipe). Note that the axle number doesn't relate directly to chassis or engine number.

This voltage control box bears the date 11 68 (November 1968).

LEFT: Steering box usually has a date stamp or a casting date. A Series III is shown here.

Identifying a Series II, IIA and III Land Rover

The following parts can often be dated:

Differentials: usually stamped on the machined face round the mounting flange.
Brake drums: often cast into the drums.
Steering box: stamped into the casing; later models have a casting date.
Dynamo: stamped into the body.
Fuse box: marked on the underside of Series II/IIA fuse boxes.
Voltage control box: marked on the base.
Radiator: either stamped into a round tag soldered to the top (early models) or on the tag for the cap chain (later models). Note that not all radiators were dated from new.
Choke switch: on early models with spring-loaded switch.
Wiper motors: on the underside of the FW2 wiper motor.
Wheel rims: on vehicles up to the late 1960s it was stamped on the rim beside a wheel nut hole, but dropped on later vehicles.
Distributor: the 25D distributor was often, though not always, date stamped in the 1950s and 1960s.
Glass: Triplex had a unique dating format based on the words 'Toughened' and 'Triplex' etched into the corner of the glass. Dots above the nine letters in T-O-U-G-H-E-N-E-D note the year within the decade (no dot = 1960, dot above T = 1961, dot above O = 1962 and so on). Further information on the quarter or month of the year is based on a code of dots above the letters in 'Triplex'. The 1960s format was in a circle, the 1970s and 1980s was horizontal.

NUMBER PLATES

Obviously there will be variations depending on your country of registration, but in the UK there are official rules regarding the registration of vehicles and the types of number plates that can be displayed. In the UK number plates have a local area identification code as well as a unique number sequence.

Until 1963 there was no specific dating within the number plate, although a letter/number sequence could be deduced with experience. From 1963, a year suffix letter identifier was added, beginning with A and running alphabetically to Y (excluding O, Q, U and Z). The author's Series IIA is KCW 53G, where CW is the local identifier for Burnley, K is the sequential identifier (L would follow) and a G-suffix is 1968. Af-

ABOVE LEFT: *6 60 on this Series II radiator disc dates it to June 1960.*

ABOVE RIGHT: *The date on later Series IIA radiators was on the chain tag.*

FAR LEFT: *Date can be found on the underside of the FW2 wiper motors. It can be faint and 2-67 is just visible here.*

LEFT: *Series II Lucas 25D distributor date stamped 2 60.*

Identifying a Series II, IIA and III Land Rover

ABOVE LEFT: *Triplex glass is date coded. The dot below the letter U (3rd letter) of 'toughened' marks this Series III as manufactured in 1983.*

TOP RIGHT: *Yellow and white number plates were introduced from around 1967, gradually replacing pressed black and white plates by 1973.*

ABOVE RIGHT: *Pressed black and silver plates give a classic look, but they are historically wrong on any vehicle post-1973.*

ter 1983, once the sequence had got to Y, the order was reversed with the year identifier as a prefix, for example A345 KSB (in this case SB is the local identifier for Argyll).

Note that the DVLA registration system was computerised in the early 1980s and some vehicles 'fell off' the system. It was not uncommon for vehicles to be registered on 'age related' or age neutral (pre-suffix) plates with unissued numbers from lower registration volume areas such as the Highlands of Scotland (AS) and Wales (FO).

Most number plates from 1958 to 1965 were made from pressed aluminium with a black background and silver letters. This was supplemented with the option to have a black background with individual plastic or aluminium letters riveted on. From 1966 white (front) and yellow (rear) reflective plates with black letters were introduced, although black and silver plates remained a legal option until 1973. Most white and yellow plates had individual plastic letters clipped on, although pressed aluminium plates were available in the late 1970s. Laminated plastic plates became widely available from the mid-1980s.

Black and Silver Plates and Historical Vehicle Status

There was an odd oversight on the legality of black and silver plates with the arrival of forty-year rolling MOT and VED exemption in 2018. Initially the rules allowed forty-year-old tax exempt vehicles to display black and silver plates (even though anything post-1973 would have been historically incorrect), but this was overturned in 2020, meaning any vehicle post-1980 has to display white and yellow plates.

Back when Series Land Rovers were common everyday vehicles, many owners desired to make their vehicles look newer by fitting modern laminated plates (or a simple expedient when a new plate was required). As Series vehicles became considered classic cars, owners then desired to make their vehicles look older by fitting 'classic' black and silver plates. Now as time has moved on, traditional individual letter white and yellow reflective plates are gaining popularity and are age-appropriate for any vehicle from 1966 to 1984. Obviously the choice is down to the individual owner and their personal preferences within the law. It is worth noting that the standard font size changed in 2001 to accommodate a different number plate format. Many modern black and silver pressed plates are made with the new-style font and therefore look modern.

Military Vehicles, Number Plates and Dating

It is worth noting that when ex-military Land Rovers were first road registered on release after approximately ten years of service, they were often allocated the then current new registration letter: for example, TEC 897R was a Series IIA built in 1966, released in 1977 and given a 1977 registration number. It's not uncommon for owners to want to have an age-appropriate number allocated and this is best applied for via a recognised owners club. It is also worth considering that when changing the registration number you can lose a significant amount of vehicle history. A 'wrongly' applied number plate date is actually a perfectly legitimate part of a Land Rover's story.

Personal Preference and Legalities

Whatever you decide, make sure it's legal and consider what is important to you: preserving the history of your vehicle or reflecting its age. Within the law there is no right or wrong in terms of personal preference, but if you want to be historically correct, there are specialist manufacturers who will make a plate up to your requirements. Specialist, historically accurate plates are not cheap, but they do make a significant difference to the visual impact of a vehicle.

RESEARCHING VEHICLE HISTORY

Most people are fascinated by what their vehicle has done and who has owned it over the years. After all, we're not simply owning a functional vehicle but a little piece of social, agricultural and industrial history. Very basic information can be gleaned from the official factory records by applying to the British Motor Museum for a Heritage Certificate. This will give the basic body type, date of build, dealer destination, engine type and occasionally key number and 'line number'.

Beyond the official factory records, the current UK V5C registration documents no longer list the previous owners. Old documents and receipts are often a good way of building up the jigsaw puzzle pieces, as are requests on social media and in club circles. The DVLA online vehicle checking service can give information on current tax, MOT status and when the last V5C was issued, so a recent change of ownership can be identified.

You can also look up a vehicle's MOT history if tested from 2005, when the system was computerised. This will give an insight into mileage covered, details of advisories and fails, and the reasons for those fails. This can build up a picture as to how the vehicle has changed, how the owner has treated it and can highlight inconsistencies such as mileage and repairs.

Applying for a Registration Document

It is potentially something of a minefield when dealing with a government agency that is not particularly interested in the minutiae of Series Land Rover history or sentimental attachment to a vehicle. If applying for a registration document for a vehicle that has fallen off the system or been imported, it is highly advisable to contact the Registrations Officer of a DVLA-recognised owners club to guide you through the process (the Series 2 Club would be the most appropriate). Significant documentary evidence is often required, as well as a physical inspection of the vehicle to confirm its identity.

If a vehicle has previously been registered, it may be possible to retain the original registration number. If imported or documentary evidence is insufficient, it will be allocated an age-related/ageless plate. Once an application has been unsuccessful, it is often very difficult or even impossible to resubmit without significant impediment.

LAND ROVER SERIES II, IIA AND III CHASSIS NUMBER CODES

The following tables contain information to decipher the chassis number codes on common Home Market production Series II, IIA and III Land Rover models. It can be considered a guide only as there were some irregularities and oddities in the systems over the years and does not include export or CKD vehicles. Factory dispatch records, held at the British Motor Museum (BMM), will confirm the build and dispatch dates of a vehicle built at Solihull; a Heritage Certificate containing the information can be purchased from BMM.

Series II

Note that the prefix would have been followed by the unique vehicle serial number, which would have commenced with 00001.

	1958	1959	1960	1961
88in models				
Petrol	1418	1419	1410	1411
Diesel	1468	1469	1460	1461
109in models				
Petrol	1518	1519	1510	1511
Diesel	1568	1569	1560	1561
SW Petrol	N/A	1619	1610	1611
SW Diesel	N/A	1669	1660	1661

Series IIA

With the introduction of the Series IIA model, the chassis number no longer included a year-model code. Any engineering updates were denoted with a sequential suffix letter. Suffix letters went from A to H before the arrival of the Series III model. Note that the unique serial number would have commenced 00001, followed by the appropriate suffix letter.

Approximate Series IIA Suffix dates are as follows:

A	September 1961 – March 1963
B	March 1963 – September 1965
C	September 1965 – April 1967
D	April 1967 – March 1968
E	March 1968 – January 1969
F	January 1969 – April 1969
G	April 1969 – February 1971
H	February 1971 – August 1971

88in and 109in 2286cc models

	88in (Utility and Station Wagon to March 1965)	109in Utility	109in Station Wagon
Petrol	241	251	261
Diesel	271	276	281

88in 2286cc Station Wagon

(A separate numbering system was introduced from 1 March 1965)

Petrol	315
Diesel	320

109in 2625cc Models

	Utility	Station Wagon
Petrol	345	350

Lightweight/Airportable 2286cc Petrol

88in Lightweight	236

Series III

The Series III broadly had three different chassis numbering systems:

- To October 1979 it followed the Series IIA type pattern with the first three digits denoting the vehicle type.
- From November 1979 a new Vehicle Identification Number VIN system was introduced. This meant vehicle type information was denoted by letters and numbers.
- From 1981 the VIN system was modified to include an internationally recognised vehicle manufacturer prefix code: in the case of Land Rover, it became SAL.

88in 2286cc Models (up to October 1979 – pre-VIN)

	Utility	Station Wagon
Petrol	901	921
Diesel	906	926

109in 2286cc Models (up to October 1979 – pre-VIN)

	Utility	Station Wagon
Petrol	911	931
Diesel	916	936

109in 2625cc Models (up to October 1979 – pre-VIN)

	Utility	Station Wagon
Petrol	941	946

Airportable (88in Lightweight) 2286cc

Petrol	951

88in models from November 1979
(NB VIN numbers were preceded by the SAL identifier from 1981)

	Utility	Station Wagon
Petrol	LBAAH1AA1	LBABH1AA1
Diesel	LBAAG1AA1	LBABG1AA1

109in models from November 1979
(NB VIN numbers were preceded by the SAL identifier from 1981)

	Utility	Station Wagon
2286cc Petrol	LBCAH1AA1	LBCMH1AA1
2286cc Diesel	LBCAG1AA1	LBCMG1AA1
2625cc Petrol	LBCAP1AA1	LBCMP1AA1

109in Stage 1 V8 models
(NB VIN numbers were preceded by the SAL identifier from 1981)

	Utility	Station Wagon
Petrol	LBCAV1AA1	LBCMV1AA1

4

Assessing the Viability of a Project Land Rover

REALITY CHECK

A wise person once said, 'there are good Land Rovers and there are cheap Land Rovers but there are no good cheap Land Rovers'. While bargains can be had if you get lucky, Land Rovers usually cost more in terms of time and money than most people imagine. There is a romantic belief that Land Rovers last for ever, that every vehicle is worth saving and it would only take a few weekends to get an absolute scrapper back on the road. It's true that Land Rovers usually last longer than a normal vehicle, but there are broad reasons why this is true.

Land Rovers are easy to repair, but historically repairs were often expedient bodges simply to keep the vehicle going as cheaply and quickly as possible. When the vehicles were of little financial value, owners weren't willing to spend a significant amount of money on garage repairs. There is also the fact that a Land Rover could still perform its function, even when badly dented and knocked around. Nails used instead of split pins, hammers used as spanners and baler twine used to hold bodywork on isn't just apocryphal but rooted firmly in reality.

Many people hang on to Land Rovers with a romantic notion that they will restore them one day and so they remain unused, unloved and semi-abandoned. Whatever your reasons for wanting to buy a Land Rover, you need to go in with your eyes wide open as well as your heart full of enthusiasm. Sad to say, some vehicles aren't worth saving and will only be good for parts. Some vehicles are beyond economical repair and may well cost more to restore than they will be worth. However, it's fair to say that often emotional attachment will overlook reality. That's fine if a vehicle means a lot to you, but you need to have a reality check on the potential time and cost involved.

In the UK vehicles over forty years old have become both tax and MOT exempt. While this is very welcome when it comes to the economics of running a classic Land Rover, it may mean that a significant number of vehicles that should have been scrapped or in need of significant repairs are still on the road. An MOT should pick up on structural corrosion and the function of safety-critical items such as brakes and steering. While an MOT may not be legally required, it does at least give a certain assurance that a vehicle is not about to collapse round you. The author is aware of a number of vehicles being driven on the public road that could only be described as having downright dangerous levels of corrosion.

Who Are You?

There is more information about confirming the identity of a vehicle in

This Series III had been in the author's family for many years and was only fit for scrap, but nostalgia outweighed the financial value and it was restored.

Assessing the Viability of a Project Land Rover

While often not legally necessary, a good MOT history adds value to a Series Land Rover.

Chapter 3, but it is vital that the vehicle you intend to restore is what you think it is. There are plenty of good 'bitsa' – bits of this and bits of that – vehicles in service that have evolved over the years. Beyond the good honest bitsa, there are vehicles blatantly running the identity of an earlier one. There are complex legalities round this, so it is hard to be cut and dried (used replacement chassis, for example, were common thirty plus years ago and not explicitly illegal), but it is a consideration. In addition, in the 1980s and 1990s there were a good number of 'hybrid' vehicles built on modified coil spring Range Rover chassis. Many very good hybrid vehicles were built for everyday use and motor sport using the Series vehicle identity and it was not illegal at the time. There were also companies that offered a new Series type chassis built to take coil springs and Range Rover axles. Some look down on these vehicles today and apply the current rules to vehicles that were not subject to them when they were built. However, you must be fully aware of what you are buying: no Series Land Rovers were originally built with coil springs.

Check the identity of the vehicle thoroughly and check any accompanying paperwork. The guidance in Chapter 3 will help, but if in doubt or concerned, seek additional expert advice. If a vehicle has been extensively modified and you wish to return it to original specification, make sure it's worth doing. Finding those rare, age-correct parts can be fun, but equally it can be time-consuming and potentially expensive. There is little point in buying a Series III blatantly run on a Series II/IIA identity and trying to rebuild it to the logbook specification. Equally well, if a vehicle has had legitimate in-service modifications, then it would be a viable and enjoyable undertaking. Do your research and, if necessary, get a second opinion from an experienced person.

A classic Land Rover doesn't make a lot of rational sense on a purely functional basis, but an old vehicle can be so much more than just a vehicle. It is as much about how it makes you feel as much as it is a functional item. Yes, people still use them for work purposes but that will mostly be based on an underlying enthusiasm rather than pure functionality. Take a reality check, weigh up your options, cost things up and go in with your eyes wide open,

Many Series vehicles have been assembled from second-hand parts over the years, but beware of vehicles that are clearly wearing the wrong identity. This is a Series III/Range Rover hybrid on coil springs and is correctly registered as such.

Assessing the Viability of a Project Land Rover

Owning and restoring a Series Land Rover should be fun and its financial value should come second – tell yourself that when it breaks down again.

but don't forget the value of how something makes you feel.

CHASSIS ASSESSMENT

The chassis is the backbone of your vehicle and has to be the starting point of any vehicle assessment. Poor historical repairs are common, often just from the expediency of getting the vehicle through an MOT. Chassis usually rust from the rear crossmember forward, the dumb irons backwards and from the inside out. You need to inspect the chassis carefully and thoroughly using a wire brush, scraper, a small hammer and screwdriver (with the owner's permission if inspecting for purchase, and remember to wear eye protection). A galvanised chassis is a massive plus point, but do be aware that even galvanised chassis corrode, especially round the forward rear body and fuel tank outriggers. Beware of large areas of thick underseal: very often it hides poor repairs and can act as a moisture trap. Having said that, a lot of military Land Rovers were heavily undersealed in service and this can offer very effective protection, hence the need to carry out a thorough inspection.

Rear Crossmember

In the UK it is very rare to find a vehicle on an original chassis that hasn't had a rear crossmember replaced and it's common to see these fitted badly. Replacements are usually supplied with extensions, and it's common to see these simply slid over the chassis rails and welded round three sides of the box but not the top. Quarter and half chassis repair sections have long been available and again these may have been fitted with varying degrees of accuracy and weld quality. If the work has been carried out to a good standard, there's no reason to reject a vehicle. Comprehensive information about chassis repairs and replacement may be found in Chapter 18.

Dumb Irons

The dumb irons carry significant forces from the front suspension and steering as well as attaching the front bumper and taking any recovery forces, so it is vital that they are in good condition. Very often they rust from behind the bumper, underneath the spring hangers and from the inside out, so often the extent of the corrosion is not immediately obvious. Comprising multiple layers of steel, they have moisture traps and unprotected metal behind the spring hangers. Repair sections are available and again you need to inspect the quality of the work. Lower quality repair sections sometimes have a slightly different profile to the original and it's not uncommon to see these fitted out of true, compromising the suspension geometry and orientation of the bumper.

Also note that the chassis number should be stamped on the right-hand dumb iron, so a replacement or repair may have removed these. It is always wise for the number to be restamped following a repair, although different countries have different rulings on this. It is possible to buy a front quarter chassis that includes the dumb irons and front crossmember.

Thick underseal is often used to cover poor repairs and areas of corrosion, so needs a thorough inspection.

This rear crossmember is deeply corroded and replacement is the only option, but how far does the corrosion extend?

Assessing the Viability of a Project Land Rover

ABOVE LEFT: *Dumb irons must be strong to carry the weight of the front suspension, but they are a significant rot spot.*

ABOVE RIGHT: *All outriggers are structural items on the chassis. The outrigger on this 109in carries the rear leaf spring.*

Outriggers

Outriggers play a vital role in supporting the bodywork and should always be considered a structural component. Bulkhead outriggers are exposed to road grit and are constantly in the firing line, so you can expect these to have either corroded or been repaired or replaced. Standards of repairs vary from very good to downright lazy. Replacements are relatively cheap and usually come with a backing plate; using the plate makes for a quick functional repair, but can often cover corrosion in the main chassis rails behind. It's also common to see poor-quality welding and inaccurate positioning leading to poor body alignment. 109in models have outriggers that support the rear springs and again these suffer from the same issues as the bulkhead outriggers. Rear body outriggers rust readily and act as mud and moisture traps, causing corrosion to spread to the main rails; again replacements come with backing plates and often are fitted covering further rust damage.

Main Chassis Rails

It is vital to inspect the full length of the chassis rails. Common rot spots are under the axle bump stops and the bottom of the main rails, in particular at the rear. Commonly they corrode from the inside out and from the bottom up, but the top of the main rails under the rear body often trap mud and moisture. There has to be a judgement call as to whether a chassis has isolated areas of corrosion or whether the whole structure has started to rot and delaminate. You need to be able to cut back to solid metal to execute any form of structural repairs. 88in and most 109in models have a simple box-section construction with welds in the corners: repairing is relatively straightforward but time-consuming to do it well. Later 109in models were constructed in twin C-section pressings and are harder to repair to a high standard. It is not uncommon to see 88in models with a new rear half chassis fitted, joining in just behind the forward rear spring hangers. If done well, this is no major cause for concern, but do be aware that homemade box-section chassis rails are all too common.

Repair or Replace?

Replacement chassis are readily available and in the grand scheme

ABOVE LEFT: *Main chassis rails tend to rust from the bottom up with moisture sitting on the inside.*

ABOVE RIGHT: *On this late model Series III 109in the chassis is made from twin C sections and is harder to repair neatly than the standard box section.*

Assessing the Viability of a Project Land Rover

If your bulkhead is this bad, just throw it away and buy a new one.

of things are relatively cheap and good value for money. If originality is important, repairing an original chassis is very rewarding but can be very time-consuming. This is less of a concern if you're doing it as a hobby, but commercially it can work out significantly more expensive to repair to a good standard than to replace. An original vehicle with provenance and a fully restored original chassis will always be more desirable to a collector, but for an everyday vehicle there may well be a point when you need to accept that a new chassis can be considered a long-term replaceable component. New chassis usually come galvanised for longevity and represent a very good investment albeit at the expense of provenance. (For further help regarding making the decision whether to repair or replace, see Chapter 18.)

BULKHEAD ASSESSMENT

Beyond the chassis, bulkhead condition has to be the next most important consideration when assessing the viability of a vehicle. Bulkhead repairs can be challenging and time-consuming to execute to a high standard. Original bulkheads were made from multiple layers of pressed steel, making moisture traps and creating problems when restoring correctly.

Footwells and Door Pillars

Footwells are relatively straightforward to replace and are now available with the correct pressings in the toe board. To do properly will require drilling out multiple spotwelds and usually having to repair other areas such as the lip to the lower dashboard and inner footwell side. Side pillars are available although these are often generic later parts with small details slightly different from the originals. Bottom feet that attach to the bulkhead outriggers are also available. Replacement is well within the abilities of an amateur welder, but to do it accurately and tidily takes time.

Top Corners and Vent Panels

Top corner sections often rust through. When corrosion sets in, it can often compromise the lower layers of steel creating time-consuming and fiddly repairs. A number of small companies specialise in producing good-quality repair sections, but be aware that to restore well takes time and skill.

Series II and IIA models have complicated dashboard sections that are very difficult to repair and this can often be the death knell when it comes to viability. Be aware that repairing an extensively corroded bulkhead might require a jig to ensure it is repaired accurately and straight.

Professional Repairs and New Bulkheads

There are a number of companies that specialise in fabricating complete new

Footwells are likely to have corroded away and have historically bad repairs.

RIGHT: Top corners rust like this. They can be a challenge to repair if internal gussets have also corroded away.

Assessing the Viability of a Project Land Rover

bulkheads as well as restorers who will rebuild your original one. Both are justifiably relatively expensive because of the complexity of the work involved. Be aware that changing a bulkhead will be as time-consuming and a similar cost to replacing a chassis. (For further information on assessing and restoring a bulkhead, *see* Chapter 19.)

ENGINE ASSESSMENT

First up, what engine is in the vehicle? It is relatively rare for a Land Rover to still have its original engine. When the vehicles were just common everyday working vehicles, a worn engine would commonly be replaced with a better one. In addition, Land Rovers have been fitted with a broad range of engines from different manufacturers by amateurs and professionals alike. If it's important to you, confirm the engine is original to the vehicle; the engine number usually begins with the same prefix as the chassis number on vehicles up to approximately 1980. (For more specific information on identifying engines, *see* Chapter 5.)

You also need to decide what engine is best for your needs. A 2286cc petrol will return anything from 15 to 23mpg, depending on use and how heavy you are on the loud pedal. The standard 2286cc petrol engine is robust and will often keep on running reasonably well, even when very worn. A healthy petrol engine should run very quietly but top-end rattles are common, usually due to poorly adjusted or worn valve gear. Valve stem oil seals often go hard causing blue smoke on start up.

A 2286cc diesel will return anything from 18 to 30mpg depending on use and condition: what you gain in fuel economy, you'll lose with being late for everything because it will be abysmally slow. Obviously there is deliberate humour in these comments – a well-maintained 2286cc diesel can give reasonable performance, commensurate with the technology of the time. Diesels suffer from stretched timing chains, worn timing gear and poorly set injection timing. This is usually evidenced by poor starting, excessive smoke and generally lethargic performance.

Both engines suffer from oil leaks from a variety of places. While this is often part of the character of owning an old Land Rover, the leaks should really only be a weep and not excessive to the point of being a noticeable cadenced drip. Crankshaft rear oil seals are particularly prone to going hard with age and dripping from the flywheel housing. The advantage of oil leaks is the natural rust-inhibiting qualities! Both petrol and diesel 2286cc engines are very easy to work on and parts are plentiful and good value. Having said that, costs do add up and it is always best practice to buy the best-quality parts you can afford. If rebuilding using new old stock genuine parts, you can expect to spend significant amounts of money.

On the road a 2286cc petrol should pull well and achieve 50–60mph without undue problems. A standard 2286cc diesel in good condition should also be able to achieve a similar speed, but will be noisy and you'll feel like you're thrashing it. This is a feature of Land Rover's cunning theory of 'the longevity of the Land Rover is directly proportionate to the discomfort of the driver'. I jest, but there is no doubt that further up the rev band you go the noisier the vehicle gets and that's just to be expected, not necessarily a fault.

A 2625cc 6-cylinder will usually return an abysmal 11–18mpg, but you'll be rewarded with smoothness and a sense of reassuringly expensive exclusivity. These engines are lovely but historically unloved when they were functional working vehicles, mostly because of the running costs. When in good condition they run beautifully and are perfect for a Sunday driver – not fast but effortless performance with a lovely soundtrack. Parts are expensive and harder to find, so factor that in.

In terms of engine conversions, later 90/110 engines make perfect sense if a vehicle is going to be used on a regular basis. The 2495cc petrol is a direct replacement for the 2286cc and the 2495cc naturally aspirated diesel fits with little more than a small modification to the RHS engine mount. 200Tdi and 300Tdi engines are commonplace, offering significant performance and economy at the expense of originality, and there is also the knock-on effect that other ancillary components need to be upgraded or modified, such as the exhaust and cooling system. The quality of these conversions varies significantly from beautifully executed

ABOVE LEFT: Most Land Rover engines leak oil, but a good 2286cc petrol engine should start and run sweetly even when worn.

ABOVE RIGHT: The 2286cc diesel is known to develop poor starting and running when poorly maintained.

Assessing the Viability of a Project Land Rover

The 2625cc petrol is a lovely smooth engine but is not known for its economy or parts availability.

and looking factory fit to bodged over a weekend with whatever was to hand.

GEARBOX ASSESSMENT

Series Land Rover gearboxes do suffer from common problems such as jumping out of gear and general noise. Having said that, it is not a weak part per se. Be aware that there is no synchromesh on first and second on a Series II or IIA box, so you can expect a crunchy gear change if unaccustomed to driving one. A full gearbox rebuild is not technically hard for a reasonably competent amateur mechanic, but if there are multiple worn internal parts, costs can rise rapidly. If a test drive is possible, all gears should engage and while transmission noise is common, it shouldn't sound like a tray of spanners having a fight!

The transfer box is known to be robust, so is less likely to have mechanical failures than the main gearbox. High and Low range should engage and 4WD should engage. It is common for a vehicle that has sat for a while to have seized 4WD linkages: thankfully this is usually just a case of removing the floor to gain access and free off the sliding rods.

On a vehicle that has sat for a long time, it is very common for the clutch to seize on. This is usually caused by light corrosion on the flywheel and gearbox input shaft. A stuck clutch friction plate can often be freed off by starting the vehicle in gear in low ratio, but if this fails the only option is to separate engine and gearbox, at which point the clutch might as well be replaced. Clutch pedals and hydraulics also seize and perish, so plan to replace all rubber hydraulic components. (For further information on gearbox identification and restoration, *see* Chapter 10.)

AXLES AND STEERING

Rear axle cases are prone to corrosion, in particular the differential oil pan and the lower reinforcing section. Repair sections are available but the welding must be carried out to a high standard. Expect oil leaks on the differential pinion seals.

Chrome steering swivel balls on the front axle are very likely to have corroded, causing oil leaks and destroying the swivel pins and bearings. While temporary fixes can be made on slightly corroded swivel balls, the only long-term solution is replacement. Full rebuild kits with all bearings, pins, seals and gaskets are readily available but costs do add up.

If a vehicle has sat up for a long time, it is likely that most of the steering ball joints will have suffered: rubber seals perish allowing moisture in and

Gearbox wear is common, but many will soldier on for years and transfer boxes generally last well. Removal is quite an involved task.

RIGHT: A vehicle that has sat for a long time is likely to have a seized clutch, either through corrosion on the flywheel or a failed hydraulic system.

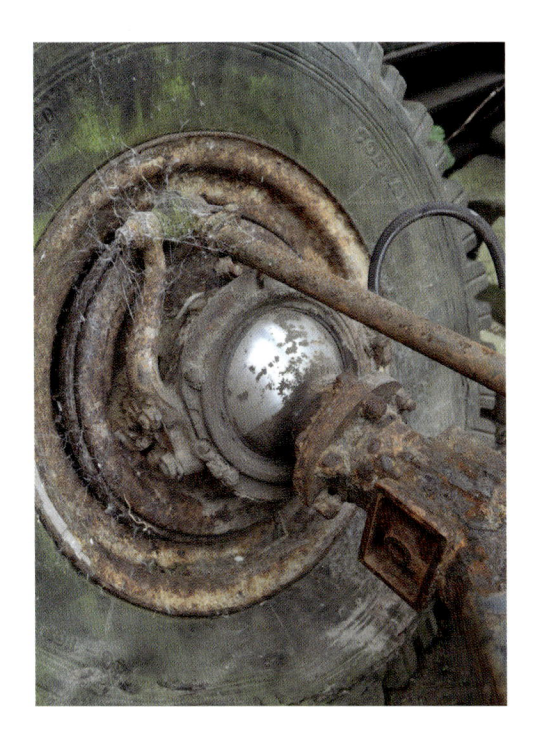

Assessing the Viability of a Project Land Rover

FAR LEFT: *Axle swivel balls are notorious for corroding. Severely pitted chrome means oil leaks, and oil leaks mean heavy steering.*

LEFT: *Leaf springs are always rock hard after a vehicle has been sat up but should free off. If they are splaying apart, like this, they will likely need replacing.*

grease out. Ball joints are also very prone to seizing in the steering rods and the rods can and do suffer from strength-compromising corrosion. The steering relay is prone to leaking: on a vehicle that has sat for a long time, there might be no oil left in it. It is also likely to have corroded solid in the chassis crossmember. (For further information *see* Chapters 12 and 13.)

SUSPENSION

All Series Land Rovers have leaf springs. The original design was a multi-leaf semi-elliptical spring, although many vehicles will have been fitted with tapering parabolic springs that have fewer leafs. Multi-leaf springs are prone to corrosion between the leafs, causing them to blow apart, seize and potentially crack. Sprung steel also goes flat over time, causing the vehicle to sit low or lopsided. While it is sometimes possible to dismantle and rebuild springs with good results, it is significantly easier to fit new, so budget accordingly for a full replacement set along with a full set of dampers/shock absorbers. (For further information *see* Chapter 15.)

WIRING ASSESSMENT

Many Land Rovers have had multiple wiring bodges. Home-made looms are common, as are potentially dangerous modifications and make-do repairs. Series II/IIA wiring is cloth covered and this tends to turn to dust, compromising the wiring identification colours. Series III looms are more robust but still prone to the same poor repairs. Wiring is a safety critical part of a vehicle and should be high on the priority list for any full or partial restoration. A bodged loom is often (though not always) indicative that the rest of the vehicle will show the same cavalier attitude to maintenance. (For further information, *see* Chapter 17.)

BRAKES

If buying a project vehicle that has sat for some time, budget for a full replacement of all the safety-critical braking components. This should normally include master cylinder, wheel cylinders, brake shoes and flexi pipes. In addition, it is likely that the fixed

Unfortunately this sort of wiring bodge is all too common on a Series Land Rover.

37

Assessing the Viability of a Project Land Rover

Any corroded brake components or old rubber hoses should be replaced as a matter of course.

brake pipes will have corroded. It's rare to see a vehicle still on the original steel pipes, but there are some out there. In-service replacement copper pipes might also be compromised by seized unions, which are often poorly made and/or not clipped securely in place. Poor brake pipes are another potential barometer for the quality of other jobs: if time has been taken to make good brake pipes, it is likely a similar approach has been taken on other jobs. (For further information, *see* Chapter 16.)

BODY AND PAINTWORK

It is a common misconception that because Land Rover bodywork is primarily aluminium, it doesn't corrode. The area where the body contacts the steel chassis is likely to have suffered from bimetallic corrosion, causing it to turn to white powder. This is usually evident on the rear body along the lip below the rear door, the forward rear body attachment points and the rear floor. The corners of the seat box, the floor panels and the front wings where they contact the chassis and bulkhead also corrode. Functional repairs are simple enough

ABOVE LEFT: *Aluminium corrodes when in contact with raw steel. The bottom of the rear tub is particularly prone to this.*

ABOVE RIGHT: *The bottom of the door bottom is a common rot spot. Note the aluminium skin is prone to bimetallic corrosion.*

ABOVE LEFT: *This is an all too common sight on the bottom of a front panel, but thankfully good quality repair sections are available.*

ABOVE RIGHT: *Patina or scruffy? You decide – beyond structural integrity, the look of the bodywork is a personal choice.*

Assessing the Viability of a Project Land Rover

with patches, rivets and appropriate adhesive and a range of repair sections are readily available, but it takes considerable time and skill to achieve a high-quality repair.

Door bottoms and tops are steel with an aluminium skin and are very prone to corrosion. Many lower-quality aftermarket doors from the past had no protection between the steel frame and aluminium skin, causing bimetallic corrosion. Good quality replacements are now available, as are correct profile repair sections, should there be a desire to retain the original doors.

Front panels corrode from the bottom up, but fortunately good-quality repair sections are available with all the correct pressing details.

The overall look of the bodywork is something of a personal choice. There is a fine line (according to one's own opinion) between patina (age-related wear, but otherwise in tidy functional condition) and scruffy. Hand-painted panels are very common, as is peeling paint and multi-coloured panels. A quick refresh with a paintbrush and coach enamel is easy and cheap. However, a full professional respray to a high standard with all the background preparation and repairs will be very expensive. (For further information, *see* Chapter 20.)

INTERIOR

Utility Land Rover interiors are very basic with minimal interior trim. Seats are available at a reasonable cost with the quality and availability improving significantly over recent years. Series III dashboard tops crack and the lower dash/heater duct is likely to have corroded badly behind the vinyl, reducing the effectiveness of the heater. Aftermarket covers are available but the thin steel backing is not currently available, so expedient repairs or a better second-hand unit is the only option. Station Wagons, however, have multiple trim panels and replacement is disproportionally expensive compared with other elements of a restoration. (For further information, *see* Chapter 22.)

Land Rover interior trim doesn't usually last well. It's all available, but costs rise if kitting out a 109in Station Wagon.

Series III lower dash panels are notorious for corroding behind the vinyl covering and top plastic tray.

5
Engine Restoration and Conversions

Series Land Rovers were fitted with a number of different engines from 1958 to 1984. It is beyond the scope of this restoration manual to cover every single detail on every different engine option, so the decision has been made to concentrate on a general overhaul on the ubiquitous and well-loved 2286cc petrol. The 2286cc diesel shares a block design and a significant number of components with its petrol counterpart, and the simplicity of the engines means that many of the rebuild tasks are simply a variation on the theme. For minute details on technical jobs and machining specifications it will be necessary to consult the official Workshop Manual, but this chapter gives an overview of the wear you are likely to encounter and the process of rebuilding an engine in a DIY environment.

SERIES II, IIA AND III ENGINE HISTORY AND EVOLUTION

The very first Series II 88in petrol models were fitted with the 4-cylinder 1997cc IOE (inlet over exhaust) engine from the outgoing Series I. The Series II 109in was launched with the then new 4-cylinder 2286cc ohv (overhead valve) petrol engine and this soon also became standard fitment in the 88in model. The Series II diesel option was the 4-cylinder 2052cc developed for the Series I in 1957. These engines were usually painted grey.

With the launch of the Series IIA model in 1961 came a new 2286cc version of the diesel engine and an update to the petrol engine, rationalising the petrol and diesel blocks. Both engines share the same three main-bearing crank design, although the diesel crank is significantly stronger. A petrol crank should not be used in a diesel, although a diesel crank can be used in a petrol. These engines were usually painted blue/green.

In 1967 the 6-cylinder 2625cc IOE engine from the contemporary Rover 110 car was repurposed as an option for 109in models. The basic engine design was based on the old 1997cc IOE engine design from the Series 1, but significantly re-engineered with two extra cylinders as well as roller cam followers. It offers improved power and torque over the 2286cc engine and is praised for its smooth running qualities – but not for its economy. Parts are relatively scarce and therefore significantly more expensive. The block and timing case were also painted blue/green.

The same engine options continued into the Series III era with minor updates, mostly to comply with stricter emissions regulations and a gradual engineering evolution. The 1980 model year saw the end of the 6-cylinder model, replaced from 1979 by the 3528cc Rover V8-powered Stage 1 model. This engine was a detuned version of the Range Rover engine, coupled to a version of the Range Rover's permanent 4×4 transmission. These models are easily identifiable by the flush front required to accommodate the length of the engine and drive chain.

Late 1980 also saw a new five-main bearing version of the 2286cc petrol and diesel engines. Acknowledged to be smoother and stronger than earlier

ABOVE LEFT: *The ubiquitous three-bearing 2286cc petrol engine was introduced in 1958 and was subject to engineering upgrades for the launch of the Series IIA. It remained pretty much unchanged until 1981.*

ABOVE RIGHT: *The 2286cc diesel was launched with the Series IIA in 1961 and replaced the underpowered 2052cc.*

Engine Restoration and Conversions

ABOVE LEFT: *The 2625cc 6-cylinder engine was an option in 109in vehicles from 1967 until 1980.*

ABOVE RIGHT: *The aluminium 3528cc Rover V8 became an option in 1979, replacing the heavy 2625cc.*

The 2286cc block was re-engineered with five main bearings in 1981 and can be identified by a terracotta block with extra strengthening ribs.

units, these can be easily identified by a terracotta painted block and a black cylinder head and timing case. Note that military versions of these engines may be painted green all over. Beyond the colour, the block can also be identified by strengthening ribs in the bottom of the block.

The basic design of the original 2286cc block, which in turn had been based on the 2052cc diesel, continued to be used with engineering upgrades in the coil spring Land Rover era, all the way through until the launch of the electronically controlled TD5 engine in 1998. It is this commonality in basic block design that makes it easy to install later engines such as the 2495cc petrol and naturally aspirated diesel, the 19J Turbo Diesel and the 200 and 300Tdi engines. Indeed, the pushrod part number from a 1957 2052cc is the same as a 1998 300Tdi. Sections on engine modifications and conversions are also included below, acknowledging that many classic Land Rovers have already been modified and that performance upgrades are still very much part of the Land Rover scene.

COMMON ENGINE PROBLEMS

2286cc Petrol

The 2286cc petrol engine is generally known to be a robust unit that will run reasonably well, even when fairly worn. The 1958–1961 variant is perhaps more prone to wear and harder for parts due to the unique block, crank and bearings, but these engines are definitely worth restoring if original to the vehicle. Later variants are common and parts readily available, although in recent years the value of the once 'cheap and cheerful' engine has risen considerably.

General age- and mileage-related wear and tear is to be expected, as is historically poor maintenance. Worn rocker shafts are common, often related to carbonated oil at the top of the engine. Valve seals are known to become brittle, causing high oil consumption, often with a noticeable puff of blue smoke on start-up.

Water galleries also suffer from rust blockages and rusty core plugs, especially in engines that run on water rather than coolant with anti-corrosion properties. The rear crankshaft oil seal on the three-bearing unit is known to leak and can be tricky to replace due to being a split design.

The later five-bearing variant petrol engine is acknowledged as being the better design with a stronger block and crank as well as a simpler one-piece rear crankshaft seal. Having said that, there is absolutely nothing wrong with a good three-bearing engine.

2052cc and 2286cc Diesel

The 2052cc and later 2286cc diesel engines are often considered by many to be poor, noisy and underpowered. This reputation is slightly unfair and performance was comparable to contemporary diesel options from other manufacturers.

A well set-up 2286cc diesel will give reasonable performance, economy and longevity, but is more sensitive to set-up and timing than the 2286cc petrol. Correct injector pump timing is essential to ensure good cold starting and clean running. Timing chains are prone to stretching, in turn causing poor valve timing and poor performance. The engine is noisy at higher

Engine Restoration and Conversions

ABOVE LEFT: *Carbon build-up at the top of the engine is common and causes rapid valve-train wear.*

ABOVE RIGHT: *Water galleries commonly fill up with rusty sludge that causes poor cooling.*

Poor pump and valve timing is the Achilles heel of the 2286cc diesel.

speeds and acceleration is, at best, steady. The diesel was often chosen for agricultural use and used at low speeds in rural environments, potentially leading to poor maintenance and excessive carbon build-up.

Despite the 2286cc diesel's debatable reputation, when set up well it is a reliable unit and will give performance appropriate to the vehicle's design era and doesn't suffer the fuelling and electrical sensitivities of the 2286cc petrol: 2286cc diesels have propelled many adventurers all over the world.

IN-SERVICE ENGINE ASSESSMENT AND REPAIRS

The 2286cc engine is as simple a design as you are likely to encounter on any classic vehicle. Consequently, there are a number of significant repair jobs that can be carried out while in the vehicle, including cylinder head, pistons, big-end bearings, oil pump, timing chain and camshaft. The engine, however, is simple to remove and gives the advantage of easy access.

Bear in mind that a tired engine is likely to have multiple worn components and may soldier on for many years without significant change. A decision has to be based on use, budget, mileage travelled and environmental considerations from emissions. If an engine is running and performing acceptably well, it may well be expedient to leave it be. When the can of worms is opened, it may end up becoming a seriously time-consuming and expensive project. However, there are a number of larger in-service repairs that are critical to the use of the vehicle and simply cannot be put off.

Compression Test

A compression test is an essential measure of engine condition and will reveal issues such as leaking cylinder heads, poorly sealing valves and bore and ring wear.

- Ensure the battery has a healthy charge and can turn the engine over at normal cranking speed.
- The test should normally be carried out on a warm engine, although a cold engine will still give an idea of condition – compression is usually higher when cold.
- Remove the coil feed so the engine doesn't start.
- Remove each spark plug in turn and screw in a compression tester – the press-in type requires an assistant.
- Crank the engine over for a few seconds with the throttle fully depressed.
- Keep a note of the reading for future comparison.

A reading above 120psi suggests a reasonably healthy engine; anything below 100psi is a significant concern that will require investigation. A significant difference in compression in one or a pair of cylinders is also an immediate concern, often caused by a failing cylinder head/head gasket or a poorly seated/damaged valve. Generally low but evenly matched compression is likely just general bore wear. Pouring a small quantity of oil down the bore and checking for an improvement in compression is a good test. If it improves, it indicates bore and/or ring wear. It is worth noting that an engine that has sat unused for a long time could suffer from stuck piston rings. Again, a decision can be made on the immediacy of the repair.

Engine Restoration and Conversions

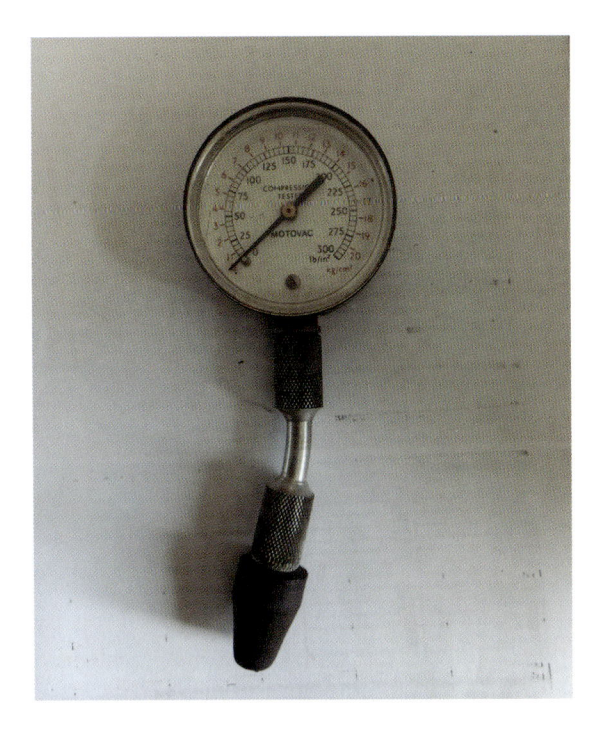

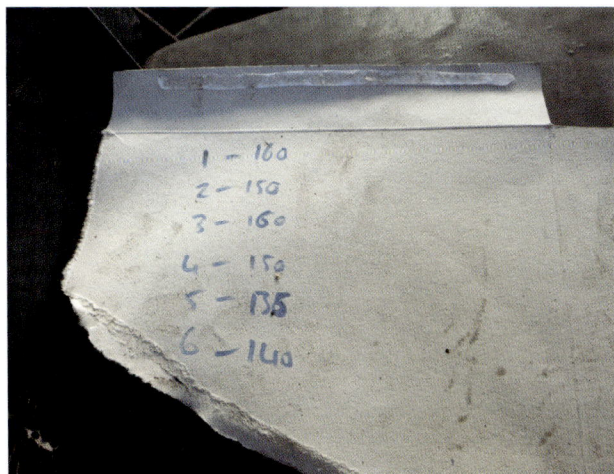

The compression results on this 6-cylinder are mostly healthy. Note that cylinder 5 and 6 are a little bit lower than the rest, so investigation was required.

LEFT: *A typical old-school cylinder pressure gauge.*

Cylinder Head Gasket Failure Symptoms

The cylinder head gasket seals the coolant and oil galleries as well as the compression of the cylinders. Typical symptoms of a failing head/head gasket are:

- Oil contamination in the coolant leading to 'mayonnaise' in the cooling system.
- Coolant contamination in the oil leading to 'mayonnaise' in the oil. Note that cold starts and short runs will naturally create moisture in the rocker cover and some emulsification may not be a cause for concern and should clear after a long run.
- Pressurisation of the cooling system caused by leaks between cylinder and coolant galleries.
- Pressurisation of the oil system caused by leaks from cylinder to oil galleries.
- 'Chuffing' and low compression caused by cylinder head gasket failing between cylinders.

Removing the cylinder head also gives an insight into the general condition of the engine and should be a first point of call to assess an unknown engine. While you're at it, there are a number of additional jobs that might be worthwhile doing while the head is removed, such as inspecting the valves, changing valve oil seals, if

This head gasket has blown between cylinders.

LEFT: *Typical 'mayonnaise' on the rocker cover indicating coolant in the oil. This was actually a head cracked between the core plugs.*

43

Engine Restoration and Conversions

Cylinder head removed from a 2625cc to gauge bore wear.

suspect, as well as changing inlet and exhaust gaskets.

In-Service Cylinder Head and Gasket Removal

It is significantly easier to completely remove the bonnet. Not only does it give much better access and light, but it means it won't fall down on your head. It is far easier to have an assistant to help remove it, as it's not uncommon for the hinges to be tight.

- Remove the air cleaner and pipes, electrical connections to the head and disconnect the battery.
- Drain the cooling system, either by removing a bottom radiator hose or via the radiator drain valve, if fitted. It's also advisable to drain the block via the valve on the LHS: this minimises coolant getting into oil galleries and bolt holes.
- Remove the remaining coolant pipes from the top of the engine including the radiator, heater and water pump bypass hose clips.
- Disconnect the throttle linkages, choke cable and fuel supply to the carburettor, as well as the distributor and brake servo vacuum pipes.
- Remove the exhaust downpipe. Access is tricky but a deep socket on a long extension can be used from underneath to remove the nuts. These are often very tight and studs are prone to snapping. A bit of heat and easing fluid may be required.
- Remove the spark plugs and leads. There is no need to remove the distributor body, but do note the orientation of the HT leads before removing them.
- Remove the oil feed pipe from the back of the block. The later type engine lifting bracket can get in the way of removing the banjo, so it's often easier to remove it.
- Back off the cylinder-head bolts slightly. Best practice is to start at the outside and working inwards, the reverse order of the tightening sequence.
- Remove the rocker shaft bolts – this includes the head bolts on the posts. As this is unbolted, any compressed valves will gradually close, but it is better to back off the rocker adjustors.
- Hold the shaft assembly at either end as it will tend to spring apart with the pressure of the rocker springs, and they can be a pain to have to reassemble if they ping everywhere. An old school trick is to upend the rocker cover and bolt it loosely on the studs on the posts.
- Lift out the pushrods from the cam followers. Best practice is that these should be kept in order and go back in the same position on reassembly as the components will have worn together. A card with holes in it is ideal to keep a track of them.
- Once all the bolts are removed, the head can be lifted off. The head is quite heavy and, coupled to the fact you have to reach at arm's length, it is advisable to have an assistant. If not, it is easier to lift the head if you can actually position yourself directly over it and lift off with an appropriate strap round the lifting eyes. Note that on occasion the head can stick to the block, especially with a composite gasket. A block of wood can be used to knock it free.

Remove all ancillary connections – access to the exhaust can be awkward.

Engine Restoration and Conversions

ABOVE LEFT: *Spark plugs out, but the distributor can stay in place.*

ABOVE RIGHT: *Backing off the head bolts – they will be tight.*

ABOVE LEFT: *Take care when backing off the rocker bolts – they can snap.*

ABOVE RIGHT: *Holding the rocker shaft assembly to stop it springing apart.*

ABOVE LEFT: *Best practice is to keep the push rods in order: a simple piece of scrap cardboard is ideal.*

ABOVE RIGHT: *With all the bolts out the head is ready to be lifted off, but sometimes a composite gasket will stick fast.*

Cylinder Head and Bore Inspection

There is no better time to gauge the general health of the engine than with the head removed, as it gives an insight into bore wear and piston condition. A really healthy bore may still have honing marks but is more likely to have a slight lip at the top of the piston stroke. Any lip large enough to catch a fingernail indicates an engine that is very worn and in need of a rebore and oversize pistons. Inspect the top of the pistons for cracking and other damage. Again, a decision can

45

be made on use, budget, expediency and urgency.

Thoroughly inspect the head and gasket on a bench. Any blow pattern should be obvious and that area in particular should be checked for damage such as cracks and imperfections in the surface. A straight edge and feeler gauges can be used to check for warping; if in doubt, have it professionally assessed.

Inspect the valves. You can expect a grey/brown deposit on the valves and some carbon build-up. Any significant oily build-up will need further investigation and could be due to worn oil control rings, excessive bore wear or from failed valve stem oil seals. A puff of blue smoke on start-up is usually valve stem oil seals; more regular blue smoke is more likely to be worn bores and/or oil control rings.

Mismatched cylinder condition is a cause for concern: if this is washed clean it is coolant entering the cylinder, or if very oily it is likely to be a broken piston oil control ring. Serious overheating will be obvious with blooming and could even lead to valve seats falling out.

If the engine was known to have a top-end tapping noise, it is worth carefully dismantling the rocker shaft assembly to examine the shaft for wear. The shaft is particularly prone to wear, especially when rocker oil flow is compromised by sludgy, carbonised oil. Any noticeable wear means a new shaft should be fitted and potentially new rocker bushes, although engines often soldier on for years with worn components like these, depending on use and expected performance.

Inspect the pads of the rockers. It's not uncommon for the pads to wear to the shape of the top of the valve if oil flow has been compromised. If so, the rocker is pretty much scrap and should be replaced. It may be possible to have them refaced but it may work out more costly than simple replacement.

Thoroughly clean off any deposits and remains of old gaskets on the cylinder head. A blunt scraper can be used but take care not to leave any scores. An air line is invaluable for blasting out rust deposits in the coolant galleries.

This is also a good time to consider the condition of the valves, valve guides and seats, and whether it is worthwhile to have hardened valves and seats fitted. The initial concerns regarding unleaded petrol causing valve recession in old engines has proved to be less of a problem than initially thought, but this would be a good time to do the work.

If in doubt, have the head inspected and tested by a machine shop who will be best qualified to advise on any remedial work required. Reconditioned heads are readily available, including

ABOVE LEFT: *Take time to inspect the bores for wear or scoring as a decision can then be made on the best course of action.*

ABOVE RIGHT: *This particular head is scrap from significant overheating – note the blooming.*

A typical rocker shaft with significant wear – in this case the shaft and rockers are scrap.

LEFT: *This head has got so hot the valve seats have fallen out.*

Engine Restoration and Conversions

the option to fit a performance head with ported valves.

Removing, Lapping and Refitting Valves

A valve spring compression tool should be used to compress the valve springs so the collets can be removed. Before fitting the compression tool, it is advisable to use a hammer and socket to knock down on the top of the valve cap to loosen off the collets as they can jam in place. Once compressed, the collets can be hooked out and the valves and springs removed.

Inspect the valves and valve seats for damage to the sealing surfaces and significant wear in the valve guides. If in doubt, have a machine shop assess the condition.

Valves in good condition with minor imperfections can be lapped in by hand using a hand-held suction stick and grinding paste. Oil the valve stem, smear grinding paste onto the valve sealing face and work the valve back and forth until it has a consistent dull grey sealing surface. Periodically turn the valve through 180 degrees. Always number valves so they go back into their original position. When refitting the collets, it is helpful to put a smear of grease on them to hold them in position on the valve until the valve spring has been released.

Change the valve seals as a matter of course: a new set is usually supplied with a head gasket kit. When they are old, the seals turn hard and brittle, causing oil to leak down the valve stems into the bores.

Refitting the Cylinder Head

Originally most cylinder head gaskets were made from copper. Since then gasket technology has moved on and modern composite gaskets are known to have better sealing properties, especially on older components. While new copper gaskets can and do work, it is commonly accepted that composite is the more forgiving option.

FAR LEFT: *The head must be thoroughly cleaned off before refitting.*

LEFT: *Valve spring compressor in use. Note that a new top-hat valve seal has been fitted.*

ABOVE LEFT: *Look for a consistent dull grey surface on a well-fitting valve and seat.*

ABOVE RIGHT: *Using a hand suction tool to lap valves in. Note that the valve positions have been numbered.*

Engine Restoration and Conversions

Composite gasket is fitted dry – a petrol engine is shown here.

LEFT: *Given the choice, go for a good-quality composite gasket over a copper one.*

Copper gaskets are often fitted with a smear of oil or with a compound such as Wellseal, but composite gaskets should be fitted dry. Note the correct orientation of the gasket to align the coolant gallery holes. Also note there is a difference between the petrol and diesel gaskets. While the blocks are the same, the head is different and the shape round the combustion chamber is different to accommodate the diesel hotspots.

- Thoroughly clean all mating surfaces, ensuring that there is no oil in the bolt holes or it will be impossible to achieve correct torque down.
- To assist in lowering the head back into place, a pair of head bolts with the heads removed to create studs can assist in lining it up correctly: put a groove in the top to allow them to be screwed in and out easily. Again, it can be a massive help to have another pair of hands to lower it into place.
- Fit all the bolts and tighten down lightly before refitting the pushrods back into their original holes. It is important to ensure that the pushrods locate fully in the cam followers. If they don't, it's common for them to break the edge off the follower as the rocker shaft head bolts are tightened down.
- Refit the rocker shaft assembly, ensuring that the post dowels locate correctly and the back of the rockers locate correctly in the pushrods. It is advisable to back off the adjustors on any rockers that are 'on cam' (that is, opening a valve).
- Start to torque the head down, working systematically out as per the Workshop Manual diagram: quality aftermarket gaskets often come with a diagram in the information slip. Ensure the valve assembly pulls into place.
- When nipped up, gradually work though half torque to full torque. On a 2286cc petrol the main bolts should be torqued to 65lb ft, the smaller rocket shaft bolts should be torqued to 18lb ft.
- Reset the valve gaps to 0.010 (*see below for two different techniques*).
- Turn the engine over a few times and recheck the valve gaps to ensure that the pushrods have fully located in the cam followers. If a rocker adjustor has significantly more thread showing than another, it's a likely sign that the pushrod is not fully located.
- Clean (or replace) and re-gap the spark plugs before refitting. Do this after setting the valve clearances to avoid having to turn an engine with compression.
- Refit the rear of head oil feed with a new copper washer. Refit all the coolant pipes, exhaust, carburettor pipes and all wiring and ignition components. Refill the cooling system and check for leaks.
- It can be helpful to leave the rocker cover off on first start-up to check the flow of oil from every rocker oil hole. It also makes it easier to listen for any valve train noises.
- If a copper head gasket is fitted, it is often best practice to re-torque it after a few miles of running.

Setting Valve Clearances

Valve clearances should be set at 0.010in, either hot or cold. This is important not only for smooth and quiet running, but to ensure that the valve opens and closes at the correct time. The clearances must be set with the valve in the fully closed position. The clearance is adjusted by backing off the lock nut and using a wide flat-blade screwdriver to alter the gap between the rocker and the valve. The 0.010in feeler gauge should be a sliding fit and the adjustor should be counter-held while the lock nut is nipped up. The most common method for checking and setting valve clearances is to use the 'Rule of Nine' technique. An alternative technique is known as the 'On the Rock' method.

Engine Restoration and Conversions

Inserting the pushrods into the original location. Ensure they seat properly in the cam followers.

LEFT: *Studs with slots fitted to help guide head into place.*

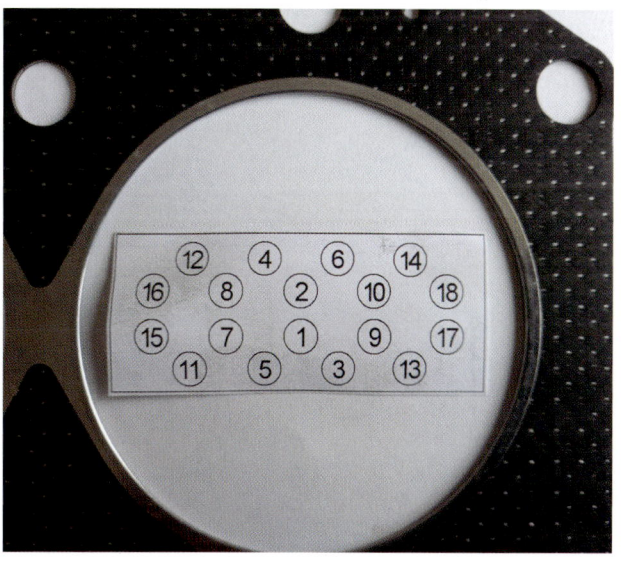

Good-quality gaskets often come with tightening sequence information, or consult the Workshop Manual.

LEFT: *Ensure the rocker shaft locates on the dowels before nipping up.*

While these techniques should result in perfectly set valve clearances and a rattle-free engine, sometimes it is expedient to locate the cause of an individual rogue tappet. This can sometimes be found by carefully feeding an old 0.010in feeler gauge under each rocker with the engine running on tick-over and listening for any change. Remember that wear on the rocker shaft and rocker bushes will give a rattle even if the gaps are set correctly.

The simpler of these methods is the common 'Rule of Nine', in which the valve numbers add up to nine. Turn the engine until valve no.1 is fully open with the rocker arm fully down and check and adjust valve no. 8. Continue with the remaining valves.

Valve Fully Open	Check and Adjust Valve
1	8
2	7
3	6
4	5
5	4
6	3
7	2
8	1

49

Engine Restoration and Conversions

ABOVE LEFT: Petrol main head bolts should be gradually torqued to 65lb ft.

ABOVE RIGHT: Rocker shaft bolts torqued to 18lb ft.

Checking for good oil flow at the rockers before fitting the rocker cover.

LEFT: Setting valve gaps with a 0.010 feeler gauge.

Engine Restoration and Conversions

On the Rock Method

An alternative to the Rule of Nine is to set valve clearances 'On the Rock', a technique that might take a while to get used to but once mastered has the advantage of being able to set two valves at the same time. 'On the Rock' is used to describe the inlet and exhaust valves on a cylinder when one is just closing and the other opening. As one just starts to drop the other one rises and this can be observed at the rockers. The pistons work as pairs on the crank shaft. When the valves serving a piston are On the Rock, the valves at its twin will be fully closed. On a Land Rover engine, piston 1 is twinned with 4, piston 2 with 3.

- Initially it is easiest to set the engine towards top dead centre (TDC), firing on piston no.1. At this point the valves at piston no.1 (valves 1 and 2) will be fully closed and the valves serving piston no.4 (valves 7 and 8) will be on the rock. The gaps at 1 and 2 can be set to 0.010in.

- The Land Rover firing order is 1-3-4-2, so piston 3 will have closed valves next (valves 5 and 6) as the engine is rotated clockwise. The point at which they are fully closed is when the valves at piston no.2 are on the rock (valves 3 and 4). Valves 5 and 6 can be set.
- Piston no.4 is next to fire, so valves 7 and 8 can be set when valves 1 and 2 at piston no.1 are on the rock.
- Finally, valves 3 and 4 at piston no.2 can be set when valves 5 and 6 are on the rock.

As a concise résumé:

Valves on the Rock	Check and Gap	Firing on Cylinder
7 and 8	1 and 2	1
3 and 4	5 and 6	3
1 and 2	7 and 8	4
5 and 6	3 and 4	2

ENGINE REMOVAL AND REFITTING

Engines are heavy, unwieldy and potentially dangerous if lifted incorrectly. A 2286cc engine weighs just over 200kg and the 2625cc 6-cylinder weighs nearer 300kg. A properly rated engine crane is usually the safest and most convenient lifting method, although owners have come up with ingenious methods with varying degrees of safety over the years. It is worth noting that it is significantly easier if the crane legs will fit between the tyres and the length of the jib is sufficient to reach to the engine balance point. Note that the further the jib is extended, the lower the lifting capacity.

All engines have the facility for lifting eyes screwed into the back and front of the head. These should be used for engine removal and refitting with an appropriately rated lifting strap, chain or engine leveller. It is possible to remove an engine without them, but far harder to get the appropriate balance point.

Whilst it is possible to remove an engine without removing the front panel, it is far easier to do so, not only for ease of access but to avoid accidental damage to the radiator. When removing the 2625cc 6-cylinder engine, it might even be necessary to remove the bumper (depending on the length of the jib) to reach the balance point.

Disconnecting the electrics, fuel, cooling pipes, exhaust and ancillaries is straightforward. The floor and transmission tunnel will also need to be removed to gain access to the bellhousing bolts. It is often easier to take the engine out if it is first lifted sufficiently to fully remove the mounting rubbers and right-hand side wedge, before lowering slightly and levering the bellhousing and flywheel housings apart.

FULL ENGINE STRIP-DOWN

Engine Stand vs Working on the Floor

Land Rover engines are heavy and stripping and rebuilding is easier with an engine stand. The only issue is that they don't fit the generic type particularly well. In addition, most engine stands hold the block at the back and having access to timing marks on the flywheel is essential for setting the valve timing accurately. A useful adaptation is to fabricate a bracket that can hold the block via the camshaft side plates. Experience suggests the block is sufficiently strong enough, though using all the fixing bolts ensures the

ABOVE LEFT: An engine hoist is essential. Here a 2625cc engine is being rigged with an appropriately rated lifting sling.

ABOVE RIGHT: While not essential, removing the front panel makes engine removal much easier.

Engine Restoration and Conversions

A home-fabricated side mounting for the engine stand allows the crank to be turned and valve timing to be set during the build process.

A 2286cc engine strapped to a pallet to support it during strip down.

considerable weight of the engine and the additional fulcrum effect is spread over the largest possible area.

Knowing that many amateur mechanics do not have access to an engine stand, the following series of strip-down photos show a method that does not require one. An engine can be stripped and rebuilt on the floor and a sturdy bench, as long as care is taken when manoeuvring the heavy sections. However, an engine crane or hoist is essential for any significant lifting: it's not just about an assessment of personal strength, but ensuring the health and safety of both the engine and the person carrying out the work.

Work with the engine on a firm but forgiving surface. A very solid pallet is ideal or a thick rubber mat on a concrete floor. This will allow the engine to be rolled over with less likelihood of causing damage.

A standard Land Rover sump has a fairly flat bottom so the engine is reasonably stable sat upright. The weight distribution, however, means it will tip forward and a block of wood can be used to chock it in place. Before beginning strip-down, it is advisable to strap it in place to stop it being pulled over when releasing tight head bolts. A ratchet strap round the engine mounts and flywheel housing is perfect to hold it onto a pallet, bolstered by additional blocks of wood.

Preamble to Stripping

Obviously the engine should be drained of oil and thoroughly cleaned before stripping down. Removal of the head is as per in-service head gasket replacement.

Remove all the ancillary components such as alternator/dynamo, fan, carburettor, manifolds, fuel pump and backing plate, oil filler tube, dipstick, starter, clutch and oil filter housing. This will then create a 'short engine' that is a reasonably manageable size and weight.

Different minds come up with different solutions to keep track of parts, their location and assembly/disassembly. Taking photos is invaluable, as is compartmentalising parts and their storage, whether in boxes or sealable bags. Bolts can often be loosely put back into their original location or put into a cardboard cut-out pattern.

It may help to break the process down into obvious locations on the engine and have separate storage containers for each general area. This is how the following strip-down sequence has been written.

Front of Engine Block

Remove the crankshaft starter dog/bolt (it should have a lock tab). A rattle gun is ideal but a suitable socket and breaker bar or large spanner can be used. A short, sharp shock with a suitable hammer will usually knock it free. Remove the pulley: it usually comes out easily enough with a pry bar, but if stuck a puller might be necessary.

Remove the water pump from the timing case. The small bolts are UNC thread. All the bolts are extremely prone to seizing, especially the long ones that go through the timing case into the block. Heat, easing fluid and patience is much better than having to deal with a sheared bolt. A socket on a short breaker bar is ideal for working the bolts back and fore.

Remove the timing case taking note of the length of the bolts – a cardboard template can be helpful. There are three bolts in the front of the sump to the bottom of the timing case. The case might be stuck and might need levering off, but do not lever against a machined surface. A careful knock with a soft mallet might also help to free it off – it will be held by the old gasket and a tight fit on the dowels.

Before removing the timing chain tensioner and timing chain, take a careful note of any timing marks on the cam wheel and any additional scribed timing marks. *See* sections below on removing the camshaft and setting valve timing for details.

Rear of Engine Block

Remove the cam rear cover plate and head oil feed pipe union. Remove the flywheel bolts. A rattle gun is ideal as it will allow the bolts to be removed without having to counter-hold the crank. If using a ratchet or breaker bar, the flywheel can be counter-held with a piece of soft metal against the starter ring in the timing inspection hole or by inserting two clutch bolts and using a lever between them to counter-hold the rotation.

It is easier to remove the flywheel off the crank spigot if the clutch cover bolts are fitted to assist gripping it and,

Engine Restoration and Conversions

ABOVE LEFT: *Using a pry bar to remove the front pulley.*

ABOVE RIGHT: *Take care when removing the long studs that go through the water pump and timing cover into the block.*

ABOVE LEFT: *Do not remove the cam wheel until a note has been taken of the timing marks.*

ABOVE RIGHT: *The flywheel might need to be counter-held when removing the bolts.*

if necessary, carefully levering against. Do not put your fingers in the gap between the flywheel and the flywheel housing – it will hurt if it traps them. The flywheel housing can now be removed. It might need a careful thud with a soft mallet.

Camshaft Removal

Remove the lock wire, special retaining bolts and lift out the cam followers and rollers. A piece of welding wire can be used to hook under them or use a suitable pair of long-nose pliers. Keep these in order so they can go back as they came out, if still in reusable condition.

Inspect the cam lobes from above. If deemed in good serviceable condition the cam can be left in place, depending on whether further work and machining is required on the block. Generally speaking, the cam and cam bearings survive well as they have good oil flow. If in doubt, take it out or seek a professional opinion.

To remove the cam, the skew gear for the distributor drive has to be removed. It is held in place with a long grub screw behind the oil filter housing; the old gasket will need to be trimmed back to find it. With the grub screw out, the skew gear can be lifted out with a pair of long-nosed pliers. The quill shaft to the oil pump can also be lifted out at this point.

53

Engine Restoration and Conversions

Cam followers being lifted out with long-nose pliers.

RIGHT: *Skew gear retaining screw is hidden behind the oil filter housing gasket.*

A puller might be required to remove the cam wheel.

LEFT: *Note P markings on cam wheel perimeter and on woodruff key spline.*

Before removing the cam wheel, it is important to note the position of the cam woodruff key and any additional timing marks. On later engines there is a P-marker on the woodruff key slot and on the perimeter of the wheel. If there are no marks, make some either with a sharp punch or correction fluid. Note that earlier petrol and all diesel models had a multi-spline cam wheel, which allows an accurate setting of the timing chain on the Exhaust Peak (EP) mark. *See* the section below on setting cam timing.

The cam wheel can often be carefully levered off once the bolt and locking tab have been removed, but if tight it will need the correct puller. Once off, the cam thrust bearing can be removed and the cam carefully withdrawn. Support it through the block apertures as it comes out to ensure it doesn't get damaged.

Crank and Piston Removal

At this point the block with crank is significantly lighter and can be carefully turned over to rest on a forgiving flat surface, such as wood or thick rubber.

Remove the sump. A small rattle gun makes this a much quicker job as there are a lot of bolts to remove. The sump is likely to have stuck to the block: a firm thud with a soft mallet should remove it. Take care not to damage the lip if levering it off.

Remove the oil pump and drive shaft if not removed during camshaft removal.

Remove the big end (con rod) journal caps. It is vital that these are kept paired with their con rod as they are machined together and must not be swapped. They are number-coded to assist with pairing. Push the pistons to the top of the bore.

Remove the crank main journal caps. They are numbered and must only go back where they came from: this is obvious on a three-bearing crank, less so on a five-bearing.

With all the caps removed, the crank can be lifted out, but note that it's pretty heavy. Retrieve the two half-moon thrust bearings from the top side of the centre bearing housing. The pistons can then be pushed out the top. Note that if there is significant bore wear, it is common for the piston rings to catch on any lip at the top. A block of wood and a hammer can be used to drive them out. In the extreme case where wear is very severe and the lip so defined that the rings will not compress in, the piston skirt can be broken off and the pistons extracted out the bottom.

It is always best practice to gather all matching components together, such as putting the bearing caps back in the

Engine upturned on a pallet and sump being removed.

RIGHT: *Removing the oil pump.*

ABOVE LEFT: *Note that con rod bearing caps are unique and must not be mixed up.*

ABOVE RIGHT: *Front main cap removed to reveal a healthy crank journal.*

Engine Restoration and Conversions

Pistons have to be tapped up the bore and out the top of the block.

LEFT: *All caps removed and crank ready to be lifted out.*

ABOVE LEFT: *These main and big end bearings have seen better days; note that all the white metal has worn off.*

ABOVE RIGHT: *It is essential to lay out the components in a logical order to avoid mixing them up.*

correct matched place in the block or on the end of the correct con rod.

Extract the remaining bearing shells and note the bearing size; it will be marked on the underside of each shell. Likewise note the size of the pistons, which will be marked if oversized. If there are no size markings then they can be assumed to be standard size. This gives an indication of any previous reconditioning and options for regrind and rebore.

Lay out all the components in a logical order for inspection and storage until reassembly. If unsure, note their origin and bag up. This is particularly useful with items such as fixings.

ASSESSING AND PREPARING STRIPPED ENGINE COMPONENTS

Block

The block is clearly the basis of the engine and carries the engine number. Remember that the 2286cc petrol and diesel blocks share the same casting and it is common for engine rebuilders to have built a diesel block up as a petrol and, occasionally, vice versa.

Carefully inspect the block for cracks, in particular looking for frost damage round any water galleries. Depending on the severity, cracks can be professionally repaired if the engine is unique, original or historically important.

As a basic assessment, running finger nails up the bores can be a good indication of excessive wear. If a nail catches on the lip at the top, a rebore is necessary. Otherwise a judgement call has to be made, but there is no better

Using a heel bar to hook a core plug out.

LEFT: *Using a drill-operated honing tool to remove slight imperfections from the bore.*

time to 'go to town' on an engine than when it's already stripped.

Inspect the bore for glazing. A bore in very good condition will still have evidence of the original honing marks and if there is minimal wear, the bores can be re-honed with a simple honing tool in a drill. If in doubt, have a professional machine shop make the assessment.

A 2286cc block can be rebored up to 0.060 (+1.5mm) and can also be relined back to standard. Appropriate size pistons can be readily purchased. Many machine shops will require a sample piston and rebore to actual size rather than a book size to account for tolerances.

A raw block will be very grubby. Before contemplating a rebuild it will have to be thoroughly cleaned. A professional clean would be the ultimate approach, although for a DIY job they can be degreased and washed off with a jet wash (ideally a hot one). Consideration must be given to the potential environmental impact of such actions.

All coolant galleries must be cleaned out and core plugs should be replaced as a matter of course. Large blockages from a build-up of corroded material are commonplace on these engines and will cause poor, uneven cooling and potential for overheating. Core plugs rust from the inside out and a plug that may seem in good condition on the outside could well be seriously compromised and ready to leak under pressure.

To remove a core plug, carefully strike the inside edge with a chisel or punch and collapse it inwards from one side. It should then pivot round and can then be hooked out with a pry bar. If it pushes fully inwards, it can usually be easily hooked and pulled through sideways with little effort. A jet wash or air gun can be used to clean out the galleries.

Cam bearings are fitted into the block by a line borer and replacement is generally best left to a machine shop. Generally speaking, the cam bearings survive well as they are not under any significant stresses. The bearings can be easily inspected through the block apertures. Note they do have small cut-outs by design.

The cam followers and rollers run in a slider housing. These can be removed from the block but are not generally prone to excessive wear.

Block decks (the machined top) rarely suffer damage causing poor head gasket sealing, but as always inspect thoroughly, and if in doubt have a professional machine shop check the block over.

Block Preparation for Rebuild

If machining has been required, the block should come back from the machine shop honed and ready to build up with new pistons. If the bores are deemed not to need machining, they should be given a light honing to bust any glazing and help ensure good compression and oil control.

All block oilways should be blown out to remove any residue of machining or any contamination.

Once scrupulously clean, the block can be repainted. A number of companies sell the correct high-temperature paint and supply instructions regarding surface preparation. *See* the section on engine history for a guide on the correct block colour. A small paintbrush is ideal to work into every nook and cranny. Any overpaint on machined surfaces can be cleaned off when dry to give a clean, crisp finish.

New core plugs are best fitted after painting to maintain the sharp finish. Ensure the edges of the core plug holes are clean and smooth. Emery cloth can be used to remove any rough edges. New core plugs can be tapped in using a suitably sized drift and hammer. A socket that just fits in the cup is ideal. A generous smear of Hylomar or equivalent should be used on the block and

Engine Restoration and Conversions

ABOVE LEFT: *Block thoroughly cleaned and repainted the correct blue/green for a Series IIA.*

ABOVE RIGHT: *Using a socket to drift the rear core plug in.*

core plug before fitting and any excess can be wiped off.

Crank Assessment and Preparation

Thoroughly inspect the crank journals for scoring. Slight marks can be polished out by a machine shop, maintaining the same journal and bearing specification, but otherwise a regrind will be required. Retain the old bearings to gauge the size required, they are marked either STD or oversize specification. The 2286cc petrol crank can be reground up to 0.060. As a matter of course, all bearings should usually be replaced with good-quality parts whether a regrind is required or not.

The crank should be thoroughly cleaned and all oilways blown out. If necessary, a new timing chain cog and woodruff key can be fitted if deemed to have worn. The rear crankshaft oil seal should also be replaced as a matter of course. On a five-bearing engine, it is pressed into the flywheel housing, on a three-bearing engine it is a split seal that has to be opened up for removal and fitting. *See* below for fitting guidance.

Piston and Con Rod Strip and Assessment

If the block is to be rebored, the old pistons are likely to be scrap. If a rebore is not required, the pistons may be reusable but should be inspected for scoring, blow-by, cracks and ring recess wear. Even if in good condition, best practice will always be to fit new piston rings.

Remove the circlips from the piston gudgeon pins and push them out. Inspect the small end bearings for wear. New pistons will come with new gudgeon pins, which should be a push-fit

Using circlip pliers to remove the piston gudgeon pins.

LEFT: *A seriously scored crankshaft journal.*

Engine Restoration and Conversions

into the small end. Note that the con rod has an oilway that must be oriented towards the camshaft when fitted in the block. Ensure that the oilways are clear by blowing through with an air line. Ensure that the original caps remain matched when cleaning thoroughly.

ENGINE BLOCK REASSEMBLY PROCESS

Crank Fitting

A side-mounting engine stand comes into its own when assembling the block, but it can be done on the floor or on a solid bench. The camshaft can be fitted before the crank and sometimes it is easier to do so (*see* below).

Cleanliness is vital during the whole process and all parts should have a generous smear of engine oil brushed on during assembly.

With the block upside down, oil and fit all the main bearing shells into place. The lugs ensure the bearings locate into the correct position for the oilways. On the three-bearing engine, the rear crankshaft seal retainer 'half-moons' are bolted to the block and the corresponding rear bearing cap. If these are to be replaced, they should be fitted with non-setting joint compound.

On the three-bearing engine, fit the new rear crankshaft seal to the crank before fitting the crank to the block. Note it comes as two sections – a hinged seal and a spring – and it's one of the most fiddly jobs on the engine build. Open the hinge seal as little as possible and fit it round the crank. Open up the joint in the spring seal, fit it round the crank and loop the ends together, ensuring they are securely fastened. Use a flat screwdriver to push the spring into the recess in the seal, ensuring that the seal joint and spring joint are at 90 degrees to each other. Smear the seal in silicone grease.

Lower the crank into place in the block, ensuring that the rear seal locates squarely into the upper seal housing section with the joint in the seal pointing to the top of the engine.

Fit the two half-moon thrust bearings to the centre bearing housing with the oilways towards the crank journal. These stop the crank from being pushed forward, in particular when the clutch is pressed.

Fit the bearings to the main caps with a smear of oil and loosely fit to the block. Before fitting the rear cap, oil and fit the cork T-seals. Care must be taken when fitting the rear cap so as not to damage the T-seals. A thin feeler gauge can be used to help it to slide down into place, ensuring that the main real seal locates squarely in the opposite half-moon. Alternatively, a pair of special bolt-on wedges can be used to compress the cork as it is pushed down.

The main bearing caps can now be gradually torqued down to the final setting of 85lb ft. With each gradual torquing, ensure that the crank still turns freely. If it starts to bind, back off each cap in turn to locate the issue and

ABOVE LEFT: *Fitting new main bearings into a three-bearing block.*

ABOVE RIGHT: *Split rear oil seal components: a hinged seal plus a fiddly spring that has to be hooked together.*

The spring has to be pressed into the recess with a flat-blade screwdriver.

RIGHT: *Crank lowered into place and fitting the main thrust washers.*

59

Engine Restoration and Conversions

Rear cap T-seals in place and ready to push down with a thin feeler gauge.

RIGHT: *Torquing down the main bearing caps to 85lb ft.*

investigate any potential cause. The crank may need some mechanical assistance to turn, but it shouldn't be excessive. It's a good idea to fit two pairs of flywheel bolts and use a pry bar between each pair to turn the engine.

Piston Fitting

Fit the pistons to the con rods, ensuring that the circlips fully locate in their recesses with a good click. If not, there is a good possibility that the gudgeon pins will migrate sideways and damage the bores.

Note that the oilway in the con rod must be oriented towards the camshaft. It is therefore best practice to orient any size markings on the piston crown to the same direction and to mark piston number and orientation with an arrow on the top of the piston to assist during fitting. A sharpie marker pen is ideal for this.

Thoroughly oil the piston and orient the piston rings so the gaps are staggered. Fit a well-oiled piston ring compression tool firmly round the piston.

Turn the crank so the piston to be fitted is at bottom dead centre, with the crank journals directly below the centre line of the bores. This will make it significantly easier to line up the con rod big-end bearings and fit the caps. If working on an engine stand, turn the block the correct way up and insert

Using a pry bar to turn the crank over with flywheel bolts in place.

RIGHT: *Fitting new pistons to the con rods. Marker pen arrows help with orientation of the oilway holes.*

Engine Restoration and Conversions

Note con rod oilway goes towards the cam.

RIGHT: *A well-oiled piston ring compressor is essential for fitting the pistons.*

and orient the appropriate piston into one of the bores with the crank at the bottom of the stroke. Note again that the oilway in the con rod should point towards the camshaft.

Using the butt end of a mallet or similar, drive the piston down through the piston ring compressor and into the bore. Push it down until the con rod engages with the crank journal. Flip the engine over again and fit the correct bearing cap, again checking orientation. Note that the con rod bolts have an eccentric head that must locate correctly. Nip the self-locking cap nuts up: final torquing can be done later. If working on the bench, it helps to lay the block on its side and have an assistant receive the con rod and guide it onto the crank journal. If the eccentric bolts push out, it can be tricky to realign them in the bore.

Fit the next piston in the bottom dead centre position, then turn the crank 180 degrees so the next pair of pistons can be fitted at bottom centre.

Torque the con rod nuts up to 25lb ft and ensure the crank can still be turned. It will have more drag on it with the pistons fitted but it should still turn over without undue effort with a bar between flywheel bolts.

All pistons in, journals torqued down and the crank turning over freely – perfect.

LEFT: *Big end bearing caps torqued up to 25lb ft.*

61

Engine Restoration and Conversions

Camshaft Fitting

Assuming the bearings are in good condition, they can be left in the block and the cam can be refitted. If new bearings are required, it is a job best left to a machine shop. Inspect the cam for any lobe wear before fitting: they are usually pretty robust as they have good oil flow, but replace if in doubt. Note that petrol and diesel cams are different and are marked accordingly (petrol has a P marker).

It is easier to have the block sat on its back when fitting the camshaft. It must be carefully supported and guided through the bearings. If working the correct way round on a bench, put your fingers through the block apertures to guide and feed it through to avoid scoring the bearings.

Fit the front thrust washer bolts with new locking tabs. Fit the chain wheel and check the end float is acceptable. Fit the rear aperture cover with a new cork gasket.

Drop the cam rollers and followers into place with plenty of oil. Note that the followers must be oriented correctly (they are marked Front). If deemed to require replacement, buy the best you can afford or fit a good set of used ones. Low-quality followers have been known to wear ridges worryingly quickly. Refit the locating screws with new washers: on Series engines they were additionally held in place with lock wire as a belt and braces approach.

Camshaft/Distributor/Oil Pump Skew Gear Fitting

This can be another of those tricky, fiddly jobs as the skew gear needs to be accurately fitted to correctly orient the distributor body, as well as ensuring that the oilway and grub screw locating holes are correctly aligned. The official Workshop Manual makes this sound like an easy job but it can be far from it, so a bit more time is dedicated to it here.

It is often better to fit the skew gear before the oil pump and quill drive as it makes it easier to align. With the timing chain fitted (*see* below for details), the crank shaft needs to be set at TDC and the cam closing valves 1 and 2 (firing on piston no.1). Look through the camshaft side aperture to check the followers are on the back of the lobes and additionally feel the cam followers are fully down.

Different manuals describe the orientation of the skew gear slots in different ways with varying degrees of clarity. The reference photo makes it significantly easier, but when looking

ABOVE LEFT: *Installing the cam. Make sure it is supported as it passes through the middle bearings.*

ABOVE RIGHT: *Thrust washer controls the cam end float.*

ABOVE LEFT: *Cam roller in and follower ready to drop (note Front).*

ABOVE RIGHT: *At top dead centre (TDC), skew gear king spline should point towards 2 o'clock and distributor slots at 11 and 5 o'clock.*

Engine Restoration and Conversions

ABOVE LEFT: *Using a small screwdriver to help align the grub screw hole in the bush.*

ABOVE RIGHT: *Older type splined distributor drive and plate.*

ABOVE LEFT: *Later type distributor drive adaptor and plate.*

ABOVE RIGHT: *Correct orientation of the distributor. Note the lead for no.1 is at 2 o'clock when viewed from the right-hand side.*

at the engine from the cam side, the slots in the skew gear for the distributor drive adaptor should point at 11 and 5 o'clock and the wide king spline should point to 2 o'clock.

The skew gear turns anti-clockwise through almost 90 degrees as it is lowered into place and picks up on the cam drive gear, so start with it approximately 90 degrees clockwise from its final resting point. Note also the position of the grub screw locating hole in the bush.

Lower the skew gear in using a pair of long-nose pliers. Once it has dropped home and the correct alignment is

ABOVE LEFT: *Skew gear incorrectly installed means no.1 lead will be in a different location – finger pointing to no.1.*

ABOVE RIGHT: *Diesel skew gear master spline is oriented to 4 o'clock.*

63

Engine Restoration and Conversions

achieved, check the position of the grub screw locating hole in the bush. If it doesn't align with the grub screw hole (it probably won't unless you're very lucky), push the skew gear back up sufficiently to get a small screwdriver or pick to rotate the bush until the grub screw hole can be aligned. Once the grub screw has been fitted, recheck the alignment of the skew gear as it is likely to have changed as it rotated upwards.

Note there are two different types of distributor drive adaptor. The early type is fully splined, the later type is a simple disc with male and female slots. Fit the distributor housing and adaptor. When fitted the slots in the distributor drive adaptor should now point at 2 o'clock and 8 o'clock: note they are slightly offset to ensure the distributor is correctly oriented.

Note that when the skew gear and distributor are fitted correctly, spark plug lead for no.1 piston sits at approximately 2 o'clock when viewed from the right-hand side of the engine. When timed up, the vacuum advance should point towards the rear of the engine.

If the skew gear is found to have been fitted incorrectly, this is not ideal for a rivet-counter approach, but not necessarily a reason to dismantle the engine. It will just mean that orientation of the plug leads will need to be in a different place and the vacuum advance will be oriented slightly differently. To ascertain the position of lead no.1, turn the engine to TDC on the compression stroke for no.1 (valves closed and feel for air being expelled from the plug hole as the engine is being turned over and align the TDC timing mark). Note the orientation of the rotor arm at this point: the terminal it points towards should be connected to plug no.1.

Diesel Skew Gear

While this manual focuses primarily on the 2286cc petrol, it is worth noting that the orientation of the skew gear is different on the 2286cc diesel. On the diesel engine, the skew gear is oriented so the king spline sits at the 4 o'clock position.

TIMING CHAIN FITTING

On later vehicles the petrol cam wheel has a single spline and is marked with a P on the perimeter. Some have multi-spines and P markers. Early vehicles had a multi-splined wheel and no timing marks, so if not previously marked, the correct position may need to be set up on the EP (Exhaust Peak) marker on the flywheel. Ideally the cam wheel should be marked before disassembly, but if not, *see* section below on EP timing. Note that if fitting a performance cam, a multi-spline wheel is necessary to set up precise timing.

Later Type with P Marking

Set the perimeter P mark to the timing case hole at 11 o'clock and set the crankshaft so the keyway on the crank is pointing vertically (TDC). Fit the timing chain with no slack.

Fit the timing chain tensioner: engage the tensioner wheel in the chain, align it in the slot in the block and compress the body of the tensioner until the dowels locate and the mounting bolts and nut can be fitted. Tighten the fixings, ensuring the pawl spring is correctly positioned. Turn the engine two full revolutions and recheck that the timing marks align.

Timing chain and tensioner all fitted and ready for the timing cover to be fitted.

BELOW: *P mark on the cam wheel pointing towards the bolt hole at 11 o'clock on the block.*

Engine Restoration and Conversions

Early Type Using the EP (Exhaust Peak) Mark

If there are no timing marks on the cam wheel, the timing must be set using the EP mark on the flywheel. This can seem complex, so in addition to this outline, it is essential to consult the official Workshop Manual.

Turn the crank until the EP mark on the flywheel aligns with the timing pointer in the aperture in the flywheel housing.

Fit the cam wheel on one of the splines, but do not fit the retaining bolt. Turn the cam until the follower on valve no.1 (the exhaust valve serving piston no 1) is at its highest point. Fit a dial gauge to the follower or, if on an assembled engine, on the rocker or valve and turn the cam wheel side to side to ascertain the exact exhaust peak point.

Fit the timing chain with no slack. If the dial gauge changes in the 'no slack' position, remove the cam wheel and try it in the next slot round. Repeat the procedure until the chain can be fitted with no slack and the exhaust peak mark is achieved and maintained.

At this point, the timing position should be marked to assist in future maintenance. The timing chain tensioner can be fitted as above.

LEFT: Lining up the EP (Exhaust Peak) markings on the flywheel.

BELOW LEFT: Using a dial gauge to find the exhaust peak.

BELOW: With the timing chain fitted, the keyway slot and an external reference point should be marked for future maintenance.

Flywheel Housing, Timing Case, Oil Pump and Sump Fitting

None of these are particularly challenging to fit, but it is worth mentioning that, if working on the bench, it makes sense to leave the oil pump and sump to the end of the short engine stage of the build. This keeps the block compact and easy to turn over.

The flywheel housing is a straightforward bolt-on affair but it should be fitted with a new O-ring round the rear crank seal housing. On a five-bearing engine a new rear seal should be pressed in (lip and spring to the inside). To fit the five-bearing housing, a special plastic collar should be used to enable the seal to slide over the rear of the crankshaft. Most seals come with the collar as part of the kit.

Engine Restoration and Conversions

Refitting the flywheel housing with a new O-ring.

It is easier to leave the oil pump off until the camshaft and skew gear have been fitted. Inspect the pump before refitting: remove the cover to inspect the gears and clean them thoroughly. If in doubt, replace or overhaul the pump with new gears. Remember to fit the quill drive or the pump won't pump.

As a matter of course, fit a new front crankshaft seal to the timing case. The old seal can be driven out and a new one pressed in until it reaches the front mud shield. Note that the lip of the seal and the spring should face to the inside. Originally the mud shield was riveted on, but it's not unusual for these to have been drilled out and replaced with either self-tappers or drilled and tapped to take small (often 2BA) screws. This is to allow the front seal to be replaced without having to remove the timing case. It is best to fit the timing case before fitting the sump as the sump gasket also seals the bottom of the timing case.

Before fitting the front pulley, inspect it for any grooving or damage. Replacements are inexpensive unless it's a double one, as fitted to military vehicles, or a later one fitted to run a power steering pump. A speedy sleeve is an option or, as a temporary expedient, two seals just fit in the timing case recess, meaning the inner seal will run on fresh metal.

Note that three of the timing case fixing bolts also seal the water gallery to the water pump, so it is advisable to use a smear of Hylomar on the small gasket to ensure it seals effectively. Fit the long bolts and all the water pump bolts with copper grease to stop them from seizing.

Thoroughly clean the sump – it will likely have some sludge in it – and fit with a good-quality gasket. Additional sealing compound is a sound idea to reduce the likelihood of leaks.

Once the sump has been refitted, the short engine can be turned the correct way up and chocked in place ready for the top end to be refitted as per cylinder head fitting instructions.

Engine Start-Up after Full Rebuild

An engine test bed is invaluable when checking a rebuilt engine before installing. It allows for fine tuning, ignition set-up and checking for leaks. While it might not be practical for an amateur restorer to have one, simply fitting the engine into the chassis and running it up to temperature before fitting the wings is a good alternative. It is always advisable to turn the engine over on the starter with the ignition off/disconnected to get the oil circulating before attempting to fire up.

Installing the front crankshaft seal from inside the timing case with a large socket as a drift.

LEFT: *Front dust cover is often removed to replace the seal without removing the timing case.*

Engine Restoration and Conversions

Timing case and water pump refitted with new gaskets and sealing compound.

COMMON ENGINE CONVERSIONS

Historically, Series Land Rovers have been fitted with a range of different engine conversions over the years. While the stock 2286cc petrol and diesel engines were perfectly serviceable in their day, it was common for owners to fit engines from other manufacturers. The driving force was usually better economy for everyday use or for more power for motor sport and leisure.

In the 1970s and 1980s Perkins 4203 diesel engines were commonplace in working vehicles and the Rover V8 was fitted to competition vehicles, even before the company offered it in the Stage 1 model from 1979. Peugeot, Ford and Daihatsu diesel engines were fitted in the 1980s and 1990s, as well as the Ford V6 'Essex' engine. While these engines offered some advantages at the time, there are knock-on effects such as the availability of parts as the donor vehicles all passed into scrapyard history.

We do still see period conversions in classic Land Rovers today, but the tendency now is to go back to standard or to fit commonly available engines from later Land Rovers or derivatives of the same basic block design. Here follows a résumé of the common Land Rover/Rover-derived engine conversions with brief notes on fitting them.

Post-1981 2286cc Petrol and Diesel Engines

As noted in the section on Land Rover engine history, the 2286cc block was re-engineered in the early 1980s with a five-bearing crank. It is common to see these engines fitted to earlier vehicles as in-service expedient replacements. They are a nice upgrade and slightly easier to work on, but do not offer any significant power improvements. They bolt directly into place but it's worth noting that many, although not all, of the fixings are metric. The 2286cc petrol was fitted to coil spring vehicles up until 1985 and the 2286cc diesel was fitted to 110 models up to 1984.

An engine test bed is invaluable for uncovering any faults before fitting.

2.5-Litre Petrol

For the 1986 year model, a new version of the five-bearing engine was launched

67

Engine Restoration and Conversions

A Perkins 4203 in a Series III was a common conversion in the 1970s and 1980s.

with a displacement of 2495cc, achieved by lengthening the stroke of the crank. It is also a direct fitment into earlier vehicles. Note that this and the late 2286cc engine were fitted with the Weber 32/34 DMTL twin-choke carburettor. This can be retained to benefit from the extra power offered, although the corresponding exhaust manifold outlet sits slightly further forward, necessitating a small modification to the Series type downpipe. A suitable link hose to the original oil bath air cleaner will be required if using the 32/34 DMTL carburettor.

2.5-Litre Naturally Aspirated (N/A) Diesel (12J code)

This was an engineering development of the five-bearing 2286cc engine fitted to coil spring Land Rovers until 1991 (although longer in military applications). It has a different injector pump, operated by a timing belt, not the old-style cam skew gear. While it will bolt up directly to a Series gearbox, the shape of the timing case means that the RHS engine mount needs to be modified to suit. It is not a complicated job for a reasonably competent DIY welder. This engine will not break any performance records but does offer a significant improvement over the 2286cc diesel. It will operate comfortably with the Series radiator. It is common to fit the Series-type thermostat housing for ease of using standard hoses. The Series exhaust pipe will connect up with minor modification to the fitting flange or a Series exhaust manifold can be fitted. The battery tray will also need to be trimmed down and it is common to relocate the battery under the seat.

Note that the same basic engine was also fitted to Sherpa vans (*see* engine number table). These engines were fitted with a different timing case that mounts the injector pump higher up, meaning it will fit directly in place with no modifications to the engine mount. The battery tray will still need to be trimmed down and a suitable air cleaner arrangement fitted.

2.5-Litre Turbo Diesel (19J Code)

This engine was fitted to coil spring Land Rovers from about 1987 to 1991. It was developed from the 12J engine with an improved lubrication system to run the turbo. It is generally not a well-loved engine and some did suffer piston cracking. However, if in good condition and looked after well, it does make a good conversion in a Series motor. Again, the RHS engine mount has to be modified, the battery moved under the seat and a suitable exhaust made up or purchased from a specialist manufacturer. A suitable air cleaner needs to be sourced/adapted.

200Tdi Discovery/Defender

This conversion was ubiquitous in the 2010s as the original host vehicle succumbed to terminal corrosion. The 200Tdi is famously reliable with very few known faults. In Discovery form, it is very easy to fit as the shape of the timing case allows for the original mounts to be used without chassis modifications. The battery tray does need to be trimmed and many choose to relocate it under the seat.

The engine bolts straight onto a Series gearbox, although a small dowel and one stud needs to be removed from the flywheel housing. In addition,

The ubiquitous 200Tdi is an easy and common fitment in a Series Land Rover and requires very few modifications.

Engine Restoration and Conversions

in Discovery form, the bottom four (now unused) flywheel housing bolts should be really replaced with countersunk M10 bolts to ensure it remains oil-tight and four lower studs need to be fitted: the casting has blanks for them but they need to be tapped out. Many choose not to do this without any significant problems, but it is always best practice to do it to reduce the likelihood of oil leaks.

In an 88in Land Rover there is sufficient clearance between the turbo and the LHS chassis rail, although it is common to 'clock' the turbo to point the outlet pipe into a more convenient location to avoid cutting the bottom of the inner wing. Another alternative is to fit a turbo and exhaust manifold from a 300Tdi engine (it bolts straight on) or indeed the turbo and manifold assemblies from a 200Tdi Defender can be fitted, although sourcing these can be a challenge. A suitable larger bore exhaust must be made up or bought off the shelf from a specialist. These are available for both 200Tdi and 300Tdi manifolds.

On a 109in model the Discovery 200Tdi turbo usually sits too close to the LHS chassis rail, so it is common to either fit an appropriate packer on the engine mount or to make a small scallop in the chassis rail. As above, a Defender 200Tdi or 300Tdi turbo and manifold is another solution.

A suitable air cleaner and pipes need to be made up. It is often advisable to use/modify standard Land Rover parts as it makes buying service parts easier in the future.

Not all owners choose to fit an intercooler or oil cooler and broad enthusiast experience suggests that this doesn't usually cause any issues in cool climates. Many choose to reuse the original Series radiator and this seems to work fine when in good condition. Another alternative is to use the 200Tdi radiator and fabricate a suitable mounting frame. An intercooler can be fitted either down the left-hand side or in front of the radiator. Again, kits of parts can be bought off the shelf from specialists.

It is also possible to fit the 200Tdi without the turbo. This means that it is simpler to fit and can be run with a standard Series exhaust. It will require appropriate blanking plugs in the turbo oil pipes and the turbo fuelling boost pipe at the injector pump.

The 200Tdi is known to be a noisy, rattly engine in a Series vehicle. This can be mitigated to a good extent by soft engine mounting bobbins (a common fitment is good-quality Ford Transit/Granada engine mounts) and plenty of sound proofing. Note also that the Tdi is not a fast revving engine and benefits from higher gearing. It's common to fit higher ratio transfer boxes, overdrives or higher ratio differentials.

300Tdi Engine

This was an engineering development of the 200Tdi and benefits from being a slightly smoother engine. As 200Tdi Discoverys became less common, so 300Tdi engines became the norm. They bolt onto the Series gearbox but the engine mounts require a bit of thought as the original type cannot be easily reused. It is most common to fit the 300Tdi mounting brackets from the donor chassis. In addition, consideration needs to be given to the fact that the engine has a serpentine multi-v drive belt, which includes a power steering pump.

Rover V8

This engine fitment dates back to the late 1960s when Rover were developing the engine for use in the Range Rover. The company actually fitted a version of the engine to a handful of Series IIAs during the testing process and the engine became a favourite fitment for classic Land Rover motor sport from the 1970s onwards. It remains a competitive and loved engine right up to the present day. It is not known for its frugality, but does offer similar mpg to a 2286cc petrol and usually better than the 2625cc 6-cylinder engine.

This engine requires a conversion plate to connect to the Series gearbox. It also requires new engine mounting brackets on the engine to connect to the chassis (the chassis doesn't normally need to be modified). The LHS manifold position requires a modification in the bulkhead footwell. There are a range of specialist suppliers who can supply all the parts and instructions to fit these engines including gearbox adaptor plates, oil filter adaptors (the oil filter sits very close to the front diff),

ABOVE LEFT: *A 300Tdi fits onto a Series gearbox but requires new engine mounts.*

ABOVE RIGHT: *A 3.5-litre Rover V8 retrofitted in a Series III. This requires a gearbox adaptor plate and a small modification to the bulkhead.*

Engine Restoration and Conversions

bolt-on engine mounts and exhaust pipes. Note that when Land Rover offered this engine in a Series III, the company connected it to the permanent 4WD LT95 gearbox from the Range Rover as well as moving the front panel forward. The original front panel position can be retained if connecting the V8 to the original gearbox.

LAND ROVER ENGINE NUMBER PREFIX CODES

The following list is a guide to identifying a Series II, IIA and III Land Rover engine. Note that the prefix code would be followed by the unique engine serial number beginning 00001. It is important to remember that engine changes are very common and an all-original vehicle is a relative rarity. Also, the 2286cc petrol and diesel share the same block design and it is common for diesel blocks to be rebuilt as a petrol (and vice versa, though less common).

The first three numbers of the engine code would normally (though not exclusively) match the chassis number on an original vehicle in the pre-VIN era (up to about 1979).

With the advent of the VIN number sequence, the engine type was denoted by a letter code within the VIN: H = 2286cc Petrol; G = 2286cc Diesel; P = 2625cc Petrol.

In acknowledgement that Series Land Rovers are frequently fitted with later engines, the list also includes common conversion engine numbers.

Series II Engine Codes

Petrol 2286cc
141
151

Diesel 2052cc
146
156

Series IIA Engine Codes

Petrol 2286cc
236
241
251
252
253
286 (IIA Forward Control)
325 (IIB Forward Control)

Petrol 2625cc
345
300 (IIA Forward Control)
330 (IIB Forward Control)

Diesel 2286cc
271
276
335 (Forward Control)

Series III Engine Codes

Petrol 2286cc three-bearing
901
902
903
904
951

Petrol 2286cc five-bearing
361
364

Petrol 2625cc
941

Diesel 2286cc three-bearing
906
895

Diesel 2286cc five-bearing
366

Stage 1 V8 Engine Codes

10G
11G
12G

Common Rover Origin Engine Conversions

Petrol 2286cc and 2495cc

10H	90/110 petrol 2286cc 8:1 CR
11H	90/110 petrol 2286cc 8:1 CR
13H	90/110 petrol 2286cc 7:1 CR
17H	90/110 petrol 2495cc 8:1 CR

Petrol 3528cc V8

10A	Rover SD1 3528cc V8
14G	90/110 petrol 3528cc V8
15G	90/110 petrol 3528cc V8
956	101 Forward Control 3528cc V8
961	101 Forward Control 3528cc V8

Diesel

10J	90/110 diesel 2286cc
11J	90/110 diesel 2495cc late military specification
11L	Defender 200TDI diesel 2495cc
12J	90/110 diesel 2495cc
12L	Discovery 200TDI diesel 2495cc
13L	Discovery 200TDI diesel 2495cc
14J	London Taxi 2495cc
14L	Range Rover Classic 200TDi diesel 2495cc
15J	Sherpa Van 2495cc
15L	Range Rover Classic 200TDi diesel 2495cc
16L	Discovery/Defender 300TDI diesel 2495cc
19J	90/110 Turbo Diesel 2495cc
21L	Discovery/Defender 300TDI diesel 2495cc
23L	Discovery/Defender 300TDI diesel 2495cc

6
Fuel and Exhaust Systems

PETROL SYSTEM: THE BASICS

Conventional internal combustion engines work on the principle of Induction, Compression, Power and Exhaust. The petrol engine internal combustion system operates when a controlled mixture of petrol and oxygen from the carburettor and inlet manifold is compressed in the cylinder and ignited by the spark plug, creating an explosion. The resulting force moves the piston down, creates rotational movement of the crankshaft and the exhaust gasses are expelled through the exhaust valves, manifold and exhaust system.

Carburettors

The 2286cc engine was fitted with two different carburettors from the factory: the Solex SX 40 on early vehicles and Zenith 36IV on later Series IIA (from 1967) and Series III models. The Zenith is fitted with an adaptor plate that turns the carburettor body through 90 degrees, but is otherwise a direct replacement on the manifold. However, the bell crank linkage systems are different: the Solex throttle arm is pushed up and the Zenith arm is pulled down. While the Zenith is considered the better carb in terms of engineering and off-road performance, there is a growing desire to put vehicles back to standard specification.

The Weber 34ICH was and indeed still is a common aftermarket alternative carburettor. It is a direct replacement on the Zenith 36IV adaptor and was often fitted as an economy measure as it can offer improved mpg, although at the expense of performance. It is a simple carburettor, easy to work on and inexpensive to buy. The Weber kit usually comes with a new universal choke cable since, due to the positioning of the choke levers, a standard Series III Zenith choke cable does not quite reach. This does mean that some small modifications may be necessary to fit the choke cable in the Series III ignition lock assembly. Some owners swear by them, others feel it strangles the power.

A number of aftermarket copies of the Zenith 36IV are available with varying quality, some very good, some not so. A well rebuilt original Zenith should continue to give good performance for many years.

The 2625cc 6-cylinder engine used either the SU (early models) or Zenith Stromberg 175 CD-25 carburettor (later IIA and Series III). The Stage 1 V8 was fitted with twin Zenith Strombergs. In recent years, adaptor kits have been manufactured to fit both the SU and Stromberg to the 2286cc as a performance upgrade.

Fuel Pumps and Filters

All Series 2286cc engines used a mechanical fuel pump bolted to the side of the block and operated by a lobe on the camshaft. The petrol fuel pump has an additional glass bowl sedimentor and gauze filter. Note that

ABOVE LEFT: Solex carburettor as fitted to Series II and IIA models to April 1967.

ABOVE RIGHT: Zenith 36IV carburettor as fitted to Series IIA from April 1967 to the end of Series III production with minor changes.

Fuel and Exhaust Systems

Weber 34ICH was never a factory option but was, and indeed still is, a popular fitment.

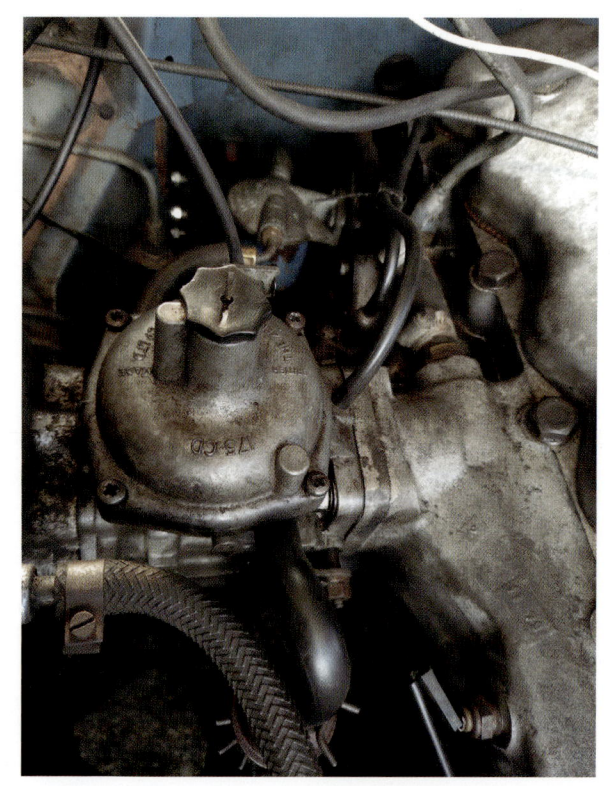

RIGHT: *Zenith Stromberg 175 CD-25 as fitted to the 2625cc 6-cylinder.*

ABOVE LEFT: *Manual fuel pump as fitted to most 2286cc engines. The lever on the bottom is for manual priming.*

ABOVE RIGHT: *Blue pot houses a replaceable filter on 6-cylinder and V8 models.*

early coil spring versions of the 2286cc engine used a Facet electric fuel pump, so if fitting one to a Series motor a mechanical pump and mounting plate will need to be fitted (unless choosing to fit an electric pump).

The 6-cylinder and Stage 1 V8 are fed by a Facet electric fuel pump mounted on the inside of the chassis rail forward of the right-hand rear spring. A replaceable element fuel filter enclosed in a blue filter housing is mounted on the inlet manifold (6-cylinder) or on the bulkhead (Stage 1).

PETROL FUEL SYSTEM PROBLEMS

Fuel Pump Issues

Mechanical fuel pumps are robust but do fail, often after a lack of use. Diaphragms harden and pumps seize. Dried fuel deposits can clog up the gauze filter and the rubber seal on the glass bowl can perish. The seal is on the suction side of the pump, so if it fails the pump will simply suck and pump air. The pick-up pipe in the tank also has a gauze or a push-on plastic filter, which is also prone to clogging.

The mechanical fuel pump has a manual priming lever, which can be pumped by hand. It must be 'off-cam' to pump, that is not on the top of the lobe of the cam. Turn the engine over to bring it off cam if the lever doesn't pump freely. Fuel should pump to the top of the system and fill the carburettor float chamber at which point a change in resistance should be felt. If suspect, it is worth taking off the connection to the carburettor and seeing

Fuel and Exhaust Systems

if fuel is actually being pumped – catch any fuel in a suitable container.

Facet electrical pumps have an internal filter that does clog and pumps do fail. Listen for the telltale ticking of the pump: the ticking should slow down as the system primes.

An engine that runs then gradually dies, becoming difficult or impossible to start, is likely to be suffering from fuel starvation.

Replacing/Rebuilding a Fuel Lift Pump

Removing and replacing the mechanical fuel pump is a straightforward job, though access is slightly tricky if working on a complete vehicle. The pump is mounted via two studs/nuts to the camshaft cover plate. It helps to use a ³/₈in or ¼in drive socket (½in or 13mm) on a short extension to make access easier. Fit the new pump with a new gasket that is usually supplied with the new pump.

It is also possible to rebuild an original pump with a rebuild kit consisting of a new diaphragm, seals and valves. If rebuilding a petrol pump, take time to clean the mesh gauze and fuel ways in the sedimentor bowl: dried fuel deposits can build up and clog them. Replace the rubber seal in the top of the bowl glass as a matter of course: they become hard, crack and fail to seal.

Carburettor Issues

Common carburettor problems include:

- Blocked jets
- External leaks from gaskets
- Worn throttle spindle
- Blocked float valve cutting off fuel
- Jammed float valve causing over-fuelling
- Poorly adjusted float level
- Flooded float causing over-fuelling: they can become porous or simply develop cracks
- Failed accelerator pump
- Blocked accelerator jet (common on the Weber 34ICH)
- Blocked inlet gauze filter
- Warped body and/or top cover, especially on the Zenith 36IV
- Failing emulsion block O-ring on the Zenith
- Fine powder deposits from old fuel
- Poor-quality aftermarket copy carburettor

There are a number of running issues that could be traced to a carburettor problem. In addition, a fault might be fuel related but not directly a problem with the carburettor itself. Air leaks from the carburettor to the inlet manifold and manifold to head can cause vacuum leaks and leaning up, especially on acceleration. The gauze filter on the fuel tank pick-up pipe is particularly prone to clogging, especially if on a late Series III with the removable plastic filter.

Before rushing to assume the carburettor is at fault, a back to basics on the ignition system should be carried out as well as a thorough visual inspection on vacuum advance hoses, servo vacuum hoses, emissions control pipes, filters and mechanical linkages. If a spare known carburettor is available, it can be a quick way to isolate the problem component.

Remember that rough running could be down to factors in the ignition system, such as a failing coil, failing condenser and closed-up points. Sometimes it is hard to tell the difference between a fuel problem and an ignition problem. (For more details, *see* Chapter 7.)

REPLACING AND SETTING UP THE CARBURETTOR

Removing the carburettor is a simple task but access to the fixing nuts is tight, especially on the Zenith. Bending or trimming down a ½in or 13mm spanner can assist. The throttle linkage and choke cable will need to be removed as well as the fuel supply and vacuum advance pipe. Note that the choke cable on the Zenith has a fiddly spring clip.

ABOVE LEFT: *Full rebuild kits are available for fuel pumps, but complete pumps aren't expensive.*

ABOVE RIGHT: *A cut-down spanner may be required to fit the inner carburettor nut.*

Fuel and Exhaust Systems

A new gasket should be fitted to the new carburettor and traces of any old gasket removed to ensure an airtight seal. Reconnect the linkages, choke cable, vacuum advance and fuel pipe and any emission control pipework.

Once fitted, the carburettor needs to be set up. However, before doing so, check and set the spark plug gaps (0.030in), valve clearances (0.010in), points gap (0.015in) and ignition timing (nominally 6 degrees BTDC, but open to modification depending on fuel).

- For faster starting after fitting, use the priming lever on the fuel pump to fill the carburettor float bowl.
- Turn the mixture (air) screw fully in and then turn out approximately two turns.
- Turn the slow running (throttle stop) screw in until it just starts to move the stop, then turn one full turn to slightly open the throttle butterfly. This should give a basic set-up that should allow the vehicle to start and run.
- Operate the choke as necessary, start the vehicle and let it get up to normal running temperature.
- Adjust the mixture screw until the vehicle runs smoothly and then adjust the slow running screw until the idle sits comfortably around 500–750rpm.
- Ensure the engine returns back to idle position when the throttle is blipped: if it stalls, the idle speed should be increased.

STRIPPING AND REBUILDING A CARBURETTOR

Unlike the diesel injector pump, the carburettor can be easily serviced by an amateur mechanic. The Zenith 36IV and Weber 34ICH are both very simple to overhaul. Comprehensive rebuild kits with exploded diagrams and instructions are available for all Land Rover carburettors. Kits include new seals, gaskets, butterflies, spindles, jets, diaphragms, air screw and O-rings. If you are unsure, there are specialists that will rebuild the carburettor for you. This is particularly important for very original vehicles with correctly date-stamped components.

It is common for the top cover and body of the Zenith to warp, causing poor sealing. This can usually be rectified by rubbing the contact surfaces flat using a sheet of fine abrasive paper glued on a sheet of glass.

Lay out all the individual parts in a logical order as they come off and inspect carefully. Floats should be carefully inspected for any evidence of fuel ingress through damage or

ABOVE LEFT: *Location of the air screw on the Zenith 36IV.*

ABOVE RIGHT: *Location of the slow running screw on the Zenith 36IV.*

ABOVE LEFT: *Location of the air screw on the Weber 34ICH.*

ABOVE RIGHT: *Location of the slow running screw on the Weber 34ICH.*

Fuel and Exhaust Systems

An ultrasonic cleaner is invaluable for cleaning carburettors and injectors.

LEFT: Typical dust and grime build-up in a carburettor float chamber.

ABOVE LEFT: Stripping a carburettor is simple enough, just be methodical. Rebuild kits come with exploded diagrams.

ABOVE RIGHT: Flatting a warped Zenith top on fine paper on a sheet of glass: both top and main body are prone to warping.

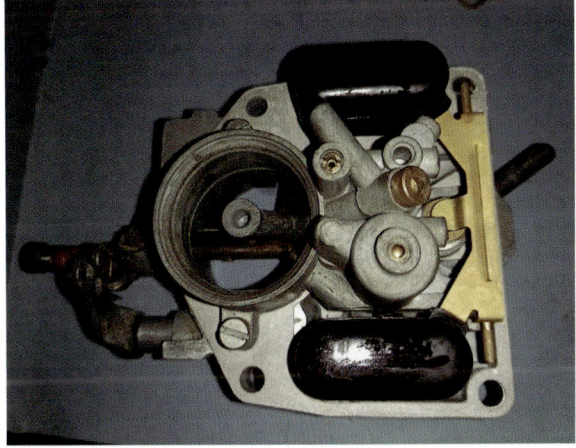

New jets installed and float level checked on the Zenith.

LEFT: Replacing the O-ring on a Zenith: they commonly fail.

75

Fuel and Exhaust Systems

ABOVE LEFT: *Fully cleaned and rebuilt Zenith. This is well within the capabilities of a home mechanic.*

ABOVE RIGHT: *Location of the main jet and pump inlet valve in the Weber 34ICH. Being at the bottom of the float chamber, they are prone to clogging.*

becoming porous. Float valves can build up deposits and jam open or closed. The carburettor and all components must be scrupulously clean before reassembly. An ultrasonic cleaning bath is ideal for this, as well as careful use of an air line to clear any build-up in any crevices.

INLET AND EXHAUST MANIFOLDS

The petrol inlet and exhaust manifolds bolt together with four long 5/16in studs. These are prone to seizing and corroding. If the two sections of the manifold have to be separated, plan for the studs to break. Plenty of heat and patience is required to remove them. If this proves a significant problem, it may well be expedient to replace the whole exhaust manifold.

The downpipe studs are also prone to wasting away, corrosion and seizing in place. Again, plenty of heat, a proper stud extractor (although a good self-grip wrench will often suffice) and patience will be time well invested. If the stud does break, use a centre punch, drill a hole and use a stud extractor. If that fails, drill the stud out very carefully and re-tap the thread (5/16in UNF).

Note that the exhaust manifold is also prone to cracking, especially adjacent to port no.4. While it is possible to have a cast exhaust manifold repaired, it will far outweigh the cost of a new one. Good-quality replacements are readily available at a reasonable price unless it's an early 'swan neck' type.

The manifolds should be loosely bolted together and then fitted to the cylinder head with a new gasket before fully tightening the four fixing studs. This is to ensure a good manifold-to-head seal. Note that originally the inlet manifold had twin 'tin' gaskets. These are available, but most choose to fit the one-piece inlet and exhaust manifold gasket as it seals better. Access to the manifold is far easier if the engine is out or the left-hand wing removed. A slightly blowing manifold gasket can make some alarming problems, from the obvious chuffing and gruff exhaust note through to serious backfiring, depending on where the blow is.

ABOVE LEFT: *Studs joining inlet and exhaust manifolds corrode and waste away and can be a challenge to replace.*

ABOVE RIGHT: *Expect to have to replace the exhaust manifold studs. Use plenty of heat and drill out if necessary.*

Fuel and Exhaust Systems

ABOVE LEFT: Check for hairline cracks in the exhaust manifold. New ones are relatively cheap.

ABOVE RIGHT: Typical blown exhaust gasket. This one made a terrible racket and even caused backfiring.

Later type single-piece combined inlet and exhaust manifold gasket is a better fit than the original two-piece inlet type.

The bottom oil pan is prone to rusting, causing pinholes that allow the oil to leak out. It is not uncommon to find the bottom of the mounting bracket is either damp or dripping in oil. This, of course, means significantly reduced air filtration. The best solution would be to acquire a better replacement, but it is sometimes possible to weld up small holes. A copper or aluminium backing plate will assist to prevent blow-through. An alternative is to thoroughly degrease the area and use an epoxy repair paste. The oil in the air cleaner should be changed at every major service: it should be filled up to the level line with normal engine oil (20/50).

The intake hose is prone to cracking and splitting. Replacements are cheap, but many aftermarket ones are less flexible than the originals. The intake elbow to the carburettor attaches via

AIR CLEANER BOX AND INTAKE HOSE

Apart from the V8 variant, Series Land Rovers originally had an oil-bath type air box mounted at the back of the battery tray. Note, though, that the 6-cylinder model had a taller air cleaner mounted at the front of the battery tray.

ABOVE LEFT: 6-cylinder oil bath cleaner on the left, 4-cylinder on the right.

ABOVE RIGHT: Typical pin-hole corrosion on the oil bath base.

77

Fuel and Exhaust Systems

K&N style filter was a common upgrade, but it makes very little difference to performance and is just noisier.

a rubber collar. The later type intake elbow had an extra spigot for an emissions control pipe to recycle crankcase oil vapours.

It was a common 'upgrade' in the 1980s and 1990s to fit a K&N style air filter to petrol vehicles. This adds very little in terms of performance but is an interesting period modification that makes the engine sound slightly throaty. For originality and a quieter engine, fit the original air intake system.

FUEL LINES

Fixed Fuel Lines

Most Series IIA and III fixed fuel lines were originally made from flexible nylon pipe. This generally survives well, although it does become brittle with age. If replacing fuel lines, individual replacement pipes can be bought, but correctly sized and appropriately rated nylon pipe can also be bought as a roll and cut to length. Old unions can be reused: to push them back on, warm the nylon in hot water to soften it. In addition it can be softened by carefully tapping it against a hard surface such as the anvil section of a vice – make sure you don't damage the pipe though.

Rubber Fuel Lines

Petrol vehicles have short rubber sections attaching pipes to carburettors. These should be changed as a matter of course on a vehicle that has been left unused for any significant length of time. At the time of writing, E10 fuel was becoming the norm in the UK and there are concerns regarding the longevity of rubber pipes with the higher ethanol content. New fuel lines and rubber seals *should* be more resistant to ethanol but there are still concerns. Old, already slightly perished rubber is unlikely to last very long with high ethanol fuels.

Note that it is very common for fuel lines to have been made from general rubber fuel hose, especially on a budget rebuild or an engine conversion. Take careful note of the condition and routing of home-made pipes and rectify if necessary. Very often they are left dangling and could snag, rub through or pop off, spraying fuel onto hot surfaces. This is a particular concern on the 2286cc petrol as the rubber link to the carburettor is immediately above the exhaust manifold.

DIESEL SYSTEM: THE BASICS

The diesel internal combustion system does not require an electrical ignition system and relies on compression ignition. Diesel is injected at high pressure into the combustion chamber and the high mechanical compression of the piston causes the air temperature inside the cylinder to ignite the fuel.

The 2286cc diesel engine is 'naturally aspirated', that is the air entering the air intake is at atmospheric pressure. In contrast, a turbo system forces air into the induction system, creating more power.

Injection Pump and Injectors

The 2286cc diesel was fitted with a CAV injector pump, operated by the skew gear from the camshaft: effectively it takes the place of the distributor in the petrol engine variant of the engine. The pump efficiency is very dependent on accurate cam timing and pump timing. Series IIA and early III models were fitted with a fully mechanical throttle linkage; later Series IIIs were fitted with a cable-operated throttle. All Series CAV pumps were fitted with a mechanical fuel cut-off: a pull cable operated from the dashboard (Series II/IIA) or on the steering column (Series III). The 2286cc variant fitted to the early One Ten had an electric stop/run solenoid.

The injector pump distributes fuel at high pressure to the injectors, which in turn fire a metered atomised spray of diesel into the combustion chamber. Even official Land Rover literature notes that only a competent service engineer with access to specialist equipment should attempt to repair the injection pump and injector nozzles.

Fuel Lift Pump and Filter

The diesel fuel system also has a mechanical fuel pump operated by a cam lobe. Early variants also had a sedimentor bowl that was deleted on later models. Fuel purity is vitally important for a diesel engine to run efficiently, so a large canister fuel filter is mounted on the bulkhead, incorporating a flow and return system.

DIESEL FUEL SYSTEM PROBLEMS

Fuel Lift Pump

Problems are as per the petrol lift pump. When the priming lever is pumped, the fuel filter housing should fill. Back off the return pipe banjo bolt and keep pumping until bubbles have been expelled. If not, ensure the pump is not 'on cam' by turning the engine over. If fuel does squirt out, suspect a failed lift pump.

CAV Injector Pump

The official Workshop Manual notes that the fuel injector pump is not a normally serviceable item and should be entrusted to a specialist, although by modern standards they are simple units. Common problems are leaks and internal components seizing, especially on a vehicle that has sat for a significant time and poorly set pump timing.

Fuel and Exhaust Systems

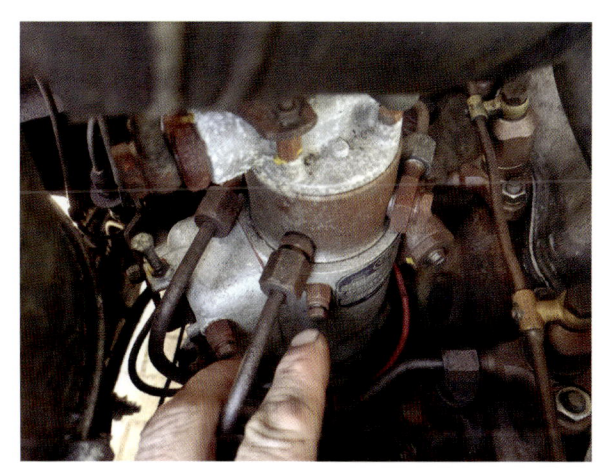

ABOVE LEFT: *Diesel fuel filter can be bled with the pump priming lever from the top return banjo bolt. Fuel should spurt out if the lift pump is in good condition.*

ABOVE RIGHT: *Location of the two bleed screws on the CAV pump body. Pump the priming lever until fuel flows out.*

The basic function of the injector pump can be checked by cracking off each injector pipe in turn and checking for fuel delivery. Note that if air has entered the system, the pump itself must be bled via the bleed screws on the side of the main body and control cover. Accurate pump timing is vital for clean and efficient running. If pump timing is out, it will cause poor starting, smoking and poor performance.

FITTING AND TIMING THE INJECTOR PUMP: A SIMPLE INTRODUCTION

The injector pump locates in the keyway on the screw gear from the camshaft. The pump is held in place by three 5/16in studs/nuts and the stud holes are slotted, allowing the pump to be rotated to set the timing. In addition to this introductory guide, it is essential to consult the Workshop Manual for the minutiae of the details required to do this accurately.

- Turn the engine clockwise until the appropriate timing mark on the flywheel lines up with the pointer with piston no.1 on the compression cycle (valves 1 and 2 closed). Note that different eras of diesel engine had different timing marks: 16 on early vehicles, 15 on later models and then 13 was suggested in later manuals. It is therefore necessary to consult the official Workshop Manual and any revision to determine the appropriate setting for your engine.
- If the engine is rotated too far, continue clockwise until the pointer lines up again on no.1 compression stroke. It is important not to turn the engine back if the engine is turned too far as this will put slack into the timing chain.
- At this point, the keyway on the skew gear should be pointing to 4 o'clock when viewed side-on from the right-hand side of the engine.

Diesel skew gear king spline identified at 4 o'clock position ready for pump to be fitted.

LEFT: *Looking through the timing aperture on the flywheel housing. Note that the pointer has been removed on this engine, but the 14 degree mark is just visible.*

Fuel and Exhaust Systems

ABOVE LEFT: *Looking through the aperture in the injector pump and aligning the A mark to the timing ring.*

ABOVE RIGHT: *Red screwdriver pointing out the adjustable external timing pointer for the injector pump.*

- Remove the pump timing cover plate. Turn the pump in the direction of travel to align the A mark on the drive plate with the line on the timing ring. Insert the pump into place with the skew gear adaptor.
- Use a mirror to check the alignment of the timing marks and rotate the pump to realign the marks. Nip up the three fixing bolts and fit the injector pipes.
- Note that later pumps had an external timing marker. This requires a special timing plate, which is bolted on with a key to take the slack out of the skew gear. The timing mark on the plate is marked with a bolt-on pointer. The timing plate is then removed and the pump fitted, aligning the timing mark on the base of the pump with the pointer. You might find that some engines have both an external and internal pointer.

Note that the timing of the pump is also dependent on accurate valve timing. If the timing chain has stretched or the timing set up with any inaccuracy, the vehicle may still smoke, even with the pump set as per the book. Advancing the pump slightly is a common method of mitigating chain stretch and can be done by ear and eye to obtain a compromise position. Loosen the pump mounting nuts and turn the body of the pump with a large pair of stilsons: this can actually be done with the engine running, noting the change in the emissions. Note that it is common to see a tired engine with the pump fully advanced in the slots and even additional advance created by filing the holes out.

Bleeding the Injector Pump

Unlike the petrol fuel system, the diesel system must be bled/primed to remove any air before it will start.

- Pump the arm on the lift pump until a steady flow of fuel appears at the bleed screw on the top of the fuel filter housing. If the lift pump lever doesn't pump, the arm might be 'on cam': turn the engine over to move the cam position.
- Ensure the fuel stop lever is in the run position with the stop lever pushed fully home.
- Close the top bleed screw on the filter header and open the bleed screw on the side of the injector pump.
- Continue to pump the lever until clear fuel flows and close the screw. Repeat for the second bleed screw on the injector pump.
- Loosen the injector pipes at the injector end and crank the engine over until fuel emits from each pipe. Tighten the pipe unions, heat the glow plugs for approximately twenty seconds and start the engine.
- It is not uncommon to have to turn the engine over for a while before it fires up, so ensure the battery is healthy.

INJECTORS

The injectors are a precision component and must be in perfect working

Injectors should be overhauled and set by a diesel specialist. The yellow paint is a tamper mark from the last professional service.

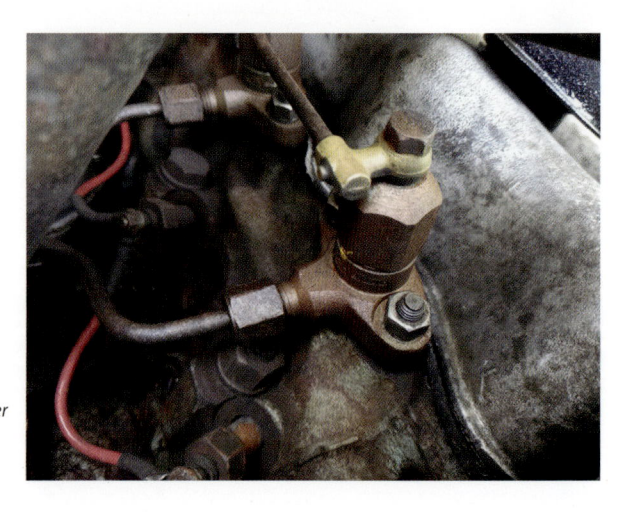

condition to atomise the fuel and produce the correct spray pattern. Wear and build-up of carbon deposits compromise this. While it is possible to DIY test the 'pop' and spray, for the minimal cost it may well be better to entrust this to a diesel specialist.

Injectors are prone to sticking in the head and may need working out. When fitting new injectors note that there are two sealing washers: a steel washer at the tip and a copper one round the body. Don't forget to remove the old lower washer. When replacing the lower steel washer, drop it down the shaft of a thin screwdriver.

GLOW PLUGS

While relatively modern direct injection diesel engines will often start without the need for glow plugs, the 2286cc engine requires them to be fully operational or it simply won't start from cold. The glow plugs preheat the air in the cylinders to assist the cold combustion of the fuel: 15–20 seconds of heat is usually required to start the vehicle from cold. The Operation Manual says the vehicle should be started with full throttle.

If an otherwise healthy engine struggles or fails to start but puffs out white smoke (unburnt diesel) when cranking, the glow plugs would be the first suspect. Plugs can be simply tested for continuity with a multimeter and if out of the engine, a failed plug should be obvious. The plugs simply screw into the cylinder head and are generally easy to remove.

Series Wired Type

The original type was wired in series through a resistor on the bulkhead. While these are very effective for cold starting, the fact that they are wired in series means that the integrity of the circuit relies on all plugs being operational. If one fails, none of the plugs work. They are immediately recognisable with large insulation washers and 'pig tail' shaped elements.

Parallel Type

The newer parallel type is a common upgrade that allows the plugs to operate even when one or more has failed. These can be bought as a kit complete with the associated wiring loom. These do not need to be run through the resistor: it can be left in place on the bulkhead and simply used as a junction box.

DIESEL EXHAUST AND INLET MANIFOLDS

Until approximately 1974 the exhaust manifold exited horizontally: the pipe was attached with four studs and came through the inner wing. The later manifold exits downwards and has three fixing studs. The manifolds are interchangeable with the appropriate exhaust pipe.

The inlet manifold on the 2052cc diesel had a central intake spigot whereas the 2286cc engine had a curved intake at the front. The inlet manifold was modified from approximately 1981 to accommodate a throttle-controlled butterfly to create a vacuum to operate the servo-assisted brakes on later models. This operated with an additional vacuum reservoir tank mounted on the inner wing.

Note that the diesel manifold gasket is not the same as the petrol.

FUEL TANKS

Broadly there were three main types of fuel tank fitted to the Series II/IIA and III models.

10-Gallon Under-Seat Tank with External Filler

This was standard fitment to all 88in and 109in 4-cylinder models from 1958 until approximately 1973. Originally it mounted on three fixed front bolts and one flexible rear fixing, allowing for some chassis flex. It is common to see aftermarket tanks fitted with six fixed mounting bolts. Both petrol and diesel tanks are the same: the aperture for the return pipe is simply blanked off on petrol models.

While it is possible to repair some leaking fuel tanks, replacement is always going to be the long-term solution. Aftermarket tanks are generally of reasonable quality, but on occasion the

ABOVE LEFT: Original in-series glow plug (left) with the new parallel type (right).

ABOVE RIGHT: Side-exit diesel exhaust manifold as fitted up to 1974.

Fuel and Exhaust Systems

10-gallon under-seat fuel tank as fitted to 88in and 4-cylinder 109in up to about 1973.

angle of the filler tube spigot can foul on the hole in the rear body. This can usually be mitigated simply by fitting an appropriately sized spacer between the rear tank mounting and the chassis outrigger.

The fuel filler pipe can be awkward to fit and many replacement parts are slightly too long. It is sometimes necessary to cut the pipe slightly to make it fit (use the old one as a template). Plenty of lubrication such as washing-up liquid can help. Sometimes it is easier to unscrew the filler tube from the tub mounting to make it easier to push the rubber pipe on.

10-Gallon 'Military' Type Under-Seat

These were fitted to military Land Rovers and had no external filler. These could also be fitted as extra-capacity tanks on the left-hand side of civilian models.

15-Gallon Rear-Mounted Tank

This was standard fitment to all 6-cylinder and V8 models. It was also fitted to 4-cylinder 109in models from approximately 1973. There are some small differences between the years and between petrol and diesel models. V8 and diesel models had a pipe for a fuel return line. Early fuel sender units were held in with 2BA screws; later ones were held in with a retainer ring.

EXHAUST SYSTEMS

Exhaust systems are readily available for all models in both mild steel and stainless pipe. Stainless pipes will of course last significantly longer, but depending on the grade of material they will tarnish and develop surface rust. The author's own 1972 Series III has had the same stainless steel exhaust for the last thirty years despite developing surface rust in the first couple of years. Mild steel systems have a limited life and usually last only a handful of years in normal use.

The later 2286cc petrol and diesel exhausts follow the same route, but note that the diesel front pipe is slightly longer, despite looking almost identical. In addition, the diesel tailpipe is usually angled down to direct particulate matter down.

Note that in the last couple of years of production, the Series III 88in petrol was often fitted with a twin silencer exhaust that exited on the left-hand side of the vehicle. The front pipe remained the same as the earlier type and the systems are interchangeable.

15-gallon rear-mounted fuel tanks were fitted to 6-cylinder, V8 and all 109in models from 1974.

RIGHT: As well as looking beautiful, a stainless exhaust is a good long-term investment.

Fuel and Exhaust Systems

The unusual twin-silencer exhaust as fitted to some late model 88in Series IIIs.

LEFT: *General layout and routing of most 88in exhaust pipes.*

The 6-cylinder and V8 models have unique exhaust systems that have a larger bore to cope with the increased cubic capacity. The 6-cylinder exhaust has been commonly used on 200Tdi and 300Tdi powered 109in models with appropriate modifications to the downpipe. This means common off-the-shelf parts can be fitted and replaced as necessary with ease.

The exhausts mount on rubber straps and clamps to brackets on the chassis. The rubber straps should have tube inserts in them to stop the rubber being over-compressed and splitting. It is always advisable to use a new fitting kit when replacing an exhaust. While a fitting kit might seem disproportionally expensive, given the relatively low cost of a mild steel exhaust, it is worth it to avoid the hassle of the inevitability of corroded fixtures and fittings and perished rubber straps.

Note that some aftermarket exhausts are slightly inaccurate round the rear silencer and tailpipe. This can sometimes cause issues when fitting larger tyres, but the pipe and brackets can usually be tweaked to fit. Always take time to fit the exhaust correctly and securely. A loose exhaust, especially on a diesel, can make an alarming noise when it touches the chassis or gearbox mounting.

Note that if fitting the common petrol or later diesel downpipe, the vehicle will need to be raised sufficiently to manoeuvre the pipe into place over the gearbox crossmember. A ramp or pit is ideal or jack it up and secure on an axle stand before lying on your back underneath.

ABOVE LEFT: *Do not scrimp on exhaust hangers and ensure the tailpipe is adjusted to clear the rear tyre on full upward suspension travel.*

ABOVE RIGHT: *It is usually necessary to jack the vehicle up to pass the front pipe over the gearbox crossmember and up to the exhaust manifold.*

Fuel and Exhaust Systems

It is always advisable to use exhaust jointing paste on all exhaust pipe joints. Even a slightly blowing exhaust can make worrying noises from quiet chuffing to worrying ticking noises. Briefly covering the tailpipe with your hand in a welding gauntlet is a little hack that can help to identify leaking joints.

Engine Conversion Exhaust Systems

Bespoke exhaust systems are available for the common engine conversions. While these might seem expensive when already spending significant amounts of money on an engine change, they also represent very good value for money. Not only will they usually follow the standard fitment route, fit correctly and be the correct diameter bore, they save hours of fabrication time making sections of exhaust fit.

If the choice is to fabricate an exhaust, it is always advisable to fit off-the-shelf Land Rover parts and adapt as necessary. This will ensure that future replacement parts can be easily sourced.

Specialist exhausts for engine conversions are designed to follow the original routing in an appropriate bore for the increased performance. They may not be cheap but they represent good value for money.

LEFT: *A multi-bend specialist downpipe to allow the fitment of a Discovery 200Tdi into a Series vehicle.*

7
Ignition System

The ignition system on a classic Land Rover is as simple as you can get on an internal combustion engine. A petrol engine requires an ignition spark to be delivered into the combustion chamber at exactly the correct time to ignite a mixture of compressed fuel and oxygen. While the system isn't complex, set-up and tracing faults can be frustrating and requires a good overall understanding of the components and their function.

IGNITION SYSTEM BASIC OVERVIEW

The ignition system consists of high and low tension circuits that work together. The high tension circuit consists of the spark plugs, HT (High Tension) leads, coil, distributor cap and rotor arm. The low tension circuit consists of the points, condenser and a 12V supply from the battery via the ignition switch. The distributor is a rotary mechanical device that controls the interface between the two circuits.

In simple terms, the coil is an electromagnet and transformer that ups the 12V from the battery to approximately 30,000V via primary and secondary windings. The coil function is controlled by the 12V contact breaker points in the distributor, which open and close via cam lobes on the shaft. When the points are closed, the current flows through the primary winding, creating a magnetic field. When the points open via the movement of the lobed distributor shaft (driven by the camshaft), the flow through the primary 12V circuit is interrupted and the magnetic field collapses. This collapse sends current through the secondary winding with the coil acting as a transformer upping the output to 30,000V: 30,000V is then passed down the HT king lead to the distributor cap and, via a sprung carbon brush, to the rotor arm inside the cap. As the rotor arm turns on the distributor shaft, it sends the current to the appropriate distributor cap terminal, which in turn flows to the correct HT lead and spark plug. The spark plug then sparks inside the cylinder at the correct time to ignite a compressed mixture of fuel and oxygen. A condenser (a capacitor) is fitted across the contact breaker points to control the sparking as the contacts open and close.

IGNITION SYSTEMS: THE MAIN COMPONENTS

The Distributor

Standard 2286cc Land Rovers were fitted with a number of different distributors over the years. The most common types are Lucas 25D, Lucas 45D and Ducellier. The 2625cc engine was commonly fitted with the Lucas 25D6 or 45D6. All work in the same way but the internal components are different. The distributor is fitted with a mechanical centrifugal advance; as the vehicle speed increases, so the timing of the ignition spark must advance. In

ABOVE LEFT: The Lucas 25D was the standard distributor fitted to the 2286cc (25D4) and 2625cc (25D6) engine.

ABOVE RIGHT: The Ducellier distributor, as fitted to late Series IIIs, is not known for being the most robust option.

Ignition System

Distributor drive has an offset keyway, but it's still just possible to fit it wrongly.

addition, the distributor is also fitted with a vacuum advance controlled by a vacuum pipe from the bottom of the carburettor. The distributor is driven via an offset keyway driven by the skew gear on the camshaft to ensure it can only be fitted in one orientation. A clamp holds the distributor body in place on its mounting plate and allows it to be rotated to set the timing. Note, however, that it is *just* possible to get the keyway to drive the distributor in the wrong orientation if it is not fully located home in its housing. The common clue that it hasn't fully located is the distributor body oscillating, coupled with rough running.

Points

Points should be considered a service item as they do wear as they act on the distributor cam lobes and wear away on the contact-breaker point surface. The points gap is usually set to 0.015in for basic set-up, although the 'dwell angle' is the more accurate measurement. Having said that, very few amateur restorers have a dwell meter and many old school mechanics set the gap with a cigarette packet! While a 2286cc engine will benefit from a really good set-up, the engine is not exactly a performance unit and will often run well out of specification. To set the gap, turn the engine clockwise until the points are fully open on the lobe of the distributor cam. Slacken the securing screw and use a wide flat screwdriver to adjust the gap and use the appropriate feeler gauge (not a cigarette packet).

When replacing the Lucas points, take careful note of the position of the top hat insulator before dismantling. It should attach the coil wire and condenser to the sprung contact, but isolate the spring from the body.

Condenser

The condenser is a capacitor that connects in parallel to the points. Its function is to prevent arcing across the points as they open. A failing condenser usually causes rough running, misfiring and potentially the vehicle

The condenser is a capacitor that controls the sparking across the points as they open.

LEFT: *Correctly set points gap (0.015in) is essential for good performance.*

will fail to start. A condenser function can be checked with an ohm meter, but for the sake of the small cost it is often easier to have a new one in stock and to think of it as a basic service item. On the Ducellier distributor, the condenser is mounted on the outside of the distributor body; on the 25D and 45D it is located under the distributor cap.

Rotor Arm

The rotor arm is a push-fit on the distributor shaft and directs current from the coil king lead terminal to each of the cylinder terminals on the distributor cap. Again, this can be considered a service part. The keyway to the distributor can wear and the plastic can crack. If the rotor arm is not a tight fit on the shaft, it can wobble and will not give a reliable spark distribution.

Distributor Cap

This should really be considered a service item and has the potential to be the cause of poor running. On occasion, a cap can develop hairline cracks that are not obvious to the naked eye. The king lead terminal connects to the top of the rotor arm via a spring-loaded carbon brush and this will wear and can fall out. Check that it is still attached and still spring loaded. The contacts to each plug lead also wear. Early 25D distributor caps had side-exit HT leads held in with grub screws, but it is more common to find the more conventional push-in type terminals.

Spark Plugs

Spark plugs are another consumable service item. The commonly used part numbers for the common 8.0:1 ratio compression is RTC 3570 or RTC 3571 for 7.0:1 compression ratio. This usually cross references to NGK BP5ES/BP6ES and Champion N12Y as commonly available parts. The spark plug gap should be set to 0.029–0.032in. Very often the gap is reasonably accurate out of the box but should always be checked before fitting and during servicing. If too wide, gently tapping on a firm surface will close the gap or gently lever open.

Before removing a spark plug, use a blow gun to clean the area round the base of the plug to ensure no foreign matter enters the cylinder. A proper plug socket with rubber insert is the best tool to remove and refit a plug to avoid potential damage.

Spark plugs are also a good indicator of the health of the engine. A healthy plug will be reasonably clean, usually with light brown deposits. An oily plug is often indicative of a worn engine with poor piston oil control rings or badly leaking valve stem oil seals. A sooty plug is indicative of over-fuelling/mixture too rich or running on choke/engine not warmed up/idling from cold. A clean, glazed plug is indicative of overheating or ignition timing too far advanced. Wet plugs suggest no spark, usually caused by either a defective plug or HT lead.

HT/High Tension Leads

Old school HT leads had a wire core, whereas modern leads tend to have a flexible graphite core. The older plug leads had a screw-in acorn terminal with an insert washer and were directly screwed into place; later ones have the more common push-on terminal. HT leads do break down and terminals do corrode and fail. For a 'rivet counter' restoration, the old school lead can be bought and simply made up to the appropriate length. Modern-style leads can be bought off the shelf.

Coil

The coil mounts up out of the way on the bulkhead and is supplied by a white ignition feed wire. The low tension contacts are marked either +/- or SW (switch)/CB (contact breaker). Early coils had screw-in acorn terminals, later ones had push-in terminals. Coils have two internal windings (primary and secondary) in oil and can break down over time, especially when hot. There are original coils more than sixty years old still going strong, but they do fail, leading to rough running, misfiring and potentially failing to start. A healthy coil should read approximately 3–3.5 ohms between the low tension terminals and approximately

ABOVE LEFT: It is essential that the rotor arm is a good tight fit on the shaft.

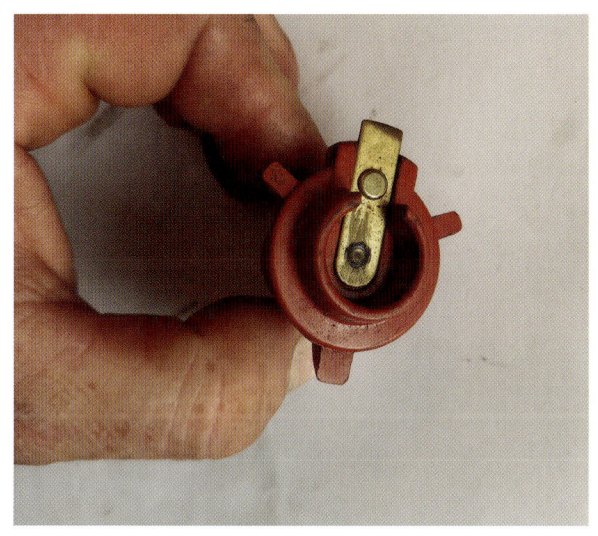

ABOVE RIGHT: Ensure that the terminals and carbon brush are in good condition. If in doubt, replace the cap.

Ignition System

Spark plugs give a very good indication of the health and set-up of the engine.

LEFT: *Plug gaps should always be checked and set to 0.029–0.032in as part of an ignition service.*

It is essential to connect the polarity of the coil correctly for best performance, making a note of the + (ignition) and − (contact breaker points).

LEFT: *Old school HT leads can be made up, but modern leads offer improved performance.*

7,500–10,000 ohms from the HT terminal to the 12V supply terminal.

Note that most Series Land Rovers have standard 'non ballasted' coils but some were fitted with ballasted coils, in particular V8 models. The ballasted coil normally operates at 9V with a ballast resistor to lower the 12V supply in normal running conditions. However, when the starter motor is operational via the exciter wire, the ballast resistor is bypassed and the coil is supplied with the full 12V, giving a stronger spark. This was a common feature on cars in the 1970s and 1980s to assist starting in cold weather. The ballast resistor is usually an external unit mounted beside the coil itself. If retaining the ballast, a ballasted coil must be fitted. If bypassing the ballast (a common in-service modification), a standard 12V coil should be fitted. A ballasted coil will normally have a primary winding resistance of approximately 1.5 ohms. If a ballast coil is constantly run on 12V, it will overheat and fail.

If going 'full rivet counter' on the coil, an age-appropriate type or appropriately branded unit adds a bit of extra authenticity. Lucas branded coils were common throughout the 1970s and Unipart were the common supplier in the 1980s. Beyond the age-correct details, it is wise to buy the best quality coil you can afford. Some companies offer performance coils that can offer improved performance.

SETTING IGNITION TIMING: FIRST PRINCIPLES

Accurate ignition timing is vital to good engine performance, but it should be noted that a Land Rover engine is very basic and will often run reasonably well even when significantly out of adjustment. The engine was designed to work on a wide range of fuel qualities and octane levels all around the world, and a lower ratio compression engine was available on export 2286cc models. Nominally, the timing was set at TDC for the low octane fuel that was common at the time. However, timing was commonly advanced to 6–8 degrees BTDC (Before Top Dead Centre) for higher octane fuels. Many owners find it advantageous to further advance the timing for the current fuel options of 95 and 99 RON.

TDC is the point at which cylinder no.1 is at the top of its compression stroke. The ignition is set so the no.1 spark plug fires just before the piston reaches the top of the stroke, giving sufficient time for the fuel to burn to return the piston on the power stroke.

Ignition timing can be set either statically or dynamically. Static timing is used for the basic set-up and does not require any specialist tools. Setting the timing dynamically requires a stroboscopic timing light.

SETTING STATIC TIMING AND DISTRIBUTOR ORIENTATION

Locate, clean and mark the timing marks on the crank pulley with chalk for visibility. Two different timing marker systems were used: either a multi-point marker bolted to the timing case with a single mark on the front crankshaft pulley or a single-point marker on the timing case and multiple marks on the crankshaft pulley. On the multi-point marker, the points correspond to 6 BTDC, 3 BTDC, TDC and 6 ATDC (After TDC). The single-point marker system has the appropriate numbers on the pulley.

Rotate the engine on the cranking shaft towards the TDC mark on the *compression stroke*. Note that there are two TDCs in a full combustion cycle. To find TDC on the compression stoke, remove no.1 spark plug and hold your finger across the hole. Rotate the engine clockwise until you feel pressure rising and air being expelled as the piston rises. Turn the engine until the appropriate timing mark lines up.

When the appropriate timing mark is aligned, the distributor timing position can be set. The timing should be set at the point when the contact breaker points are just opening. With experience this can be done visually for a very basic set up simply to get the vehicle to run, but can be more accurately found by using a test lamp. With the ignition on, put the test lamp clips between the distributor low tension wire and a good earth point. Turn the distributor body until the test lamp only just lights – this is the point when the coil will deliver power to the spark plug – and tighten the securing clamp.

Note that when TDC is set on the compression stroke, the rotor arm points towards the terminal on the distributor cap for no.1 HT lead. When the camshaft skew gear is correctly positioned, the distributor orientation should put no.1 terminal at approximately 4 o'clock when looking from the front of the vehicle (2 o'clock viewed from the RHS). The vacuum advance should be pointing towards the rear of the vehicle.

Note that if the engine has been dismantled, it is not uncommon for the skew gear to have been refitted in the incorrect location. If this is the case, the rotor arm and orientation, and therefore plug no.1, might be in a different location. The orientation of the distributor body may have to be adjusted to give the best orientation to ensure the vacuum advance doesn't sit too close to the cylinder head.

Note that the firing order on the 2286cc is 1-3-4-2 and the distributor turns anticlockwise. Once the no.1 position has been confirmed, it is a simple case of connecting the leads anticlockwise in firing order. The firing order on the 2625cc engine is 1-5-3-6-2-4.

Once the static timing has been set, the engine can be started. With experience the timing can be set to a certain

Going 'full rivet counter' with this Unipart-branded coil on a concourse restoration.

RIGHT: *Later-type timing marks: a single pointer and (faint!) marks on the front pulley.*

Ignition System

Correct location of distributor terminal serving piston no.1.

LEFT: *Static ignition timing: when the test lamp lights, the points are just opening.*

extent 'by ear', listening to the engine note rising and falling and setting to a 'happy spot'. Note that the distributor turns anticlockwise, so turning the distributor clockwise will advance the timing, anticlockwise will retard it. A well-used road test technique is to drive up a hill with the engine on the cusp of labouring and advance/retard the ignition timing so it doesn't quite 'pink' with pre-ignition.

DYNAMIC TIMING

To set the timing dynamically, the static timing must be sufficiently accurate to run. A stroboscopic timing light is required: this fires a light beam in time with the spark at no.1 cylinder, and when pointed at the timing marks it causes the timing mark to appear static. A range of different timing lights is available from very basic to multi-function offerings with rpm and dwell angle functions; the manufacturer's guide should be referenced for details. The following is a brief guide:

- Mark the timing pointers with chalk or correction fluid.
- Clip the timing light power leads onto the battery.
- Clip the pick-up sensor to no.1 HT lead.
- Disconnect the vacuum advance.
- Start the engine and ensure it is up to running temperature with the choke in.
- Ensure the idle is about 750rpm.

- Point the gun at the timing marks and note the position of the pointer.
- Advance or retard as necessary by turning the body of the distributor.
- Ensure the body is clamped tightly in place and reconnect the vacuum advance.
- Take the vehicle for a road test and recheck/adjust the timing as necessary.

ELECTRONIC IGNITION

Ignition technology has moved on and electronic ignition offers a far more accurate system. A pickup and trigger ring directly replace the conventional mechanical moving points and condenser. There are a number of options available, either as a kit to fit inside the existing distributor or a full distributor already built and ready to fit. Externally, electronic ignition is not usually visible but note that it will usually benefit from silicone HT leads and, depending on the manufacturer, may require a specific or recommended coil and rotor arm. Full kits with all components are available from a range of manufacturers and suppliers. Electronic ignition systems will come with full fitting instructions and only an overview is possible here.

Note that you cannot use the usual static timing technique when fitting electronic ignition. It is important to note the orientation of the old distributor before removing it. Setting the new distributor in the same orientation as the old one should be close enough to get the vehicle running, but accurate timing will have to be set dynamically with a strobe light.

There are two wires on an electric distributor: one goes to the + side of the coil, the other to the – side. There are different kits available for positive and negative earth systems.

IGNITION SYSTEM PROBLEMS

Ignition system problems will mean the vehicle runs poorly or doesn't run at all. A systematic approach must be taken to diagnosing problems and isolating problems. A return to first principles is usually the best plan of attack. On occasion it is hard to identify whether a problem is ignition or fuel related.

Engine Fails to Start

The following questions might help to isolate the problem:

- Is this a new problem or a developing one? What is the history of the starting/running?
- Does engine turn over at a normal speed?
- Is there fuel to the carburettor?
- Does the carburettor pump fuel via the accelerator jet when accelerator is pressed?
- Is the choke out as appropriate for the weather conditions?
- Is there a 12V supply to the coil?
- Do the points give a small spark when flicked open? There should normally be a visible spark, but a

Ignition System

TOP LEFT: *The skew gear has been inserted incorrectly here, so terminal 1 is clocked round and the timing had to be set accordingly.*

ABOVE LEFT: *Clipping the strobe pick-up clamp to the lead serving cylinder no.1.*

TOP RIGHT: *With the strobe light pointed at the pulley, the timing mark will appear static. Adjust the distributor to set the correct level of advance.*

RIGHT: *Electronic ignition offers a more precise timing set-up and dispenses with the need for points and condenser.*

significant spark could suggest the condenser has failed.
- Do the points open and close as the engine is cranked over?
- Has the points gap closed up/opened up?
- Is the distributor cap dry inside?
- Is the carbon brush in the distributor cap intact?
- Are the wires inside the distributor correctly connected and insulated? Note that the braided insulation can fail.
- Has the timing slipped?
- Does the rotor arm turn when the engine is turned over?
- Remove each spark plug lead in turn and connect to a known good or new plug and earth to the engine block. Is a strong spark visible at all leads when cranking over?

If there is no spark at any plug, suspect coil or king lead. If there is spark at some, suspect some faulty HT leads or poor connections.

Engine Starts but Runs Poorly

A range of factors could cause the engine to run poorly or misfire. Again it is a process of elimination. The problem could still lie in the fuelling system leaning up.

- Check each plug connection in turn and listen for any changes in running as a process of elimination. Use insulated spark plug removal pliers (not your bare hands, unless you want a 30,000V shock). Listen for any change in engine note to identify whether one (or more) plug is failing to spark: investigate whether it is a lead or plug at fault.
- Recheck the ignition set-up timing as outlined above.
- Note that ignition components can fail as they warm up, or can function sufficiently to start the vehicle but not run correctly.
- Coils break down and overheat and can cause misfires.
- Condensers short circuit and break down, often causing significant misfires.
- Insulation can break down within the low tension circuit, especially the fabric-covered points wires in the distributor.
- Check valve clearances to ensure valves are closing correctly
- Carry out a compression test on all cylinders

8
Cooling System

The Land Rover cooling system was designed to be effective in a range of different climates. When in good condition it is more than capable of controlling the temperature of the engine. Briefly, the block and head have coolant galleries and the coolant is pumped round a closed, pressurised system by the water pump, which is housed on the front of the timing cover. The temperature is controlled by a thermostat at the top of the engine. This diverts coolant to either the bypass circuit when cold or, when sufficiently hot enough to open the thermostat, through the radiator. The cooling fan, coupled with airflow from vehicle movement, reduces the heat of the coolant within the radiator core. If a vehicle heater is fitted to the system, this acts as an additional radiator/water-to-air heat exchanger, cooling the engine and warming the cab.

EVOLUTION OF THE COOLING SYSTEM

The basic design of the cooling system changed very little throughout Series II, IIA and III production, although a number of different radiator and water pump designs were used over the years.

Series II

Early engines had a cast aluminium thermostat housing and bypass system and a unique water eight-hole pump. The early water pump attached with eight bolts/studs. The very early engines also had an aluminium timing cover, although this changed to the standard cast iron type on later Series IIs. The early radiator design was usually manufactured by Serck and looked very much like the Series I diesel radiator, but with a different mounting frame to match the new front panel design. It has a thin steel fan cowling screwed onto the radiator frame.

Series II/IIA

The water pump became the standard nine-hole type on civilian specification vehicles. Military vehicles were usually fitted with a seven-bolt type pump, which is matched to a different timing case design. The newer radiator design was wider with a larger flat top tank. Later IIA vehicles were additionally fitted with a catch tank to capture any overflow from the radiator cap vent pipe. The bottom hose exits straight back on the right hand 4-cylinder model. The 6-cylinder radiator had different top and bottom hose connections on the left-hand side to match the different thermostat and water

Original Series II radiator (note the date stamping). If originality is important, an old-school radiator can be re-cored, so do not scrap it.

LEFT: *Thermostat and bypass on an early 2286cc. It also has a unique 8-hole water pump, which is obsolete and so the original would have to be rebuilt. Kits are available.*

Cooling System

pump. The last Series IIA radiators were the same design as the Series III.

Series III

The Series III radiator had a rounded top tank and larger diameter hose connections. The bottom hose connection comes up at an angle and is matched to a U-shaped bottom hose. The fan cowl is made from plastic, held in place with screws and spiral springs with an additional thin steel side cowling braced to the battery tray. The 6-cylinder radiator had an angled top hose on the left-hand side and a straight bottom hose on the left-hand side. The Stage 1 V8 radiator is a derivative of the contemporary Range Rover across the full grille width, mounted on rubber bobbins. Instead of the usual bult-in pressurised header tank, it had an external pressurised expansion tank.

Radiators for 2286cc models of different generations are interchangeable, as long as the appropriate hoses, fans and cowls are used. Budget modern aftermarket radiators are often aluminium cored with a crimp-on plastic tank and based on the Series III type. While these do look very modern, generally speaking they last well and are efficient.

While new old stock 'correct' radiators are very hard to come by, an original copper core radiator can be repaired or re-cored by a specialist at a reasonable cost. With the relative values of the vehicles rising and the growing enthusiasm for originality, this would seem the best option on a higher level restoration. Stage 1 radiators are very hard to obtain and re-coring or adapting a Range Rover radiator is pretty much the only option unless going for a bespoke build.

Nine- and seven-hole water pumps are commonly available, but eight-bolt and 6-cylinder types are rare and

ABOVE LEFT: *Later Series IIA type with larger header tank. Note the plastic catch bottle to return any overfill back to the radiator as it cools.*

ABOVE RIGHT: *Series III 6-cylinder type radiator. Note plastic fan, cowl and offset top hose position.*

If originality isn't important and the budget is tight, just fit a modern radiator with an aluminium core and plastic header tank – it will work just fine.

LEFT: *Standard Series III 4-cylinder type radiator with central top hose position.*

Cooling System

If your radiator looks like this you can expect overheating and leaks.

usually only available as genuine new old stock. However, rebuild kits are readily available, consisting of a new shaft, bearings and seals that need to be pressed in. Alternatively, there are specialists that will recondition water pumps on an exchange basis.

COOLING SYSTEM PROBLEMS

With the exception of the V8, which can be quite sensitive in hot conditions, Land Rover engines are generally well cooled or even over-cooled for some climates. An overheating engine is therefore a significant concern, potentially leading to terminal engine damage, so any problem with the cooling system should be rectified with urgency. Be aware that temperature gauges can be unreliable, reading over or under. While there is seldom any need to be paranoid and constantly watching the gauge, it is important to work out what is 'normal' for your vehicle and be aware when it becomes 'abnormal'.

Common reasons for overheating are as follows:

- Low coolant level: on an old vehicle this should be part of any 'first parade' pre-use check.
- Corroded radiator fins reducing the efficiency of the cooling process.
- Blocked radiator: externally by mud/chaff/debris or internally by rust deposits and oil contamination.
- Defective thermostat failing to open.
- Cylinder head gasket failure. This can cause combustion gasses to leak into and over-pressurise the cooling system, for coolant to enter the cylinders, for oil to enter the cooling system or coolant enter the oil.
- Loose or broken fan belt causing the water pump to lose drive.
- Water pump failure, either through a corroded impeller or through significant external leaks.
- Failure of the radiator pressure cap allowing coolant to leak out through the overflow pipe.
- Ignition timing significantly out.

Note that the top tank on the radiator also serves as an expansion tank as the engine heats up. The coolant should be topped up to just cover the fins and should not be filled right up to the top. If the radiator is overfilled, it usually vents to find its natural level and this is often confused with over-pressurising of the system or a leak. The catch tank fitted to the later model Series IIA and III was introduced to catch any overfill and to allow it to siphon back into the radiator as it cools down.

Checking for 'mayonnaise'. There is nothing to worry about if it clears when the engine warms up, but could be a sign of coolant in the oil.

RIGHT: *Overfilled radiators will usually blow off to find their own level. Just covering the fins is fine, so do not overfill.*

COOLING SYSTEM MAINTENANCE

Pre-Use/Post-Lay-Up Checks

Checking the coolant level should be routine on a classic vehicle in regular use and should definitely be checked before a long journey or when bringing a vehicle out after a lay-up. Rubber hoses do degrade and dry joints and gaskets do weep. Very often they will hold up fine until the vehicle is up to running temperature and then proceed to dump boiling coolant everywhere. Look for traces of dried coolant on hose clips, rusty weeps from core plugs and for any rusty cracks in the block, especially down the left-hand side of the block near the starter motor.

The expansion cap should never be removed when the coolant is hot: boiling water at high pressure is likely to cause serious scalding. While this is blatantly obvious, when you're out in the field with a suspected overheating vehicle, it is very easy to ignore the risks and take a chance. Even the most experienced Land Rover mechanics will have risked it and regretted it afterwards.

Coolant vs Water

The cooling system should normally be filled with ethylene glycol (blue) summer coolant and winter antifreeze to the appropriate concentration for the expected temperatures. Water expands as it freezes and a deeply frozen block is likely to crack down the left-hand side between the cylinder coolant galleries. In addition, coolant has anti-corrosion properties, an important consideration in a cast iron block. A build-up of rust particles often lodges in the cooling jackets round pistons 3 and 4 and corrosion in the core plugs can go unnoticed until they let go under pressure. If filling the system after a major overhaul, it is advisable to initially fill the system with water and check for leaks before adding the appropriate amount of coolant concentrate.

Cooling system maintenance should be part of a regular service regime. It is recommended to change the antifreeze/coolant every five years as the anti-corrosion properties degrade over time. Knowing that it is common to have to do small top-ups to the system, it is easy to lose track of the concentration and for the coolant to become diluted. It is therefore important to know the antifreeze concentration level as winter approaches. This can be checked with a refractometer or hydrometer, which should give an accurate freezing point. The old school 'taste test' is not to be recommended as it is wildly inaccurate and ethylene glycol is harmful to the central nervous system. Its sweet taste is actually rather pleasant to humans and animals alike, so it is important to dispose of any waste responsibly.

Fan Belts

Fan belts degrade and replacement should again be part of a regular service regime. Old belts crack, fray, stretch and slip. It is always advisable to carry a spare and replacement is straightforward, although occasionally fiddly if bolts are tight, and you'll no doubt skin your knuckles on the fan. If the charge light comes on and the vehicle starts to overheat, inspecting the fan belt should be the first point of call. Again, this may seem obvious, but even the most experienced Land Rover owners do get caught out miles from home with the most obvious and simplest of problems. It has been known for the 2286cc engine to be run without the fan belt for reasonable distances without damage, but that is purely down to luck rather than good mechanical judgement. No fan belt means no circulation through the radiator, no circulation means overheating, significant overheating means a damaged engine.

Flushing the Coolant System

2286cc engines are very prone to internal corrosion, especially if used for long periods with plain water. Antifreeze was not always used when the vehicles were new: sixty years on you can now expect a significant build-up of sludge and coolant that looks like dirty Irn Bru. Rust deposits build up and often lodge in the water jacket around cylinders 3 and 4 as well as in the radiator. A garden hose can be used to reverse-flush the radiator from bottom to top. A suitable bung/cloth/duct tape can be made up to pack the diameter of the bottom hose to give a watertight seal.

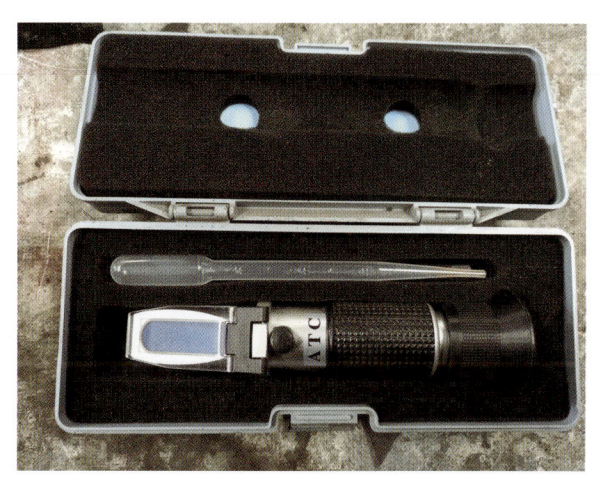

ABOVE LEFT: Note the traces of rusty water. Clearly those old hose clips have been leaking and the coolant galleries are probably full of corrosion.

ABOVE RIGHT: Antifreeze not only protects from frost damage but significantly reduces internal corrosion. Use a refractometer to check the freezing point.

Cooling System

To flush the block, run the hose through the heater connections in the back of the head and remove the drain plug from the left-hand side of the block. Note that the drain wing-bolt is one of the very few left-hand threads on a Series Land Rover. Continue to run the hose until the water runs clear. Note that if there is significant rusty build-up, it may be necessary to remove the core plugs to remove it completely. If suspect, it is worthwhile to check the block with an infrared thermometer, looking for hotspots, in particular around cylinders 3 and 4. The side plugs can be removed with the engine in place (it's easier if the wing is removed), but access to the rear plug is hampered by the bulkhead, so engine removal is pretty much the only option unless you cut an access hole (not recommended). (For more detail on changing the core plugs, see Chapter 5.)

Water Pump Replacement

Typically the water pump leaks before it fails. When the internal seal fails, coolant leaks past and comes out of the weep/witness hole in the casting. As the bearings wear, they can also become noisy and loose. A worn water pump can often be heard as a rattle when the vehicle is idling. As part of a service routine, it is worth feeling the fan for any play. Any more than slight play is a cause for concern, as is any roughness when spinning the fan.

Replacing a water pump is a straightforward, though occasionally fiddly, job. The fan and cowling need to be removed for access. Note that water pump bolts commonly seize in place, in particular the three that pass through the timing case and into the block around the water jacket. Do not heave at these bolts if they're tight as they can break in the block. Careful application of heat and easing fluid, and carefully working the bolts, should release them. Time carefully working the bolts out is well invested: it will always take longer to rush the job and have to drill them out. Note that the small, top fixings into the timing case are coarse-threaded ¼in UNC, not the more common UNF.

Thermostat Replacement

The cooling system is designed to run with a thermostat, although it is

ABOVE LEFT: *This pile of rust was removed from the coolant galleries of just one engine after prising out a core plug – there would have been no coolant flow round the rear cylinders.*

ABOVE RIGHT: *Location of the block drain point below the exhaust manifold. Also check for rusty crack marks from frost damage.*

ABOVE LEFT: *A telltale hole in the water pump warns of a leaking seal, hopefully before the bearings give out.*

ABOVE RIGHT: *These three water pump bolts pass through the timing cover and into the block. Take care not to snap them.*

not uncommon for it to have been removed for some expedient reason by a previous owner. The thermostat is designed to maximise engine efficiency, allowing it to get up to normal running temperature quickly and then maintain it by opening and closing as necessary. A defective thermostat can, of course, fail to open at the appropriate temperature, causing overheating. A thermostat can be tested by putting it in boiling water and ensuring it opens fully. However, it is a cheap part and if going to the effort of removing it, it is probably best to have one in stock in preparation. There are two types of thermostat used: the early type ethyl-alcohol type and the later wax-filled type. The standard thermostat opens at between 71 and 78°C and should be fully open at 90°C.

While removing the thermostat housing should just be a case of draining some coolant out, removing the top hose and undoing the three long bolts (¼in UNF or 6mm on later vehicles), they are likely to have seized in place. *Do not* force them if they're tight: if they snap off, it will take far longer to deal with the hassle than to invest a bit of time working them out.

Use a powerful blowtorch to get some heat into the housing and threaded section in the head. Soak in easing fluid and repeat. Use a tight-fitting six-sided socket on a short breaker bar to rock the bolt backwards and forwards: it is far easier to use than having to keep reversing a ratchet and gives much better feedback when the bolt is starting to release. Do not celebrate too soon and rush the removal process when the bolt starts to turn. Keep working it, feeling if it's 'springy', suggesting the bolt is twisting rather than unscrewing.

If a bolt does snap, it can often be drilled and extracted with a stud extractor or the hole retapped. Use a centre punch on the remains of the bolt and drill carefully, ensuring it does not wander.

Fit the new thermostat with a new housing gasket/gaskets. It is advisable to use a smear of jointing compound such as Hylomar to ensure a good seal as they are very prone to weeping, especially if the casting has corroded round the machined faces. Smear the mounting bolts in copper grease to ensure they come out easily in the future.

Coolant Hoses and Hose Clips

Coolant hoses should be considered a disposable item on a vehicle that has been out of service for any length of time. Rubber degrades over time, potentially leading to weeping joints or sudden failure under pressure. Old hoses will often pick up rust deposits from the cast connection spigots, which can cause poor sealing. Replacements are cheap and easy to fit – apart from the bypass hose on the water pump. While it is just possible to fit that without removing the thermostat bypass, it is often easier to do so but do be warned that the bolts may be seized. Rusty spigots on connections such as the thermostat housing and water pump need to be cleaned off to ensure a good sealing surface, and occasionally a smear of jointing compound is necessary.

Early vehicles were fitted with wire hose clips. These are a lovely period detail that look fantastic on an accurate restoration, but it is important that the clips used are exactly the correct size. They are not particularly adaptable to variations in diameter and often don't seal as well as a good-quality 'Jubilee' type worm hose clip. Irrespective of whether you choose period design or

Look, no thermostat! This is likely to be masking a problem with the cooling system and may need further investigation.

ABOVE LEFT: *Take the time to get plenty of heat into the thermostat bolts – they snap for fun!*

ABOVE RIGHT: *Using a small breaker bar allows the bolt to be worked backwards and forwards.*

Cooling System

A coolant system leak-stop pellet was fitted on the production line to minimise tiny leaks: this is a modern equivalent.

LEFT: *Plan ahead when fitting hose clips: make sure you can get a screwdriver in for routine maintenance.*

functional performance, always use good-quality clips: budget ones often strip when nipped up tight. Also plan ahead with the orientation of the clips to make tightening/loosening easy in the future, and make sure you can get a screwdriver in when the wings, radiator and front panel are back in.

Frustrating Coolant Leaks

When recommissioning a cooling system after significant work, it is always advisable to initially fill it with plain water to check for leaks to minimise the loss of any coolant. While coolant is more 'searching' than water, at least this will give an opportunity to find and rectify any obvious leaks without wasting additive. When the system is confirmed as watertight, an appropriate amount of water can be drained and replenished with coolant.

Note that the Workshop Manual informs us that Land Rover actually added a sealing pellet to the cooling system from new to deal with any potential weeps. This would suggest a product such as Bars Stop Leak or Holts Radweld would be expedient to cure small leaks.

Temperature Gauge, Sender and Choke Otterstat

The temperature gauge works through the variable earthing resistance of the temperature sender in the head. In normal running conditions the temperature gauge should sit somewhere in the middle of the normal zone. However, the components can be inaccurate and, while the gauge might read on the high side, the actual temperature might be perfectly normal. Because the components are pretty basic, they do vary and it is important to know what is normal for your vehicle. If suspect, it is worthwhile ascertaining the actual temperature of the coolant with an infrared thermometer. Aftermarket temperature senders are frequently inaccurate and when a vehicle is fitted with an engine conversion, there is often incompatibility between the gauge and sender. For example, the Discovery 200TDi temperature sender will often make a Series gauge read somewhere near the red at normal running temperature.

A failing voltage stabiliser can be one of the reasons for an inaccurate reading. The function of the stabiliser is to average out the output voltage

The voltage regulator behind the dash can cause the temperature gauge to give a false high reading.

Cooling System

to 10V to reduce the fluctuation in the temperature and fuel gauge readings and so were fitted to late Series IIA and III models. If both fuel gauge and temperature gauge are overreading, the stabiliser is likely to be faulty.

Note that it is common to confuse the temperature sender with the Otterstat switch. The Otterstat switch is fitted to the top of the cylinder head on some petrol models and illuminates an amber dash light to inform the driver that the vehicle has got to temperature and to feed the choke in. It is a simple on/off bimetallic switch, not a resistor like the sender: if the sender wire is attached to the Otterstat, it will read hot as soon as the vehicle is up to temperature.

ABOVE LEFT: Location of the temperature sender on the 2286cc petrol.

ABOVE RIGHT: Location of the temperature sender on the 2286cc diesel.

ABOVE LEFT: Location of the 2625cc sender with wire attached.

ABOVE RIGHT: This is an Otterstat for the choke light, not a temperature sender.

9 Clutch

Series II, IIA and III clutch systems comprise of a pressure plate and a dry friction plate, operated by a hydraulic system. The hydraulic system comprises a pedal-operated master (primary) cylinder and slave (secondary) cylinder that operates a clutch release mechanism within the bellhousing. The clutch components are matched to the gearbox as well as the engine. Knowing that Land Rovers are often modified over the years, a broad overview is required. You cannot assume that your vehicle has the same engine, gearbox and clutch that it left the factory with.

CLUTCH SYSTEM EVOLUTION

Series II and IIA System

On Series II and IIA models, the clutch release mechanism is an integral part of the gearbox and the clutch release bearing is lubricated by gearbox oil. While it is a hydraulically operated system, it uses the same basic engineering as the mechanical release system used on the Series I models. The slave cylinder is attached to a bracket that is bolted to the bellhousing via the flywheel housing bolts on the right-hand side of the engine. The master cylinder shares a reservoir with the braking system though with a separate compartment for safety (note that the smaller, central compartment serves the clutch).

Series III System

The Series III clutch release system is simpler than the earlier design. The slave cylinder is bolted directly onto an aperture in the bellhousing on the left-hand side of the vehicle. This operates a rod, which in turn pivots a heavy-duty clutch release fork mounted inside the bellhousing. This then moves a sealed clutch release bearing to control the pressure of the clutch diaphragm. The master cylinder has an integral reservoir pot and is completely separate to the braking system.

Clutch Sizes and Compatibility

Four different clutch sizes were fitted to Series Land Rovers:

- 9in with coil spring pressure plate and three-lever release in Series II and IIA.
- Optional (later standard) 9.5in with diaphragm pressure plate with a release boss in Series II and IIA.
- 9.5in diaphragm release with no release boss in Series III.
- 10.5in diaphragm release in Stage 1 (109 V8).

The clutch type needs to be matched to both the gearbox (specifically the bellhousing and clutch release mech-

Series II/IIA slave cylinder bolts onto a bracket that is attached to the side of the bellhousing.

LEFT: *Clutch release mechanism on Series II and IIA models was based on the Series I.*

Clutch

ABOVE LEFT: *Series III clutch release mechanism was far simpler than the Series II/IIA.*

ABOVE RIGHT: *9in clutch pressure plate with three release levers locates with two flywheel dowels.*

ABOVE LEFT: *Series IIA 9.5in clutch diaphragm pressure plate with central boss and three flywheel dowels.*

ABOVE RIGHT: *Series III type diaphragm pressure plate with no boss and three flywheel dowels.*

anism) and the engine. If fitting a Series III gearbox to a Series II/IIA, you will need the Series III clutch and vice versa. There is further information in Chapter 10, but it is important to have a good overview of gearboxes when it comes to choosing the appropriate clutch for your vehicle. It is very common for a Series III gearbox to have been fitted in a Series II/IIA to benefit from the synchromesh on first and second gear. Also, in-service gearbox changes are extremely common and often whatever was available would have been chosen.

Note that because of the larger bulge in the bellhousing for the slave cylinder, if fitting a Series III gearbox into a standard Series II/IIA chassis, it is necessary to trim the engine crossmember gusset or the gearbox will foul on it. There are significant overlaps and compatibilities with the different generations of gearboxes, hence why it is best to think more about matching the clutch to the clutch release mechanism and bellhousing and less with the internals and serial number of the gearbox. For example, it is possible to fit a later Series IIA bellhousing and clutch release mechanism (along with the primary pinion and constant gear) to a full synchromesh Series III box to allow it to be fitted without trimming the chassis. It is also possible to fit a Series III bellhousing and clutch release mechanism to a later Series IIA box. This exact modification was an expedient change fitted to the author's Scottish Series III simply because that was all that was available in the remote Highlands of Scotland in 1991.

The flywheel has pressure plate location dowels: two dowels for 9in, three for 9.5in. The holes are pre-drilled in the flywheel, but if fitting a different clutch it will be necessary to add/remove dowels to match the pressure plate.

DIAGNOSING CLUTCH PROBLEMS

The most common clutch problems are slipping, juddering, failing to release and noise. A well-known simple test of the clutch system can be carried out by trying to move off gently in second gear with the parking brake applied. The vehicle should stall before the clutch starts to slip significantly.

There should be no significant grumbling noises when the pedal is depressed and the bite point should be predicable and not at the top or very bottom of the pedal travel. Note that it is common to get a slight crunch when selecting first or second gear

101

Clutch

Series III slave cylinder sits close to the engine crossmember gusset.

with the engine running from a standstill on a non-synchromesh gearbox (Series II and IIA). Try selecting third or fourth gear beforehand and it will usually select without crunching.

Clutch Slip

Slipping is usually caused by a worn friction plate and is often accompanied by an acrid burning smell, especially when under load. Additionally, the springs or diaphragm in the pressure plate do wear, causing or exacerbating the wear on the friction plate. It is always best practice to replace both together given the relatively small extra cost versus the time and labour costs of removing the gearbox.

Significant oil contamination on the friction plate can also cause clutch slip. Oil contamination can come from either engine or gearbox – to determine which, inspect the viscosity of the oil at the wading plug hole in the bottom of the flywheel housing. Gear oil is thick and usually clean, engine oil is thinner and often dirty, especially in a diesel. Gear oil will most likely be from the clutch release mechanism. On all but the very last Series IIA models, the clutch release mechanism was unsealed and relied on a scroll on the primary motion shaft to 'wind' oil back into the gearbox when the engine is running. If a vehicle is parked facing steeply downhill, oil can leak out of the front of the gearbox and contaminate the clutch. All Series III gearboxes have a sealed clutch release system but the primary pinion seal in the front cover of the gearbox can leak.

Any engine oil contamination on the clutch will be coming from a failing rear crankshaft seal and replacement will involve removal of the flywheel and flywheel housing (for further information, *see* Chapter 5), which is not a nice job on a three-bearing 2286cc. Note that a slight weep of oil from the rear crankshaft seal is not uncommon and can often be lived with unless it is severe and causing problems. The original design has a threaded hole in the bottom of the flywheel housing specifically to allow oil weep to escape. The hole can be fitted with a 'wading plug', designed to keep water out of the bellhousing as water ingress can also cause the clutch to slip. The wading plug was originally fitted to a carrying bracket attached to one of the bellhousing bolts, ready to be fitted.

Clutch Judder

Clutch judder, especially when moving off, can be a symptom of oil contamination. It can also be caused by a loose pressure plate or worn springs on the friction plate. Friction plates are damped by springs round the splined output and wear or damage can cause uneven release. Note also that a binding handbrake, especially in reverse, can also give clutch judder symptoms, so check this first. Also, severely worn propshaft universal joints can also cause judder.

Leaking rear crankshaft main seal can contaminate the clutch friction plate.

LEFT: *Typical worn clutch friction plate worn down to the rivets.*

Bellhousing oil drain hole and wading plug in place on bolt-on bracket adjacent.

LEFT: *Scroll on the Series II and IIA primary pinion is designed to wind oil back into the gearbox. It doesn't work when parked on a hill.*

Failure to Release

This is most likely to be caused by a failure or maladjustment of the hydraulic system, although collapse of the pressure and friction plates can also cause a failure to release. Feel the pedal resistance: if solid throughout the stroke, it's likely to be a plate problem or other mechanical issue; if it's slack, it's most likely to be a hydraulic issue.

Check the fluid level at the reservoir, also check for leaks throughout the system and check the condition of the flexible hose. Note that on a Series II and IIA, the flexible hose connects directly to the slave cylinder, on a Series III it connects to a fixed pipe across the back of the engine.

If a Series II/IIA pedal is completely slack with no resistance with a full hy-

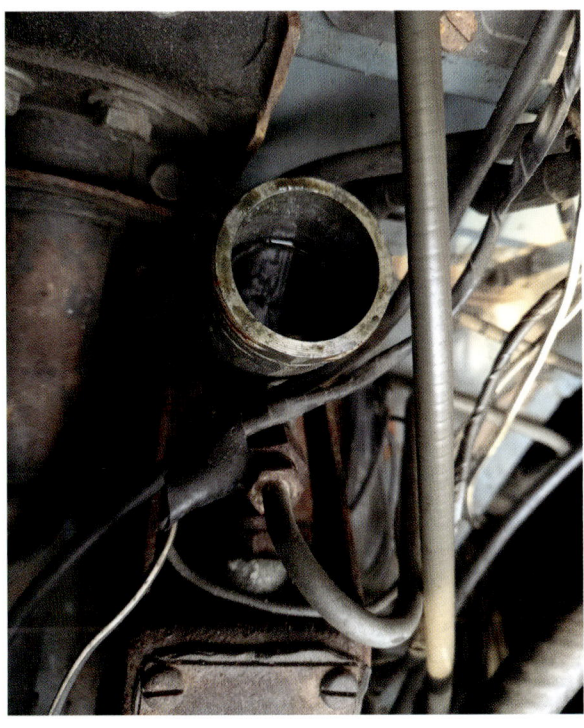

ABOVE LEFT: *Checking the fluid level on a Series III. The integral reservoir is small and the cap often a tight fit.*

ABOVE RIGHT: *Series II and IIA has a combined clutch and brake reservoir can. The clutch pot sits in the centre of the can.*

Clutch

Clutch cross shaft, collar and pins on a Series II and IIA are prone to wear and snapping.

draulic system, it's possible that a pin in the clutch release connecting rod has sheared or fallen out. In addition, sometimes the pin can break at one end and still allow the pedal to feel OK but not fully release the clutch. Note also that the collar is prone to wear and so can lead to poor adjustment.

On a vehicle that has been left standing for a long time, especially in damp conditions, it's possible that the friction plate has stuck to the flywheel. A stuck pressure plate can often be freed off by selecting low range and starting the vehicle in gear. Another cause could be corrosion on the gearbox/friction plate input splines. Note these should be lightly lubricated on assembly.

A spongy feeling clutch pedal, which could also cause a failure to release, can be caused by a collapsing flexible hose. You might be able to detect this by noticing it bulging when the pedal is pressed down.

Noisy Clutch

A grinding or grumbling noise while the clutch is pressed down is likely to be a worn clutch release bearing. A screeching noise is likely to be a dry or worn flywheel spigot bearing.

CHANGING THE CLUTCH

Gaining Access

Changing the clutch is a fairly involved job and can be executed in a variety of different ways. The gearbox will have to be separated from the engine: some people choose to remove the engine, but most choose to remove the gearbox.

To gain access to the bellhousing bolts, the floor plates and transmission tunnel have to be removed, which is not a difficult job but the floor screws are likely to be seized or the heads rusted. A useful trick to remove corroded floor screws is to cut a slit in them with a 1mm disc and get a wide-bladed screwdriver on them. As well as giving good purchase on the head, the heat generated can also help to loosen them. A trick for removing the driver's side floor plate, which snags on the pedals or handbrake, is to select low range and press brake and clutch pedals down sufficiently to lift it up from the front – back off a brake adjustor if necessary to give sufficient pedal travel (readjust afterwards, of course).

On the 6-cylinder and Stage 1 V8 models it may be easier to remove the engine as access to the bellhousing bolts is easier. The large centre tunnel comes out of the 6-cylinder model without having to remove the floors, and the long bellhousing on the LT95 gearbox on the V8 means the bellhousing bolts are accessible without removing any internal fixings.

Removing the Gearbox for a Clutch Change

Note that the gearbox does not have to be fully removed from the vehicle. It can just be moved back sufficiently to gain access to change the clutch, although space is tight and the exhaust often gets in the way. For vehicles with a bolt-on gearbox crossmember, the gearbox can be removed from below. If fitted with a fixed gearbox crossmember, the seat box will need to be removed to fully remove the gearbox upwards.

An engine hoist is the safest way to remove, support and manoeuvre the

ABOVE LEFT: *Pressing down on both brake and clutch to allow the floor plate to be lifted up.*

ABOVE RIGHT: *Access to the bellhousing bolts requires the floor and transmission tunnel to be removed.*

gearbox. Complete with transfer box it weighs in at around 80kg and it is an unbalanced weight. A lifting strap round the waist of the gearbox where it joins the transfer box, biased to the right-hand side, is a good balance point for lifting. Once the propshafts and handbrake linkages have been detached and the bellhousing nuts removed, the gearbox and engine can be gently levered apart. Put a small block of wood between the flywheel housing and the engine crossmember to maintain the engine angle when the gearbox is off. If an overdrive is fitted, it will need to be removed to slide the gearbox back sufficiently to change the clutch.

Note that for complete removal, the speedo cable will have to be removed: a magnetic screwdriver is invaluable as the grub screws are very fiddly. Alternatively a tight-fitting screwdriver blade will help. On a Series II/IIA the clutch cross shaft will have to be split at the joint; on a Series III the slave cylinder will have to be unbolted from the bellhousing. The hydraulic system should not normally need to be disconnected for a clutch change, although if removing the engine the Series III pipe bracket on the fuel pump plate will need to be removed.

Clutch Removal, Inspection and Replacement

With the gearbox removed or moved back sufficiently, the clutch cover can be removed from the flywheel. Note that old clutches contain asbestos, so do not blow the dust; soapy water will minimise the likelihood of breathing it in, in addition to wearing appropriate PPE.

With the clutch removed, examine the clutch components and flywheel. Significant oil deposits will need to be investigated and remedied, although do note that sticky oil (a mixture of EP90 and clutch dust) is common in the bellhousing, especially in a Series II/IIA with no seal on the primary pinion. The flywheel should not be scored, rough or show signs of overheating, which are common if the clutch has been slipping for a while. A damaged flywheel should be assessed professionally and re-faced as necessary.

For the cost of a new clutch kit, and given the significant background work involved, there is little point in risking putting old components back in. A wide range of clutches is available from entry-level aftermarket through OEM to specialist heavy duty options. Buy the best you can afford based on your expected use. It is safe to say there is little point in fitting a premium heavy duty clutch to a vehicle you use lightly and infrequently.

Inspect the condition of the gearbox primary pinion and the flywheel spigot bearing. If the bearing is suspect, loose or broken, it should be replaced. The old bearing can be 'hydrauliced' out by packing it with grease and knocking in an appropriately sized drift. An old primary pinion is ideal for this and for use as a clutch alignment tool. A new bearing that has already been pre oil-soaked can be carefully drifted in.

Examine the clutch release bearing. This is easy on a Series III as it is a sealed external unit and a new one is usually supplied in a clutch kit. Note it has a plastic clip that retains it in position on the fork during assembly. The release fork is held in place on the pivot ball with a sprung clip and the slave rod is held in place with a slightly fragile plastic clip. Ensure this is in place before re-fitting the gearbox as it is fiddly to refit when the box is in place.

On a Series II/IIA the clutch release bearing is contained in the clutch release housing in the gearbox. They are robust and, being lubricated by gearbox oil, seldom cause issues but replacement is straightforward, if re-

Gearbox being removed with lifting strap at the balance point.

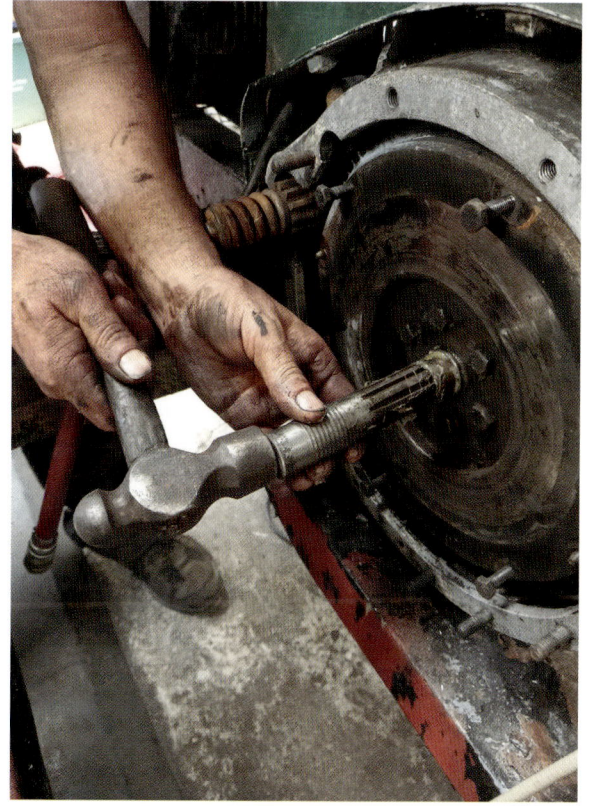

RIGHT: Using grease and an old primary pinion to 'hydraulic' out the old flywheel spigot bearing.

Clutch

quired. With the release assembly removed from the gearbox, fold back the fork and drift the release tube off the bearing. Press a new bearing onto the tube and refit the release assembly to the gearbox with a new gasket.

Thoroughly degrease the flywheel and pressure plate with brake and clutch cleaner. Hold the friction plate in place with an old, lightly greased, primary pinion (or clutch alignment tool) and bolt the pressure plate in place. Leave the alignment device in place until you have fully fitted the pressure plate. Note that the flywheel side is marked, although the friction plate can only go in one way on the flywheel (note that this is not always the case on some other vehicles). Tighten the plate gradually, working to opposite bolts and ensure the bolts have anti-vibration spring washers. These should be torqued up to 25lb ft. Ensure you can remove and refit the clutch alignment tool with ease to ensure correct alignment has been maintained.

Refitting the Gearbox

Possibly one of the tasks that people struggle with the most, fitting a gearbox should never require strength or roughness. There should be no need for heavy manhandling. It should be controlled and calm, and misalignment should be carefully adjusted with lifting equipment. The aforementioned wooden block should be in place between the flywheel housing and engine crossmember. The input shaft/primary pinion splines should be lightly greased.

An engine hoist is the best tool for supporting the gearbox as you line it up, but in addition a trolley jack can be used. Once the input shaft has started to locate in the clutch, select a gear and turn the handbrake drum while pushing forward to line the clutch/primary pinion splines up. When the drum no longer turns, the splines have started to engage. The gearbox can then be wriggled forward to fully mate the bellhousing and flywheel housing. As soon as studs show through the bellhousing, nuts can be fitted to pull the gearbox into place, carefully and progressively.

If the gearbox does not push home, it will either be down to poor clutch alignment (check it with the old input shaft) or simply poor gearbox-to-engine alignment. Practice makes perfect, but if it doesn't go, don't get frustrated, don't use force, stay calm and work on the bellhousing to flywheel housing alignment.

The hydraulic system can then be reassembled, refitting the clutch slave cylinder assemblies. It is always advisable to ensure the clutch operates correctly before reassembling the rest of the vehicle, just in case you've overlooked something.

REPLACING THE MASTER CYLINDER

When carrying out a major overhaul or significant recommission, replacing the master and clutch cylinders as a matter of course should be considered. A typical sign that a master cylinder is leaking is to find a drip of fluid in the footwell, often accompanied by bubbling paint. Dark fluid is usually a sign that rubber seals or the flexible link in the system are starting to degrade.

While the master cylinder can be replaced in situ, it is usually easier to remove the pedal box assembly. With the six bolts in the footwell removed, it can

A cut-down primary pinion (gearbox input shaft) is the best tool for clutch alignment.

ABOVE LEFT: *It is vital that the clutch is correctly aligned or the gearbox won't fit.*

ABOVE RIGHT: *Leave the alignment tool in place until all the pressure-plate bolts are torqued up.*

Clutch

be easily lifted out when the hydraulic connections have been removed. On the Series III type the reservoir is built in; on the Series II/IIA it shares a reservoir with the brake system, although there is a separate section within the reservoir. To reduce the spillage of fluid, use a syringe to suck the majority of it out. Brake fluid is a very effective paint stripper.

The master cylinder can then be removed from the pedal box, removing the two retaining bolts and the two nuts on the push rod. While the seals can be replaced in the cylinders, it is easier to replace the complete unit unless originality is of utmost importance.

When fitting the new cylinder, use the original self-locking nuts or equivalent. The push rod should have 1.5mm free play – that is the length of the rod should be adjusted so that it doesn't quite push the piston when the pedal is in the top position.

When fitting the pedal box back into the footwell, note the condition of the rubber gasket and replace as necessary – it stops (or at least minimises) you getting wet feet! Remember to refit the return spring.

Check the height of the pedal tip from the floor. For hydrostatic systems this should be 140mm (most models); for early adjustable systems with a return spring on the slave cylinder, this should be 158mm. There is an adjustor bolt on the rear of the pedal box on early pedals.

Reconnect the hydraulic system and bleed the system.

REPLACING THE SLAVE CYLINDER

Series II/IIA Type

The slave cylinder is attached to a bracket bolted to the bellhousing. The right-hand floor plate needs to be removed to gain access. The slave cylinder is easy to replace, but note the presence of a spacer on the bracket: if originally fitted it should be refitted. The length of the slave cylinder operating rod should be adjusted to give 1½in of free travel at the pedal before resistance is felt.

ABOVE LEFT: *It is far easier to remove the pedal box to change the master cylinder, but it can be done.*

ABOVE RIGHT: *It's fiddly setting the free play to 1.5mm. A cut-down ½in ring spanner helps with the lock nuts.*

Checking the clutch pedal height is set correctly (140mm on most IIA models).

RIGHT: *Set the slave rod to give 1½in free play at the pedal.*

Clutch

Series III Type

On a Series III gearbox the slave cylinder is bolted to the casting of the bellhousing. When withdrawing the old slave cylinder, take care not to disturb the push rod, which is held onto the release fork with a fragile plastic clip. If it pops out, it is just possible to refit without removing the gearbox, but it can be fiddly and access is poor. Removing the left-hand floor plate will make access much easier, especially if replacing it on the ground rather than on a lift or ramp. Fit the new slave cylinder, taking care as you push the dust seal in the hole – a touch of red rubber grease can help if it's tight. Because the fixed steel supply pipe is inflexible, sometimes it is easier to start the threads of the supply pipe to the slave cylinder before you tighten the slave cylinder fully into place.

BLEEDING THE CLUTCH SYSTEM

Clutch systems can be tricky to bleed, especially if being filled for the first time after replacing both master and slave cylinders. Series III systems in particular seem to be more challenging than the Series II/IIA, possibly because of the larger bore pipe and poor access to the bleed nipple. Traditional bleeding techniques with one person pumping and another opening and closing the bleed nipple normally work, but a pressure bleeder can make life easier and achievable with one person. Be aware that the volume of the reservoir is small, so it will need topping up every few pumps unless using a pressure bleeder.

If the system fails to bleed in the usual manner, experience tells us that

Be careful not to disturb the plastic retainer for the Series III slave push rod.

RIGHT: *The Series III slave bleed nipple is easy to access with the floor out, but very tight with it in.*

ABOVE LEFT: *Bleed nipple can be accessed behind this grommet on a Series II/IIA.*

ABOVE RIGHT: *A pressure bleeder is a significant help when bleeding both brake and clutch, especially on your own.*

sometimes simply leaving it overnight to settle can solve the problem. Occasionally a small airlock gets trapped in the Series III slave cylinder (as it lies horizontally) and this can sometimes be removed by removing the cylinder and pressing the piston fully home while opening the bleed nipple.

CLUTCH UPGRADES

While the Land Rover clutch pedal should be relatively light, if a driver has limited left leg strength, there are a couple of modifications that can reduce pedal pressure.

Fitting a Remote Servo

Just like a servo fitted to a braking system, a remote servo can also be fitted in line with the clutch system. The servo operates via a vacuum (from the inlet manifold or separate pump) and reduces the physical effort required to press the pedal. From experience, a 1.5:1 ratio servo works well and the unit itself can be hidden under a wing or seat box.

Fitting a Clutch Booster System

A clutch booster system is available from Red Booster. This is a complete, compact system with servo, bracketry to fit to the existing pedal box and a separate vacuum reservoir tank. While it was designed to fit later Land Rovers, it can also be fitted to Series vehicles.

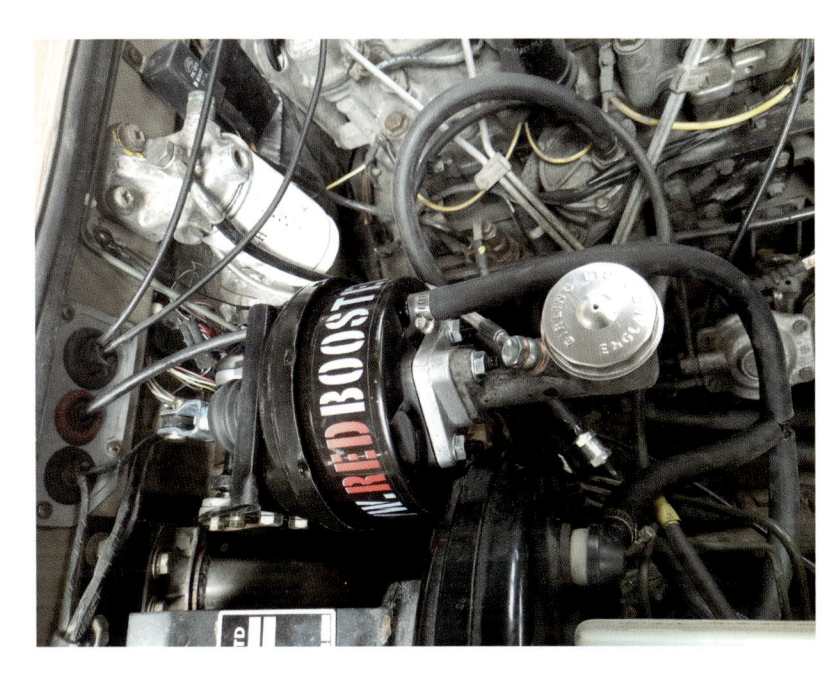

An off-the-shelf clutch servo system to reduce the effort required to press the pedal.

10
Gearbox

Apart from the Stage 1 V8 model, all Series Land Rovers were fitted with a variation of the LT76 main gearbox. The basic gearbox design can trace its origins back to the first Land Rovers in 1948 and indeed the design was based on 1930s Rover car gearboxes. The LT76 code refers to Leyland Transmissions (LT) and 76mm between the centres of the main and layshaft. The code is slightly misleading in as much as it is a relatively late nomenclature that has been retrospectively attributed to all four-speed Series Land Rover gearboxes. That aside, it is a useful code that helps us name the common Series gearbox and make a distinction between the LT95 fitted to the Stage 1 V8 and the LT77, which was used in coil spring models from 1983.

Despite the apparent homogeneity suggested by the LT76 code, there were a number of significant gearbox changes throughout the production period from 1958 to 1984. These changes are identified by different suffix letters on the end of the gearbox number. In the Series IIA era the changes went from A to F, denoting changes to components such as bearings, shaft sizes and gear ratios. It is important to note that the suffix code started again for the Series III era with suffixes A to D. You can therefore have a Series IIA Suffix B gearbox and a Series III Suffix B gearbox and they will be very different inside.

SYNCHRO OR NON-SYNCHRO?

For the general owner who doesn't need to get involved in the minutiae of gearbox internals, we may broadly identify two basic types of LT76 gearbox: non-synchro and synchro. From 1958 to 1971 the Series gearbox had no synchromesh between first and second gear, requiring either a double declutch or a carefully timed rev-match to change down into these gears and a small pause when changing up. With the launch of the Series III, a synchromesh was fitted to all gears, although for completeness it is worth noting that a handful of late Series IIA models also had full synchromesh.

As a basic guide, a non-synchro gearbox has a hole in the right-hand side of the bellhousing for the clutch release linkage and an external slave cylinder mounted on a bracket bolted to the bellhousing. A Series III synchro gearbox can be identified by an extra bulge below the starter on the left-hand side of the bellhousing for a bolt-on clutch slave cylinder.

UNDERSTANDING GEARBOX NUMBERS

Broadly speaking, the basic first three identification numbers on the gearbox number would usually have matched up to the vehicle chassis and engine prefix codes, but the numbering system is not directly or sequentially connected. For example, a 271 chassis vehicle (Series IIA 88in diesel) would have been built with a 271 engine and a 271 gearbox, but the serial numbers would not have been the same. Neither would they necessarily have had the same suffix letter. The suffix was added to denote an engineering modification to the component and this is what should be used as a reference for parts.

The same basic numbering system continued during the Series III era: a 901 chassis vehicle (88in petrol), for example, would likely have had a 901 engine and gearbox. With the introduction of the

ABOVE LEFT: Series II/IIA non-synchro type gearbox with a single 'ear' on the bellhousing.

ABOVE RIGHT: Series III full synchromesh gearbox with extra ear for the clutch slave cylinder.

Gearbox

Location of Series II/IIA and early Series III gearbox number.

RIGHT: Gearbox number was stamped on the transfer box on most Series III gearboxes.

VIN type system from 1979, the connection between chassis, engine and gearbox was less apparent. While the basic engine and gearbox prefix connection continued, the chassis/VIN number had a different code to distinguish between models. The introduction of the five-bearing engine also saw a change to the gearbox numbering system: for example a 361 engine (2286cc petrol) would likely be fitted to a 361 gearbox.

It is also important to note that some rebuilt gearboxes could have been assembled with components from a different suffix to that noted on the casing. It's not uncommon to see serial numbers crossed out or a suffix restamped on factory rebuilt units. Also, most Series III boxes had the serial number on the transfer box that it was matched to at the factory, so if gearbox and transfer box have been separated at some point, it might be a challenge to work out exactly what is in there.

BASIC ENGINEERING CHANGES TO THE LT76 AND NOTES

It is vitally important to consult the Parts Manual when it comes to ordering the appropriate parts for the gearbox as there were both obvious and subtle changes over the years. The following is an overview, but should be used as a guide to assist and the Parts Manual is essential reading.

Series II Gearboxes

The gearbox changed very little during this time, other than the prefix code matching to general vehicle type. The gearbox number was stamped on the right-hand side of the top cover. It is worth noting that the first 88in Series II petrol models retained the 1997cc IOE engine from the outgoing Series I and these gearboxes had a bellhousing that matched the IOE engine. It can be identified by the bellhousing top stud pattern with a hole at 11.55 and 12.05. Bellhousings that matched to the 2052cc diesel and 2286cc petrol engines had a top hole at 12 o'clock. Both bellhousings had a hole in either side for left- and right-hand clutch release mechanisms, although with the introduction of the hydraulic clutch in 1958, the left-hand hole was redundant. These early gearboxes had a dipstick and a top filler held in place by a spring clip; note that many later military gearboxes also had a top filler.

Series IIA Gearboxes

The change to the Series IIA was mostly to introduce a system for noting engineering changes with a sequential suffix. Note that the 6-cylinder gearbox had the same bellhousing hole pattern as the 1997cc type, although they are not interchangeable due to having a larger layshaft bearing.

Suffix A	Pretty much the same as the Series II type, dipstick deleted, top filler retained for some time
Suffix B	Introduction of a larger front layshaft bearing
Suffix C	Revised gearbox ratios
Suffix D	Introduction of a stronger layshaft design
Suffix E	Minor revisions from Suffix D
Suffix F	Sealed clutch release introduced

Series III Gearboxes

Suffix A	Introduced with the launch of the Series III in 1971. Synchromesh on all forward gears. The Series III box also saw the introduction of a one-piece layshaft. The reverse gear operates on a shaft with a bronze bush on Suffix A
Suffix B	Introduction of a reverse gear with roller bearings
Suffix C	Introduction of a stronger case with extra webbing and different gear ratios
Suffix D	Introduction of improved synchromesh with 'tombstone' teeth. The Series III suffix D gearbox is considered by many to be the best of the bunch

Gearbox

Updated layshaft design for suffix D onwards with sprags to retain gears.

LEFT: *Half-moon locators for the gears on Series II and IIA to suffix C layshaft.*

ABOVE LEFT: *A one-piece layshaft was introduced for the Series III.*

ABOVE RIGHT: *Later type Series III case with extra ribbing.*

GEARBOX PROBLEMS

While the Series transfer box is known to be a robust unit, the LT76 is nowhere near as strong. That's not to say it's a bad gearbox, but problems are not uncommon. Higher performance engines can kill off old gearboxes and many will have been worked hard over the last few decades. The following is a non-exhaustive list of common ailments:

Wear on mainshaft output splines: This causes backlash and a clunk when the power goes on and off. This is often caused by a loose mainshaft nut (*see* below).

Loose rear mainshaft nut: Often causing gears to pop out on overrun. All too common after poorly executed repairs. The nut needs a special socket to tighten correctly as well as a special lock washer. It's common to find a hammer and chisel have been used to loosen and tighten it.

Broken 3rd/4th synchro springs: This usually causes crunching when changing gear. The springs are curved sprung steel and these wear through over time, causing them to snap in half. The broken sections often fall out when draining the oil. The gearbox will often limp on for a long time but it's not going to get any better.

Broken 2nd/3rd bronze bush: One of the most common failings in an LT76, often causing it to drop out of gear. Having said that, often they will soldier on with no apparent problems with a broken bush. A later engineering upgrade actually made it into a two-part bush to overcome the problem.

Broken layshaft or failed layshaft bearings: Often giving no drive except in fourth gear. Fourth gear is direct drive using the primary pinion and, while it will turn the layshaft constant gear, it does not depend on the layshaft being intact. Depending on where the break is, sometimes other gears will drive but will sound like a

Gearbox

ABOVE LEFT: All too often a loose mainshaft nut can cause the gearbox to jump out of gear.

ABOVE RIGHT: Another common sight: the remains of the 3rd/4th synchro springs coming out with the oil.

Pre-suffix D layshaft commonly breaks at the half-moon recess.

LEFT: Typical broken 2nd/3rd gear bush.

handful of spanners having a fight in a metal dustbin.

Worn bearings: Causing noise, backlash, dropping out of gear or difficult to engage gears.

Oil leaks: Very common and to some extent to be expected, especially from the selector shaft seals. Note that all but the very last Series IIA gearboxes did not have a seal on the primary motion (input) shaft. Instead it relied on a scroll that 'wound' the oil back into the box. This works fine when the engine is running, but if parked pointing down a steep hill gearbox oil can run into the bellhousing. This is not a fault that can be rectified, just a design flaw, so park appropriately. The Series III gearbox (and very last series IIA) does have a proper seal in the mainshaft/layshaft cover.

General noise and whine: This is to be expected to some extent, especially in straight cut gears like first and reverse. However, the hardening on gears does break down, gears do wear and on occasion teeth break off, often causing significant further damage as the broken parts get churned around.

Crunching going into 1st or 2nd when stationary: This is common and usually no cause for concern on non-synchro boxes. A good trick is to select third gear before selecting the non-synchro gear.

Sloppy gear lever or difficult to select reverse: Reverse gate springs are prone to breaking, making it difficult to differentiate between first and reverse. Reverse can be difficult to select on late Series III boxes as the gear lever gets very close to the dashboard. The grub screw in the gear lever ball housing is prone to wear, causing the lever to pivot round and jam between gears.

Gearbox

Series III (and some very late IIA) had a seal for the primary pinion.

LEFT: *Primary pinion scroll on Series II and IIA winds the oil back in when the engine is running.*

Broken gate springs make it very hard to differentiate between 1st and reverse: there should be two springs here.

TO REPAIR OR NOT TO REPAIR?

Depending on the use a vehicle is put to, a range of gearbox problems can be 'lived with'. The occasional jumping out of gear might be a mild nuisance in an otherwise perfectly functional gearbox. However, if the vehicle is being driven in challenging off-road conditions, jumping out of gear could be a safety concern. A whining gearbox and a slight crunch when selecting a gear might not get any worse and might just be working within the limitations of the underlying 1930s engineering. If in doubt, it is worth having a drive in a well-sorted vehicle to compare and contrast what can be deemed 'normal'. It is always worth asking an experienced owner to pass judgement. However, at some point a properly worn or catastrophically failed gearbox will have to be exchanged or repaired.

Note that when a gearbox is in bits, it might be opening a can of worms when significant numbers of components have to be replaced. Rebuilding a Series gearbox is not difficult per se, but it does require a methodical approach, and on occasion assembling components can be fiddly. If in doubt, an exchange unit may well be the easiest option. Also do not underestimate the potential cost of good-quality parts. Sometimes it can be worth fitting a good known used box, but if taking pot luck it is a time-consuming exercise should a replacement not be up to scratch.

REMOVING AND REFITTING THE GEARBOX

Removal

The process of removing and refitting a gearbox is straightforward but can be time-consuming. Unless a removable gearbox crossmember is fitted, it means removing the floor and seat box, which often means fighting with seized fixings. The following tips might be helpful:

- Remove both propshafts. While they can be disconnected at just the gearbox end, they often get in the way of manoeuvring the gearbox in and out, so it is easier to completely remove them. The speedo cable needs to be removed: this is fitted with three small 2BA grub screws that are very fiddly to access.
- The handbrake pivot mechanism has to be disconnected. The clevis

Gearbox

pins are quite fiddly to undo and refit. Note they should have an anti-rattle spring and a split pin fitted. It is sometimes helpful to remove the pivot from the chassis to allow more wriggle room round the right-hand-side gearbox mounting.

- Note that the gearbox mounting 'wedges' that bolt onto the chassis are handed: the smaller, shallower angle wedge goes on the right-hand side. It's a common mistake to swap these around and means the gearbox fits out of line, often clashing with the edge of the seat box.
- On a Series III gearbox, the clutch slave cylinder needs to be removed, though there is no need to break into the hydraulic system. On a Series II/IIA gearbox, the slave cylinder and cross-shaft assembly needs to be removed. The cross-shaft pins have fiddly split pins in the ends.
- The rear of the engine needs to be supported on a small block of wood to the engine crossmember. When everything is unbolted, the weight of the gearbox can be taken up and the engine and gearbox carefully levered apart until the input shaft clears the clutch cover.
- The gearbox and transfer box combined weight is around 80kg, so an engine hoist through the passenger door makes it significantly safer. Note that the balance point of a gearbox and transfer box combination is pretty much at the join between the two and biased to the right-hand side. A short strap, as illustrated, is a simple balanced rigging point.
- If the gearbox is to be stripped for repair or the transfer box reused, another approach is to separate transfer box and gearbox on the vehicle. The individual sections can be lifted by hand with care. (For more guidance, see Chapter 11.)

Refitting the Gearbox

This is possibly one of the tasks that people struggle with the most. Fitting a gearbox should never require strength or roughness. There should be no need for heavy manhandling, it should be controlled and calm, and misalignment should be carefully adjusted with lifting equipment. Everyone has their own approach, but the following tips might be helpful:

- Put a block of hardwood between the flywheel housing and engine crossmember to keep it supported and level. Use a jack on the rear of the transfer box to adjust the angle to match the bellhousing and flywheel housing. Take extreme care not to get fingers trapped as the gearbox is wriggled into place.
- It can help to remove the mounting brackets from the transfer case to give better clearance around the handbrake pivot and the exhaust.
- If you don't have access to lifting equipment, there is the option to fit the gearbox and then the transfer box. This is easier and indeed can just be done without fully removing the seat box.
- The input shaft/primary pinion splines should be lightly greased.

A lifting strap round the balance point of the gearbox/transfer box.

- Once the input shaft has started to locate in the clutch, select a gear and turn the handbrake drum while pushing forward to line up the clutch/primary pinion splines. When the drum no longer turns, the splines have engaged.
- The gearbox can then be wriggled forward to fully mate the bellhousing and flywheel housing. As soon as studs show through the bellhousing, nuts can be fitted to pull the gearbox into place, carefully and progressively.

GEARBOX STRIPPING

Preamble to Stripping

The gearbox illustrated is a Series III type, but the Series II/IIA is a variation on the theme (indeed it is simpler). Most gearbox fixings require Whitworth/BSF sockets/spanners and it is worth investing in these.

A gearbox removed from a vehicle will be filthy and oily, but the insides need to be kept scrupulously clean, so spend time getting the gearbox as clean as possible. Plenty of degreaser, a jet wash and plenty of scrubbing will be required. Always drain the transfer and gearbox of oil before separating them: on a Series III box there are holes in the rear of the case to enable the rear layshaft bearing to be tapped out, but as soon as it is separated from the transfer box it will leak.

Note that some gearbox repair jobs do not require the transfer box to be removed. For example, changing the front seal on a Series III box and changing the 3rd/4th synchro or synchro springs. In fact it is known for the synchro springs to be replaced without removing the gearbox, although it is incredibly fiddly. The bellhousing can be removed and the front layshaft and mainshaft bearings can be replaced.

A standard Land Rover wheel is invaluable as a makeshift stand for separating main and transfer boxes and for stripping the main gearbox.

Removing the Top Cover and Selectors

Remove the side detent plates (3rd/4th and Reverse). The bolts are very

Gearbox

ABOVE LEFT: *The correct drain plug key: a wide spanner does the job too.*

ABOVE RIGHT: *Gearbox and transfer box upended on a wheel to aid dismantling.*

close together and benefit from a narrow wall, deep drive socket. Remove the springs and the detent ball from both sides.

Remove the middle (1st/2nd) detent spring (under the brass cap). The ball is hard to remove, so leave it until the cover is off. Note that the top cover and gearbox case are a matched pair and code marked. They should not be mixed up as doing so is likely to cause the selectors to jam.

Remove the top cover fixings and lift the top off: it might need a gentle tap with a soft hammer. Do not lever under the mating surfaces: there is no gasket and oil sealing relies on a smooth machined surface. Carefully collect the 1st/2nd detent ball and the two side detent rollers. Before removing the selector shafts, it helps to remove the two cover studs.

Removing (and refitting) the selector shafts can be a bit of a puzzle. It helps to lift them all up slightly, then lift, turn and remove the reverse selector. Use a wide screwdriver to select second gear and lift the 1st/2nd selector out. Deselect second and select third, and lift out the 3rd/4th selector.

Removing the Clutch Release and Bellhousing

Stand the gearbox on end, supported on a Land Rover wheel or other suitable stand; a robust bucket also works well.

Unbolt the clutch release mechanism assembly/front cover. On the Series III it also houses a seal. The Series III layshaft has a bolt ($5/8$in socket size) that should be fitted with thread lock.

ABOVE LEFT: *Removing the side detent components.*

ABOVE RIGHT: *Gearbox case and top are a matched pair and cannot be swapped.*

ABOVE LEFT: Removing the reverse selector shaft.

ABOVE RIGHT: Select 2nd and remove the 1st/2nd selector shaft.

Deselect 2nd, select 3rd and lift the 3rd/4th selector out.

RIGHT: The gearbox balances nicely on a wheel or in a bucket.

It is common for it to have worked loose, but if not it could be tight. The Series II/IIA layshaft has a castle nut and split pin. To assist in undoing these, it helps to select two gears at the same time to lock the shafts to stop them turning. With the selector shaft removed, reverse will tend to slide and select itself.

Remove the four main fixings holding the bellhousing on and lift up the bellhousing. As it lifts, the primary motion shaft and layshaft gear will tend to bind, stopping it from fully lifting off. Carefully wriggle the layshaft gear off its shaft and lift the bellhousing off. Note the orientation of the layshaft conical spacer with the tapered end towards the bearing. Lift off the 3rd/4th synchro and note the orientation: it fits with the tapered spline to third gear (to the rear of the box).

Removing Layshaft, Reverse Shaft and Mainshaft

Lift out the layshaft. The Series III type is a one-piece unit (apart from the front constant gear), the Series II/IIA is a shaft with individual gears. From suffix B, the layshaft had a larger front bearing but the rear bearing remained the same all the way through. From Series IIA suffix D the layshaft was redesigned to be stronger and simpler.

Using a long thin drift, drive out the reverse shaft and remove the gear. If on a late Series III box, note the order of the thrust washer followed by the spacer. The mainshaft can now be driven out of the back bearing with a soft-faced mallet. On a Series III box, it is important not to let the 1st/2nd synchro assembly spring apart as it can be fiddly to reassemble.

Lay out the shafts and gear on a clean bench in order to ensure components do not get mixed up. While some things are obvious and can only go one way, other items such as thrust washers can be assembled incorrectly, causing functional problems and premature wear. Note at this stage, second and third gear will still be on the mainshaft.

Gearbox

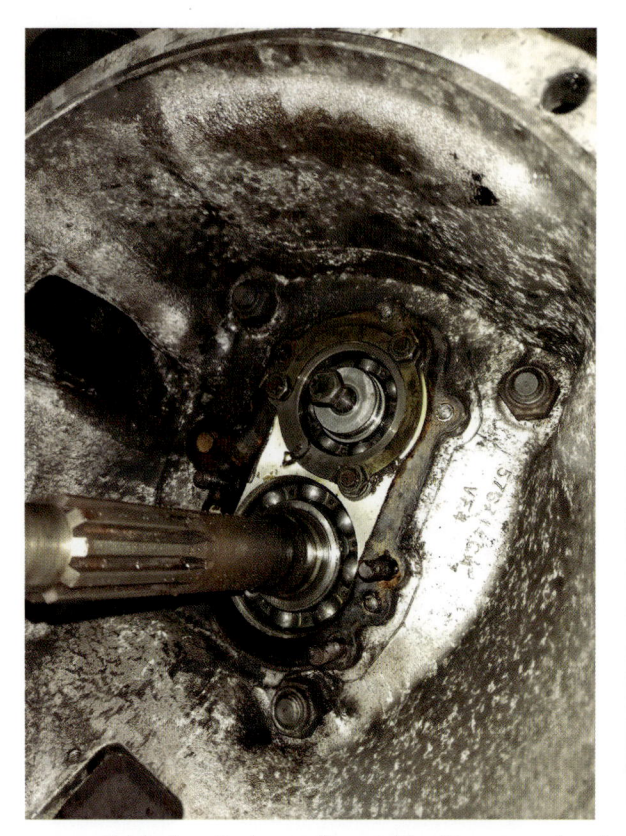

ABOVE LEFT: Clutch release/front cover off to reveal the all too common loose layshaft bolt.

ABOVE RIGHT: Lifting off the bellhousing.

ABOVE LEFT: Lifting out the 3rd/4th synchro hub.

ABOVE RIGHT: Lifting out the one-piece layshaft.

Hold the mainshaft in a vice with a soft covering to protect it from damage from the jaws. Prise out the spring clip holding third gear in place and slide the gear off. While it sounds easy, it can be very fiddly; a trick is to use a series of wood drill bits to lever it out of the recess and to wrap them together with a zip tie before tapping the gear up and off. Alternatively, a series of appropriately sized split pins (5mm seems to work well) can be used to hold the ring out of the recess while third gear is driven off the shaft. The mainshaft bush and second gear can now be removed. The bush is very likely to have split in two.

INSPECTING THE COMPONENTS

Any catastrophic problems with a gearbox should be obvious. However, a generally worn gearbox may have multiple components starting to wear. The following list might assist in whether to keep or replace.

Shafts

Look for wear in splines, in particular the back of the mainshaft where it enters the transfer box. Reverse shafts are prone to the hardening breaking down. Layshafts tend to break catastrophically, but note that the half-moon retainers on pre-suffix D Series IIA boxes can

ABOVE LEFT: On a Series III box it can help to remove the reverse shaft and gear before lifting out the mainshaft.

ABOVE RIGHT: Lifting out the mainshaft.

ABOVE LEFT: Be careful not to let the 1st/2nd synchro spring apart.

ABOVE RIGHT: Mainshaft on the bench ready to be dismantled.

break. This is also the weak point where shafts tend to break. The one-piece Series III layshaft means that any wear necessitates replacement of the complete unit rather than a single gear.

Gears

Look for obvious damage such as chipped or worn teeth. Also check for a breaking down in the hardening on the gear surface. Note that the gear on the primary pinion and the layshaft constant gear should be kept as a matched pair: if they are mis-matched they are likely to whine. It is also good practice to keep/replace other gears as a matched pair, but this is not as critical as the primary gears.

Bushes

As above, the 2nd/3rd bush is likely to have broken. If so, it should be replaced with the best replacement you can afford. Spending a little extra will usually mean it will fit perfectly with no extra machining required. Check the other bushes such as first (Series III box) and reverse (Series II, IIA and III Suffix A).

Bearings

Generally speaking, it is best practice to replace all bearings if a gearbox has been stripped. These can often be bought as a complete gearbox set. Always buy the best bearings you can afford.

Gearbox

It makes sense to lay out all the components to see how they will go back together.

RIGHT: *Using wood drill bits to open up the spring clip on the mainshaft.*

BELOW LEFT: *Significant wear on the end of this mainshaft means it's scrap.*

BELOW RIGHT: *Examine all gears for wear: the synchro teeth on this 2nd gear are badly worn.*

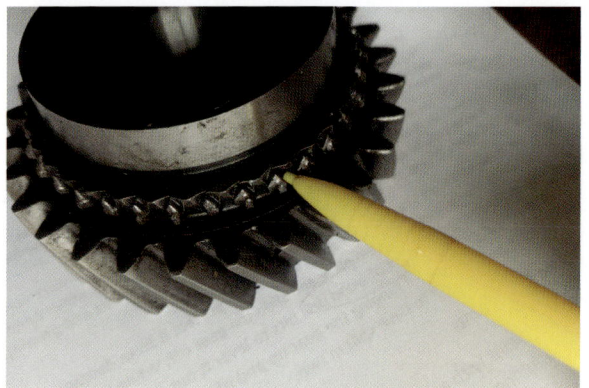

This mainshaft/primary bearing has clearly twisted.

FITTING BEARINGS

Rear Mainshaft Bearing

This is held in a housing held in place with a large circlip. It is easier to remove the seal before removing the housing. Undo the large main circlip and carefully drive the housing out into the casing. The bearing circlip can be removed (a robust pair of circlip pliers is essential) and the bearing can be tapped out. Tap a new bearing in and carefully refit the bearing housing into the gearbox from the inside using a soft drift. Refit the outer circlip and a fit a new seal. The seal fits flush to the housing.

Front Mainshaft Bearing

This is held in place by the clutch release housing fixings and held onto the primary pinion with a circlip. It is simply a case of tapping the clutch release fixings back and tapping out the bearing and primary pinion as a unit. With the primary pinion circlip removed, the bearing can be tapped off the primary pinion and a new one carefully drifted on. Tap in the new bearing/primary pinion assembly and refit the fixings.

ABOVE LEFT: Refitting the rear bearing carrier circlip: strong circlip pliers are necessary.

ABOVE RIGHT: Refitting the primary pinion to bellhousing bearing.

Rear Layshaft Bearing

On most Series III boxes, the rear layshaft outer bearing race can be tapped out via the holes in the rear of the casing. On earlier casings the official technique is to 'hydraulic' the bearing out by packing the bearing recess with grease and driving in a tight-fitting wooden drift. While this does work, another approach is to carefully and accurately drill two holes in the appropriate places behind the bearing race like the Series III case. The only drawback is that, when disconnected from the transfer box, the gearbox will not be oil-tight. The outer bearing can be carefully drifted into the case using a suitably sized socket and an appropriate length extension bar. It is advisable to put the outer race in the freezer to shrink it slightly to allow it to fit more easily. Be careful not to crack the casing while drifting the bearing in. Tap the new inner layshaft bearing onto the layshaft.

Front Layshaft Bearing

This is held in place with two retaining rings with offset holes (meaning the rings only fit in one orientation). It is simply a case of carefully bending back the lock tabs, removing the fixings and driving the bearing out. It is advisable to fit a new lock tab washer. Note that

Driving out the rear layshaft outer bearing through the drift holes.

RIGHT: Driving in the new outer rear layshaft bearing with a suitable socket and extension bar.

Gearbox

Front layshaft bearing fitted in the bellhousing.

the clutch release bearing is not included in most gearbox bearing kits.

MAINSHAFT ASSEMBLY

Assembling the mainshaft can be tricky and a bit of a head-scratcher. It is therefore essential to have the appropriate Parts Manual to hand to see the exploded diagram. This overview covers and illustrates the main tasks, but the official Workshop Manual will confirm some of the extra details that might be required.

Fitting and Shimming the 2nd/3rd Bush

If the rear thrust washer has been removed, refit it but do not fit the locating pegs at this stage. The small peg holds the thrust washer in place, the larger peg stakes the bush in place. If the bush is intact and deemed to be in usable condition, refit it to the shaft. If broken or worn, replace it with a good-quality part, noting that the updated version often comes in two parts.

Slide second gear onto the bush with the synchro cone to the rear and fit the bush onto the mainshaft. Fit third gear to the bush and fit the assembly with the front thrust washer and the old spring ring (this will be much easier to fit and remove as they can be fiddly). Push third gear hard against the shoulder of the bush and measure the end float between second gear to the shoulder of the bush. Repeat pushing second gear to the shoulder and measure between third and the shoulder. The book specification is 0.004–0.007in. If the end float is insufficient, the bush should be replaced. If excessive, the appropriate end of the bush can be reduced by rubbing on a piece of fine sandpaper on a piece of glass.

Once the gear end float is correct, remove the bush and gear assembly from the mainshaft and refit the bush with the thrust washers and spring ring. Now measure the end float of the bush on the shaft. The book specification is 0.001–0.008in, but should be kept as low as possible with different thickness thrust washers.

Once the bush end floats are confirmed, the 2nd/3rd gear assembly can

Confirming the end float of 2nd and 3rd gear is correct with feeler gauges.

LEFT: *New 2nd gear thrust washer fitted to a new mainshaft: the stake pin is still to be fitted.*

Checking the end float of the 2nd/3rd bronze bush on the shaft: it should be as low as possible.

be finally assembled onto the shaft. Fit the pegs for the rear thrust washer and bush (they may have been left on if re-using the mainshaft). Fit the bush with second and third gears onto the shaft and fit the front thrust washer and a new circlip.

Assembling the 1st/2nd Synchro onto the Mainshaft

On Series III models, the 1st/2nd synchro is a fiddly affair if the ball bearings and springs pop apart during assembly. If it does, consult the Parts Manual. Slide the synchro assembly onto the mainshaft, followed by first gear and its bush, and finally the thrust washer. Note the orientation of the thrust washer to allow oil flow to the rear of first gear. The mainshaft is now ready to be fitted into the case.

GEARBOX ASSEMBLY

Fitting the Mainshaft

With 2nd/3rd gears and bush fitted to the shaft, as above, and first gear and synchro assembly slid on the mainshaft, insert the mainshaft assembly into the rear bearing of the casing. It is sometimes easier to insert the mainshaft with the case vertical (rear of case upwards) to stop the synchro assembly falling apart. Once in, the shaft should push through the bearing but may need a tap with a soft-faced mallet to push it fully home. Take care that the first synchro doesn't pop apart while you're tapping the mainshaft home.

Reverse Shaft and Gear

On a Series III box, it is easier to fit the reverse gear and shaft after the mainshaft is in place because of the intricacies of the 1st/2nd synchro and its tendency to ping apart. Note the order of the thrust washer and spacer on the shaft: the spacer sits against the case, then the thrust washer sits between the spacer and the gear. Line them up and drive the reverse shaft into place. It is sometimes advisable to warm the casing or freeze the shaft to make it easier to fit.

On the Series II/IIA box, the reverse gear assembly has two gears. Up to suffix B these are 17/20. From suffix C these are 16/19.

Assembling and Fitting the Layshaft

On all Series III boxes, the layshaft is a one-piece part (apart from the front constant gear) and simple to fit. The inner rear bearing is simply tapped onto the shaft and the assembly can be inserted into the outer rear bearing in the casing. At this point it is easier to

ABOVE LEFT: *1st gear and synchro hub assembly. Take care not to let them ping apart when refitting.*

ABOVE RIGHT: *Mainshaft reassembled and ready to be refitted into the casing.*

Gearbox

ABOVE LEFT: Mainshaft being pushed or carefully tapped into the rear bearing.

ABOVE RIGHT: On a Series III, it's easier to refit reverse gear and shaft after the mainshaft has been fitted.

ABOVE LEFT: Reverse gear shaft being pushed into place. If necessary, put it in the freezer to make it easier to fit.

ABOVE RIGHT: Layshaft installed. It needs a wriggle to mesh into the mainshaft.

have the gearbox placed upright in a wheel rim or other suitable stand.

On Series II/IIA, the layshaft is an assembly of individual gears on the shaft with a spacer sleeve between third/fourth. On Series II and IIA suffix A, the layshaft has a smaller front bearing than suffix B onwards. The rear bearing is the same size throughout LT76 production. Up to suffix C, second gear is held in place by two half-moon split rings. From suffix D, the shaft has sprags on the shaft to hold the gear in place. First gear is pressed onto the shaft and is prone to wear, so is likely to need to be replaced.

Assemble all gears in order on the layshaft and ensure they fit with no end float by temporarily fitting the front bearing and nipping up the front castle nut. Once assembled, the shaft is installed the same way as the Series III type.

Fitting the Bellhousing

This can be one of the more fiddly jobs when assembling the gearbox. The issue is that the primary pinion and layshaft constant gear need to be in mesh as the bellhousing is fitted. Add to that the need to keep the layshaft distance piece and primary pinion/front mainshaft roller bearing in place.

The following technique works well and with practice can be achieved very quickly, even with the gearbox horizontal, but it is significantly easier with the gearbox supported upright.

- Fit a new gasket to the bellhousing. Greasing the gasket helps as it holds it in place but allows for repositioning. Sealing compound is also fine, but there is less manoeuvrability as it goes off.
- Fit the 3rd/4th synchro to the mainshaft. Note that the synchro fits with the tapered end of the splines towards third gear, that is pointing to the back of the gearbox. Fit the mainshaft end roller bearing.
- Position the layshaft conical distance piece and constant gear in mesh with the primary pinion. Note the thin end of the distance piece points towards the bearing. The trick is to hold the gears in mesh and insert the ends on the mainshaft and layshaft into their respective holes at the same time.
- Once almost aligned, it can help to rock the primary pinon slight-

ly to help the splines on the constant gear to line up. Once lined up correctly, the bellhousing should push home with ease. Do not try to force it. Fit and tighten the casing fixings and check that the layshaft has at least 0.005in end float and is not binding. Different size conical spacers are available to achieve this as necessary.
- Select two gears at the same time to lock the gearbox and tighten the layshaft bolt/nut. On a Series II/IIA the nut should be tightened to 75lb ft and secured with a split pin. On a Series III the bolt should be fitted with thread lock as it is prone to working loose.

Clutch release

The clutch release assembly can now be fitted. Note that the gasket set comes with three different options: Series II/IIA small layshaft, Series IIA large layshaft and Series III all have different gaskets. On the Series III, replace the primary pinion seal as they go hard over time and leak oil into the bellhousing.

Selector Shafts

This is another potentially fiddly job that is relatively easy once sussed. If necessary, replace the selector shaft seals, which involves removing the selector fork from the clamp. There are various methods to fit the selectors but the following works well on a Series III box:

- Insert the reverse fork in first and ensure it locates in the recess in the gear.
- Select second gear by levering the gear forward and fit the 1st/2nd selector fork completely in the recess, then select neutral again.
- Select third gear by levering the synchro hub backwards, then lift the 1st/2nd selector shaft sufficiently to insert the 3rd/4th fork into place on the synchro hub.
- Reposition all the selectors fully in place.

ABOVE LEFT: Bellhousing gasket fitted with grease to allow it to move slightly but not fall out.

ABOVE RIGHT: Installing new 3rd/4th synchro springs can be fiddly.

RIGHT: Synchro in place – don't forget the end bearing.

BELOW: Note that the chamfered end of the splines goes towards 3rd gear.

Gearbox

ABOVE LEFT: This is how the layshaft constant gear meshes with the primary pinion before dropping the bellhousing into place.

ABOVE RIGHT: Bellhousing dropped into place. Give the pinion a wriggle to align the splines.

RIGHT: Note there are three different clutch release housings and gaskets in a normal gasket kit.

BELOW: Tightening the Series III layshaft bolt to 65lb ft with thread lock.

Gearbox

ABOVE LEFT: Locating reverse gear selector shaft into place.

ABOVE RIGHT: Select 2nd gear with a screwdriver blade and fit the 1st/2nd selector shaft.

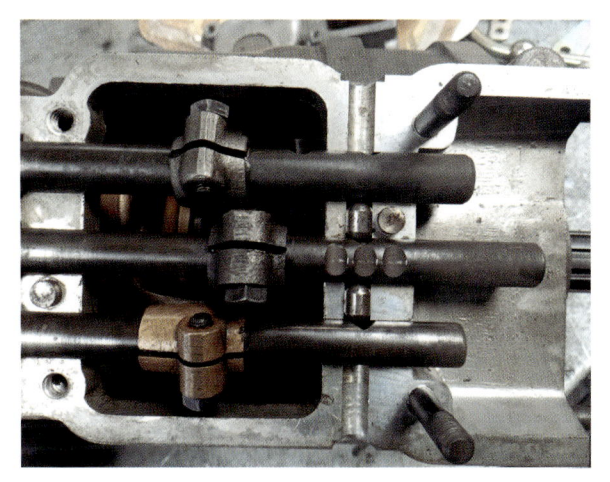

ABOVE LEFT: Select 3rd gear, lift the other selectors up slightly and fit the 3rd/4th selector.

ABOVE RIGHT: Don't forget the selector rollers between the shafts.

Top Cover Fitting

Note that the top cover is line-bored with the casing and cannot be used on another casing. There are telltale stampings to distinguish the pairs. It can help to remove the mounting studs to assist fitting the selector shafts. There is no gasket between the top and the case. Note that the rollers between the shafts must be fitted. Also check that all gears select smoothly before and after fitting the top. Take care to ensure the selector shaft seals locate correctly in their

ABOVE LEFT: Refit the detent balls, springs, seals and retainers.

ABOVE RIGHT: Gearbox fully assembled and ready to be refitted.

127

Gearbox

recesses between the case and the bolt-on end covers.

Detents and Springs

Refit the detent balls, springs and seals. Note that the stronger spring is for the reverse selector. Press firmly against the spring while positioning the retaining plate. On the 1st/2nd detent (on the top cover), press down against the spring and make sure the cap screws in straight and doesn't cross-thread.

GEARBOX/TRANSMISSION MODIFICATIONS

In-Service Exchange Units

Land Rover offered service exchange units and these are marked with a plate on the bellhousing. The internals of the gearbox may have been changed from the original specification, so the above outline on the basic engineering changes may help to identify the suffix for ordering parts.

Expedient Changes

As a relatively weak component in the drive chain, it is very common for second-hand gearboxes to have been fitted. Because of the basic interchangeability of the main units, a vehicle could have been fitted with a gearbox from a range of different eras. Again, further investigation will be required.

It was a common upgrade to fit a full synchro Series III gearbox to earlier models. On an original Series II/IIA chassis, this involves trimming the web on the engine crossmember to clear the bulge in the bellhousing for the slave cylinder. An alternative is to fit the bellhousing, clutch release assembly, primary pinion and matching layshaft constant gear from a post-suffix A Series IIA gearbox.

Fitting an LT77 Five-Speed from a Coil Spring Land Rover

There are a few options when fitting the LT77 to a Series vehicle. It can be fitted complete with the LT230 transfer case with some modifications to the chassis and new appropriate-length propshafts. The LT230 transfer box is normally permanent 4WD with a centre differential. Technically, the universal joints in the front axle are not compatible with permanent 4WD, although many enthusiasts have run this combination for many years with no real issues other than slight feedback in the steering on full lock. To rectify this, it is possible to buy a kit that makes 4WD a selectable option on the LT230.

An alternative is to fit an Ashcroft conversion kit to fit the main LT77 to a selectable Series transfer box. The kit comes with a gear cluster, a rear cover plate and an adaptor plate. This again is not a straightforward conversion as the LT77 is 4in longer than the LT76. The options are to either leave the transfer box in place and move the engine 4in forward or to leave the engine in place and move the transfer box 4in further back. The first option can be achieved by modifying the bolt-on engine mounts; the latter option requires custom-length propshafts and gearbox mountings. No matter which option is chosen, it is a significant amount of work, both underneath and inside the vehicle. The advantage is a significantly stronger, quieter gearbox that is much easier to operate, leaks less oil and has an overdrive fifth gear.

FITTING AN OVERDRIVE/ INCREASING FINAL DRIVE RATIOS

A factory-fit overdrive option manufactured by Fairey was introduced in the mid-1970s. These are old now and have a tendency to be noisy, even

A 5-speed LT77 fitted with a Series transfer box with an Ashcroft adaptor and gear.

RIGHT: *A factory-approved Fairey overdrive became available in the late 1970s.*

when new. Having said that, a good one can be quiet and easy to use, and it has the advantage of being operational as a splitter between gears.

The Toro/Bearmach overdrive was another option similar to the Falrey, but with a significantly larger oil capacity. While generally known to be a robust unit, parts are harder to come by.

Roamer/Roverdrive units, manufactured in Canada, are a significantly improved design over the original Fairey. These are the current go-to for a simple method of up-gearing a Series vehicle. The kit comes with a comprehensive fitting kit and instructions.

For more information on fitting higher ratio differentials, *see* Chapter 12.

High Range Transfer Box

Ashcroft Transmissions produce a gear kit that increases the High Range gearing by around 30 per cent but leaves Low Range at the factory ratio. The conversion requires the transfer case to be modified to account for the different position of the intermediate shaft. Modified transfer box cases are available on an exchange basis.

An Ashcroft high-ratio transfer box offers a cost-effective and simple 30% ratio increase in high range.

LEFT: *A Roamerdrive offers the same increase in gearing as the Fairey but with significantly improved engineering.*

11

Transfer Box

Standard Series II, IIA and III Land Rovers have a selectable four-wheel-drive system with high and low ratio gearing options. The transfer box bolts on to the rear of the LT76 gearbox and comprises an input gear from the main gearbox, an intermediate gear cluster and a rear output shaft that has high and low gear wheels. In High Range and in normal road driving conditions, the transfer box only delivers power to the rear wheels through the rear output. When 4WD is required, the front output sends drive to the front axle, controlled by a dog-clutch assembly within the front output housing. Low and high ratio are selected by a long transfer lever bolted to the main gearbox bellhousing. Additionally, a yellow knob selects 4WD in High Range and selecting Low Range automatically selects 4WD.

The exception to this is the permanent 4WD LT95 gearbox as fitted to the Stage 1 V8 model. This is a combined gearbox and transfer box as fitted to contemporary Range Rovers.

TRANSFER BOX DRIVE OPTIONS

High Range 2WD and 4WD

High Range 2WD sends drive to the rear axle and is used for normal road driving. Drive from the main gearbox exits into the transfer box and via the high gear wheel to the rear output shaft.

There is the option to engage 4WD in High Range by depressing the spring-loaded yellow knob on the transmission tunnel. This releases a plunger and a spring on the 4WD selector shaft that locks up the dog clutch in the front output housing. This shares the drive 50/50 between front and rear axles and there is no centre differential. This is ideal for situations where ground conditions are slippery but a reasonable speed can be maintained, for example driving on wet grass or snow. It should not be used on high grip surfaces as there is no mechanism to vary the required speed differential between the axles when cornering. To do so will result in poor handling, excessive tyre wear and potential to damage the transmission. Selecting High Range 4WD can be done on the move, but it is recommended to keep speeds below 30mph.

To deselect 4WD in High Range, stop the vehicle and select Low Range by pulling the red knob transfer lever backwards. Doing so will cause the yellow knob to spring up. The transfer lever can then be pushed forward to return to 2WD.

Low Range 4WD

Low Range 4WD is for driving in off-road conditions or hard pulling at low speeds. To select, stop the vehicle and pull the red knob transfer lever backward. Selecting Low Range automatically selects 4WD via a pivot assembly on the transfer gear selector shaft, which operates the front output dog clutch. There is no option to have Low Range 2WD (unless achieved via freewheeling hubs and this is not normally recommended). To deselect Low Range 4WD, push the lever forwards: it is recommended to stop the vehicle to avoid damage.

TRANSFER BOX EVOLUTION

The transfer box only had minor changes throughout the Series Land Rover era and shares many components with Series I variants from 1952 onwards. Broadly speaking, we can consider two generations: small and large intermediate shaft types. While some internal components are different, they are interchangeable as a complete unit and either will fit on any variant of the LT76 main gearbox. Rough dates for changes can be given, but in-service changes are to be expected so inspection is required to ascertain which box is fitted. Transfer boxes were not individually numbered, although during the later Series III period the gearbox number was stamped on the transfer case rather than the gearbox case. This can cause confusion when it comes to identification if main components have been swapped.

Small Intermediate Shaft

The small intermediate shaft was fitted to transfer boxes up to and including Suffix A. It has a corresponding intermediate gear, bearing set and shims. The low gear set has a 2.81:1 ratio, although the lower gear ratio did continue into Suffix B with the larger intermediate shaft. Parts for these are less readily available than the later type and are therefore significantly more expensive.

Large Intermediate Shaft

This was introduced from Suffix B onwards although, as above, the Suffix B intermediate gearset retained the 2.81:1 ratio. Suffix C and onwards had the larger intermediate shaft with a higher 2.35:1 ratio low gear set. It is worth noting that using a Suffix B transfer gear set is advantageous when running higher ratio differentials as it offers better low speed control in low range, but leaves high range unaffected.

Transfer Box Problems

Generally speaking, the transfer box is remarkably robust and suffers fewer

Transfer Box

ABOVE LEFT: Transfer levers in road-going 2WD mode: yellow knob up, red knob forward.

ABOVE RIGHT: Transfer levers in 4WD High Range: yellow knob down.

LEFT: Transfer levers in 4WD Low Range: red knob back, yellow knob pops up.

problems than the main gearbox. Having said that, the following problems are noteworthy.

Common Simple Fix Problems
- Oil leaks from front and rear output seals, the latter in danger of contaminating the parking brake
- Oil leaks from the bottom cover plate
- Seized 4WD selector shafts

Less Common but More Complex Problems
- Worn intermediate shaft, bearings and shims
- Worn rear output shaft bearings
- Worn gearsets
- Worn splines on rear output shaft

FRONT OUTPUT SEAL REPLACEMENT

There is no separate oil filling point for the front output housing, but it does get oil from the main transfer box to keep the front bearing and selector shafts lubricated. The front seal (FRC 1780) is the same as the rear output seal and is retained in a bolt-on housing.

- Remove the front propshaft, split pin and castle nut and pull off the front output flange. Engage 4WD

Gearbox and Transfer Box Fixings

Note that most transfer box fixings will require BSW (Whitworth)/BSF spanners and sockets. While some AF and metric tools will just about fit in an emergency, for best practice and safety the correct tools should be used. For the sake of a small investment in rebuilding a gearbox, it is worthwhile buying a rack of Whitworth sockets. Whitworth sizes are based on the size of the shank of the bolt/stud, not the size of the head. This is in contrast to the more common Across Flats (AF) system used on UNF (Unified National Fine), UNC (Unified National Coarse) and Metric sets.

Transfer Box

and a low gear to lock the transmission for removing the nut. The seal can be replaced without removing the seal housing, but the dust shield will need to be removed as it can be easily damaged when prising the seal out. For the small extra effort, it is beneficial to remove the seal housing as the seal and dust shield is tricky to refit in situ. Note that a new gasket (part no. FRC 1511) may be required if the housing is removed.

- The oil seal can be prised out using a suitable prying tool or a heavy-duty flat-blade screwdriver. If removing the seal housing, you can knock the seal out from the rear, meaning the dust shield can stay in place. Clean up the seal housing before pressing a new seal into place. Always buy the best seals you can afford: a good-quality seal should press in reasonably easily and not pinch round the edges.
- Refit the seal housing with a new gasket. If the dust shield has been removed, it can be a challenge to refit as access is awkward and it is easy to chip the edges of the housing. A little bit of heat to expand it slightly will allow it to be knocked home more easily.
- Inspect the drive flange before refitting. Any slight pitting can be polished out with emery cloth or a tiny amount can be removed in a lathe, but any significant damage or ridges means it should either be replaced or fitted with a speedy sleeve. Refit the drive flange, washer and castle nut, torque to 85lb ft and fit the split pin. Engage 4WD to assist tightening the nut and refit the front propshaft.

REAR OUTPUT SEAL

A leaking rear output seal is one of the main causes of poor parking brake performance. As oil leaks out, it runs down onto the brake shoes causing contamination. The Series Land Rover parking brake is actually very efficient when in good condition, so if the brake mechanism is adjusted correctly and it fails to hold on an incline, then suspect contamination.

- Remove the rear propshaft and tie it out of the way. Remove the parking brake drum fixings and drum. Remove the split pin, castle nut and washer. Engage a low gear to stop the transmission from turning.
- Note also that there is a 'fluffy' seal behind the washer that should be replaced on reassembly. This is also a common cause of oil leaks and often is not fitted or replaced during poor maintenance.
- Note that if the oil is still up to the correct level it will leak out when the rear output flange is removed, so it is advisable to drain sufficient oil out – or use this as an opportunity to change the oil anyway.
- The brake backplate can now be unbolted. There is no need to disconnect the handbrake linkages as there is sufficient room to swing it out of the way. Note that there should also be an oil catcher plate.
- It can help to remove the speedo housing to change the seal, but it can be done with it in place.
- The oil seal can then be hooked out with a suitable prying tool. The new seal (FRC 1780) can then be tapped carefully into place; a hub spanner or other suitable tube is ideal for this. If the seal becomes twisted during fitting, it should be replaced or it will leak.
- Reassembly is a straightforward reversal of disassembly. Refit the brake backplate and assess the condition of the brake shoes. Oil-soaked shoes are really only fit for scrap – even if degreased, any soaked in oil will track to the surface again. If changing the brake shoes, do this before refitting the rear output flange as it is far easier to fit the springs.
- Note that the 'fluffy' seal (part number 622042) can be tricky to fit. It goes with the rubber side facing outwards and it is often easier to fit it to the flange first rather than the shaft. When refitting the flange, place the washer over the

Front output seal housing complete with mud shield ready to be refitted.

LEFT: *Pressing a new front output seal into the housing.*

Transfer Box

ABOVE LEFT: Handbrake assembly can be removed complete from speedo housing.

ABOVE RIGHT: Examine the output flange – scoring will lead to leaks.

Using a hub spanner to press the new rear output seal into the speedo housing. This is a useful technique if the housing is still on the transfer box.

LEFT: Using a pry bar to hook the rear output seal out.

fluffy and hold in place with both thumbs as you push the flange onto the splines.

- Tighten the output nut to 85lb ft and secure with a new split pin. Degrease the brake drum before refitting and refit the rear propshaft.

BOTTOM COVER LEAKS

The bottom cover is held in by multiple fixings with a thick gasket. This is prone to weeping as the thin cover expands and contracts at a different rate to the aluminium casing. In addition, the thin cover can be distorted if not tightened evenly. New heavy duty cover plates are available, but often the sealing properties of the original set-up can be improved by using Hylomar or equivalent sealing compound on the thick gasket. Note also that the quality and fit of the gasket can vary, so ensure it is a good fit on the studs before fitting. Note also that the drain plug copper washer compresses and should normally be replaced after removal.

4WD SELECTION PROBLEMS

The transfer and 4WD selector shafts protrude outside the front output housing and the ends are protected by a cover plate. If the vehicle has been sat up for a long period, or 4WD has not been selected for a significant time, it is common for the shafts to corrode and seize in place. The 4WD selector rods are spring loaded, not directly moved by the transfer lever, so any corrosion will mean that the internal spring on the shaft may not be able to overcome the resistance.

The most common symptom of seized selector rods is simply not selecting 4WD in either high or low range. When the yellow knob is depressed, there should be a distinct clunk as the selector shaft springs forward. When the red transfer lever is pulled back, the yellow knob should pop back up promptly. If the yellow knob is pressed down and the spring

Transfer Box

comes straight back up, the rod or rods are seized and the selector will not operate the dog clutch.

Unseizing the rods is usually straightforward, although the driver's floor panel will need to be removed to gain access. It is worth trying a 'thermal shock' trick by pouring hot water on the output housing before unbolting too much, but if this, coupled with operating the controls, doesn't work, the mud shield will have to be removed (the pivoting selector lever, locking pin and the transfer lever operating ring will need to be removed)

ABOVE LEFT: *The front output houses the transfer and 4WD rods.*

ABOVE RIGHT: *Typical corrosion on the end of the shaft means 4WD won't select.*

ABOVE LEFT: *Using self-grip pliers to free off the seized 4WD rod.*

ABOVE RIGHT: *Correct position of the rods for each Transfer/4WD selection option: Selectors in 2WD High with arm and yellow knob up.*

ABOVE LEFT: *Selectors in 4WD High with yellow knob and arm down and 4WD selector springs forward.*

ABOVE RIGHT: *Selectors in 4WD Low: yellow knob springs back up as red knob goes back.*

Transfer Box

and the ends of the shaft can then be cleaned up. Dowse the shafts in easing fluid. Careful use of a pair of self-grip pliers can be used to wriggle the shafts in and out. Once the shafts have freed off, refit the mud shield assembly with a generous smear of grease on the ends of the shafts.

REMOVING THE GEARBOX/ TRANSFER BOX FROM THE VEHICLE

The transfer box attaches to the main gearbox with eight fixings, three of which are inside the case itself, requiring removal of the input and intermediate gears. The transfer box can be removed from the main gearbox in the vehicle without having to remove the seat box, although this is significantly easier if done on a ramp or pit. The complete transmission weighs about 80kg: approximately half of this is the transfer box, so separating them on the vehicle does break it down into manageable sections that can be moved by hand.

To remove the gearbox as a complete unit from the vehicle usually requires removal of the seat box, unless a removable engine crossmember is fitted (see Chapter 10 for additional information). Briefly, however, the weight of the complete gearbox is such that an appropriate engine hoist is a necessity for safety and accuracy. Good technique and the correct tools mean that strength is seldom required for any Land Rover restoration task – don't try to be a hero. The centre of gravity for a complete transmission is offset, making it hard to handle. A short lifting strap around the waist between gearbox and transfer box, offset to the right as shown, is a simple balanced rigging point allowing for easy, controlled movement.

SPLITTING GEARBOX AND TRANSFER BOX

- Drain the oil from both gearbox and transfer box. While the two boxes have different fill points, on a Series III gearbox the rear layshaft bearing has two removal holes that are sealed by the transfer box gasket, so it will leak when removed. In addition, drilling removal holes was a common in-service modification on earlier boxes.
- If splitting on the vehicle, prop the back of the engine to the engine crossmember with a suitable block of wood. This will support the engine and main gearbox as the transfer box mounts are removed.
- If splitting the unit out of the vehicle, it is often easier to upend the gearbox. Usefully, the bellhousing is a good fit for a Land Rover wheel, which works as a very effective stand.
- Remove the bottom cover plate to give access to the internal workings of the transfer box. There will be residual oil in there. Note also that the high/low lever will need to be removed as it pivots on the bellhousing but acts on the transfer box.

Gearbox lifted out with a strap round the waist on the balance point.

ABOVE LEFT: *Transfer box can be removed with gearbox remaining in the vehicle, which means the seat box can stay in place.*

LEFT: *Main gearbox can remain in place with a packer under the engine crossmember.*

Transfer Box

- Remove the rear output/PTO cover and top cover plate. This gives access to the special nut on the back of the gearbox mainshaft. Bend back the tab washer and remove the special mainshaft nut using the correct special socket.
- It's common for 'bush mechanics' to use a hammer and chisel, but this is only acceptable if you intend to replace the nut as it is likely to damage it.
- If using the correct tool, the transmission will have to be locked, either via the parking brake or by jamming the transfer gears with a suitable piece of soft metal such as copper or lead. Alternatively, a rattle gun should work.
- Remove the parking brake drum and rear output flange. Again it may be necessary to lock the transfer gears. Remove the complete parking brake assembly complete with shoes on the backplate, unless intending to replace them.
- This will now allow access to remove the intermediate shaft gear, which is held in place with a nut and tab washer. Once these have been removed, the intermediate shaft can be carefully levered out on one of the flats.
- It is not uncommon for the shaft to seize in place or for it to be a tight fit. Take great care when levering out, using a pry bar on either side to work it out. The end of the shaft can be brittle and can break off. The shaft is also threaded so a stud can be wound in to assist pulling it out and Land Rover produced a special tool for this particular job. The rear of the shaft is only accessible when the boxes are separated, so it cannot be driven out from the rear.
- When the shaft is withdrawn, the intermediate gear can be slid out to give access to the internal fixings. Note that there are thrust washers at either end and potentially a shim or shims, as well as two roller bearing cages. Note the shaft is prone to wear with the hardening breaking down and causing pitting.
- Note the internal fixings have locking nuts and should not be mixed up with the plain external fixings. Once all the fixings have been removed, the two boxes can be separated.
- If splitting on the vehicle, there is leverage to wriggle the transfer box off. If separating off the vehicle it can be more challenging as the gasket and any sealing compound can stick like glue.
- Do not pry apart with a screwdriver as this is likely to damage a sealing surface. It is sometimes possible to break the adhesion by placing the gearbox assembly across a lump of wood and pressing down on both sides.

ABOVE LEFT: *Gearbox can be upended on a wheel rim as a stand to remove the transfer box.*

ABOVE RIGHT: *Using the correct tool to remove the rear mainshaft nut – it's worth the investment.*

LEFT: *Carefully prising the intermediate shaft out with a pry bar: a special puller is available.*

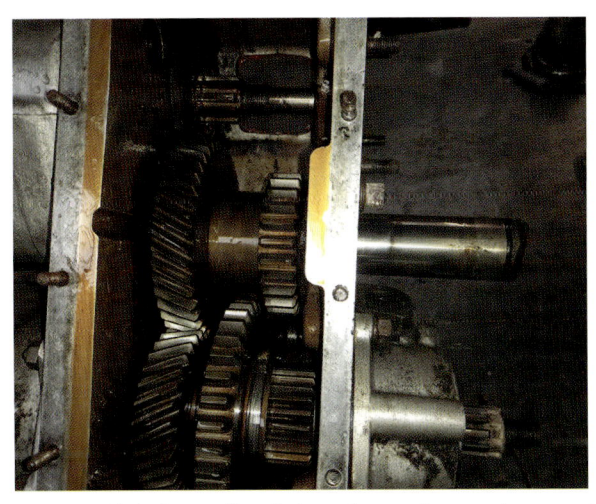

ABOVE LEFT: With the intermediate shaft out, the gear cluster can be removed.

ABOVE RIGHT: Carefully remove the intermediate gear thrust washers and any shims.

ABOVE LEFT: Removing the three internal fixings, which should be fitted with locking nuts.

ABOVE RIGHT: Gearbox sections separated on the bench. Sometimes the gasket sticks them together.

STRIPPING THE TRANSFER BOX

Front Output Housing Removal

- Remove the front output flange. This will need to be counter-held: a pair of bolts through the fixing holes and a pry bar can be used to hold it while the castle nut is undone.
- The front selector cover can be removed along with the 4WD operating pivot and high/low selector loop.
- Remove the transfer box top cover. Undo and fully remove the clamp bolt on the high/low operating fork. Remove the detent cap, spring and plunger.
- Remove all the front output fixings and tap the housing with a soft mallet to release. As the housing is withdrawn, assist the selector rod to slide through the selector fork.
- Take time to note the orientation of all the selector rods and dog clutch assembly and how they operate: they can be tricky and frustrating to reassemble at the best of times.
- The front output shaft can now be tapped out of the front bearing. Note that it has a bolt-on oil thrower to assist splash lubrication.
- Note also that the dog clutch is a loose fit on the end of the front output shaft with notable backlash: this is normal to assist in selecting.

Rear Output Shaft Removal

The rear output shaft is held in place by two taper roller bearings. The front bearing is retained by a large circlip, the rear one is tensioned by shims on the rear of the speedo drive. The requirement to remove the shaft is based on the need to replace worn bearings and/or gears. Generally speaking, both are pretty robust and seldom cause issues, but if the box is being stripped for full overhaul it is always advisable to replace the bearings and ensure the pre-load is correct.

- Remove the speedo drive housing and associated shims at the rear of the box.
- At the front of the box, remove the large circlip. The shaft can then be tapped back with a copper-faced mallet to drive the rear bearing race out of the casing.
- Use a chisel to carefully lever the front inner bearing race forward on

Transfer Box

Removing the transfer rod cover, 4WD selector pin and Low Range selector loop.

RIGHT: *Removing the Low gear selector fork bolt. Note the orientation of the fork before removing the front output.*

BELOW LEFT: *Pulling the front output housing off the transfer case: it has a long spring inside.*

BELOW RIGHT: *Front output internals laid out as they sit in the housing. Note the arrangement now as it can be confusing when reassembling.*

Note the front output shaft is always a loose fit in the selector dog – it seldom wears.

It is always advisable to line everything up in order on the bench to understand the assembly order.

CLEANING AND ASSESSING THE TRANSFER BOX COMPONENTS

Cleanliness is absolutely essential when it comes to assembling a good transmission. As a minimum, a thorough cleaning and degreasing should be carried out on the cases. Professional steam cleaning or vapour blasting will ensure it looks good and is squeaky clean. All internal components need to be thoroughly cleaned in a parts washer for assessment and reassembly.

- the shaft to give access to remove the circlip holding the high gear wheel in place (it is sometimes found to have broken).
- The shaft can then be withdrawn out the back and the gears lifted out of the case. The rear inner bearing can then be removed off the shaft.

Transfer Box

ABOVE LEFT: Driving the transfer gear shaft out the back of the case with a copper hammer.

ABOVE RIGHT: Pull the shaft back to access the front bearing.

LEFT: Removing the High gear wheel-retaining circlip can be fiddly.

BELOW: Levering the front inner bearing off the shaft with a chisel.

ABOVE LEFT: Lay the transfer box output shaft components out on the bench in order to understand the assembly process.

ABOVE RIGHT: Using a chisel to remove the rear inner bearing from the shaft.

139

Transfer Box

ABOVE LEFT: *Cleanliness is vital: this case has been vapour blasted.*

ABOVE RIGHT: *Three separate containers have been used here to ensure the components and fixings do not get mixed up.*

To aid assessment and reassembly, it is vital to keep all the components in a logical order. Keeping different component groups in different containers helps. Here the transfer box internals have been separated into buckets for front output components, rear output components and fixings/housings.

If disassembled, it is always advisable to replace any bearings and seals as a matter of course. As always, buy the best quality you can afford for ease of fitment and longevity.

Carefully examine all shafts and gears. While they are robust, gears suffer from wear, a breakdown in the hardening and potentially from corrosion if from a vehicle that has sat unused for years. Note that the low gear wheel is always a loose sliding fit on the shaft.

TRANSFER BOX REASSEMBLY

Reassembling the Rear Output Shaft

- Before reassembling the rear output into the case, check the high gearwheel end float is 0.006–0.008in
- Tap the rear inner bearing race onto the shaft with a suitable drift. Pass the shaft into the casing from the back and slide on the low and high gears, securing in place with the circlip.
- Slide on the front inner bearing and tap it home on the shaft. Tap the outer front bearing into place and secure in place with the large circlip.
- The shaft can now be positioned and the rear outer race can be tapped in place to secure the shaft in place.

Inserting the shaft and installing the High and Low gear and circlip.

LEFT: *Using a feeler gauge to check the High gear end float is 0.006–0.008in.*

ABOVE LEFT: Using a box spanner to carefully drift the front bearing into place on the shaft.

ABOVE RIGHT: Rear bearing installed. Now to set the pre-load with the speedo drive housing and shims.

- The preload on the rear bearing can now be set using the speedo drive housing and the appropriate thickness of shims (*see* below).

Setting the Rear Output Bearing Preload

The rear bearing outer race is secured in place with the speedo drive/rear seal housing and the preload set with an appropriate number of shims between the housing and the transfer case.

- Fit the rear output seal to the speedo drive housing.
- The preload can be measured with a spring balance attached to a string wrapped round the low gear selector fork recess with a constant measurement of 2–4lb.
- As a basic set-up, fit the speedo drive and the housing without any shims, and hold in place with two fixings on opposite sides. Tighten gently and evenly until the appropriate preload resistance is reached.
- The appropriate number of shims can be inserted in the gap between the housing and casing to give an initial pack size guide. The pack can then be fitted and bolted up and the preload resistance checked again: add or remove as necessary and confirm preload when all fixings are tight.

Refitting the Front Output Housing and Shafts

Once the rear output shaft has been fully fitted, the front output can be reassembled. This can be fiddly due to having to line up the shafts, so take time to lay the shafts out on the bench to understand the mechanism.

- Replace the front output bearing as required. It's a simple roller bearing that simply taps into place. Replace the front seal as a matter of course (*see* above for details).
- Insert the front output shaft into the bearing, assemble the rods into the housing and align the dog clutch 4WD assembly.
- Slide the selector fork into place on the low gear wheel, check the orientation is correct with the threaded side of the pinch bolt on the left.
- Fit a new gasket and slide the front output housing assembly into place, aligning the high/low rod into the selector fork as it slides into place.
- Once fully aligned, the front housing should push into place reasonably easily against the spring and can be bolted up. Fit the selector clamp bolt, refit the 4WD operating pin and mud shield (with some grease on the rods), and ensure that the rods operate correctly.
- Final torquing of the front output nut is easier when assembled on a vehicle, but to tighten on the bench either counter-hold the flange with bolts and a bar or select 4WD and jam the intermediate gear with a piece of soft metal. Fit a new split pin.

Refitting and Shimming the Intermediate Gear

The Intermediate gear has thrust washers on either side. These do wear and can become scored, although if in

Transfer Box

Preload set to give a consistent draw pull of 2–4lb on the shaft.

LEFT: *Speedo housing in place and gauging the number of shims required.*

BELOW LEFT: *Installing the front output shaft with a new front bearing.*

BELOW RIGHT: *Sliding the transfer rod into the High/Low selector fork can be fiddly.*

good condition they can be reused. However, the end float does need to be measured and adjusted as necessary.

- Hold the thrust washers in place with sticky grease. Insert the intermediate gear and bearings and slide the intermediate shaft into place.
- Insert an appropriate feeler gauge into the gap between the thrust washer and gear cluster: the end float should be 0.004 to 0.008in. The gap can be adjusted with shims behind the thrust washers as necessary.
- When the appropriate gap has been achieved the shaft can be

Transfer Box

ABOVE LEFT: *Pushing the front output casing back into place and compressing the spring.*

ABOVE RIGHT: *Hold the thrust washers and any shims in place with grease while you refit the intermediate gear and shaft.*

Using a feeler gauge to check the intermediate gear end float is 0.004–0.008in.

secured in place with the locking tab. Note that the shaft has an O-ring that should be replaced as a matter of course.
- Note, of course, that once the correct set-up has been achieved, the intermediate gear will have to be removed to refit the transfer box to the gearbox.

REFITTING THE TRANSFER BOX TO THE GEARBOX.

Refitting the transfer box to the gearbox is a simple case of nuts and bolts. If attaching to a gearbox off the vehicle, it's easy to upend the gearbox on a wheel rim and drop the transfer box on, using a new gasket.

- Use the self-locking nuts on the internal fixings. Once bolted to the gearbox, the intermediate gear, along with any required shims, can be refitted.
- Refit the intermediate gear and shaft with the previously determined thrust washers and shim(s).
- Fit the rear distance piece with oil thrower followed by the rear output gear, washer and locking tab.
- Lock the transfer gears with a piece of soft metal and tighten the special rear nut to 85lb ft using the correct socket tool (not Stilsons or a hammer and chisel), and bend the appropriate locking tab over.
- Refit the rear PTO cover with a new gasket (and rear bearing, if necessary).
- The handbrake assembly, oil catcher and rear output flange can now be refitted.
- Fit the lower cover plate and fill both the gear and transfer box with oil.

A fully rebuilt gearbox fitted with a fully rebuilt transfer box ready to be fitted – a very satisfying job.

143

12

Axles and Propshafts

Land Rover Series II/IIA and III axles share a significant number of internal components with a gradual evolution from 1958 to 1984. Even the basic design was little changed from the outgoing Series I model, which in turn had its origins in 1930s Rover cars. In addition, complete axles are compatible with many models and it is common for vehicles to have acquired different axles as an expedient repair. With this in mind, it is important to have a broad understanding of the evolutionary process to ensure correct identification and to ensure the correct parts can be ordered.

Axle cases are numbered for basic identification purposes: the number can be found on the top of the case adjacent to the axle breather. The identification code broadly follows the pattern used for chassis numbers, although it is never the same as the chassis number. It doesn't differentiate between petrol and diesel models and will likely have a different suffix number to the chassis. For example, the author's own all-original 1967 Series IIA is a 271 suffix E vehicle with 241 suffix B axles. It is common for the number to have corroded to the point of being unreadable, in particular on the rear axle. In addition, it will only confirm the age of the axle case but not necessarily the rest of the components.

AXLE CASE TYPES

Front Axles

- 1958–80 approx.: The basic standard Rover type axle case changed very little over this time.
- 1980–84 approx.: Flat bottom axle case with offset drain plug.
- 1979–83 approx.: Stage 1 V8 with CV (constant velocity joints) and 3.54:1 ratio differentials. These axles had unique swivels to accommodate the CV joints and a slightly different spring perch. The case serial number has an 88 prefix.
- Heavy-duty ENV axles on 110 Forward Control and one-Ton models: identifiable by the large round diff casing.
- Heavy-duty axle cases with additional lower strengthening brace (often found, though not exclusively, on military vehicles).
- Heavy-duty Salisbury (Dana 60) axle with unique case and differential with a bolt-on differential oil pan.

Note that Series III 109in models had 24-spline halfshafts (at the drive flange end). The Rationalised Axle introduced about 1981 had 24 splines on both 88 and 109 models, as well as different hubs, bearings and stub axles.

Rear Axles

88in and 109in rear axles are not directly interchangeable as the springs attach in a different location. On an 88in, the front and rear springs are directly below the chassis rails; on a 109in the rear springs sit outboard of the chassis rails on outriggers. Note,

ABOVE LEFT: *Location of the axle number adjacent to the axle vent. Note the modern extended breather fitted here.*

ABOVE RIGHT: *Standard front Rover-type axle case with central bottom drain.*

Axles and Propshafts

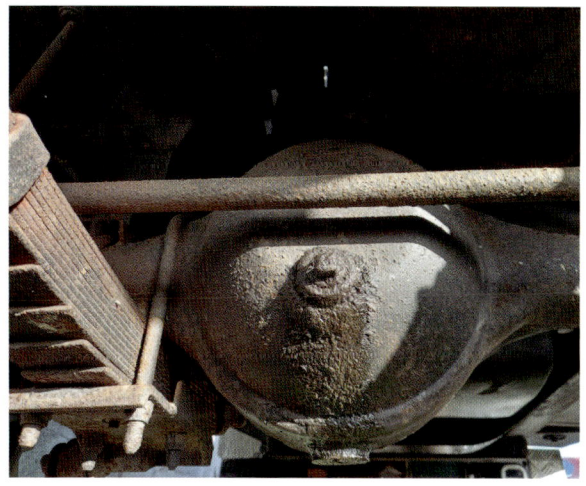

Heavy-duty ENV front axle as fitted to 1-Ton and Forward Control.

LEFT: Later flat-bottomed front axle case fitted from 1980 to 1985.

BELOW LEFT: Optional heavy-duty Salisbury/Dana front axle fitted to late 1-Ton and some military vehicles.

BELOW RIGHT: 109in Salisbury rear axle modified to fit an 88in. Note the old outboard spring mount is still in place.

however, that it was a period upgrade to modify a heavy-duty rear Salisbury 109in axle to fit an 88in.

88in Models
- 1958–80: 10-spline axles (both drive flange and differential end). Internals and case remained pretty much unchanged throughout, except for heavy-duty option and a change in wheel stud size.
- 1980–84: Flat bottom 24-spline axles (drive flange end) with unique hubs, stub axles and bearings

Standard rear Rover-type 88in axle case. Note no filler in the oil pan.

145

ABOVE LEFT: Late type 88in rear axle case with flat bottom and filler plug.

ABOVE RIGHT: Standard Salisbury Series III 109in rear axle.

Rear ENV axle as fitted to 1-Ton and Forward Control.

109in Models
- 1958–71: Rover rear axle. Differential is the same as the front axle.
- 1971–84: Salisbury/Dana 60 axle.
- 1979–84: Stage 1 V8 Salisbury/Dana axle with 3.54:1 differential.
- Heavy-duty ENV axle on 110 Forward Control and 1-Ton Models.
- Later 1-Ton models had a rear Salisbury axle.

AXLE PROBLEMS AND ASSESSMENT

Land Rover axles are generally fairly robust but do suffer from a range of common problems. The following list, though not exhaustive, outlines the common issues you're likely to encounter.

Leaking hub seals: Identifiable by grease/oil round the brake drums. Note that leaking wheel cylinders can also produce dampness in the same place. A leaking hub seal will eventually cause contamination on the brake shoes, significantly reducing brake efficiency and balance.

Worn wheel bearings: Identified by droning/grumbling/knocking and associated play. To assess the bearings, jack up the wheel and feel for play gripping and rocking the wheel at 12/6 o'clock and 9/3 o'clock positions. A worn or loose bearing will have play in both positions. Spin the wheel both directions and listen for unhealthy noises.

Corroded differential pans: Most common on rear axles. Replacement pans are available, although most are the later type with an oil filler hole.

Corroded rear axle strengthener: These can be repaired or replaced with an appropriate sized U-channel section or with an off-the-shelf repair section.

Broken halfshafts: Most common in the rear axle leading to a loss of drive and a lack of an effective handbrake in 2WD. The shorter (right-hand) halfshaft is the most common one to break. Typically it will break at the differential end, requiring the differential to be removed to change it. As a temporary expedient, the vehicle can be driven in 4WD to a point of safety, but there will be metal on metal creating a grinding paste that will soon destroy diff bearings.

Rusted and pitted steering swivel balls: A common failing that often remains unrepaired due to the perceived cost and difficulty level. Slight corrosion in the chrome surface may not cause too much of a problem, but deep pitting or damage to the swept section of the ball will lead to oil leaks.

Leaking swivel seals: A failing often overlooked when the oil leaks stop after it has all leaked out. Again, this is one of those tasks avoided due to the perceived difficulty. Filling the swivel with 'one shot' semi-fluid grease is a known 'solution' to leaking seals, but this is delaying the inevitable. Note that a slight weep is common, especially on a vehicle that is used infrequently, and this may not be a significant issue as long as levels are checked regularly. Replacing seals will require removal of the chrome ball: the occasionally used 'bodge' of splitting the seal to pass it round the ball without dismantling seldom works well.

Wear in swivel bearings and upper Railco bushes: Both lead to poor steering and 'death wobble'. Play can be identified by jacking up and rocking the wheel, feeling for play at 12/6 o'clock position (additional play at 9/3

ABOVE LEFT: Typical oil contamination from a leaking hub seal.

ABOVE RIGHT: Extremely worn-out bearings as a result of seal failure and water contamination.

A very rusty steering swivel ball. All the oil will have leaked out.

LEFT: Typically a halfshaft breaks at the diff end and the short one breaks more often than the long one. This is the twisted remains removed from the diff end.

o'clock is likely to be wheel bearings). Also, feel for play between the swivel housing and the chrome swivel ball.

Worn differentials: Often resulting in significant noise and transmission slop. Bearings, shims and gears wear. Depending on use and the extent of wear, this can often be lived with but may be delaying the inevitable. It is common to feel play when turning the differential drive flange: a few degrees is necessary backlash, but any significant angle of movement will require investigation. Rebuilding a differential to a good standard is a reasonably specialist job and is often beyond the

Clearly this diff pinion seal has been leaking for a while. Note the old-type metal and leather seal.

Axles and Propshafts

amateur mechanic. A good used unit would be an expedient replacement and, if originality is important, it would be advisable to have it professionally rebuilt.

Leaking differential pinion seals: A reasonably straightforward job. Note that the seal running surface on the pinion often wears as well. Small imperfections in the flange can be polished out using emery cloth.

General transmission slop: Often caused by a combination of wear in the multiple splined joints such as differentials, halfshafts and drive flanges. Very often this can be lived with and mitigated by taking up the drive carefully, but, again, should be investigated to find the cause – whether a combination of slight wear or significant wear in one component.

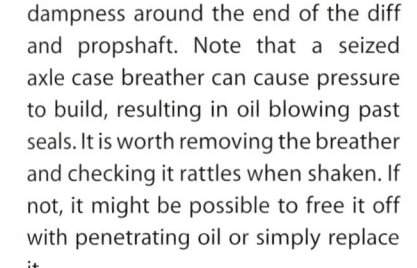

REPLACING DIFFERENTIAL PINION SEALS

A leaking pinion seal will show as dampness around the end of the diff and propshaft. Note that a seized axle case breather can cause pressure to build, resulting in oil blowing past seals. It is worth removing the breather and checking it rattles when shaken. If not, it might be possible to free it off with penetrating oil or simply replace it.

- Remove the propshaft, pinion split pin, nut and washer and remove the drive flange. Often the nut will have loosened in service.
- Use a seal removing tool or a large, old flat-blade screwdriver to lever the old seal out.

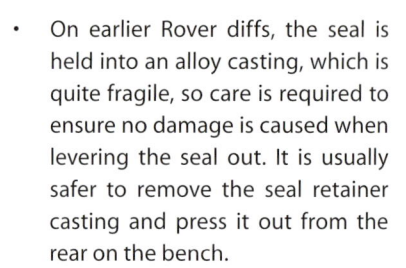

Seal carrier removed to make it easier to fit a new seal.

- On earlier Rover diffs, the seal is held into an alloy casting, which is quite fragile, so care is required to ensure no damage is caused when levering the seal out. It is usually safer to remove the seal retainer casting and press it out from the rear on the bench.
- Note that the earlier type has a steel mud shield pressed onto the seal retainer, which is best removed when replacing the seal. These can be a very tight fit when it comes to refitting, so it pays to warm it up to expand it.
- Carefully press the new seal into place using a suitably sized drift. Always fit the best-quality seals you can afford, the extra cost is usually worth it. Be very careful to ensure it goes in straight and doesn't warp. A damaged seal is very likely to leak straightaway.
- Refit the seal retainer with a new gasket and bend the lock tabs over. Note that the gasket looks very similar to a transfer box front output seal retainer, but it has an extra tab shape at the bottom.
- On later diffs without the separate seal retainer, the new seal can be tapped into place and home with the aid of a large tube or socket: a hub box spanner is ideal.
- Carefully inspect the drive flange, as damage to the area that the seal runs on will result in leaks. Slight damage can be polished out, but

New seal fitted, nut torqued to 85lb ft and split pin fitted.

LEFT: *Typical drive flange with a significant wear line. It might be possible to polish it out, but if in doubt replace.*

Axles and Propshafts

any significant damage will require either a speedy sleeve or a new flange. This can be bought as a kit with seal, nut, washer and split pin.
- Refit the flange and washer and tighten the nut to the specified 85lb ft to the nearest split pin hole. Secure in place with a new split pin.

CHANGING A REAR HALFSHAFT

Changing a rear halfshaft is significantly easier than the front and can be executed with the wheels on. (The front halfshaft is significantly more involved and is dealt with as part of the front axle overhaul.) If a rear halfshaft is suspected to have failed, it is frequently the shorter RHS one, so investigate this one first. Note that when investigating a failed halfshaft, often the axle will seem to turn correctly by hand but not under load. This is due to the ends of the broken halfshaft binding together.

- Removing the six bolts on the drive flange allows the halfshaft to be withdrawn from the axle. Note that it is not necessary to remove the end cap at this stage, although it is easier to do so when the halfshaft is bolted in place.
- The end cap can be levered off with a pry bar, using another as a fulcrum point. These can be firmly held in place by corrosion and might need some encouragement. They are cheap to replace, so have one to hand if in doubt.
- Have a tray to hand to catch the oil as the halfshaft is withdrawn. If you're lucky, it will have failed at the drive flange end and it can be withdrawn easily, but more often than not they break at the differential end.
- Replacing a halfshaft is straightforward but it should be fitted with a new split pin, fluffy oil seal and drive flange gasket. This is also a good time to assess the condition of the splines on the drive flanges. Slight play is common, but the more play at each splined component, the more it adds up to noticeable transmission shunt.
- A hub nut box spanner is an ideal aid for knocking the end cap home without damaging it. It is wise to put a blob of grease inside the cap, although not too much as hydraulic action will stop it pressing on.

REMOVING AND REPLACING DIFFERENTIALS

Rear Differential

To remove the differential, both halfshafts must be removed as well as the rear propshaft. A proper propshaft tool is a welcome addition to any toolbox, although it is possible to get in with a pair of 9/16th spanners. Note that early vehicles had 3/8th BSF fixings and

ABOVE LEFT: *Expect oil to leak out when you remove the drive flange bolts.*

ABOVE RIGHT: *Halfshaft being removed. This one needed a good tug to remove the twisted bit from the diff.*

Using a pry bar to prise off the hub cap.

RIGHT: *Refitting the hub cap with a hub spanner to avoid damaging the nose.*

149

Axles and Propshafts

therefore require an appropriate socket, although as an expedient a 15mm should be a tight enough fit.

- Drain the oil before removing the differential (1.5 litres). On early axles, the bung has a wide slot. This can be removed by putting the side of a spanner in the slot or with the proper slotted tool.
- A propshaft tool is also the correct size to remove the differential mounting nuts, although a narrow-wall 9/16th socket fits fine. Early axle cases had 3/8th BSF fixings. Use the correct socket or, if expedient, a 15mm socket.
- Note that the differential weighs about 25kg and is an awkward shape, especially if working on your back underneath. A trolley jack underneath is a significant help, as is a piece of carpet to help drag it out.
- Sometimes the diff jams in place on the locating dowels (early type) and/or sticks to the gasket. A firm boot heel is usually enough to free it off.
- The remains of any broken halfshaft will likely be firmly stuck on the differential centre splines. A suitably sized drift can be pushed through to knock it out.
- Thoroughly clean the axle case out and remove any trace of broken halfshaft/differential swarf.
- Remove all traces of the old gasket and fit a new one. Smear grease or, if concerned about oil leaks, sealing compound such as Hylomar. Take care not to catch the gasket with the crown wheel as the differential pushes home.
- Refitting the differential is not technically difficult, but can be

Remove the diff end first and hold the rear prop over at an angle to make access to the nuts easier.

RIGHT: *Draining the oil. Note its dark grey colour is caused by shards of metal from a broken halfshaft.*

Most diffs are fitted with 3/8 UNF nuts (9/16th socket), although early ones had 3/8 BSF.

RIGHT: *End of the halfshaft still jammed in the diff. A thin drift was required to remove this one.*

Axles and Propshafts

awkward due to weight and the requirement to be accurate with alignment. Using a trolley jack to support the weight while lining up can make the job easier.
- Sometimes a differential is a challenge to locate. Patience and bit of wriggling is usually the answer and it should slide home. When tightening up the nuts, do it gradually to pull it up square.
- Note that there are two different Rover differential castings. The early type has a bolt-on aluminium housing for the pinion seal; the later type, introduced about 1969, has no separate housing and a 'flat bottom' on the casting. The earlier differential has two locating dowels that will need to be removed if fitting to a later axle.

Front Differential

Replacing the front differential is a very similar procedure to the rear one, but to remove the front halfshafts requires removing the wheels, brake drums, backplates, hubs and stub axles. (For details, *see* the section below on swivel replacement.)

WHEEL BEARINGS

Adjusting Wheel Bearings

Wheel bearings consist of a pair of taper roller bearings (smaller outer, larger inner) on a stub axle that is bolted to either the axle case at the rear or the swivel housing at the front. The bearing pairs are the same size front and rear. Note that there was a change to the stub axles, bearings and hubs and seals for the rationalised axle from 1982 (the bearings became a matched pair rather than a smaller outer bearing).

The bearings are lubricated with an initial packing of grease and additionally by oil from the axle. The lubricant is retained by the hub seal, which runs on a distance piece on the inner edge of the stub axle. There is also a felt 'fluffy' and end cap on the drive flange.

Wheel bearings are designed to have a small amount of end float, which is usually just perceptible at the edge of the wheel. Over time the bearings wear, become loose and will require nipping up. Beyond in-service wear and settling, there will be a point when the bearings become no longer serviceable, especially if the hub has become contaminated with water leading to a loss of lubrication. Significantly worn bearings will 'grumble' when the wheel is spun or knock when laden. A loose bearing can be detected by lifting the wheel off the ground and feeling for play at 12/6 o'clock and 9/3 o'clock positions, as outlined above.

- To gain access to the wheel bearings, remove the hub cap, halfshaft nut and drive flange. On the rear, the flange can be removed complete with halfshaft.

Differential Ratios

Standard Series differentials have a 4.7:1 ratio – that is it takes 4.7 revolutions of the pinion to 1 turn of the crown wheel. The pinion has 10 teeth, the crown wheel has 47 teeth. The exception to this is the Stage 1 V8 model, which has a 3.54:1 ratio – 13 pinion teeth and 46 crown wheel teeth. 3.54:1 was also used on the Range Rover and Discovery 1 models.

For an increase in final drive ratios, especially when running powerful, low-revving engines such as 200 and 300Tdi, it is a common modification to fit higher ratio differentials. The most common choice is 3.54:1 and this gives a final drive approximately 30 per cent higher than standard. There are pros and cons to this modification. It gives quieter cruising and potentially a higher overall top speed, but the drawback is that it might not be the best compromise when towing or driving on steep hills. In addition, it also raises the low range gearing, so engine braking can be compromised on very steep descents.

Another, although less common, option is to fit differentials from contemporary Rover cars: 4.3:1 or 3.9:1 ratios offer something of a compromise between better road manners and off-road control. The drawback is the lack of availability and could really be considered a period mod these days. It's worth noting that, due to the interchangeability of parts, it is always worth checking the differential ratios before fitting/replacing. Obviously a mismatched pair of differentials will cause significant problems in 4WD.

- If simply tightening the wheel bearing, there is no need to remove the wheel. Indeed this can be an advantage when it comes to an in-service setting of the end float. If replacing the bearing and or seal, the wheel and hub will need to be removed.
- Bend back the lock washer with a hammer and chisel and use a proper hub box spanner or appropriate socket to remove the locknut. Do not use a hammer and chisel on the hub nuts except in an emergency. It is a crude, though all too common, method that should be frowned upon.
- Inspect what is visible of the bearings. If found to be in good condition, tighten the inner nut to just take the play out of the bearing. Feel for play at the edges of the wheel and adjust until it only just disappears. This end float can be set 'as per the book' with a dial gauge to 0.004–0.006in, but just taking the play out is the most common in-service technique.
- Fit a new lock washer (these should usually be considered a single-use part) and refit the outer lock nut hand-tight with the box spanner. Bend/knock the lock washer over a flat on the inner nut with a pry bar or chisel to secure the inner nut, then fully tighten the outer lock nut.
- Spin the wheel to check it runs freely. Feel for any play to check the end float has not changed during the tightening process. Bend the lock washer forward and tap into place against a nut flat to secure the outer lock nut into place.
- Refit the drive flange (and halfshaft if removed) with a new gasket (and fluffy seal, split pin and end cap if removed separately).

Replacing Wheel Bearings

- With the vehicle suitably secure on an axle stand, remove the wheel and drive flange to gain access to the hub nuts. Note it is normal for oil to leak out.
- Back off the brake drum adjustors, remove the countersink fixing screws and remove the brake drum.

Axles and Propshafts

ABOVE LEFT: Checking bearing adjustment at the wheel: a tiny amount of free play is fine.

ABOVE RIGHT: Using a chisel to bend the lock washer over an inner nut flat.

Locking washer also bent over a fully torqued outer lock nut.

- Knock back the lock washer tab and undo the lock nut, lock washer and unscrew the inner hub nut. Withdraw the hub from the stub axle – the keyed thrust washer will slide with it – take care not to overlook it. If the hub does not withdraw easily, the inner bearing race may be stuck on the stub axle and the hub may need to be tapped off with a soft mallet.
- With the hub on a clean, solid work surface, the rear oil seal can be levered out and the bearings tapped out. There is just enough room to get a punch or chisel on the edge of the outer race to knock out gradually. Take care not to damage the inner face of the hub.
- With the bearing races removed, the hub should be thoroughly cleaned before fitting new bearings.
- New bearing inner races can be pressed or tapped home, but care must be taken to avoid damage. A bearing fitting tool/drift is a useful addition to a toolbox but a useful trick is to cut a slit in the old bearing race and use it against the new race to tap it home. The slit means it can be easily levered out when the new race is driven fully home.
- To gauge whether the bearing race is fully home, either look for the significant change in pressure required in the press or, if tapping home, listen for the change in sound – change to a solid thud suggests the bearing race is fully seated.
- Thoroughly pack the taper rollers with an appropriate high melting-point grease. This will give initial lubrication during assembly.
- Locate the rear roller bearing in place and then fit a new oil seal. A good-quality oil seal should press in easily and sit flush with the lip of the hub. Do not hammer the seal home or it will likely distort and leak. A thick metal plate is ideal for pushing the seal home.
- Before sliding the hub and bearings back onto the stub axle, inspect it thoroughly for wear. In

Axles and Propshafts

particular, inspect the distance piece or 'land' that the seal runs on. If it is scored, it is likely to leak, Small imperfections can be cleaned off with emery cloth, but if there is any wear it should be replaced (*see* below).

- Slide the hub on complete with bearings and keyed thrust washer, Set the bearing end float as described above. Nipping the bearings up tighter and then backing off to give the correct end float can help to seat them fully in place.

Replacing the Stub Axle Land/ Distance Piece

The 'land' or distance piece is a replaceable press-fit ring on the stub axle that the hub seal runs on. Over time it does wear, developing a groove and/or pit-

ABOVE LEFT: *Backing off the break adjustor to remove the brake drum.*

ABOVE RIGHT: *Using a hub spanner for its correct purpose to remove the hub nuts. It has plenty of other uses too!*

Prying out a leaking hub seal.

RIGHT: *Using a chisel to drift out the hub bearing races.*

153

Axles and Propshafts

Hub seal is fitted flush with the rear hub face. A good seal will press in reasonably easily.

LEFT: *New race drifted in and bearing packed with grease.*

This hub seal was pressed in too far and leaked badly, contaminating the brake shoes.

ting leading to poor sealing properties. Note that the late stub axles do not have a replaceable land/distance piece and any significant wear means replacement is the only option. While not the official approach, acceptable results have been reported by cleaning the land up with emery cloth in a lathe, although any significant removal of material will result in poor sealing.

- To remove the distance piece, strike down firmly on it with a sharp cold chisel. This should distort it sufficiently to allow it to be levered off the stub axle.
- Drift a new one on using a suitable tube after putting a smear of sealing compound such as Hylomar on the mating surfaces. Failure to do so could result in oil seeping past the distance piece. Like the wheel bearing races, the old one can be slit through to use it to protect the new piece while drifting into place.

ADJUSTING STEERING SWIVELS

Play in swivel components is often indicated by significant wobble at the steering wheel after hitting a pothole at speed. As above, to assess play, jack up and secure on an axle stand and feel for play at 12/6 o'clock positions; if there is play at 9/3 o'clock as well, it's more likely to be wheel bearing play. Play between chrome ball and swivel housing can be felt and often observed: it can help to have an assistant.

As long as the components are in reasonable condition, often a small amount of play can be reduced by removing an appropriate thickness of shims from under the top bearing/Railco bush pin. This can be achieved by minimal dismantling, but be aware that when you remove the top pin, oil will leak out at the bottom of the swivel seal. With experience you can gauge an 'in service' removal of shims by feel. As a basic guide this is a case of just removing the play plus adding a touch of preload. Remove one shim at a time to gauge this. If in doubt, set the preload 'as per the book', as outlined below. If all shims have been removed and play still remains, the only option is to rebuild the swivels with new bearings/bushes as a minimum.

Removing the top pin will also give an insight into the general condition of the internal components in the swivel. It is common for the top bush to have corrosion on it from a lack of lubrication and an ingress of water. If it has significant corrosion, wear or pitting, it should be replaced as a unit with the Railco bush and, if stripping to replace, the bottom bearing should also be replaced. These components are available as an off-the-shelf service kit complete with seal, seal retainer and gaskets.

Axles and Propshafts

Obviously this is starting to become a larger job and a decision should be made at this point whether to also replace the chrome ball. With isolated light corrosion it might still be serviceable, but any deep pitting or significant breakdown in the chrome will cause significant oil leaks. Some DIY repairs have been made with epoxy filler, but replacement is really the only long term solution.

REPLACING STEERING SWIVELS

Good Series Land Rover steering depends on a raft of components, in particular the condition of the swivels. Rusty, pitted and leaking swivels are all too common and vehicles will often have been driven for years with worn-out components. Owners often simply accept that vague, heavy steering is the norm or turn a blind eye to the problems. While rebuilding swivels can seem daunting, it doesn't actually require anything more than reasonable DIY skills and a methodical approach.

Full swivel rebuild kits are available with everything required to carry out the job including all seals, bearings, bushes, shims, O-rings and gaskets. They represent good value for money, but note that there are two different kits available: one for the early axle (Series II and early IIA) with the steering arm on the top and the later, more common, arm on the bottom.

Removing the Swivel Assembly

- With the vehicle secure on axle stands and the wheels off, drain the remaining oil out of the swivels, remove the brake drums, hubs, brake backplates and stub axle. The backplate can be hung up out of the way to avoid having to open the brake system. The stub axle is often quite firmly stuck on the swivel housing and may require a tap from a soft mallet to remove.
- Withdraw the halfshaft complete with universal joint and inspect for wear. Note that the halfshaft bearing sets must be kept together: the inner race is pressed on and held in place with an interference fit collar. A seal runs on the collar and does cause wear over time.
- Remove the appropriate steering ball joint from the steering arm – after removing the split pin (where fitted) and nut, a firm hammer blow on the steering arm will usually shock it off. A ball joint splitter might be necessary, but can often split the rubber boot.
- Remove the bolts that hold the seal retainer and prise out the seal. The top pin can now be removed and the swivel housing can be pulled away and down to remove it from the chrome swivel.
- The swivel can now be unbolted from the axle case. The nuts are frequently very tight and might need to be cut off.
- The swivel and housing can now be stripped and thoroughly cleaned. The steering arm and pin should be inspected for any wear.

Halfshaft Bearing Replacement

The halfshaft bearing in the swivel often survives well due to it taking little load and really just acting as a support. If the bearing is in serviceable condition, it can be carefully tapped out and reused in the new swivel. If it is not reusable, the complete bearing set and collar on the halfshaft must be replaced. Carefully drift the halfshaft support bearing into the rear of the new swivel.

If installing new bearings, the inner race and new collar must also be fitted on the halfshaft. The collar and old race

LEFT: Removing a front halfshaft with universal joint.

Striking the steering arm to shock the ball joint out is a quick and simple trick.

Axles and Propshafts

ABOVE LEFT: Old halfshaft bearing can be refitted in the new swivel if it is in good condition.

ABOVE RIGHT: Using a chisel to break the press-fit retaining collar on the halfshaft bearing.

can be removed by grinding it down close to the halfshaft and then striking with a chisel to break it off.

The new bearing race should press into place using the old collar and an appropriate tube as a drift. The official method of fitting the retaining collar is to press it on with a large press; a common DIY option, however, is to heat the collar in an oven to expand it (200°C for 90 minutes usually works), hold the shaft in a vice and drop it on, using a long tube of the appropriate size to knock it home. Inspect and, if in doubt, replace the oil seal in the axle case.

Rebuilding the Swivel Assembly

- Press or drift the bearing race into the bottom of the swivel and the Railco bush into the top. Check the old one for the correct orientation as it is easy to get it the wrong way round. A packing piece inside the swivel reduces the possibility of distortion if using a press.
- Note that a known modification was to install a taper rolling bearing in both top and bottom, but Railco bearings are designed to give a small amount of dampening. Vehicles from 1958 to 1964 had a taper cone and spring in the

Pressing in the bottom swivel bearing race. Note the socket to stop the swivel distorting – note it can also be drifted in on the bench

RIGHT: Don't forget to fit the seal and seal retainer before bolting the swivel in place.

Axles and Propshafts

ABOVE LEFT: *Nipping the top pin down with a selection of shims while setting the preload.*

ABOVE RIGHT: *Using a spring balance to check the resistance is 8–12lb: note pulling on the track rod hole and with no seal fitted.*

ABOVE LEFT: *Lock stop bolt fitted. It is essential to limit steering travel on full lock.*

ABOVE RIGHT: *Refitting the front halfshaft can be a fiddly job. Wriggle it a little to align the diff splines.*

top, though many will have been changed to Railcos.
- Remember to slide the swivel seal retainer and seal over the axle flange before bolting the swivel onto the axle with a new gasket. It's a common oversight to fully assemble the swivel and then realise that the seal and retainer have been forgotten.
- The original swivel mounting bolts were 3/8th BSF, although 3/8th UNF is another common in-service change. Note the position of the steering lock stops – these need a longer bolt – and the jack guide plate on the right-hand side.
- Install a new O-ring on the lower steering arm and refit the arm to the swivel housing with new lock tabs. Leave these unbent until final torquing. Grease and fit the bottom bearing.
- It is a good idea to check the fit of the Railco pin in the bush before offering the housing up. Sometimes they are quite tight and might need oiling and working in. Also check that the Railco disc is in place in the bottom of the bush. Some kits have them supplied separately, some are already in the bush. If the disc is missing, it will be impossible to set the correct preload.
- Fit the housing to the swivel and assemble the top bush with a selection of different shims. Nip the bolts down and check the preload using a spring balance on the track rod hole: 8–12lb is the quoted figure.
- If too tight, add shims; if too loose, remove the appropriate number/size of shims to achieve the preload. Note the preload should be set before the swivel oil seal has been fitted.
- Once the preload has been set, fully tighten all the fixings, check the preload again and bend over the lock tabs.
- The oil seal can now be bolted into place with the retainer: a smear of Hylomar to the joint with the swivel housing is advisable. The steering ball joints can now be refitted with new split washers as appropriate.
- The halfshaft can now be refitted. It sometimes needs a bit of a

157

Axles and Propshafts

ABOVE LEFT: Refitting the stub axles. Use the lock tabs in the kit. Note that the later type was usually fitted with threadlock.

ABOVE RIGHT: The finished result. Note the lock stop fitted to axle and the swivel locking tabs bent over. It's not a difficult job as long as you keep being methodical.

wriggle to get it to locate fully into the diff, followed by the stub axle and brake backplate with a new gasket and lock tabs.

- Reassemble the hubs and bearings as outlined above.

PROPSHAFTS

Propshaft Problems

Propshafts send the drive from the gearbox to the differentials and consist of two universal joints and a splined sliding joint. These should be lubricated and inspected on a regular basis. The sliding splined joints are prone to wear and can seize on a vehicle that is used infrequently. Seemingly illogically, given the fact it seldom drives the front wheels, the sliding joint on the front prop is often the one with most wear. The universal joints are also very prone to wear. They are exposed and the needle bearings will wear quickly once the grease has been washed out. In extreme circumstances they can flail apart causing extreme damage. Worn universal joints usually cause rhythmic vibrations and clunks on taking up drive.

Series propshafts are set 'in phase', that is the orientation of the universal joint yokes at each end are in line. An out of phase prop can cause vibrations or grumbling noises, in particular on overrun. This will cause premature wear in the propshaft bearings and potentially the differential. It is also worth noting that when fitting parabolic springs, the vehicle is often lifted due to a greater free camber and this can also cause propshaft grumbles. This can sometimes be mitigated by fitting castor correction wedges between the springs and axle to lift up the angle of the diff. Another option is to experiment with phasing the propshaft, which is reported to have made improvements.

ABOVE LEFT: Note that the 88in rear prop universal joints have been set 90 degrees out of phase, causing grumbling noises on overrun.

ABOVE RIGHT: A dedicated propshaft tool is a very useful addition to any toolbox (9/16th head size).

Axles and Propshafts

Propshaft Removal and Refitting

Removing or refitting a propshaft is straightforward but is significantly easier with a dedicated propshaft socket tool. Note that the standard fixing is 3/8th UNF, which requires a 9/16th spanner, although early vehicles had 3/8th BSF fixings. Propshaft bolts should be fitted with self-locking/nyloc nuts. It is usually easier to remove the rear prop from the diff end first as it can then be positioned in the best place to access the nuts at the gearbox. A rattle gun makes it much quicker and easier, but is by no means essential.

Assessing Propshafts

Propshaft universal joints should be inspected as part of a regular service regime. A worn universal joint should be very apparent on inspection: look and feel for play with one wheel safely secured off the ground. Also look for any rust stains indicating a dry bearing. Propshafts are relatively cheap so a judgement call has to be made whether to change universal joints in a slightly worn prop or to replace the complete unit. If there is any wear causing backlash in the splined sliding joint, it may well be advisable to change the complete unit. The official backlash limit is 0.004in, a slightly perceptible movement. In addition, if there is wear in the yokes such that the bearing caps have become loose enough to rotate, then the propshaft should be replaced. The bearing caps should be a press-fit in the yokes and any rotation of the caps will show as a distinct shiny ring round the path of the circlip.

Changing Universal Joints (UJs)

Replacing universal joints can be very frustrating. The yoke bearing caps contain needle bearings that are prone to falling out or turning inwards during assembly. Practice fitting helps, but it is advisable to buy the highest quality replacements you can afford as budget options can be harder to fit. Note that there are two different sizes of universal joint, 75mm (RTC3291) (1958–64) and 82mm (RTC 3346) (1964–84). Because propshafts are a regularly changed component, it is important to measure which one is required rather than relying on simply what is listed in the Parts Manual. Note also that the front propshaft on a Stage 1 V8 model has a unique 'double cardan' type joint at the gearbox end.

- Removing the old universal joints is straightforward enough, but do expect it to be harder if the old joints are heavily rusted. Good-quality circlip pliers are essential: the light-duty universal/changeable head types are seldom strong enough.
- Seized clips are common and these may require tapping round with a small punch, as well as plenty of easing fluid. A vice is pretty much essential for holding the propshaft secure and for pressing the caps home.
- Once the circlips are out, the caps can be loosened by alternately striking the lower sides of the yoke with a hammer. The caps should start to loosen off and tap up and out.
- Do not strike the yoke immediately round the bearing caps. If it bruises or distorts, the caps may not come out or the recess for the circlip may be compromised.
- Once both sides of the UJ are removed, thoroughly clean the yokes,

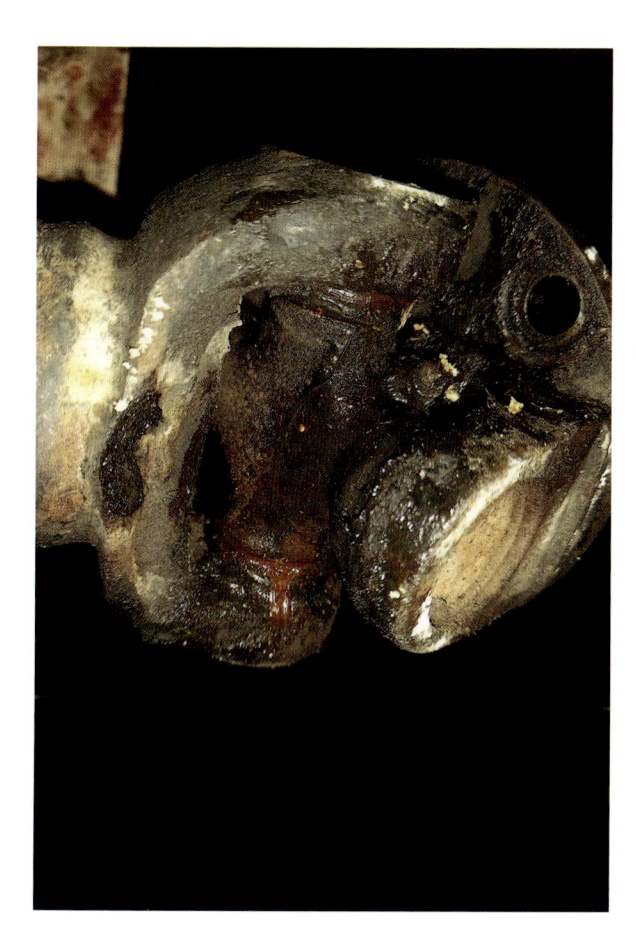

Striking the side of the yoke should drive the bearing cap out.

LEFT: *Typical failing UJ with a rust track from the bearing.*

159

Axles and Propshafts

ABOVE LEFT: Locating the bearing caps onto the UJ spider. Be careful not to let the needle bearings pop out.

ABOVE RIGHT: Using a vice to squeeze the bearing caps into place in the yokes.

A good pair of circlip pliers is essential for fitting new UJs, since light-duty ones are too fragile.

RIGHT: Repeat the process for the other side and ensure the UJ operates smoothly: they are usually slightly tight when first fitted.

including the circlip recesses. An additional good practice is to tap the old bearing caps through the yokes to ensure they go through cleanly.

There are various tips and tricks to fit UJs and practice makes it much easier. The key thing is to ensure that the needle bearings do not drop out or stick in the back of the caps during assembly. You will find that the following technique works:

- Gently press or tap one of the new caps part way into the propshaft yoke. Manipulate the UJ into place and press the cap flush with the yoke. Insert the second cap slightly in and slide the UJ body over to meet it, ensuring the needle bearings locate correctly.
- As this is done, ensure that the UJ spider still remains in the bearings

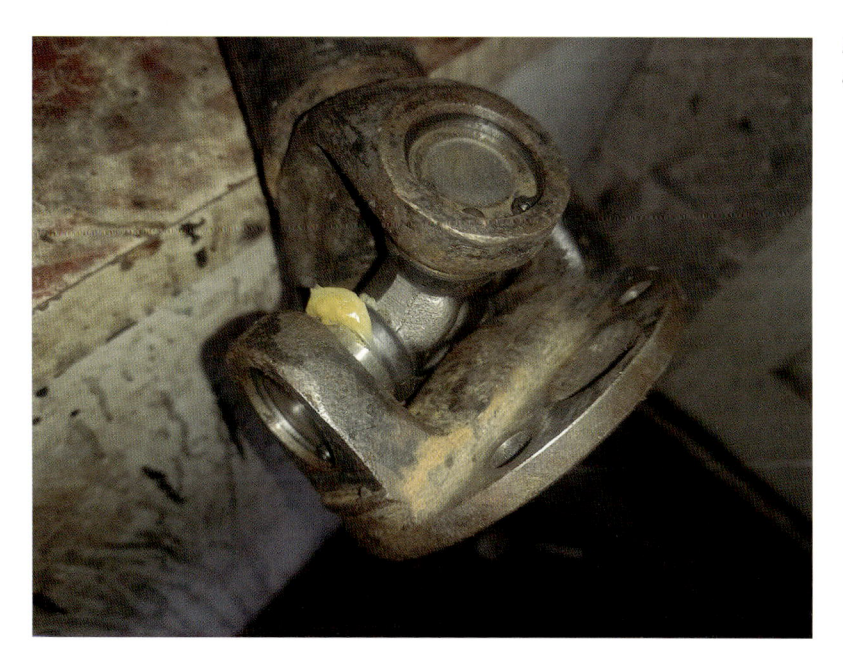

Pump grease in via the nipple until it squeezes out the side.

of the opposite cap. This method means that the needle bearings do not get knocked out or pushed into the bottom of the cap. Squeeze the caps flush in the vice.

- Use an appropriately sized socket to tap one cap fully home and fit a circlip, ensuring it fully locates in the recess. Tap the opposite cap home and fit the circlip. If the circlip doesn't fit, check the caps have pressed in sufficiently: if not, it could be that a needle bearing has dislodged and is sat in the bottom of the cap.
- Ensure the UJ rotates smoothly: if not, a gentle tap of the side of the yoke should free it off.
- Repeat for the other side of the yoke.

Fitting Rubber Gaiters

A rubber gaiter (part no. 276484) was originally fitted to the front propshaft. These commonly split and should be replaced with the best-quality part you can afford. Before splitting the propshaft, check for any alignment arrows. If none found, scribe a line to aid assembly.

Unscrew the dust cap using a pair of large slip-joint pliers or Stilsons and slide the sections apart. When reassembling, locate the jubilee securing screws at opposite sides to aid prop balance.

Propshaft Orientation

All Land Rover diagrams show the propshafts 'pointing forward' – that is the short length nearer the front of the vehicle. On the rear, the short end is closest to the gearbox; at the front the short end is closest to the axle.

13
Steering

Tradition has it that Land Rover steering is heavy and vague with a poor turning circle. However, when the components are in good condition a Series Land Rover should have reasonably light steering that is direct and shouldn't wander significantly or wobble dramatically when hitting potholes. There should be minimal play at the steering wheel rim. While a slight amount of play may be acceptable, it should always be investigated. While the turning circle is large by modern car standards, it should have the same lock each way and needn't be problematic in most driving situations. Most complaints and problems with Series Land Rover steering are caused by worn-out components, poor adjustment and tyre-related issues.

Land Rover steering changed very little throughout Series II, IIA and III production. While there were different steering wheels and boxes, the general layout remained the same. Briefly the system comprises a recirculating ball steering box with a swinging drop arm, which moves a longitudinal tube to a steering relay in the front crossmember. This in turn transmits the turning forces to a drag link that connects to the steering arm on the NSF steering swivel. The NSF steering arm also has a track rod link that connects it to the OSF wheel, completing the steering system.

INITIAL SAFETY ASSESSMENT OF THE STEERING SYSTEM

Most steering problems are simply down to worn-out components, poor adjustment and gradual decline that a driver simply gets used to. If concerned about the steering on a vehicle, it is worth driving another vehicle for comparison or asking an experienced Land Rover owner/specialist to pass judgement. It is also highly advisable to carry out a thorough annual inspection, irrespective of any requirement to have an MOT on a Historical Vehicle. The performance of the vehicle steering and safety of the driver and other road users depends on the condition of some simple parts that are easy to check.

On an MOT, a very basic safety assessment of a vehicles' roadworthiness, an assistant rocks the steering wheel side to side while the inspector works systematically from top to bottom on the steering system.

- Initially look for play in the steering box itself and any looseness in its mounting bolts and brackets. Mounting bolts do work loose and the mounting lugs on the box can break as a result. The casing is aluminium but it can corrode, compromising the strength and safety of the box. You can expect there to be flex in the mounting brackets when dry steering, but all the fixings should be tight.
- Look and feel for play or stiffness at each ball joint in turn. Inspect every rubber boot: any splits will let water in, the grease out and cause corrosion, stiffness, slop and premature failure. Inspect the security of the ball joints in the steering rods, ensuring the clamps are tight and there is no movement on the threads.
- Look and feel for any movement in the steering arms on the steering box, steering relay and on the swivels. The pinch bolts should be tight and there should be no play in the arms on the splines. The steering arms on the swivel housings should be tight and secured with lock tabs.
- Note that the axle swivels are also prone to oil leaks, a lack of lubrication and wear, and are a significant part of the steering system. (These will be dealt with in Chapter 12.)
- Remember that tyres are the only point of contact with the road, so tyre pressures should be up to normal manufacturer's guidance. Larger or wider tyres will make a significant difference in the handling and steering characteristics of a Series Land Rover.

Well-maintained Land Rover steering should be reasonably direct and not overly heavy.

Steering

Steering Box and Steering Wheel Evolution

1958–65: Series II/IIA
Wire steering wheel held in place on parallel splines with a clamp bolt. The top of the steering column is supported by a Tufnol (phenolic resin) bush. The early boxes had a shorter steering column the same length as the Series I. The earliest boxes had a separate horn button on a side bracket; later models had the horn push in the steering wheel boss and a slip ring contact arrangement.

1966–71: Series IIA
Plastic/resin steering wheel attached to the column with a taper spline (48 splines) and nut. The horn push in the steering wheel has a slip ring contact, but the push cap is smaller than the earlier design. The steering wheel is not interchangeable with the earlier type and should not be attempted. A steering wheel/box combination can be swapped between models, but note that later mounting bolts are larger. There was a lower ratio fitted to 1-Ton models to cope with the larger wheels.

1971–84: Series III
Very similar to later IIA type but with the provision of a steering lock and a different top bearing/spacer arrangement. Horn now on the horn/dip/indicator stalk. These are interchangeable as a complete unit to earlier vehicles. The very last Series IIIs had a smooth plastic steering wheel that didn't leave black marks on your hands when they got old and wet.

ABOVE LEFT: Three-spoke wire steering wheel fitted from 1958 to 1965.

ABOVE RIGHT: Series IIA plastic steering wheel fitted from 1965 to 1971.

Series III plastic steering wheel fitted from 1971 to 1985.

- Note that larger tyres can catch on the leaf springs on full lock. Look for evidence on both the tyre and the spring. The lock stops should be adjusted to prevent this.

BALL JOINTS

Removing Ball Joints/Track Rod Ends

Each steering rod has a left- and a right-handed thread ball joint. It is hard to tell which is which unless sufficient thread is protruding out of the rod, so it is always advisable to have both in stock when carrying out any steering repairs.

- To remove a ball joint from the steering arms, remove the split pin if fitted (some aftermarket ball joints have nyloc nuts) and remove the nut. A pair of old side cutters is a useful tool for removing old split pins. If the pin will not come out, turning the nut left and right will usually shear a rusted pin.
- A ball joint splitter can be used to separate the taper from the arm, but the hammer-in fork type will often damage the rubber boot. An alternative, usually quick and effective, method is to firmly strike the side of the steering arm with a hammer (do not hit the ball joint itself). This is usually enough to shock the taper out of the arm.

163

Steering

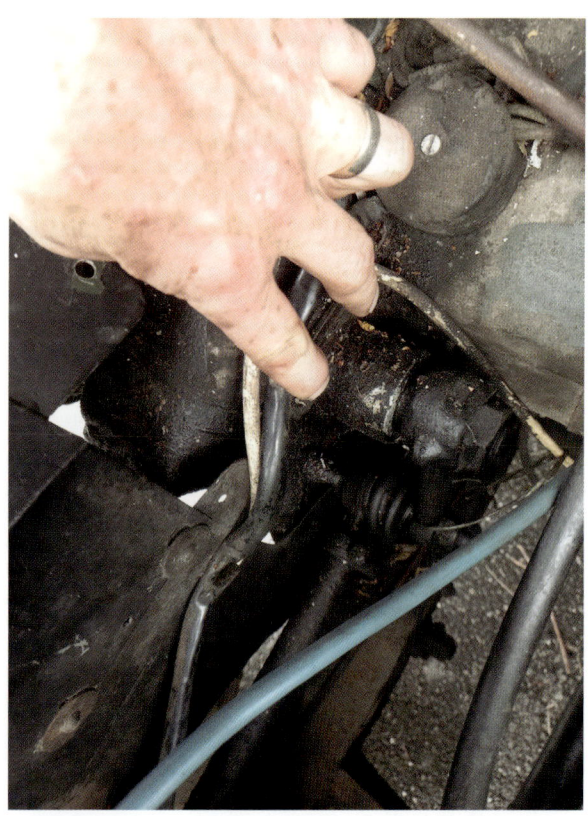

ABOVE LEFT: *Steering box cover removed to check for corrosion damage to the lower mounting lugs.*

ABOVE RIGHT: *These two top mounting bolts screw blind into the casing: early boxes had smaller bolts.*

ABOVE LEFT: *Tyres have clearly been fouling on the springs and chassis here. A Series I is shown here but the same thing happens on any leaf spring model.*

ABOVE RIGT: *Check the steering relay drop arm for security: the bolt often works loose leading to play at the steering wheel.*

- If putting the steering rod back on without further repairs to the steering system, measure the centre-to-centre length to ensure the rod goes back the same length. This will ensure the tracking remains the same and the steering wheel position remains the same. If multiple changes need to be made, *see* the section below on steering set-up.
- If you are lucky a ball joint will unscrew easily from the tube, but more often than not it will be firmly seized in place. Loosen the clamp bolt and knock it along the tube. Clamp the tube in the vice and use an appropriately sized ring spanner as a lever to unscrew the ball joint.
- If the joint won't turn, there are a few techniques that can help to loosen them. Place the tube on a solid surface like the anvil section of the vice and strike the outside of the threaded section to shock it loose, turning as you go. Heating the area with a blowlamp can also help, as can soaking in penetrating oil. If at all concerned about any damage or corrosion, the steering rod should be replaced – after all, your life may depend on it.

Steering

ABOVE LEFT: *Striking the steering arm to shock a ball joint loose is quick and usually very effective.*

ABOVE RIGHT: *Shocking the track rod to help release a seized ball joint shank.*

Using a large ring spanner to unwind the ball joint from the track rod.

Replacing the Ball Joints

Once the ball joint or joints are out, inspect the threads in the rod for damage and corrosion. If the threads are dirty, they can be cleaned out using an old ball joint with slits cut in it.

Note that there are two different types of ball joint threaded sections. Early types had a plain shank round where the clamp pinches and a corresponding plain unthreaded section on the track rod/steering tube. The later type is threaded throughout the full length of the ball joint and steering tube. It is advisable not to mix and match these different types and failures have been reported. Note also that because Land Rovers are often chopped and changed, you cannot easily trust a year-model cut-off point. You will need to inspect every tube to confirm which one you need.

- Put a good smear of copper grease on the threads before winding the ball joint in. If replacing both ball joints, wind both of them fully in, then wind both out the same number of threads to match the previously recorded length.
- Refit the steering rod to the vehicle, tightening the ball joint nuts and replace the split pins. The turning force from the steering box is transferred on the taper, not on

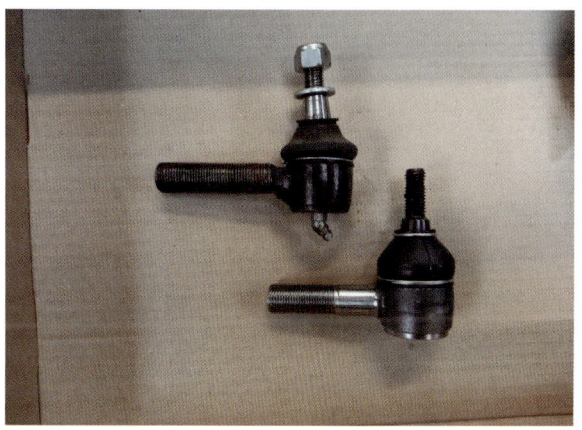

ABOVE LEFT: *An old ball joint with grooves cut in the shank is ideal to clean out track rod threads.*

ABOVE RIGHT: *Later type fully threaded and early type semi-threaded ball joints should not be mixed.*

Steering

ABOVE LEFT: *Original type castle nut (split pin must be fitted). Modern nyloc types are also available.*

ABOVE RIGHT: *Using a pair of Stilsons to adjust the length of the steering rods.*

the threaded section, but the nut should be tight and shake-proof (hence the split pin or a nyloc nut). Confirm the length of the rod and tighten the clamps.
- When adjusting the length of the rod on the vehicle, a pair of Stilsons, Footprint or a self-grip wrench will be required to turn the rod unless the ball joint threads are well lubricated.
- Note that it is possible to replace a rubber boot on an otherwise good ball joint. This can be a cost-effective alternative to replacing the whole ball joint. The retaining rings/springs can be fiddly though.

STEERING RELAY

Assessing the Steering Relay

The steering relay is bolted into a tube in the front crossmember with two long 5/16in bolts at the top and a retainer plate on the bottom held in place by four ¼in bolts. The relay is filled with EP90 oil on fitment, but over the years they do leak. Stiff or vague steering that cannot be attributed to other factors can often be traced to the steering relay. In addition, the split bushes and shaft inside do wear leading to slop and backlash.

- To assess the condition of the steering relay, get an assistant to rock the steering side to side while you feel and observe any play: play will be down to worn Tufnol bushes and/or shaft, requiring a strip-down and an overhaul or replacement.
- To assess the smoothness of the operation, remove the top steering arm and turn the bottom arm by hand (having removed the drag link ball joint), feeling for a smooth, damped action. Expect it to have some resistance but it should be a continuous action, not stiff and lumpy.
- Stiffness will usually be down to a low oil level, which can be topped up with EP90. Some have a fill hole on the top for this purpose. Alternatively, it can be filled through one of the top plate bolt holes; remove two to allow air to escape as you fill with either a syringe or a narrow-tubed pump. It's not a quick process.

Removing the Steering Relay

Removing the relay from the chassis is technically very simple, but it is very common for the body to have corroded into the chassis tube. With the bolts removed and the bottom mounting plate off, it *should* be possible to rock it out. In reality, it is likely to have seized firmly in place.

Get plenty of penetrating oil in advance and try to remove any loose corrosion jamming the sides with an air line. Applying pressure with a jack underneath (with care) might also assist.

An air chisel or even SDS drill on hammer stop can be used to carefully rattle away rust round the edges but be careful not to damage the chassis round the tube and attachment points. If all fails a press frame and a bottle jack can be used to press it out or, if the decision has been made to replace it, the relay can be broken up and taken out in pieces. Note the warning below about the internal spring before breaking it up.

Rebuilding a Steering Relay

The relay consists of a cast casing with a closure plate top and bottom. The splined shaft that transfers rotational force runs in split conical Tufnol bushes top and bottom. The large, compressed spring under significant tension sits between the two with thrust washers each end.

If the plan is to retain the original relay, it is possible to rebuild it with new bushes and seals, either on the bench or in place in the chassis, if removal is proving problematic. Do be aware that once the top plate bolts are removed, the spring may pop up with significant force with the potential to cause injury. The spring is likely to be stuck in the casing and bush and may not release straightaway, but when it does let go it will travel a significant distance with great force. A special tool is available to compress/decompress the spring, although a home-made version can be made.

Replacing the Steering Relay

To avoid potential future problems, thoroughly smear the new/rebuilt steering relay and the inside of the chassis tube with copper grease. Inspect the chassis tube thoroughly,

Steering

ABOVE LEFT: *Remove two of the steering relay bolts to top up the oil with a syringe (use EP90).*

ABOVE RIGHT: *The notorious steering relay removal task. Most are rusted in like this and can be a challenge to remove.*

ABOVE LEFT: *Steering relays can be rebuilt, but heed the warning about the compressed spring inside.*

ABOVE RIGHT: *Always fit the steering relay with a generous smear of copper grease.*

too. It is common for them to corrode out and weaken the chassis. This must be repaired before proceeding with fitting the relay – it's usually a reasonably straightforward welding job with the appropriate skills and the correct internal diameter tube.

Once inserted, refit with the top bolts and bottom plate: note that the flat boss on the side should face away from the radiator. The bottom plate must be a snug fit to avoid any lateral movement; oversize plates are available if play is excessive. The steering arms on the relay are normally oriented at 90 degrees or fractionally under.

STEERING BOX

Assessing the Steering Box

If working on a complete vehicle, you will need to remove the steering box cover and potentially the under-wing mud shield to fully inspect the steering box and mounting points.

The steering box is fairly robust but does suffer from oil leaks, corrosion and wear to the bearings and bearing track on the shaft. Have an assistant rock the steering and look and feel for wear. Rock the column up and down and look for play in the top bearings/bush. Note that on the Series III, the top bearing is tensioned with a spring held in place by the steering wheel and the indicator cancel tube.

The steering box case is made from aluminium but it can suffer from cor-

Steering

rosion. A deeply pitted steering case is potentially dangerous and fixing points can and do break off. Do not risk a heavily pitted and corroded steering box. If in doubt, have it assessed by a specialist or replace with a better one.

A small amount of play can be adjusted out using the square profile adjustor on the steering box side plate. With the road wheels off the ground (on axle stands or equivalent), back off the outer lock nut and gradually turn it by hand to just remove the free play at the wheel: do not overtighten the adjustor. Retighten the lock nut.

Removing/Replacing the Steering Box

Removing the steering box is straightforward but does involve removing surrounding components, including the driver's wing and mud shield, to gain access.

- Remove the steering wheel. On early vehicles this is held on with a pinch bolt, which must be fully removed before the wheel can be pulled off – a rubber mallet can be used to assist.
- On later vehicles the steering wheel is held on to tapered splines with a nut and lock washer. A puller may be required to remove the later wheels, although a careful strike with a rubber mallet is often enough to remove it. *Do not* hit it hard with a hammer! Additionally, pouring hot water onto the splines can aid removal. Keep the nut on until the wheel has started to move on the spines as this will stop it from pulling free and hitting you in the face.
- The steering wheels are not interchangeable between the early and later types. Note that on most Series II and IIA models you will have to remove the horn push and wiring.
- On the Series III the ignition key barrel/steering lock assembly must be removed. Unless it has previously been removed, the saddle clamp is held in place with shear bolts. These will have to be removed either by drilling or a stud extractor. It is sometimes possible to tap them round using a centre punch and hammer. New shear bolts are available or replace with cap head/security M8 bolts.
- If necessary, the ignition switch can be removed from the back of the key assembly by undoing the two small grub screws. Take care not to lose them and the internal collar and rod.
- Remove the steering column support clamps. On Series II and early IIA there is a spacer plate on the top column bracket to account for the fact that the column comes up at a very slight angle towards the centre of the vehicle. There is a corresponding twist in the upright bracket from the chassis that sets the angle: it looks 'wrong', but it is designed to be there.
- On the Series III, note that the top clamp backing plate is attached to the bulkhead with 5/16th rivet-nuts and these can strip out or pop loose. They can be easily replaced with readily available M8 rivet-nuts.
- If removing the steering box complete with brackets to chassis and bulkhead, there is no need to remove the drop arm and there is just enough room to knock the ball joint off the drop arm. However, the drop arm will need to be removed

Location of the steering box adjustor and locknut: it should just take the backlash out of the steering box.

ABOVE LEFT: *If using a soft mallet to remove the steering wheel, leave this nut on a couple of threads.*

ABOVE RIGHT: *Series III steering lock is held on with two shear bolts.*

Steering

Set the steering wheel straight in the middle position on the box.

LEFT: *Using the correct puller to remove the steering box drop arm.*

ABOVE LEFT: *Set the steering box drop arm pointing vertically down.*

ABOVE RIGHT: *Set the steering relay arms at approximately 90 degrees (slightly less is OK).*

Steering

for any remedial work on the steering box. The arm sits on a tapered spline and is likely to be very tight. Once the lock nut and tab have been removed, a special low profile puller is required. Do not hammer or lever the arm off as this can damage the aluminium casting; invest in the correct puller or borrow one.

- If removing the steering box from the chassis mounting plate, note that two bolts attach into inserts in the casting, two are nuts and bolts on cast lugs. Examine these attachment points carefully for corrosion and cracking.
- Replacing the steering box is the reverse of removal, but note the number of shims removed from the bulkhead attachment points. This sets the position of the steering box in relation to the bulkhead and removal can impact the door/body alignment.
- Note that originally the steering box brace to the bulkhead was fitted with bolts on captive plates on later vehicles, which makes refitting significantly easier. It is common for these to corrode or be misplaced, so many vehicles will be fitted with plain nuts and bolts. This is fine, although fiddly, and they should be fitted with shakeproof washers; better still, buy the correct plates.

Steering Box Overhaul

Overhauling the steering box is fairly straightforward for a competent mechanic. Full rebuild kits are available, although it is fiddly when refitting the individual ball bearings. These can be held in place using thick grease or Vaseline. Note that steering box leaks are common and usually come from the O-ring on the rocker shaft. This can actually be replaced without having to remove the steering box from the vehicle, but does involve removing the drop arm.

There are specialists who will rebuild your steering box if you don't fancy the challenge of fighting all those fiddly ball bearings.

STEERING SETUP

It is vital to set the steering up correctly after a full or partial overhaul of the system. It is not uncommon for steering wheels to be off-centre and for there to be a difference in steering lock between left and right. On 750-16 tyres or larger it is common for the inner edge of the tread to catch on the leaf spring. The easiest approach is to start from the top and work down.

- Set the steering box in the centre position. It's approximately 3½ turns lock to lock, but note the position of the steering wheel and count the turns, returning to the halfway point. Now set the steering wheel in the straight-ahead position on the splines.
- Set the drop arm on the steering box splines in the vertical position.
- Set the length of the top steering rod so the top arm of the steering relay is parallel with (or pointing very slightly forward of) the front crossmember.
- Set the lower steering arm on the relay approximately one spline off 90 degrees (officially noted at 81 degrees) to the top arm.
- Adjust the drag link from lower steering relay arm to forward hole on passenger swivel arm to put the OSF wheel in the straight-ahead position.

Set the drag link to put the OSF wheel in the straight-ahead position.

ABOVE LEFT: *Set the track rod length to give a very slight toe-in.*

ABOVE RIGHT: *Set the lock stops to ensure the tyres do not rub on the springs.*

Power Steering Conversions

Many will argue that a Series Land Rover with well-maintained steering does not require power steering. While there is some truth in that, there are a number of reasons why an owner might choose to convert to power steering: health reasons, the fitment of larger tyres, easier manoeuvring in tight spaces and simply because we have got used to it on modern cars.

Power steering was never fitted to standard Series Land Rovers, although a system was developed for armoured Series IIIs. It is very rare to find this system for sale but there are both aftermarket kits and well-known amateur conversions.

Range Rover P38A Steering Box

This conversion has become more popular in recent years due to the significant number of second-generation Range Rovers being scrapped and broken for parts. The P38A steering box can be bolted via a strengthening plate welded to the outside face of the chassis leg. A standard coil spring steering column can be fitted to existing brackets on the bulkhead and the lower linkages and universal joints can be made up from P38A parts. If a 48-spline steering column is used, a standard Series IIA or III steering wheel can be reused to maintain the original interior look. If a 32-spline column is used, the matching coil spring wheel or an aftermarket wheel can be fitted. A front steering drag link from a first-generation Discovery or Range Rover is often used. A hydraulic pump and reservoir will need to be fitted: this is usually straightforward to fit if a later engine such as a 200Tdi has been fitted as off-the-shelf parts are easy to obtain. An electric hydraulic pump is another option, often sourced from a Vauxhall Astra or Vectra. While this is not an 'off-the-shelf' conversion and does require fabrication skills, many of the parts required are readily available and some specialists will supply a kit. The time, money and skill required to carry out the conversion to a high standard should not be underestimated.

General layout of the P38A steering box in a Series vehicle.

LEFT: *A new chassis modified to take a Range Rover P38A power steering box on the outside face.*

BELOW LEFT: *48-spline Defender steering column supported on a fabricated bracket bolted to the old steering box mounting.*

BELOW RIGHT: *Heystee power steering assistor ram system doesn't require any chassis modifications.*

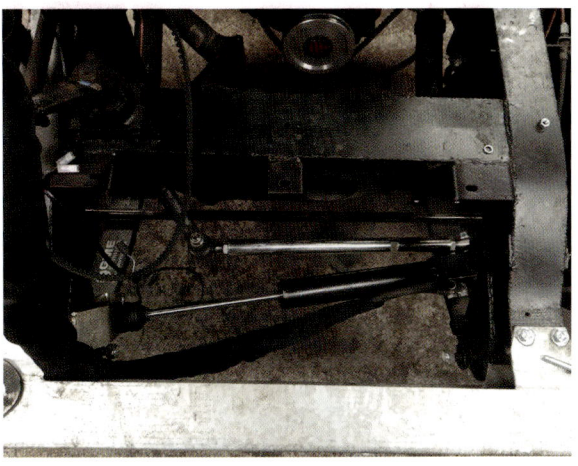

(continued overleaf)

Steering

Power Steering Conversions *continued*

The full Heystee kit comes with a pump, brackets, reservoir and extra pulley required for the power steering.

Hydraulic Assister Kits
Fitting a steering assister kit allows for power steering without modifying the steering system on the vehicle. The kit consists of a replacement drag link with a hydraulic ram that makes the steering easier to turn. The normal steering box and relay remain in place and it is simply the movement of the wheels downstream of the relay that are assisted: as the wheel is turned, a valve on the helper ram is opened and closed. This can be bought as a full kit to be fitted to a standard 2286cc engine or can be bought as individual components as necessary to fit onto an engine conversion. The kit includes a hydraulic pump, reservoir and mounting brackets.

Electric Power Steering
There are specialist companies that will modify a steering box to add electric power assistance. This can be hidden in the dashboard on a Series III and maintains a standard appearance. It comes with a control ECU giving variable assistance. Alternatively, a well-known generic amateur modification is to adapt the steering column to take the electric power steering from a Vauxhall Corsa.

Whatever power steering conversion is fitted, it should be to a high standard and will count as a modification, so should be notified to the insurance company.

- Set the length of the track rod to put the NSF wheel in the straight-ahead position.
- Set the tracking with a tracking gauge or other suitable measuring device to achieve a slight toe-in of 1.2–2.4mm (advisable to have the tracking checked at a garage).
- Remember to tighten all the ball joint clamps, nut, bolts and so on, and ensure all split pins and lock tabs are fitted.
- Adjust the lock stop bolts on the swivels to ensure that the wheels do not hit the springs and that the swivel adjustor bolt hits the stop before the steering box reaches the limit of its internal travel.
- Road test and ensure the lock is the same left and right. If necessary, reset the steering wheel position by adjusting the drag link (or moving the steering wheel on the splines if necessary).

STEERING SWIVEL ASSEMBLIES

As mentioned in the introduction, the condition and adjustment of the swivel assemblies in the front axle are a significant factor in the performance of the steering system. Low oil/grease levels, worn bearings, worn Railco bushes and pins are all too common. These are dealt with comprehensively in Chapter 12.

14
Wheels and Tyres

Series II, IIA and III Land Rovers were fitted with a number of different wheel and tyre combinations over the years. Beyond the Series era, Land Rover wheels gradually evolved, but there is a significant amount of interchangeability of wheels over the decades. Beyond what was done at the factory, there was a growth in the aftermarket wheel industry in the 1980s and 1990s with eight-spoke and modular wheels being a common 'period' modification.

Tyre technology moved on considerably in the early 1980s with cross-ply tyres giving way to radial tyres. Tyres are a vital safety feature on any vehicle so they must be in good condition, compatible for the wheels and suitable for the vehicle, but beyond that there is a lot of personal choice, depending on the desired image.

WHEELS: AN OVERVIEW

Most Series Land Rovers were fitted with 16in steel wheels from the factory. The only exception seems to be for the North American market, where 15in wheels were more common. The original wheels consisted of two pressed sections riveted together at four spoke points. The wheels were made by a number of different manufacturers over the years including Dunlop, RO and KH.

There were a number of different wheel widths and offsets available for different applications, but it was common to change for larger wheels/tyres for looks, off-road performance and raise the gearing.

88in Wheels

The standard wheel for SWB Series Land Rover carried part number 23601 and had a nominal size of 5.00×16 (5in wide and 16in tall). The same part number carried on with minor modifications from 1949 until the very end of Series III production in 1985. The wheel width is designed to carry 6.00×16, 6.50×16 and 7.00×16 tyre sizes. The part number was later superseded by STC3403.

109in Wheels

The standard wheels for a LWB Series IIA Land Rover carried either part

All but NADA (North American Dollar Area) Land Rovers had 16in wheels. Note the 5.5Fx16 stamping on this late Series III rim.

RIGHT: *231601 – the standard 5in SWB wheel for 6.00-16 tyres.*

Wheels and Tyres

272309 – early 5.5in LWB wheel with the same offset as the 231601 with the extra width on the inside.

RIGHT: *560690 or ANR7578 – the later wheel fitted to LWB vehicles (and SWB fitted with LWB tyre sizes). Note the deeper dish.*

number 272309 (1¾in offset) or 569690 (1 5/16in offset) and had a nominal size of 5.50×16. These were designed to carry 7.50×16 tyres. Note that it is common (indeed it was a factory option) for LWB wheels to be fitted to SWB models to allow the fitment of the larger tyre size. Later part number equivalents are listed as NRC7578/ANR4636/FV2000727.

Divided/Split Rims

These were fitted to some military Land Rovers and were also available as an option on civilian models. The design allowed for the two sections of the wheel to be bolted together, allowing for the tyre to be changed without the need for tyre levers. The part number for these wheels is 217267 (SWB) or 517986 (LWB).

Forward Control/1-Ton Wheels

This is a generic term used by enthusiasts to refer to wider, deep-dish rims fitted to a variety of Land Rover's models over the years. The common part numbers are 569203 and 569204 with a later ANR1534 fitted to heavy-duty Land Rovers in the late 1980s. There are small differences in the offset between the part numbers but the general look is very similar. These wheels were originally fitted for heavy-duty applications, such as the 1-Ton and Forward Control vehicles, but it became a popular modification for off-road trials and for the 'chunky' looks. In recent years these wheels have grown in popularity and genuine 569203/569204 rims have become very desirable with a correspondingly high asking price. More recently, a modern equivalent 8×16 has been manufactured and is available at a competitive price.

Tube vs Tubeless Wheels

The original design and construction of Series Land Rover wheels means that tyres should be fitted with inner tubes. This is not only because of the riveted construction but the fact that there is no tyre bead retaining hump. During the coil spring Land Rover era, the construction changed to welding the rim sections together, but these were still designed to be used with an inner tube. It wasn't until later on in the Defender era that the rim pressing was changed to accommodate tubeless tyres. The commonly referenced part numbers for tubeless rims are RRC5036000, 6H12-1007-BC or LR05384. Check with the tyre manufacturer or fitter whether the tyre is compatible with an inner tube: some tyres such as Avon Rangemaster are marked as being compatible with tubes or can be fitted tubeless.

Aftermarket Options

There was (and still is) a range of aftermarket options, commonly eight-spokes and modulars. These are usually manufactured to take tubeless tyres and give a 'period mod' look. They are not to everyone's taste, but they are part of the history of classic Land Rovers and therefore perfectly acceptable on a non-standard vehicle. A number of manufacturers are now offering modern copies/updates of the original Land Rover wheel design, including tubeless wide/deep versions.

Rostyle Wheels

These were fitted to classic Range Rovers and were a common fitment on Series Land Rovers in the 1980s and 1990s, simply for the look. However, they do not fit without modification to clear the drive flanges. It was common to heat them up round the middle and use a heavy hammer to reshape the problem area. Another known

Wheels and Tyres

569204 '1-Ton'/ Forward Control wheels with deep dish designed for 900-16 tyres.

RIGHT: All Series and many later utility Land Rover wheels were designed to run with inner tubes.

BELOW LEFT: Riveted construction on all Series wheels.

BELOW RIGHT: Welded construction on later wheels, but these are not necessarily tubeless.

ABOVE LEFT: Note TR15 valve stem with grooves to allow air to escape from around the inner tube.

ABOVE RIGHT: Narrower TR13 valve fitted with a top hat ferrule to fit the Land Rover wheel.

175

Wheels and Tyres

Rostyle wheels as fitted to the contemporary Range Rover. They were a period mod but need slight modification to fit Series hubs.

LEFT: *Typical aftermarket eight-spoke rim popular in the 1980s and 1990s.*

BOTTOM LEFT: *Tubeless Discovery 1 wheels are a direct fit onto Series hubs.*

BOTTOM RIGHT: *Late Series III wheels were only painted on the outside as a cost-saving exercise.*

modification was to use a hole saw to remove the appropriate area. It is of course inadvisable to do these modifications these days. Most Rostyle wheels were tube-type, although the last ones were tubeless.

Discovery 1 Steel Wheels

These were fitted to base Discovery models from 1989 to 1998 and will fit on Series Land Rovers. They are simple, strong and suitable for tubeless tyres – at the expense of originality. Painted Limestone they can look more in keeping with older vehicles. They offer the benefit of taking a large range of different tyre sizes.

'Wolf' Wheels

These were heavy-duty wheels fitted to military Land Rovers from the 1990s and are incredibly strong. They look good on a Series Land Rover but, because of the thickness of the metal, the wheel nuts do not go on far enough to leave any thread showing. While many enthusiasts simply torque the nuts up tight, it is strongly advisable to fit longer wheel studs, which are readily available.

Wheel Colours

The majority of Series II/IIA and III Land Rover wheels were finished in Limestone paint. However, it would seem that Deep Bronze Green vehicles were fitted with body-coloured wheels until the late 1970s and very early station wagons had body-coloured wheels. There were other variations such as red wheels on fire engines, as well as special builds and company liveries. As cost-saving measures were introduced in the late 1970s, wheels were only painted Limestone on the outside and black/grey primer on the inside. This can be replicated on full rivet-counter Series III builds!

Wheel Dating

Series II and IIA wheels often had a date stamping and a manufacturer's mark as well as the part number. The usual format was a month/date number, such as 6/68 for June 1968. Later wheels tended not to be date stamped and usually had the part number in a smaller font.

Wheel Problems

Land Rover wheels are robust but they do rust. External corrosion is obvious, but internal corrosion less so. Rivet heads can become weakened and rust flakes can cause punctures. It is also important to ensure that the wheel nut holes are round and haven't ovalled from loose wheelnuts. Rims can buckle from off-road damage and a damaged wheel is usually scrap. Unless original to the vehicle and of significant importance, it is usually not worth the effort to execute a safe, professional standard repair and used rims are in good supply. Good-quality aftermarket wheels are available at a reasonable price. Because they come fully finished and ready for tyres, they represent good value for money.

Painting vs Powder Coating

Much of this comes down to personal preference. Having wheels blasted and powder coated usually works out cheaper than having them blasted and painted. However, there is the danger that if powder coat gets damaged, it can lift and corrode underneath. However, the process is evolving with continued improvements in technology, and if well prepared and appropriately primed, there is no reason why it shouldn't be as robust as good paint. Wheels can of course be easily painted by hand and with good preparation a decent quality finish can be achieved.

Current Tyre Options

CLASSIC TYRE OPTIONS

Tyre choice mostly comes down to personal preference and the use to which the vehicle is put. For the period/rivet-counter look, Avon Traction Mile-

---

Tyres: General Period Overview

When Series Land Rovers were being built, cross-ply tyres were the norm for working vehicles: radial tyres became an option in the late 1970s. The County Station Wagon became the first model to have radial tyres as standard in 1982. A number of different tyre size and manufacturer options were available over the years, with tyre options for general purpose, on-road and off-road applications.

SWB: 6.00×16 as standard on 5×16 rims (6.50×16, 7.00×16 and 7.50×16 were optional). 205R16 tyres became available as an approved size in the early 1980s. Guidance stipulated that the 5.5×16 wheel should be used for 7.50×16 and 205R16 tyres.
LWB: 7.50×16 on 5.5×16 rims

Common period tyres fitted by the factory included:

Avon: Traction Mileage (TM), Ranger Mk. 11, Rangemaster (Radial)
Dunlop: RK 3, T29, Road Track Major
Michelin: XY, XZY, Sahara, XCM, XS, M+S (205R16 as used on the Range Rover)
Goodyear: All Service, Sure Grip, Hi-Miler, Xtra Grip

Common classic in-service tyres included:

General SAG (Super All Grip), Firestone SAT (Super All Traction), Regent Newcraft

Original specification Avon Traction Mileage tyres complete the classic show look.

RIGHT: There are numerous companies remaking the classic Goodyear Xtra Grip and Xtra Traction tread types.

Wheels and Tyres

age tyres are now being reproduced in some sizes and very good copies of the Michelin M+S Radial (Range Rover/88in County Station Wagon) are available. Genuine and modern copies of the Goodyear Xtra Grip are readily available and look particularly good on Military Lightweight models. Avon Rangemaster tyres are readily available in 750R16 size and while this was only available at the end of Series production, it is an in-keeping option. Many classic owners choose to fit Michelin XZL or Goodyear G90 tyres, both military options on 90/110 models.

Modern Tyre Options

Modern radial tyres may not offer the same 'classic' look but will usually offer far superior performance than the older options. Tyre choice should be based on the use to which the vehicle is put, but there is no doubt that many of us choose the tyre based on looks rather than pure function. 205R16 is the common replacement size for 600-16 or 650-16 and 235 85 R16 is the usual modern equivalent for the 750-16. Check out the tyre manufacturer's specification regarding the minimum rim width required for modern tyres, as it may be that a wider rim than a standard Series 5.5in is necessary: 6in is the usual quoted minimum for 235 85 R16.

Safety and Legislation First

Note that old tyres do perish, crack and go hard with UV light, so a decision to keep or replace must be based on safety and any local legislation. Hard, classic tread tyres can be absolutely lethal in the wet. Open-tread tyres are particularly prone to cracking between the tread blocks, sometimes revealing the plies below, especially having been sat with weight on them. Side walls on all tyres perish and crack over time.

Note that cross-ply and radial tyres should not be mixed on the same axle. It is deemed acceptable to have cross-ply on the front axle and radial on the rear axle, but tyre construction should only be mixed in exceptional circumstances. It is always best practice to have all matching tyres on a vehicle to give predictable handing. Land Rover did advise swapping tyres round as part of a regular service routine.

ABOVE LEFT: *6.00-16 is a cross-ply tyre and must not be mixed with radial tyres.*

ABOVE RIGHT: *7.50R16 – R denotes radial construction.*

ABOVE LEFT: *Modern tyres have date of manufacture codes: WC4918 is December 2018.*

ABOVE RIGHT: *Tyres like this are clearly unsafe to use on the road.*

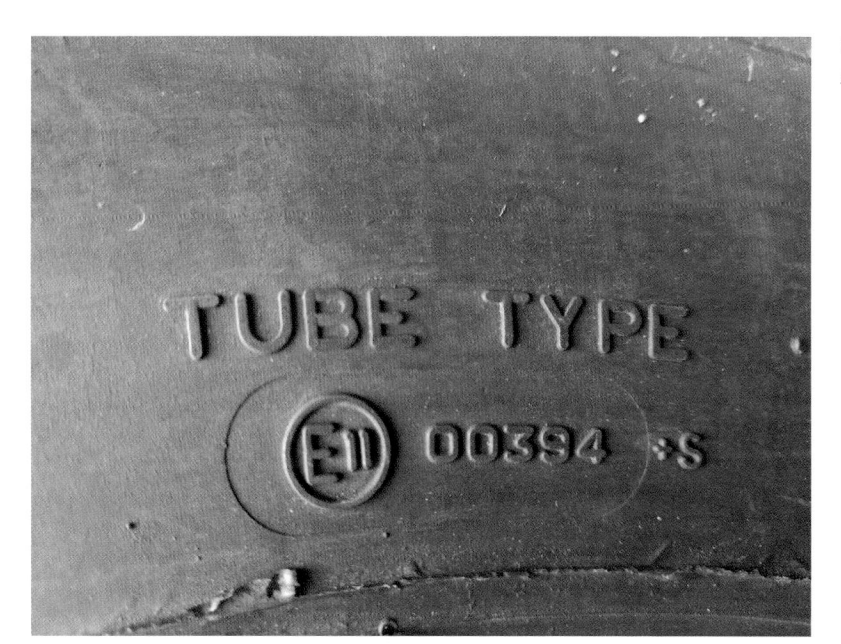

This Avon Rangemaster is marked Tube Type: some can be run tubeless.

Tyres in the UK need to have a minimum tread depth of 1.6mm across the central three-quarters of the tyre, no bulges and no cuts through to the inner plies. At the time of writing, age restrictions did not apply to non-commercial historical vehicles, but owners should carry out their own research: depending on the age of the vehicle, number of seats and registration details, age restrictions might apply and legislation does change. Irrespective of legalities, safety has to come first. Just because a vehicle might be exempt from some legislation, it is not exempt from the laws of physics.

Date Markings on Tyres

Tyres have required manufacture date codes since the early 1970s. Commonly known as DoT markings, the code has a week and year identifier. This usually a 4-digit code denoting ww/yy (or ww/y for older tyres). For example, 4419 would be the 44th week of 2019.

Fitting and Balancing Tyres

It is possible to fit tyres on a DIY basis but it can a challenge and could risk damage to tyres and inner tubes. In the grand scheme of things, it is usually safer, easier and cost-effective to ask a friendly local garage to do the work for a nominal fee. While Land Rovers are pretty crude and seldom driven fast, balancing is advisable, although many owners choose not to without significant ill effect.

15 Suspension

Basic leaf springs are part of the charm of a Series Land Rover and very few changes were made throughout production. The system comprises a semi-elliptical spring made up of a pack of leaves with a swinging shackle at the rear of each spring. The spring is attached to the chassis and shackles by steel-encased rubber bushes to allow rotational and lateral flex. The spring rebound is controlled by oil-filled telescopic dampers (the technical word for shock absorbers) at each wheel.

Land Rover retained the leaf spring system from the Series I because it was simple yet effective for a working vehicle at the time. Coil springs arrived with the launch of the One Ten in 1983 and Ninety in 1984. This represented a significant development in comfort and off-road ability, although there was opposition from some traditional customers who craved the simplicity of leaf springs. When in good condition, leaf springs offer a firm but not unduly uncomfortable ride. If your vehicle is rock solid then the problem is not so much the design but the condition and quality of the components.

ASSESSING YOUR SUSPENSION

Ride On- and Off-Road

Driving down the road, the vehicle should not crash around and there should be no need to wince every time you see a pothole. There should, however, be no creaking or knocks from underneath: it is not unknown for vehicles that are used infrequently to make some strange noises as the springs free off. Off tarmac, the ride will be firm over bumpy ground but should not rattle your teeth out. If in doubt, drive a known well-sorted vehicle and compare it to your own. The issue often comes from inexperience: if you have only every driven your own vehicle, you have no reference point. Land Rover's own Chief Engineer actually commented that the 'longevity of the Land Rover was related to the discomfort of the driver', that is, firm springs made you slow down for your own comfort before the vehicle broke. However, there should be no need for undue discomfort when travelling at an appropriate speed for the ground.

Walk Round Inspection

Park the vehicle unladen on level ground and walk around it. Does it sit level? Does the vehicle droop down at the back? Is it lopsided? Get a tape measure out and compare corresponding heights either side: the official variation was up to 1in difference. The original design of the vehicle was to have a slightly greater 'free camber' on the RHS side to compensate for the extra weight of driver and fuel tank, so this needs to be factored in. Have a look at the angle of the swing-

Leaf springs needn't give a hard ride and poor travel. It's usually down to maintenance and set-up.

Suspension

ing shackles: on the front it should sit approximately vertical or very slightly backwards, at the rear it should be angled approximately 30 degrees backwards. If the visual inspection raises issues, it's time to get underneath to explore further. An inspection ramp is a significant advantage when it comes to underbody inspection and replacement of suspension components, but it is possible on good solid ground.

Leaf Spring Inspection

Leaf springs by their very nature are prone to seizing with steel leaves clamped together. Are the leaves rusty from lack of use? If so, a good drive on rough roads may well start to loosen things up. Multi-leaf springs benefit from being used. If they are sat up for a long time, especially at an angle or weighted down, they can become seized in an 'unnatural' position. As springs start to move they can make some alarming noises, but as long as there's nothing loose, the clonks and choppy ride should gradually subside. Opinion is divided regarding oiling and or greasing springs between leaves, but it certainly reduces the possibility of them seizing. Drivers in trials competitions have long lubricated their springs to improve off-road performance and there is actually a special tool that can be used to separate leaves to lubricate between them.

Have the leaves started to blow apart? This is very common on vehicles that have been sat up for many years. This is not instantly a reason to scrap the springs, but a significant factor in deciding on the best course of action. Blown leaf spring packs can be recommissioned by dismantling, removing corrosion and reassembling, although it is time-consuming without guaranteed results. Commercially this doesn't really make sense, but for a DIY enthusiast it can be viable. Springs can also be reset and fully reconditioned to factory specification by specialists if there is a desire to retain the original springs.

Have any of the leaves cracked or fractured? Individual leaves can be replaced, but if more than one has failed it is likely that the tempering process has been compromised during manufacture and replacement is the only

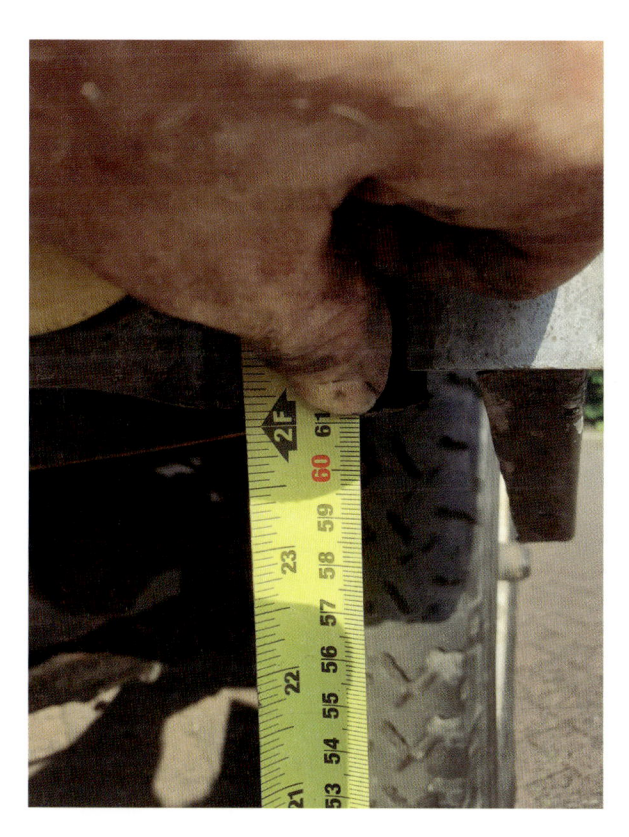

Front swinging shackle should sit approximately vertically with the vehicle on level ground.

LEFT: *Measuring the difference in height side to side on the ends of the crossmember: the factory guideline variation was 1in.*

BELOW LEFT: *Signs of a worn spring on the 109in, although the angle of the shackle is not too far out.*

BELOW RIGHT: *A healthy angle for the rear spring shackle on this 88in.*

Suspension

ABOVE LEFT: *This 11-leaf spring has clearly started to blow apart although the ride characteristics were actually OK.*

ABOVE RIGHT: *Same spring again: this leaf has clearly started to thin at the end of the leaves*

option. Have the leaves started to thin at the ends due to rubbing over time?

Inspect the spring bushes – have they started to crack? Do the springs sit twisted in the shackles? Get a pry bar on the end of the spring and look for any play. If so, replacement is required and can be a time-consuming job, especially when removing the bushes from the chassis.

Damper Inspection

Inspect the shock absorbers/dampers. Are they wet? As seals fail, oil can mist out, reducing their effectiveness. Are the top tube covers in good condition? Have they started to corrode? This doesn't affect their functionality per se, but does increase the likelihood of wear, plus it looks uncared for.

Grab and twist the body of the damper to assess the condition of the bushes. These are held in at the bottom with large washers and heavy-duty split pins: these are frequently replaced with a variety of functional alternatives like nails and staples. 109in rear dampers are fitted with a lower pin and nut and the lower bushes seem particularly prone to wear, and the nut is difficult to access when corroded in place. If carrying out a strip-down, pull the damper through the full length of its travel feeling for resistance. It should offer reasonable and consistent resistance on extension. If in doubt, replace.

Chassis/Suspension Mounting Point Inspection

Ensure that the dumb irons are solid – it's a common rot point on a chassis. Also check whether the dumb irons have been replaced badly. Assess the condition of the welding and whether they sit square to each other. It's not uncommon for them to be fitted squint and some aftermarket repair sections are not to the original profile, leading to either misaligned suspension or a misaligned bumper. Check the rear spring hangers for rot and poor repairs. If they are suspect, measure the distance from the forward mounting point on both sides. On a 109in the forward rear spring hanger outriggers are a common rot point and poor quality repairs are all too common. Obviously the geometry and safety of your suspension system depends on the condition of the chassis.

U-Bolt Mountings

Each spring is attached to the axle by a pair of U-bolts. Ensure these are in good condition and that they are tight. The whole sprung weight of the vehicle sits on just eight of these bolts, so it is essential they are correctly fitted and torqued up. It is common for them to

ABOVE LEFT: *A mist of oil clearly shows this damper is starting to fail and is ready for replacement.*

ABOVE RIGHT: *The dumb iron on this 88in had corroded to the point of allowing the suspension to droop.*

Suspension

ABOVE LEFT: This poorly executed crossmember and spring mount repair meant this Series III sat lopsided.

ABOVE RIGHT: U-bolts should be trimmed down as necessary to avoid catching off road.

Multi-Leaf Spring Options

While the basic design of Land Rover leaf springs remained the same, there were a variety of different ratings and number of leaves for different applications as well as variations for left- and right-hand sides.

Model	Leaves	RH Part No.	LH Part No.
Front Springs			
88in Petrol	9 leaves	241283	242863
88in Diesel	11 leaves	265627	264563
109in Petrol	11 leaves	265627	264563
109in Diesel	11 leaves	265627	264563
Rear Springs			
88in Normal Duty	11 leaves	517588	517589
88in Air Portable/HD	7 leaves	562631	562632
109in SW	8+2 leaves	279678	279679
109in HD	9 leaves	535173	535173

If sticking with standard leaf springs, buy the best quality you can afford. Depending on use and possible engine changes, choose the most appropriate for your vehicle use. Station Wagon springs give a softer ride until the extra 'helper' leaves come into play. 11-leaf front springs are quite firm, so some choose the 9-leaf 88in petrol option, irrespective of engine fitted and wheelbase. Land Rovers can be finely tuned to people's needs and modifications, but if you're going for originality, choose the 'correct' springs, after all they were built that way for a reason.

work slightly loose after fitting, so they should be retorqued after a test drive to settle the leaves. Check for any off-road damage: the bolts are the lowest point on the vehicle and impacts can bend and fracture them. Bolts should be trimmed so the minimum number of threads protrude below the nut.

PARABOLIC SPRINGS

Parabolic springs were fitted to Santana (Spanish licence-built) Land Rovers in the 1980s and have been commonly available as an aftermarket option since the 1990s. The spring design has fewer leaves and the leaves taper towards the ends, meaning less interleaf friction than standard multi-leaf springs and allowing for more flex. Many owners swear by them, although traditionalists tend to dislike them. It's fair to say they have their pros and cons. Many owners who fit parabolics have moved on from worn-out multi-leaf springs and feel the vehicle has been transformed. However, a similar transformation could possibly have been achieved with new, good-quality multi-leaf springs. Most trials drivers prefer light-duty parabolic springs to maximise axle travel. Many have finely tuned them to their application by experimenting with different manufacturers, different leaf numbers and different shock absorbers. Much of this comes down to personal choice, the use to which you put your vehicle, your budget and the degree of originality you want to achieve.

- Generally speaking, parabolic springs give a slightly higher ride height and many owners like the slightly lifted look. The downside is that there is the potential to require longer shock absorbers and, if too high, it can cause standard shock absorbers to top out, giving a very harsh and choppy ride. In addition, significant extra height can create problems with rear propshaft angles, resulting in premature wear or undue noise.
- Parabolics tend to give a softer ride and more flex off road. This is an advantage when it comes to trying to keep wheels on the ground on undulating terrain. The downside is that this can cause problems when cornering and carrying heavier weights.
- Parabolics have fewer leaves that only touch in the middle and ends, meaning less interleaf friction and less likelihood of corroding together. The downside is that with engine upgrades it can cause spring wrap under extreme torque

Suspension

Parabolic springs can offer softer ride characteristics and require less maintenance than a multi-leaf spring.

situations. Parabolic springs are available with different numbers of leaves for different applications, just like multi-leaf options, so it is important to consider the most common use the vehicle is going to be put to.

REVIVING OLD SPRINGS

If springs have started to blow apart or become seized together, they might be revivable if originality is desirable or budgets are low. Heat and bend back the spring clamps (or unbolt on the removable type) and undo the centre pin. Use a G-clamp to compress the leaves while you do this and then gently release the pressure. The individual leaves can be fully separated and cleaned up. This could be done on a wire wheel, using a flap disc or sandblasting. After painting, they can be reassembled with some lubricant between the leaves for added protection and flexibility. Again, use G-clamps to compress the leaves while you reassemble them and refit the centre nut and bolt. The clamps can be hammered round into place with a heavy-duty hammer on a solid surface.

CHANGING SPRING/ CHASSIS BUSHES

It is fair to say that fitting spring bushes is not high on the list of most people's favourite jobs.

- Spring bushes can usually be pressed out of the spring eye with a hydraulic press and an appropriately sized drift. Press the new bushes in with an appropriate drift that allows it to press on the outer section of the bush. An appropriate-sized socket can usually be used, although a specially turned drift with a recess is more accurate. If a press is not available, *see* the techniques below.
- Chassis bushes are very likely to be seized in the chassis tubes and impossible to knock out. A well-tried technique is to use an appropriately sized hole saw (without the pilot drill) to cut the rubber section out, thus removing the inner tube. This is also particularly useful when a bolt has seized in the bush, necessitating cutting the bolt to remove the spring.
- In the absence of a hole saw, a drill bit (a wood bit seems to work best) can be used to chain drill round the rubber section of the bush.
- An old school trick was to burn the rubber out, but this is certainly not advised these days: the hole saw trick is quicker, cleaner and more environmentally sound.
- The outer sleeve can then be cut out of the chassis using a hacksaw

A hydraulic press makes removing and fitting spring bushes significantly easier.

RIGHT: *A specially turned drift for inserting chassis bushes without damaging them.*

Suspension

ABOVE LEFT: *A die grinder or hacksaw blade can be used to remove the inner bush sleeve.*

ABOVE RIGHT: *Polyurethane bushes are significantly easier to fit at the expense of originality.*

- or die grinder. Make a couple of cuts, ensuring you don't damage the chassis, and then use a chisel to collapse the sleeve.
- Ensure you clean the tube in the spring hanger thoroughly: a small drill-operated reamer is ideal. New bushes can be fitted with a length of heavy-duty threaded bar, ensuring you press against the outside sleeve of the bush, not the inner – otherwise you're likely to damage the rubber.
- A well-fitting bush should pull in reasonably easily and indeed can often be driven in using an appropriate drift. Never hit it hard or you will 'mushroom' the bush, causing it to bind hard and potentially damage the chassis.
- Some aftermarket bushes might need to be slightly fettled to fit well: a light trim in a lathe is not an uncommon necessity. Stop, remove and take more off if you think a bush is binding significantly as it goes in. It won't get any easier but it will definitely get worse! Some light oil will assist fitting – hitting very hard won't!
- The bush through the chassis rail on the rear of the front spring can be a challenge to fit due to binding from the increased surface area. There are two versions, a full length and a split version. The split version is easier to fit and a full-length one can be cut in half to facilitate fitting.
- 'Poly bushes' made out of polyurethane with separate steel inserts are significantly easier to fit than standard 'metalasitic' ones and can be pushed in with simple tools or, indeed, often by hand. Again, they have their pros and cons/lovers and haters. Some replacement chassis are supplied pre-fitted with them because they are easier to fit in a galvanised chassis. If there is a desire to maintain the 'factory' look, black ones can be fitted.

Whatever you choose, choose the best-quality bushes you can afford – OEM and genuine parts usually fit more easily.

REPLACING COMPLETE SPRINGS

Removing Springs

If springs are to be replaced, it is advisable to soak all old fixings prior to carrying out the work. All fixings should be cracked off with the weight on the ground and significant leverage may be required. An impact/rattle gun is a useful tool, especially on shackle bolts.

- If shackle bolts are tight but 'bouncy', it is likely that the bolt has become bush bound (seized in the bush) and very often the only option is to cut the bolt. A thin slitting disc or hacksaw/reciprocating saw run down the side, avoiding damage to the chassis, may be the only option.
- Replacing the springs is straightforward on a two-post vehicle ramp. With the vehicle lifted on the chassis rails, the axle can be supported on a transmission stand/jack and the springs removed and replaced in turn.
- If only replacing the leaf spring, you can usually leave the shock absorber attached to the bottom plate and twist it out of the way. If you encounter problems leaving them on or intend to replace the whole system, obviously remove them (*see* below).
- If replacing the spring on the ground, never put any part of your body under the vehicle if it is only supported on a jack. Ensure the vehicle is on level ground and use appropriately rated axle stands. It is easier to replace one spring at a time unless you choose to remove the whole axle for other works.
- A useful trick is to lift the vehicle high enough to take the weight off the spring and support the chassis at that height on an axle stand. Leave the wheel on and then remove the U-bolts and mounting plate while supporting the weight of the spring on a jack to control any remaining tension.
- Once the spring has been unbolted from the axle, it can be unbolted from the chassis.

Refitting Springs

- When refitting, hang the new spring in place on the chassis with the shackles and bolts, but do not tighten them at this stage.
- Place the bottom mounting plate on a jack and raise it to push the

185

Suspension

spring back up to the location hole on the bottom of the axle.
- Roll the wheel, which will just be touching the ground, to align the centre pin into the location hole on the axle before refitting the U bolts.
- An alternative method of lining up the centre pin is to use a socket and ratchet on the spring shackle bolt. Nip up the bolt into the shackle plate and use it a leverage point to pull the spring into place.
- Refit the shock absorber bottom fixings as necessary.
- Do not tighten the shackle and U-bolts fully during the initial fitting process. Doing so can put undue tension in the bushes and bind the suspension, causing the vehicle to sit lopsided.
- With the vehicle on the ground, rock the vehicle side to side to allow the springs and bushes to settle. If off the public highway, take a short drive to settle everything into place. Park on level ground and fully tighten the shackle bolts and U-bolts.

If doing a full chassis-up rebuild, it is often easier to fit the springs to a rolling axle. Turn the axle over so the underside is upward and the weight of the spring can then rest on the axle. Once the spring is fitted with bottom plate and U-bolts, it's not unduly heavy to flip it over with assistance so the axle can be rolled under the chassis.

New springs should have part numbers on them or marked offside/nearside. It is important to fit the springs to the correct side due to greater free camber on the offside. If fitting used springs with no markings or parabolic springs that aren't marked as handed, fit the spring with the greatest free camber on the offside. To measure the camber, put a straight edge between the bushes and measure to the top of the leaf pack.

ABOVE LEFT: *Using a transmission jack to support the weight of the axle while the spring is removed.*

ABOVE RIGHT: *Always smear copper grease on the shackle bolts – you or the next owner will thank you for it.*

ABOVE LEFT: *Lowering the axle case down to locate the spring centre bolt on the bottom of the axle case.*

ABOVE RIGHT: *A socket and ratchet on the swinging shackle bolt can be used to flex the spring to assist in locating the centre bolt.*

ABOVE LEFT: If fitting springs to a bare axle, it is far easier to turn it upside down like this, then flip it over when the springs are on.

ABOVE RIGHT: Note springs are normally 'handed'. If the part number is not visible, the spring with the greater camber fits on the driver's side.

DAMPERS/SHOCK ABSORBERS

Choosing Shock Absorbers/Dampers

Original shock absorbers were simple oil-filled units, often manufactured by companies such as Girling, Woodhead and Unipart. Some would not have had any internal buffers at full extension and so the rear units were protected by heavy-duty canvas straps to limit downward travel. Modern dampers usually have internal buffers, so many owners choose not to fit axle straps. However, they are original fitment, do offer additional protection in extreme situations and just look right on an original vehicle. For 'rivet counter' reference, OEM Woodhead and Genuine Rover shocks were usually blue, later OEM Unipart ones were red. While a damper is just a damper and just a functional item, getting the little details right is a nice touch if undertaking a full concourse or original patina restoration.

A broad range of aftermarket and OEM dampers are available. Usually it is advisable to pay extra for quality, but even budget dampers seem to perform remarkably well. Modern options also include gas shocks that have better cooling properties and reduce oil foaming in extreme situations, such as driving at higher speeds on corrugated roads. Extended shock absorbers are often required for parabolic springs due to the usual greater free camber. Many manufacturers and suppliers have their own recommended spring/damper combination.

Removing Shock Absorbers

This is usually straightforward, although the lower split pins can corrode in place. If they won't pull out, cut the ends off with an angle grinder. The remains of the split pin can then be drifted out with an appropriate punch or drilled out. On a 109in, the bottom of the rear shock absorber is attached by a nyloc nut: access is poor and it's very likely to be seized. A self-gripping wrench or water pump pliers can be used to counter-hold or turn the body of the shock absorber when removing the nut, but if this doesn't work easily, a die grinder is a useful tool to remove the bottom nut. Don't waste time trying to be too polite to it – you'll be replacing it anyway!

Refitting Shock Absorbers

This is a simple but occasionally challenging task. It is advisable to extend and compress the shock absorbers fully a number of times before fitting. The hardest job is compressing the rubber bushes while fitting the large washer and split pin on the bottom. The easiest option is to cut a pair of slots into an appropriately sized socket to accommodate the split pin and use a G-clamp to compress it. Alternatively, a wide-throat welding clamp can often be used. A smear of red rubber grease or soapy water can also assist in compressing the bush sufficiently. On the 109in rear shocks, water pump pliers may be required to counter-hold the body of the shock while the bottom nut is tightened. Tighten until the lower bushes are slightly compressed and two to three threads show below the nyloc nut.

It is not uncommon for shock absorbers to appear too short when fitting to a vehicle that has no engine, gearbox or body on. It may be necessary to wait until the vehicle is more complete or, if very close to reaching, use a sash clamp to compress the spring sufficiently to fit it.

Axle straps being fitted to an 88in. Note the sash clamp to compress the new unladen spring for fitting.

Suspension

Access to the bottom of the 109in rear shock is tight: a chisel or die grinder might be required to break the nut.

LEFT: *Using a welding clamp to compress the bush when fitting the lower shock absorber split pin.*

Low Rider?

Note that there was an official height between the top of the axle and the bottom of the chassis rail above the bump stop, and it is actually lower than many people imagine. As said, parabolic springs tend to make the vehicle sit a little higher than standard and many of us have simply become accustomed to the taller look, which makes a standard vehicle look tail-heavy.

The official measurements from the top of the axle to the bottom of the chassis rail on an unladen vehicle are:

| 88in | Front | 112mm | Rear | 144mm |
| 109in | Front | 120mm | Rear | 160mm |

ABOVE LEFT: *Checking the front spring height on the 109in: at 100mm, this is sitting about 20mm low, suggesting the spring is getting tired.*

ABOVE RIGHT: *Checking the rear spring height on a 109in: at 165mm, this is pretty much perfect.*

16
Braking System

Tradition has it that Land Rover brakes are poor both in terms of design and reliability. This is a myth that has developed over time due to worn-out components, poor maintenance, poor adjustment and substandard parts. When in good condition and properly set up, there is no good reason why standard Land Rover brakes shouldn't be perfectly adequate and capable of stopping your vehicle promptly in a straight line. Having said that, you cannot expect the performance to match that of a modern vehicle and regular maintenance is required to keep them in top condition. Drum brakes are poor when wet and do suffer from brake fade when hot. They also need to be adjusted as the shoes wear and are prone to brake lining contamination from leaking hub seals. Vehicles that are used infrequently also suffer from rusty drums, stuck shoes and seized hydraulic components leading to poor performance and leaks. This chapter covers assessment, adjustment and maintenance through to full system replacement, upgrades and troubleshooting.

GENERAL OVERVIEW

Series Land Rover service brakes comprise front and rear drums with friction shoes operated by wheel cylinders pressurised by a master cylinder operated by the brake pedal. The parking brake or handbrake operates on a drum with friction shoes on the output shaft of the transfer box and is controlled by a mechanical lever via a rod and relay system. In good condition, both the service brake and parking brake were perfectly adequate and appropriate for the performance of the vehicle both on and off road given the technology of the era. There were gradual upgrades to the braking system during the Series III era, many of which were later fitted to earlier vehicles: these include twin leading shoes, twin line systems and servo assistance. While improved braking performance is welcome, it can create issues when working out what has been fitted to your Land Rover. In addition, a mix and match approach to components doesn't always produce the best results.

ASSESSING THE PERFORMANCE OF THE SYSTEM

Service Brake

On an assessment drive, the vehicle should be able to stop promptly in a straight line before the brake pedal runs out of free travel. Pumping the brake pedal should not be required. The pedal should feel firm and progressive, not spongy, slack or snatchy. The ultimate test is to have the vehicle assessed on rollers as used at an MOT garage as this will show not only the braking effort at each wheel but show any imbalance across the axle. If found wanting, the braking system is likely to require adjustment, overhaul or complete replacement.

Parking Brake

The parking brake cannot be assessed in the usual way on a rolling road, since because it works on the transmission output this would put excessive strain on the system. Attempting to move off with the parking brake applied will give a reasonable assessment of its performance. Most problems of inefficiency are due to oil contamination on the friction shoes from a leaking rear gearbox output seal.

REMOVING BRAKE DRUMS AND SHOES

Workshop safety is vital. While asbestos is no longer in new brake components, be aware that older vehicles may still have asbestos linings. Do not blow brake dust, ensure a well-ventilated environment, use soapy water to damp down brake dust and wear an appropriate mask.

- With the vehicle appropriately supported on axle stands and the relevant wheel removed, the brake shoe adjustor cams need to be backed all the way off. Note there are two on 11in drums on LWB and late SWB models, but only one on 10in drums.
- Brake drums are held on with (usually three) countersunk grub screws. These are likely to have seized in place and may require an impact screwdriver to remove. An appropriate-sized cold chisel can also assist to shock the grub screw before unscrewing with a wide-blade screwdriver.
- Drums often stick in place and these can often be freed off using a copper or hide-faced hammer. Do not hammer hard on the fragile edges of the cast drums as these can damage easily. A grub screw can be screwed into the threaded hole in the drum to help pry it off. You might need to take your time to carefully work the drum off.
- With the drum off, inspect for wear on the friction surface. In particular, be aware of deep scoring. Drums can be machined within the wear tolerances as marked on the drums or replaced with quality new or good used ones.
- Take careful note of the position and orientation of the shoe springs before you remove them. Reference photos in this manual should help, but do note where everything came from. Be aware that a previous owner may have got it wrong.

Braking System

Technical Specifications and Revisions

This is a general overview of the technical specifications, but vehicle modifications and upgrades are common. Cut-off points for updates can be flexible.

SWB Models
1958 to 1980
- Front 10in drums, single 1¼in wheel cylinders
- Rear 10in drums, single 1in wheel cylinders
- Brake pipe unions: UNF on fixed and flexible pipes
- Fixed brake pipes: 3/16th
- Single-line unassisted system
- Master cylinder: CB (to approx. 1967) or CV type
- Servo optional
- Single leading shoes with single adjustor cam
- Trailing shoe with no adjustor

1980 to 1985
- Front 11in drums with twin leading shoes; 2 × wheel cylinders per drum
- Rear 10in drums, 1¼in cylinders
- Brake pipe unions: initially UNF, then metric on fixed pipes on later vehicles
- UNF wheel cylinders
- Fixed brake pipes: 3/16th
- Twin-line servo-assisted system with PDWA (pressure differential warning actuator) valve
- Master cylinder: two options; imperial (early) and metric (late) threads

LWB Models
1958 to 1980
- Front 11in drums with twin leading shoes; 2 × wheel cylinders per drum
- Rear 11in drums with 1¼in wheel cylinders and twin adjustor cams
- Brake pipe unions: UNF fixed and flexible pipes
- Fixed brake pipes: 3/16th
- Master cylinder single-line on early vehicles
- Master cylinder twin-line UNF on later vehicles
- Non-servo assisted system, servo optional
- Servo assistance as standard on later vehicles
- Wider shoes, drums and corresponding wheel cylinders on 6-cylinder and V8 models

1980 to 1985
- Front 11in as per 88in model
- Wider shoes, drums and corresponding wheel cylinders on 6-Cylinder and V8 models
- Rear 11in drums with 1¼in wheel cylinders
- Brake pipe unions: initially UNF, then metric on fixed pipes on later vehicles
- Fixed brake pipes: 3/16th

ABOVE LEFT: *10in drum brake assembly*

ABOVE RIGHT: *Note 1¼in front cylinder (top) and 1in rear cylinder (below).*

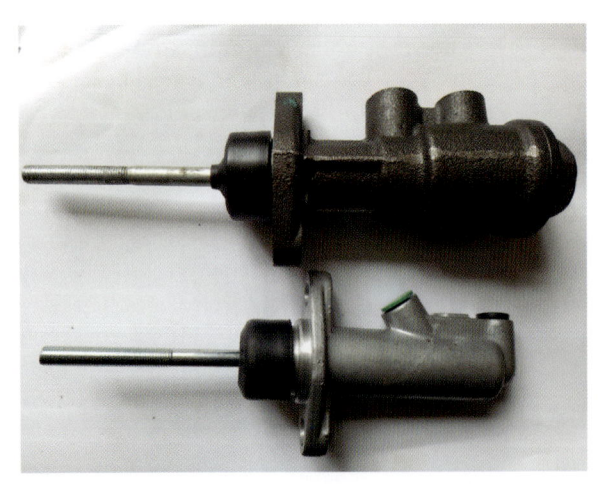

ABOVE LEFT: *CB type 88in master cylinder (top) and CV type (below) are interchangeable with a small pipework modification.*

ABOVE RIGHT: *11in twin leading shoe brakes as fitted to 109in and late 88in models.*

Braking System

Technical Specifications and Revisions *continued*

ABOVE LEFT: There is a noticeable difference in size between the 109in (top) and 88in (bottom) CB master cylinders.

ABOVE RIGHT: Single-line servo-assisted master cylinder as fitted to late Series IIA and early Series III 109in models.

ABOVE LEFT: Twin-line UNF system fitted to mid-era Series III with rounded reservoir.

ABOVE RIGHT: Twin-line metric system as fitted to post-1980 Series III with square-profile reservoir.

PDWA (pressure differential warning actuator) was fitted to later Series III models.

(continued overleaf)

Braking System

Technical Specifications and Revisions *continued*

11in rear with leading and trailing shoe adjustors as fitted to 109in models.

LEFT: *6-cylinder, Forward Control and Stage 1 V8 models had 3in wide front brake shoes.*

- Prise the shoes out of the wheel cylinders with an appropriate tool: self-grip pliers or a large adjustable spanner work well. On 10in drums you also need to remove the trailing shoe banjo.
- Inspect the shoes for wear and contamination, either from oil/grease leaking from the hub seal or brake fluid from the wheel cylinder. If there is contamination, the shoes are pretty much scrap.

REPLACING WHEEL CYLINDERS

Fold back the dust covers on each wheel cylinder and inspect for fluid leaks and corrosion. Old leaks often show up in crystalline form. Corrosion not only causes the pistons to stick but usually leads to damaged seals. Seal kits are available, but if there is any damage to the cylinder bore it will need to be replaced. It is possible to get old wheel cylinders relined with stainless steel inserts, but new cylinders are relatively inexpensive and widely available (except for the very earliest Series II 109in rears). Yours and others' lives depend on good brakes, so don't risk compromised wheel cylinders.

- The brake pipes need to be removed before removing the cylinders. If the pipes will go again, carefully unscrew the union using a tight-fitting spanner. Specific

Removing the drum grub screws may require an impact screwdriver.

LEFT: *It is essential to back off the adjustors to remove the brake drum.*

ABOVE LEFT: Using a self-grip wrench to lever off a very oily brake shoe.

ABOVE RIGHT: Note the twin leading shoes have been assembled incorrectly here: they are pointing the wrong way, effectively taking the brakes off as the wheel turns.

- brake pipe spanners are a massive help.
- If the unions round off, it is usually best just to cut the pipe and get a pair of self-grip pliers or a tight-fitting six-sided socket on the union (usually 7/16in/11mm).
- Wheel cylinders are held onto the brake backplates with two 5/16th UNF nuts (½in spanner/socket) and spring washers. These are often rounded off and hard to get a spanner on: a thin-walled six-sided socket is usually the best bet. If a nut proves challenging, it may be necessary to cut through the wheel cylinder to remove it.
- Note that new wheel cylinders don't normally come with new 5/16th UNF nuts and they should also be fitted with spring washers.
- Fit the best-quality wheel cylinders you can afford. For longevity it is worth putting a smear of red rubber grease under the dust cover.
- Note that 6-cylinder and V8 model front backplates, drums and wheel cylinders are different to standard 11in fronts due to a wider shoe design. The wheel cylinders are fitted with two 5/16th UNF bolts and spring washers.
- Note that it is possible to fit the twin leading shoe wheel cylinder back plates on the wrong side. This gives very poor braking performance: as the wheel turns, it effectively takes the brakes off. The top wheel cylinder should point forwards. Note it is normal for twin leading shoe brakes to be less effective in reverse.

FITTING BRAKE SHOES

Brakes are obviously the most critical-safety feature on your vehicle and it is worth spending just a bit extra on the best-quality shoes you can afford. Some shoes are poorly made, are almost impossible to adjust, the friction compound is too hard for non-servo applications and they take ages to bed in. There are specialist companies that will reline old shoes with softer new linings. Asbestos in brake linings has been banned since the 1990s and is not advisable for obvious health reasons.

It is essential that you fit new shoes with clean hands and ensure no grease, oil or fluid contamination. Clean surrounding components with brake cleaner and carry out any remedial work on leaking hub seals before fitting.

If the system is full of fluid, you can minimise loss and the possibility of popping seals by holding the wheel cylinder pistons in place with a cable tie.

Fitting shoes is always easier if done before fitting the hub, but this is not always convenient if working on an in-service vehicle with a fully assembled axle.

11in Fronts with Twin Leading Shoes

- These have a heavy-duty spring for each shoe. Fit the spring to the shoe and hook it onto the post on the back plate.
- Insert the wheel cylinder end into the wheel cylinder and use self-grip pliers to lever the opposite end into place.
- Ensure the adjustor posts on both shoes rest in the correct position on the snail cams.

10in Drums, Front or Rear Shoes

- The bottom spring holds the shoes together on the bottom pivot point.
- The top spring goes from the post on the leading shoe to the post on the back plate. This spring pulls the leading shoe post back onto the adjustor.
- The trailing shoe is only held in place loosely by the bottom spring with a banjo plate to stop it popping off.
- Hook the lower spring between the shoes and position them round the lower pivot point.
- Hook the long end of the top spring round the post on the leading shoe. Ensure it doesn't foul the adjustor cam and stretch the opposite end to hook round the post on the back plate. A hook or a cable tie can be used to stretch it into place.

11in Rear Shoes

- The bottom spring holds the shoes tight together into the bottom anchor post.

Braking System

ABOVE LEFT: Using a zip tie to hold the wheel cylinder closed when replacing the shoes reduces the chance of fluid loss and air entering the system.

ABOVE RIGHT: Levering the twin leading shoes into place with a self-grip wrench.

ABOVE LEFT: The correct orientation of the 10in shoes and springs, with the trailing shoe banjo still to be fitted. Note that this is the left-hand front.

ABOVE RIGHT: Using a zip tie to pull the top leading shoe return spring onto the backplate post.

The bottom banjo stops the trailing shoe from dislocating in extreme circumstances.

- The top spring, which has coils on both ends, holds the top of the shoes tightly against the two snail cam adjustors.
- Fit the lower spring between the shoes and offer them into place round the hub, but do not fit to the bottom anchor post yet.
- Hook the top spring in place between the shoes round the back of the hub.
- Position the top of the shoes into the wheel cylinder and lever the bottom of the shoes into place in turn with a pair of self-grip pliers.
- It is important to note that the 11in rear leading and trailing shoes are not identical, and the backing plates are handed. The leading shoe adjustor peg sits lower down the shoe and the adjustor cam operates on the underside of the peg. The trailing shoe adjustor operates on the top side of the adjustor peg.
- If the shoes are fitted incorrectly, it can be impossible to get the brakes to adjust correctly, resulting in long pedal travel. It is also not unknown for an axle set of shoes to be incorrectly packed at the factory with a mismatched set. Always check before starting to fit them.

ABOVE LEFT: Correct location of the springs on an 11in rear 109in assembly. Note this is a left-hand rear.

ABOVE RIGHT: Note 11in leading shoes and trailing shoes have different adjustor locations: the leading shoes are shown on the right of shot

ABOVE LEFT: Draping the shoes round and fitting the springs in place.

ABOVE RIGHT: Levering the bottoms of the shoes into place with self-grip pliers – don't grip the friction surface, obviously.

REFITTING/REPLACING DRUMS AND ADJUSTING BRAKES

- Note that there are two different sizes of wheel stud holes. Series II and most IIA had smaller 9/16in studs. Larger M16 studs arrived with late Series IIA models.
- Ensure the snail cam adjustors are on the lowest setting and put the drum on. You might need to tap the shoes up or down to position correctly.
- On 10in drums, it may be necessary to hold the trailing shoe tight against the wheel cylinder to fit the drum.
- Secure the drum with the grub screws, ensuring that they sit in the countersink.
- Some aftermarket grub screws do not sit flush. They need to be filed down so the wheel fits tight against the drum and doesn't sit proud.
- Adjust the snail cams until the shoes start to bind, then take the adjustor back one click. Repeat for both adjustors on 11in drums and check the shoes are just on the bind point.
- Shoes always need to bed in, but a good shoe should adjust up with minimal fuss. There should be a distinct point at which the adjustor goes from free to binding to locking up.
- If the shoe binds throughout the whole throw of the adjustor cam, then there may be a problem that needs investigating. Very often it is caused by poor-quality linings.
- Shoes usually come with a chamfer on the leading edge of the shoes to minimise excessive binding, especially in reverse.

FIXED BRAKE PIPES

Originally Land Rovers were fitted with coated steel brake pipes. Obviously these do corrode and it's pretty unusual to find a vehicle with the original pipes intact and in safe condition. Pipes were clipped into place with screw-in metal P-clips on most vehicles, although the later Series IIIs had knock-in plastic C-clips. Brake pipes were routed to minimise potential damage and should go back into place as per factory fit.

Braking System

Fixed pipes were originally coated steel, so most will have corroded by now.

If you're lucky, you might be able to source genuine new old stock pipes, but the most common replacement material in the UK is copper. These can either be bought as pre-made lengths with unions pre-fitted, specific to the vehicle, or can be made up by hand using a flaring tool. Some countries do not allow copper brake pipes, based on the fact that it can work-harden with vibration and fracture in extreme circumstances. Cunifer (or Kunifer), which is a copper/nickel/iron alloy, is another option with the advantage of being accepted worldwide. Steel pipes can also be made up, but some flaring tools struggle to make good flares.

Land Rover braking systems use 3/16th pipe for main high-pressure lines and ¼in for low-pressure feeds from remote reservoir to master cylinder. Series II and IIA clutch pipes are also 3/16, but Series III uses ¼in pipe for the clutch, which can be bought as a pre-bent pipe.

Making brake pipes is very satisfying. With a bit of patience and practice you can make pipes that are neat and safe. For a factory look, remove any original pipes with care and use them as a pattern. Original pipes usually have a series of distinct bends rather than long sweeping curves.

- If you have no patterns to copy, the images in this manual should help as references, as well as looking at other vehicles. Using cable or washer fluid pipe of a similar diameter to 3/16th brake pipe can be used to plot the route and help to gauge the length required. Ensure that pipes do not fret on bodywork, especially front inner wings.
- While copper pipe can be easily bent by hand, there are a number of different types of brake bending tools available. These are exceptionally useful when making tight bends. They help to recreate that factory finish and minimise the chance of kinking the pipe and creating possible fracture points. Kunifer pipe is harder than copper and a bending tool is often required.
- A brake pipe straightening tool assists in making clean straight lines and deliberate neat bends.
- Making pipe flares is very satisfying, but can take time to master the skill on different flaring tools. Consult the manufacturer's instructions for reference marks. There are two different types of flare required on Land Rovers: male and female (or single/double). The female flare is created by a second operation on the flaring tool. Don't forget to put the union on before the flare – we've all done it!
- Note that metric and imperial unions look very similar, so it's always wise to do a dry fit of the union before making the flare. UNF female unions should have a rounded profile and metric have a squarer profile.
- Note that post-1980/81 vehicles are likely to have metric fixed pipes but will have UNF wheel cylinders.
- Pipe clips are a vital safety measure and should be fitted as per factory. Rubber-lined P-clips hold the rear axle pipes on the axle strap protection brackets. These are not just for show (they do look good when new) but a vital part of ensuring the pipes do not suffer from work hardening and getting snagged off-road.

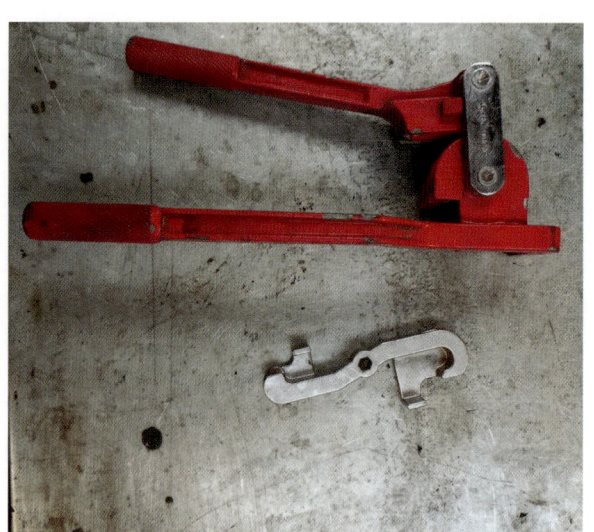

ABOVE LEFT: A good-quality brake flaring tool makes the job significantly easier.

ABOVE RIGHT: Brake pipe bending tools make for neat pipes.

Braking System

A brake pipe straightening tool facilitates a good-quality job.

LEFT: *A proper pipe slice ensures a tidy and accurate cut.*

BELOW LEFT: *A nicely made male convex flare. Take time to practise your flaring skills before committing.*

Female concave flare achieved by the second operation of the flaring tool. Check the operation instructions.

LEFT: *Note metric union with square top (left) and UNF (right) with conical top.*

197

Braking System

ABOVE LEFT: *Rubber-lined P-clips on the rear axle strap guard are good looking and useful.*

ABOVE RIGHT: *Metal P-clips ensure that the brake pipes don't rattle, fret and work harden.*

Correct route for a Series III flexi pipe to fixed pipe.

LEFT: *Correct route for the flexi pipe to fixed pipe on a Series II/IIA, keeping out of the route of the steering rod.*

FLEXIBLE BRAKE PIPES

Flexi pipes should always be thoroughly inspected on a regular basis and should be replaced if there is any evidence of degradation or damage. They should be considered age-expired service items. Note late models have metric flexi pipes. Flexis going directly into a wheel cylinder or T-piece require a copper sealing washer on the square profile end. Note that Series II/IIA and Series III chassis have different flexi pipe brackets, so if using a generic replacement chassis, Series II/IIA brake pipes will require re-routing to ensure a safe system.

MASTER CYLINDER REPLACEMENT

Series II and IIA models usually have unassisted (non-servo) brakes and the master cylinder bolts directly onto the pedal box assembly. Two different types were fitted: CB (large nut on the back) and CV (aluminium body). The changeover point was about 1967, although with minor rerouting of the pipes they are interchangeable. The CV master cylinder on an 88in model is the same as the clutch cylinder. Note that 109in models have a larger bore cylinder. Non-assisted brakes on Series II/IIA have a combined brake and clutch cylinder reservoir with two separate ports. A remote servo was fitted to 6-cylinder models.

Series III (and late IIA) models saw the introduction of integrated servo-

A compromise – a Series IIA system run on a generic Series III-type replacement chassis.

RIGHT: *Factory routing for the twin leading shoe link pipe.*

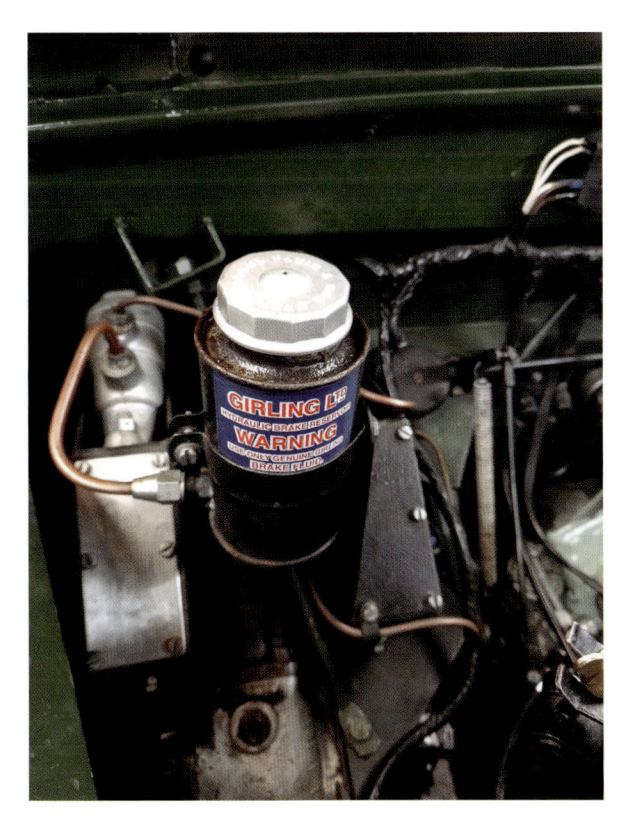

Combined brake and clutch reservoir on a Series II/IIA.

assisted brakes, initially on 109in models and then 88in models from 1980. The servo was bolted to the pedal box and the master cylinder in turn bolted to the servo. Initially this was a single-line system with twin-line systems fitted from the late 1970s. Twin-line systems also saw the introduction of a PDWA (pressure differential warning actuator) shuttle valve. Note that there were UNF (round profile reservoir) and metric (square profile reservoir) master cylinder types. Late parts books only list the metric type.

When a servo fails, it is usually due to a leak in the diaphragm and the whole unit must be replaced. Typical symptoms are a very hard pedal and very poor braking effort. To test the servo operation, turn the engine off and press the pedal a number of times to expel any air from the servo system: it will gradually go hard. Start the engine with the brake applied and the pedal should gradually depress to give a normal pedal feel and travel. If it doesn't change, suspect the servo has failed: obviously you should also check the system for air leaks at the vacuum pipes and listen for any sucking noises.

Master cylinder replacement is simple enough, although fiddly in situ on non-servo models. Sometimes it is quicker to remove the pedal box and do this on the bench. Obviously this is what you would do on a complete strip-down restoration.

It is vital to adjust the master cylinder rod on non-servo systems. There should be 1.5mm free play on the rod before it starts to push the cylinder. This is required so the master cylinder recuperates, that is it allows more fluid to enter the cylinder to pump the next push of the pedal. CB cylinders seem to be more prone to recuperating problems than CV types. If there is

Braking System

insufficient free play, the brake system can start to over-pressurise and not release with the return of the pedal, leading to the brakes gradually sticking on. Too much free play can lead to insufficient volume of fluid being pumped.

BLEEDING BRAKES

Bleeding brakes can be a challenge and there are a number of ways to accomplish this. Note that if the master cylinder hasn't been set up correctly, you will have problems getting the system to pump. Ensure that the brake shoes have been adjusted correctly.

Manual Bleeding

Using the pedal to pump fluid through the system is best carried out with an assistant. Press the pedal down, release the bleed nipple allowing air/fluid to escape, then tighten the nipple before releasing the pedal. You soon get into a rhythm of 'Down. Hold. Up'. If bleeding the brakes on your own, a one-person brake-bleed kit comprising a tube and reservoir pot can be used. Emitted fluid should not be reused, but should be caught in a transparent container via a flexible tube (ideally transparent) on the nipple. This will also help to gauge when all the air has been emitted. The normal process is to start the process furthest away from the master cylinder (NSR) and work back to the master cylinder (OSF), although the official Workshop Manual suggests a couple of different options and techniques, so it is worth a read. Pump the pedal until all air has been emitted from the system and a good firm pedal is acquired. Always ensure there is fluid in the reservoir during the bleeding process to ensure air doesn't enter the system.

If you only have to break into one part of the system, for example changing one wheel cylinder, you can use a clamp in the nearest flexi pipe to reduce fluid loss. This means that only the local part of the system needs to be bled.

Pressure Bleeding

Pressure bleeding the system means the pedal does not need to be pressed. Fluid from an external reservoir bottle is pushed through the system via a tight-fitting rubber sealed cap on the master cylinder reservoir with pressure from a tyre (maximum pressure usually about 20psi). This has significant advantages over manual bleeding as it can be an easy one-person operation. The bleed nipples can be cracked in turn to allow fluid to flow until clear. The external reservoir bottle means you don't have to keep checking the level of fluid in the master cylinder reservoir as often. This method is particularly useful on a new dry system and seems to assist with new master cylinders with dry seals (in particular on new CB type cylinders).

Reverse Bleeding

A reverse bleed kit can be used to pump fluid from the wheel cylinders up to the master cylinder. This is again useful on a dry system or on a system that is otherwise a struggle to bleed.

Problems Bleeding

If you are struggling to bleed the system and get a firm pedal, you can usually work out where the problem lies by using a clamp on the local flexi pipe.

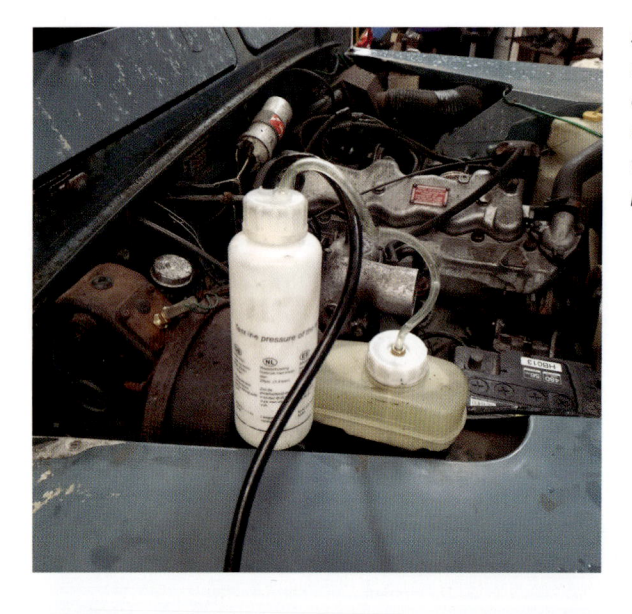

A pressure bleeder uses the pressure from a tyre to push fluid through the system without having to pump the pedal.

The intricate internal components of the handbrake expander: see the parts manual if in doubt.

Note that a pedal that comes good on second pump is often down to poorly adjusted shoes, incorrectly fitted shoes, poor quality shoes or shoes that need time to bed in. Trapped air usually causes the pedal to remain spongy on second pump.

PARKING BRAKE

It is again a myth that Land Rover parking brakes are inefficient. A correctly adjusted system should hold the vehicle firmly on a steep hill within three to four clicks. Most issues are down to contaminated shoes, poor adjustment or seized expanders. Ratchet and pawl mechanisms can wear to the point of not holding effectively and popping off at the most inconvenient moment. A firm knock on top of the lever is a good way to gauge the effectiveness and condition of the ratchet system.

The parking brake system, while simple, comprises a multitude of small components in both the handbrake lever and the drum expander and adjustor mechanisms. *See* photos and the Parts Manual for a breakdown of the components.

If the system is found lacking, investigation is required. If the travel is too long, this may be adjusted out via the adjustor on the left-hand side of the back plate or via adjustments of the connecting rods.

Parking brakes are also prone to sticking on vehicles that are used infrequently, usually caused by a seized relay, seized expander or adjustor or a broken shoe spring.

Adjusting the parking brake shoes

- To adjust, with the lever down, the adjustor should be wound in until the shoes just start to bind, then back off one click. This should achieve the required three to four clicks at the lever to hold the vehicle.
- If the travel is still too long, the relay rods may need adjusting. The main rod from handbrake to relay should be set with minimal free play. Note that it is not uncommon for the relay to be loose in its fixing point.
- Clevis pins should also be examined for wear. It's not uncommon for these to have been replaced with bolts for expediency. They are fiddly to assemble with the anti-rattle spring and split pins.
- If the adjustment is correct, inefficiency is mostly likely down to worn-out or contaminated shoes.

Replacing Parking Brake Shoes

- Remove the rear propshaft, ideally using a propshaft socket. Note that on most vehicles the fixings will be 3/8th UNF with a 9/16th head, but early vehicles did have BSF fixings.
- The drum is held onto the drive flange with ¼in BSF nuts and ideally should be removed with the correct socket/spanner.
- With the adjustor backed off, the drum should tap off and the shoes can be assessed for wear (it's very rare for a parking brake shoe to wear out) and contamination (very common).
- It is far easier to replace the shoes with the rear output removed from the gearbox: this will be required to replace the output seal in any case. (For more details, *see* Chapter 10.)
- The brake shoes can now be levered off the adjustor and expander, taking careful note of the position of the shoe springs.
- Fit the springs to the shoes, then prise into place on the adjustor and expander. Do this before refitting the output flange.
- Thoroughly degrease the drum before refitting and adjust the brake shoes as above.

BRAKE UPGRADES

A range of brake upgrades is available and this is a particularly important consideration if fitting an engine with

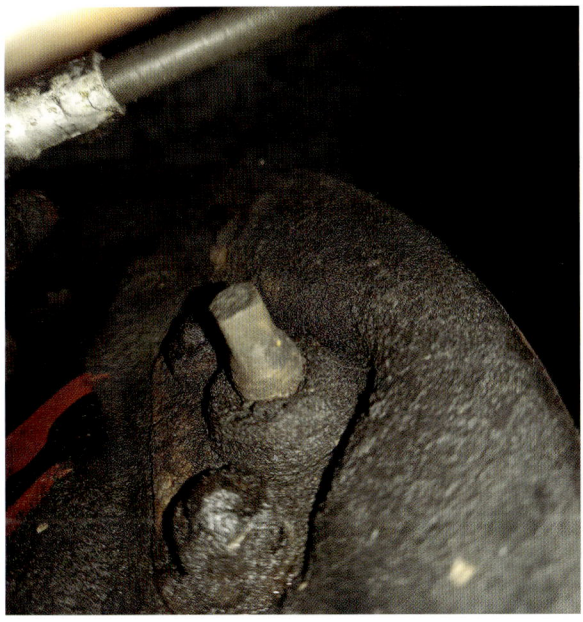

ABOVE LEFT: *Location of the handbrake shoe adjustor. Turn it until the shoes just bind and back off one click.*

ABOVE RIGHT: *It is far easier to remove the backplate to replace the handbrake shoes.*

Braking System

A remote servo can be used to boost the performance of the original braking system.

increased performance. These can be divided into simply using parts available from other Land Rover models and to using specially developed aftermarket components.

Using Land Rover Components

The most common upgrades require fitting the complete braking system from a later vehicle, the brakes from an 109in to an 88in, or a universal remote servo to the existing system. The servo principle is to use vacuum pressure from the inlet manifold or a vacuum pump to reduce the pedal effort. This is a simple system to fit: the output from the master cylinder is diverted to the servo booster cylinder and then rejoins the existing system.

Modern brake linings tend to be a harder compound than older asbestos linings. Asbestos linings are of course banned, but softer non-asbestos linings are available from specialist manufacturers. With the increasing values on Series vehicles, owners are willing to spend a bit extra for better braking performance.

Disc Brake Conversions

While good-condition drum brakes are perfectly adequate, there are significant advantages with disc brakes: less fade when hot, less affected by getting wet, a more progressive feel at the pedal and they are self-adjusting.

There are a number of aftermarket companies now offering conversions. Some involve a re-engineered swivel housing to include calliper mounting lugs, others have a conversion ring that bolts on to the swivel housing. Some use standard coil spring Land Rover parts such as callipers and discs, some use readily available parts from other manufacturers. Be aware that some of the conversions might require larger offset wheels to accommodate the discs and callipers. Conversions are available for both front and rear brakes.

17
Wiring

Wiring your Land Rover can seem one of the more daunting tasks you have to undertake and many shy away from doing it properly. However, it is not technically difficult once the task has been broken down into its individual elements. This chapter is designed to break down the spaghetti of multi-coloured wires into bite-sized chunks and give a broad overview, but for specific details it will be necessary to consult the schematic diagrams in the Workshop Manual.

Whether it's a full rewire or just a repair, addition or modification, it's important to carry out the task correctly. Obviously, the wiring is a safety-critical element on any vehicle, but sadly it is often one of the most bodged, either due to expediency or simply a lack of skill or knowledge. Land Rovers in particular seem to suffer from previous-owner wiring repairs as their simplicity often encourages a 'that will do' attitude. Fuses replaced with nails or wrapped in aluminium foil are not just apocryphal tales, they are all too common: remember these were working vehicles and often temporary solutions became permanent 'fixes' as they were forgotten about. Seven-core trailer wiring is a common sight and, while not necessarily dangerous, it does tend to raise concerns about what else has been done to the vehicle. Home wiring is often done with whatever wires were to hand and it may be a challenge to work out what does what. When multiple modifications have been carried out, sometimes it is just easier to go back to factory specification and fit a complete new loom.

Contrary to folklore, classic Land Rover wiring is actually well designed, logical and, when in good condition, works well. Yes, there may be some benefit in additional fuses and relays for upgraded lights, but on a standard vehicle there is little need to change anything. The old joke about buying a bottle of 'replacement wiring harness smoke', while funny, should not be taken in any way seriously. Electrical faults are mostly caused by age-old, worn-out components, poor repairs or modifications. Compared to modern wiring, it is very easy to understand and can

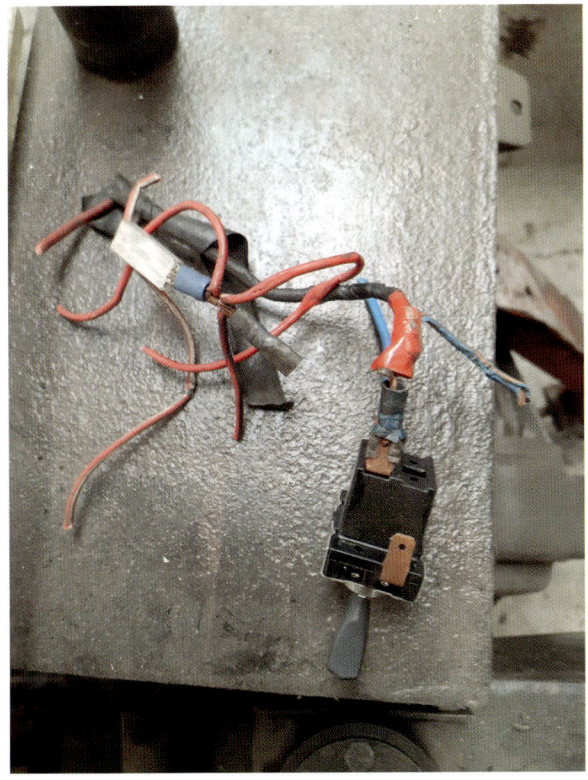

ABOVE LEFT: Please, whatever else you do, don't live with or execute wiring like this.

ABOVE RIGHT: Bodges like this are all too common – this image was not manufactured for effect.

Wiring

easily be followed due to its modular design of individual looms and the fact that it follows standard British classic wiring colours.

Schematic diagrams in the official Workshop Manual may be essential reading for details, and while it shows the connections and colours in a vehicle wiring system, it doesn't show the actual grouping of the wires, the individual looms or the physical runs of the wires. This chapter aims to give an overview, show the 'real world' distribution of power and the route of the looms.

A personal plea to all Land Rover owners: if you choose to modify the wiring, use the *correct colour-coded wires*. This is vitally important for future fault finding, both for you and future owners. You wouldn't do it on your domestic housing wiring, so don't do it on your Land Rover.

CLASSIC WIRING COLOURS

Classic British vehicles, including all Land Rovers, followed a standard wiring colour identification system. Becoming familiar with this system makes wiring and fault finding significantly easier. On twin-colour wires, the first colour is the primary colour, the second one is the stripe.

Power Distribution Wire Colours

Brown: Most non-fused permanent live feeds. This is basically the supply from the battery distributed to components such as the ignition switch, fuse box and primary supply to systems that do not require the ignition to be on. This includes the supply to the light switch, horn and dash sockets, as well as the primary feed from the charging system.

White: Ignition fed, non-fused live feeds. This includes coil, fuel pump (6-cylinder and V8) and ignition fed sections of the fuse box. These wires are often bulked together in a 'header' where a main heavy-duty white feed from the ignition switch branches out to feed other circuits.

Green: Ignition fed, fused. These circuits will run from the fuse box to individual switches and gauges such as wiper/washers, indicators, brake lights and fuel and temperature gauges.

Purple: Most non-ignition-fed fused circuits. On a Land Rover, this includes the feed to the headlight flasher.

Black: Earth (or ground) wires – but do note that on a seven-core trailer loom, black is left-hand sidelight and white is earth.

Lighting Circuit Wires

Blue	headlight light switch to dip switch
Blue/Red	low beam headlights
Blue/White	high beam headlights
Red	sidelights/tail lights
Red/Black	tail lights
Red/White	dash illumination
Green/White	right-hand indicator/turn signal
Green/Red	left-hand indicator/turn signal
Green/Purple	brake light switch to brake lights
Red/Orange	fog light

Gauge Circuits: Including Voltage Stabiliser

Green	fused supply to voltage stabiliser
Light Green	stabilised voltage supply to gauge (often with insulated female spade connector)
Green/Black	fuel gauge to fuel sender in tank
Green/Blue	temperature gauge to temperature sender

Dash Light Circuits

White	ignition feed to charge, choke light, oil pressure lights
Brown/Yellow	charge light to alternator/dynamo (red light)
Brown/White	oil light to oil pressure sender (green or red light)
White/Blue	cold start light to cold start (choke cable) switch/glow plug resistor (orange light)
Blue/White	main beam light (blue or red light)
Black	earth for main beam light
Green	fuel light feed
Green/Orange	low fuel light (diesel) (blue or orange dash light)

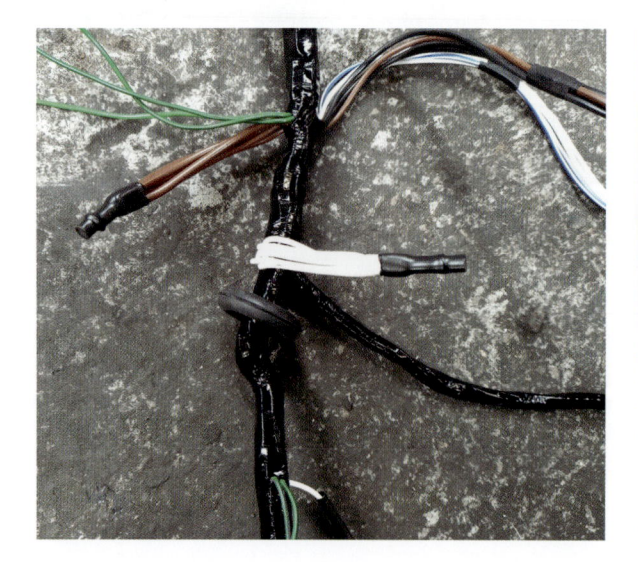

Fuse box connections: Brown = permanent live in; White = ignition live in; Purple = fused permanent out; Green = ignition fused out.

LEFT: *Brown (permanent live) and white (ignition live) 'headers' in a Series III loom.*

Wiring

Voltage regulator at the back of the dash for Series IIA gauges: light green wire is regulated feed out to the gauge.

LEFT: *Lighting circuit wires on a Series II ready to be connected into the junction box on the bulkhead.*

Rear of dash connections on an early Series IIA with combined light and ignition switch.

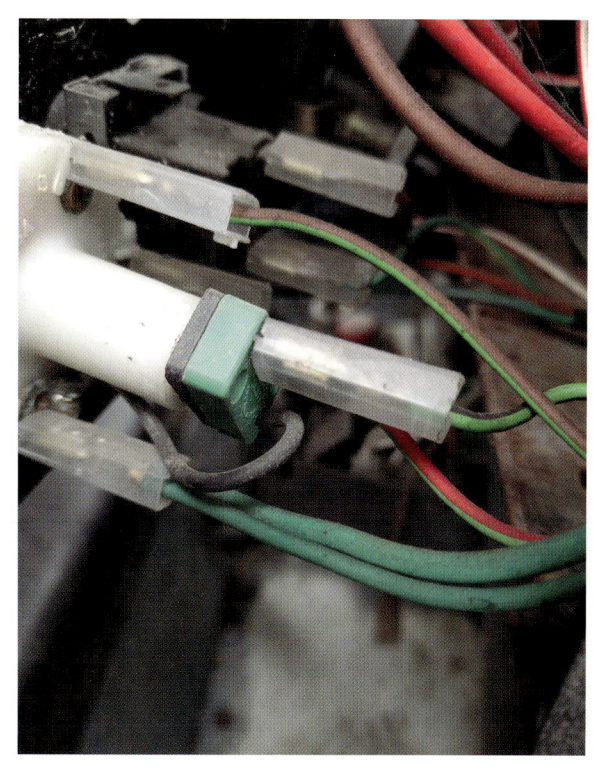

RIGHT: *Wiper motor and washer connections on a Series III.*

Wiper Motor Wires

Green	supply for individual FW2 motors (Series II and IIA to 1967)
Green/**Black**	washer motor feed
Green/**Red**	wiper feed
Green/**Brown**	wiper park switch

ASSESSING YOUR LOOM

Good wiring is a vital safety feature on your vehicle. If carrying out any significant restoration or wiring works, it is the time to seriously consider the condition of your loom. Series II and IIA looms were made from colour-coded braided cable, which, over time, breaks down turning to powder, leaving black insulation over the copper wires. While this might not compromise the insulation properties of the wires, it can make identification and future fault-finding difficult. The majority of the connections are individual screw terminals,

205

Wiring

spade connections or push-in bullet connections. Again, these suffer from corrosion leading to poor connections and potential overheating.

Series III looms were made from PVC-insulated wires and have considerably more moulded multi-plug connections for joining individual looms. Generally speaking, Series III looms last pretty well as long as they haven't been extensively modified or damaged.

New looms are available from a variety of specialist companies and represent very good value for money. It is possible to build your own loom from scratch, but by the time you've bought the correct colour of wires, the correct terminals and wrapping material, you will be pretty close to the same cost, discounting the amount of time to build it. In the end, it will always be a home-made loom that is unlikely to look as good as a professionally built one. Yes, there will be exceptions and significantly modified vehicles will no doubt need a bespoke loom, but for a pretty standard vehicle it is strongly advised to just save up and buy a professionally manufactured one. Series II/IIA looms are available finished in modern PVC or cloth-wrapped to match the original for authenticity.

FITTING A NEW LOOM

While there are variations between models, we can generally break the wiring system down into a series of individual looms that plug together. If fitting a new loom, it is advisable to take multiple photographs of the connections on the old loom. In addition, when stripping out the old loom, instead of pulling off all the old connectors, snip them off leaving a small length of wire showing the colour codes.

At first glance the main loom can be a daunting spider's web, but the easiest way to start is to work out what side of the bulkhead a wire should go. This is simply a case of identifying the large grommet(s) and laying it out on the floor to see the shape of it. It will then be obvious which orientation it fits in. If building a vehicle from ground up, it is far easier to fit the wiring loom with the bulkhead bolted to a rolling chassis but without the rest of the bodywork fitted.

New looms usually come in separate bags to help identification.

BELOW: *Grommets show the divide point between the engine bay and the dash on this Series II loom.*

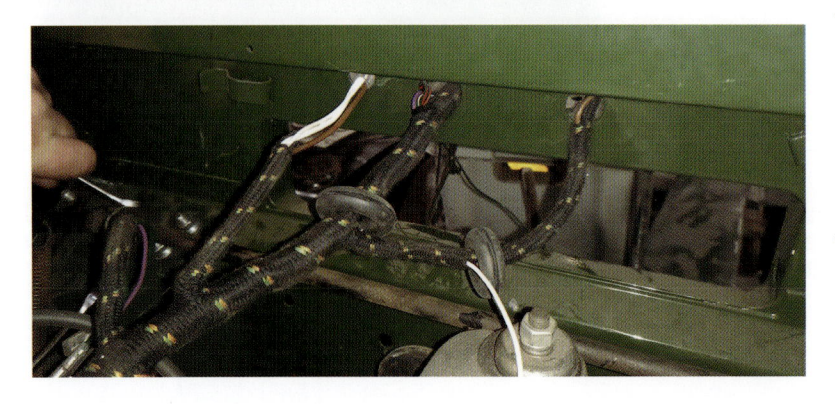

Another plea to would-be Land Rover restorers: always use grommets when passing a cable through holes in bodywork. Nothing says 'amateur' like wires needlessly rubbing through on sharp metal edges.

Main Loom Orientation: Series II/IIA

- The loom passes through the bulkhead in two places with two obvious large grommets. These can be tight, so a spray of soapy water or lubrication can assist.
- A cluster of green, white and brown wires goes to the fuse box on the engine side of the bulkhead.
- A heavy-duty brown and smaller white/red wire links into the starter solenoid: on a petrol this is on the bulkhead, on a diesel it is down by the starter motor. This acts as the main feed/distribution point for many circuits.
- A long leg of lighting wires drapes out along the side of the wing to then link into the front panel.
- A short leg with bullets comes down the side of the footwell to join into the rear wiring loom. Note that early vehicles have a separate junction box for the front lighting and horn on the top of the footwell.

Main Loom Orientation: Series III

- As with the Series II/IIA, there is an obvious divide between what goes behind the dash and what goes to the engine bay. Note that the wiring grommet sits in a hole in a plastic plate screwed on the bulkhead. The multiplugs are a tight fit through the hole, so fit the plastic plate to the loom off the vehicle and then pass it through the aperture in the bulkhead.
- Because the dash and clocks are directly in front of the driver, it is much easier to wire the vehicle with the steering wheel off. If building onto a bare bulkhead, it is also easier to leave the upper and lower dash off at this stage.
- Each subsection of wires leading to a switch is individually wrapped on a new Series III loom. Separate each section out so you have a logical drape of wires, not a tangled mess.

Wiring

ABOVE LEFT: Series II wires neatly arranged to aid identification behind the dash.

ABOVE RIGHT: The shape of the loom is as important as the colours when working out what goes where.

ABOVE LEFT: This plastic plate is the dividing point between dash and engine bay on the Series III.

ABOVE RIGHT: Series III loom neatly draped out in the correct location with individual groups of wires taped together.

- On a Series III, the fuse box is mounted in the lower steering column cowl. The bunch of white/brown/green wires can be easily identified.

Rear Wiring Loom

The rear wiring loom should run through the chassis rail. This means it is protected from the elements but not from welding repairs. If you choose to replace the rear loom, use the old loom to pull the new loom through. It is usually easier to pull the loom through from the back to the front.

ABOVE LEFT: Using an electrician's rod set to put a draw line through for the chassis loom.

ABOVE RIGHT: Rear of Series III chassis/rear lighting loom with chassis grommet in place.

Wiring

Series III chassis loom has multiplugs at the bulkhead end.

There is a variety of techniques that work to pass the loom through the chassis. While it can be a fiddly task, it is worth the extra effort for the factory finish look. A well-proven technique is to insert an electrician's rod set through the small drain hole in the rear crossmember and pull it up through the wiring hole by the bulkhead with a long pick or suitable bit of wire. Attach a length of strong string to it and then pull it through to the back, then push the string out through the rear wiring hole in the top face of the chassis rail. The string can then be used to draw the wiring loom through.

Front Wiring Loom

The front wiring on all but the early vehicles is integral to the main loom and runs down the side of the right-hand wing to distribute power to the right-hand sidelight, indicator and horn, before running through the front panel to send power to the headlights and to the left-hand side and indicator lights. The headlights are connected by individual looms. Note that the headlamp bullets are particularly prone to giving poor connections and it is always advisable to replace the four-way insulated bullet connectors if the bullets are a poor fit. Note that the earthing point in the top of the front panel is also a common poor connection point. On Series IIIs, this is a four-way sprung bullet connection point and is particularly prone to poor connections.

DASH WIRING

It is important to consult the Workshop Manual for the minute details for your own model, but there is very much a theme when it comes to wiring up behind the dashboard. There are broadly three different dashboard types:

- Body colour dash (1958–1966) with large push-button start housed below the dash (note there was a key start on diesels). Rotary light switch in the dash with a combined ignition switch.
- Rationalised black dash (1967–1971) with key start and separate solenoid on petrol and diesel models. The light switch moved to a toggle switch.
- Series III dash binnacle directly in front of driver. There were very few changes during the Series III era, little more than adding a centre dash to house the fog and hazard lighting.

Front lighting loom passes through a grommet in the front panel.

BELOW: *Earthing point on the front panel is a common poor connection, leading to dim lights or no lights at all.*

While the spiderweb of different coloured wires can seem daunting, think of it like a jigsaw puzzle where you work from the known to the unknown. If replacing a loom, cut the old wires off leaving a short section of the wire in place to identify it. Alternatively, go for an 'old wire off, new wire on' approach. If there is no previous reference, group the wires together based on the hardware they will attach to. Note that replacement looms often have holders for modern capless dash bulbs, not the original screw-in type.

Wiring

ABOVE LEFT: Body-coloured dash with separate dash lights and combined lights and ignition switch fitted from 1958 to 1966.

ABOVE RIGHT: Black dash with separate light switches, key start and dash lights in the gauges from 1967 to 1971.

Series III dash sits in front of the driver.

BELOW: Back of the dash looks daunting at first, but it's not as scary as it looks.

Systematically remove old dash wires and attach new in turn.

FUSE BOXES

Series II and IIA models had a two-way fuse box mounted on the bulkhead. These usually last well, although sprung fuse holders can break, tarnish and lose their springiness; replacements are widely available. Series III models had a four-way fuse box mounted below the steering column binnacle and an additional in-line fuse protecting the heater circuit.

It is common for a vehicle that has sat for a long time to develop poor fuse connections that create significant resistance. While a multimeter or power probe will detect a voltage, there will be insufficient current flowing to take any load. A good clean-up usually solves the problem; alternatively, fit a new fuse box.

The fuse box not only acts as a safety link in the system, it also operates as a power distribution point and can be a good point to pick up a spare feed for an additional circuit. The Series III usually has a spare fuse way, the Series II and IIA doesn't.

Ignition Switch

While the ignition switch is pretty straightforward, note that petrol and diesel versions are different. The diesel type is significantly heavier duty than the petrol and has an additional terminal for glow plugs. In addition, the 2286cc diesel has a manual stop cable and the ignition switch cuts the ignition feed when cranking the engine over meaning that it is not directly

Wiring

compatible with a petrol engine or indeed a later fuel solenoid engine so an additional feed would be required.

Note also that while they look very similar, the body of the Series III key/ignition/steering lock assembly is different between petrol and diesel models. Not only are the choke and stop cables different, the recess for the switch itself is different. Neither of these are readily available now unless you're lucky enough to find new old stock. Neither is the lock section easily changeable in the assembly.

Ignition switch and barrel assemblies for coil spring models are readily available and will physically fit on the Series III steering column. However, because the later engines ran with a separate choke cable assembly on petrol models and a stop solenoid on diesel models, they don't have the facility for a choke or stop cable, so these would have to be fitted elsewhere. It has been known to cut the relevant cast cable housing section off the old switch assembly and bond it onto the new type.

The Series III ignition switch itself is readily available but accessing it is tricky. It is held into the back of the lock assembly with two small screws. Be very careful not to lose the collar that connects from the lock rod to the switch, as they drop out very easily and not readily available.

Series II and IIA switches and lock assemblies are readily available as remanufactured parts or refurbished originals. It is also possible to order a new key by quoting the key number on the ignition barrel.

CHARGING SYSTEM

Series II and most IIA models had a dynamo and voltage regulator charging systems. The dynamo is effectively a DC brush motor run in reverse and is operated by the fan belt. The voltage output is controlled by the voltage regulator, which is mounted on the bulkhead. Most systems were positive earth until 1967, when it changed to the now conventional negative earth. An alternator became an option in 1968 and was standard fitment on the Series III. An alternator is an electrical generator that produces AC and the output is rectified to DC by a diode pack. By now, many Series II and IIA models will have been fitted with alternators.

Charging System Faults

The most common symptom of a charging system fault will be the charge light coming on with the engine running and/or the battery failing to charge sufficiently. Be aware that if a vehicle is used for short journeys, an old-school charging system might not be able to recharge the battery sufficiently. A proper battery load tester will confirm battery condition and the output of the dynamo or alternator can be measured by a multimeter. To test the output, simply test the battery voltage with the engine running. A healthy reading is between 13.5V to 14.4V, although a dynamo output is likely to be slightly less than an alternator.

Common causes for a failure in the charging system are:

- Poor connections
- Failed alternator diode pack
- Failing internal windings
- Worn dynamo brushes
- Failing or poorly adjusted voltage regulator

Dynamo brushes can be easily replaced by a reasonably competent DIY mechanic, although having the original professionally rebuilt is not prohibitively expensive. The official Workshop Manual has a section on adjusting the voltage regulator and new units are available at a reasonable cost. Alternators can be rebuilt, although it is often more cost-effective to simply replace them.

Alternator vs Dynamo: Alternator Upgrade

For a period-correct vehicle that gets little use and is seldom driven at night, a dynamo is perfectly adequate. However, an alternator is far more efficient and has fewer moving parts. By now many vehicles will have already been converted. In the past it was common to fit an alternator and bypass the voltage regulator, leaving it in place for expediency or to maintain the original look. Note that if this has been done, the supply lead from alternator to battery should also have been beefed up to cope with the additional charging current. Dynamos can work on positive or negative earth: an alternator must only be wired negative earth. A different mounting bracket is required when fitting an alternator and these are often disproportionally expensive on the second-hand market.

Series III ignition switch is held in with two tiny screws – don't lose them!

Don't lose the collar that connects the lock rod to the ignition switch either.

Wiring

ABOVE LEFT: A dynamo needs a voltage control unit, but it can also be used as a joint box if changing to an alternator.

ABOVE RIGHT: An alternator AMP multiplug was specified for this new Series II loom. Note that it still has a classic braided cable.

If ordering a new loom, specialist suppliers will have a range of off-the-shelf looms to accommodate an alternator or will build one specifically to your requirements with the appropriate connector plug. An alternative would be to fit a 'Dynamator', which is an alternator housed within a dynamo body. This has the advantage of offering the original looks but with modern efficiency.

MAKING ELECTRICAL CONNECTIONS

Land Rover loom terminals are a combination of screws, ring terminals, spade terminals and bullet connectors as well as soldered 'headers'. These are usually robust but are prone to surface corrosion leading to poor conductivity, especially on a vehicle that is used infrequently. A clean with electrical connection spray can usually restore good connections.

Being able to carry out good, safe repairs or modifications is invaluable. Always use the correct connectors and, if replacing a wire, replace it with the original colour. Invest in a good set of electrical tools such as pliers, side cutters, wire strippers and crimping tools.

Bullet Connections

The standard Land Rover bullet connectors are 4.7mm. Note that it is relatively common for replacement lamp units to come with smaller size bullets, which are too loose in the socket connectors. Factory type uninsulated crimps are widely available from specialist suppliers, although a special crimping tool is required for the uninsulated bullets to ensure a good, strong fit. Once these have been made, pull firmly on the connection to ensure it is tight. If not, the joint can also be soldered.

Wire strippers and ratcheting crimpers are essential for a professional job.

Insulated Connectors/Crimps

Many people dislike pre-insulated crimps for a variety of reasons, mostly because it is common to see poorly fitted ones nipped up with multi-purpose pliers. Functionally there is nothing wrong with a pre-insulated connector as long as it is fitted correctly with a proper tool. While the pliers type work, a ratcheting crimping tool is by far the best option. Note the standard colours of red (0.5–1.5mm wire), blue (1.5–2.5mm wire) and yellow (3–6mm wire). If the coloured insulation looks somewhat out of place, it can always be covered in black heat shrink. In addition, non-insulated crimps with separate insulation covers are also available and look more in keeping on a classic Land Rover.

Soldering

Soldering is a robust and neat way to fit terminals and join wires. A gas-powered soldering iron gives a strong heat very quickly and is far more adaptable than a mains-operated one when working on a vehicle. All solder joints should be covered with heat-shrink, not insulating tape. A caterer's size blowtorch is also very useful for larger solder joints and for fitting heat-shrink. Note that there are concerns over the durability of soldered joints if used on areas subject to significant vibrations, so wires should be clipped, taped or tied into place and not free to rattle around.

Wiring

A gas soldering iron is more adaptable than a mains-powered one for working on a vehicle.

FAULT FINDING

Beyond poor modifications and wear and tear, most wiring faults are caused by poor live terminal connections and poor earths. Typical poor earth connections often result in dim lights or lights glowing unexpectedly. Bullet connectors corrode and many aftermarket light units have bullet connections that are too small: sometimes these can be opened out sufficiently to give a tighter fit.

Multimeter

A multimeter is an essential tool and should be in every mechanic's toolbox. Even a cheap one will read voltage and resistance, the most common measurements required when testing circuits and components.

Power Probe

A power probe is invaluable and in many ways a more versatile tool than a multimeter for tracing wiring faults. A power probe reads voltage, but can also be used to supply a live feed to a circuit or component as well as earthing a component. If, for example, a light doesn't work, the power probe can be used to power up the light/bulb itself, to power up the circuit to the light or to earth the light. The probe has a sharp point on it, so can be easily pushed into terminals and can even be used to press through insulation, a massive advantage when tracing whether a circuit has a supply or not.

ABOVE LEFT: A multimeter is an essential tool for working on Land Rover electrics.

ABOVE RIGHT: A power probe allows you to test circuits and components with the facility to test if the circuit has a supply, supply a live feed or supply an earth – all necessary when fault finding.

18
Chassis Replacement and Restoration

The Land Rover chassis is, of course, the backbone of the whole build and it is also where the identity of the vehicle lies with the chassis number (VIN Vehicle Identity Number from 1980). The chassis number was originally stamped on the RHS dumb iron/spring hanger, but decades on it is likely to be difficult to read or may be missing due to chassis repairs. The chassis is often the Achilles heel on a Land Rover and when undertaking a restoration or refurbishment, there will always be a decision to be made on the viability of the chassis based on the work required to make it sound and the skills and patience of the restorer. Commercially it usually works out more expensive to repair an original chassis to a good standard than it is to buy a new one from one of the current range of manufacturers. While there are different rules in different countries, in the UK a chassis can be replaced with a new one manufactured to the same design as the original. However, given the time and appropriate skills, repairing a chassis is very satisfying and retains an originality and authenticity that is desirable to collectors, especially if the vehicle is of personal or historical importance.

REPLACEMENT CHASSIS OPTIONS

When available as a Land Rover Genuine Part, replacement chassis were usually supplied as universal generic-fit units based on the late Series III design. In terms of basic design, the chassis didn't change significantly from 1958 to 1984. However, there were slight changes over the years, such as brake pipe brackets, handbrake pivots, rear axle strap retainers, crossmember gussets, PTO hole sizes and front spring mount/dumb iron gussets. It is also worth noting that from the mid/late 1970s chassis rails for 109in models were constructed from twin C-section pressings welded along the top and bottom seams, not the earlier box-section construction. For complete authenticity to the original design, some manufacturers are offering 'replica' chassis with all the correct details for the age/suffix of your vehicle. At the time of writing, only box-section 109in chassis were available due to the development costs versus low demand for the C-section design. Most new chassis come galvanised for protection, although some companies will supply them painted by negotiation.

Painting a galvanised chassis adds extra protection and matches the original factory finish. A box-section 109in chassis is shown here.

LEFT: *Most new chassis come pre-galvanised for longevity.*

Chassis Replacement and Restoration

COMPLETE CHASSIS REPLACEMENT/BODY REMOVAL

If the main structure of the vehicle body is sound, it is possible to lift the body off as a complete unit. This is particularly useful on a patina restoration or functional rebuild/recommission vehicle. This is significantly easier on a two-post ramp/lift but can be accomplished with careful rigging of a block and tackle on a gantry or even using a forklift.

The process is fairly straightforward, requiring the following (though not exhaustively) basic steps:

- Unwire the engine bay, chassis loom and rear lighting loom.
- Unplumb the engine including the fuel and cooling system, including the radiator and heater.
- Unclip the throttle arm to carb/throttle cable.
- Remove the steering box drop arm.
- Undo the clutch and brake master cylinder pipes.
- Remove the bulkhead outrigger bolts.
- Unbolt the bulkhead/steering box upright brackets from the chassis.
- Unbolt the floor plates and seat box to chassis bolts.
- Remove the handbrake lever and actuator relay from the chassis.
- Remove the speedo, choke and heater control cables.
- Unbolt the seat belt to chassis fixings where appropriate (Series III).
- Unbolt the front panel lower fixings.
- Unbolt the rear body fixings along the rear crossmember and forward body outriggers.
- Remove the fuel tank filler and breather pipes.
- Check absolutely every other possible fixing, just in case you've forgotten anything.
- Rig up the body for lifting: on a two-post lift the front arms can go under the bulkhead feet and the rear arms can lift a box section slid under the rear body floor.
- Lift the body carefully and slowly up, knowing that things can/will snag on the way up.
- Curse as you've forgotten something as the body lifts off – we've all done it!

The rolling chassis can then be removed either for repair/assessment/strip for replacement.

Refitting the body is, as they say, the reverse of removing it. However, it is not always that simple and it can be difficult to realign all the body fixing points. Having the rolling chassis on wheel dollies/skates is invaluable for fine adjustment, but there will always be a session with pry bars to get the body bolts back in.

Note that when fitting a new chassis it's not uncommon for there to be slight variations in bulkhead outrigger mounting hole positions. A favourite trick the author uses is to put a point on the bulkhead mounting bolts to mitigate slight misalignment: as the bolt is tapped in, it should pull the holes together. Most replacement chassis from the current stock of manufacturers are very accurate and it's very unusual to find one that is substandard. Having said that, you can expect to elongate holes and fit spacers and washers – after all, that's exactly what was done in the factory. Remember also that historical repairs to bulkheads, manufacturing tolerances and general wear and tear over the years may have twisted the body slightly. Most issues with fitting a new chassis comes down to the inexperience of the person carrying out the job: Chapter 20 is dedicated to bodywork alignment for this very reason.

CHASSIS REPAIRS

Land Rover chassis usually rust from the rear forwards, the front backwards, outriggers inwards and bottom upwards! In short, expect rust everywhere except for where it has been naturally covered in a mist of engine and gearbox oil. Expect functional/poor repairs from previous owners and always endeavour to make a better job. Welding is a skill that develops with experience and patience: if you are a novice, having a trusted and experienced welder/fabricator to coach you is invaluable. A good weld should have good penetration, follow factory join points where possible and be neat

Lifting the body off to repair or replace the chassis is remarkably straightforward.

You can expect to have to use packing washers and shims when fitting a new chassis.

Chassis Replacement and Restoration

If repairing a chassis, try to match the original weld runs. Here a new 'fishplate' strengthening gusset has been fitted, matching the original weld position and length.

and tidy. You can expect to have to tidy up your welding with a flap disc but it should not be blobby or porous, neither should the flatting back process be allowed to compromise the strength of the weld.

Welding Equipment

A gas MIG (Metal Inert Gas) is the most appropriate welder for chassis repairs. Old-school stick welders will work on good, thick metal, but lack the flexibility of a MIG. While gasless (flux cored) MIGs are popular with DIY welders, these should really only be considered for ad hoc work rather than significant repairs. For the small extra cost, it is always advisable to buy a proper MIG welder that runs a shielding gas (usually an argon mix). There is a variety of companies that will supply welding gas to the hobbyist on a purchase or deposit basis. Small disposable gas canisters are expensive, wasteful and will run out in minutes, so are best avoided.

Self-darkening masks are commonplace and cheap now, although the more you spend, the better the quality. Welding gauntlets/gloves look after your hands. You will also benefit from a variety of clamps including self-grip wrenches and C-clamps, G-clamps and magnets. As you become more experienced you'll find ingenious ways of holding repair sections in place while you tack them in.

Cutting Equipment

The angle grinder has to be the Land Rover owner's best friend. A 4in grinder is ideal and can be used for cutting, grinding and flatting back. It is always best to have two angle grinders on the go, one set up for cutting and one for grinding/flatting to save having to constantly change discs. 1mm cutting discs are ideal for chassis work, but do wear quickly and are relatively fragile, so upsizing to 1.6mm may be more cost-effective.

Be aware that good-quality eye protection is vital, even for the smallest of cuts. Sparks fly everywhere and can bounce off multiple surfaces. A fractured disc at 14,000rpm can cause untold damage. The author is particularly cautious when it comes to eye safety, but has still had various trips to A&E to have specks of grinding detritus removed.

Another consideration in your armoury is a plasma cutter, which is ideal for cutting out large areas of corrosion and cutting larger repair sections. Once very expensive, plasma cutters have dropped in price significantly in recent years and while there is always an element of getting what you pay for, on a hobby basis, even a lower-end plasma cutter will save significant time and energy when it comes to long cuts or getting into small spaces. Note that a plasma cutter will also need a suitable compressed-air supply.

Repair Sections and Materials

The following repair sections are available off the shelf from a range of manufacturers:

- Rear crossmember, with or without extensions
- Rear quarter chassis, including rear spring hangers
- Rear half chassis (88in) (rear crossmember up to and including body outriggers)
- Dumb irons with short and long extensions
- Front half chassis, including dumb irons and steering relay crossmember

A range of welding clamps and magnets may be required to align repair sections.

LEFT: A good amateur/entry level professional MIG welder is fine for chassis repairs.

Chassis Replacement and Restoration

There is a broad range of replacement outriggers and repair sections available and the quality of the parts is improving with increases in vehicle values.

- Bulkhead outriggers: both 88in and 109in types (109in are a deeper profile)
- Fuel tank outriggers
- Body outriggers: 88in and 109in
- Spring hanger outriggers for rear springs on 109in
- Spring hangers for rear of 88in
- Engine crossmember
- Gearbox crossmember: 88in and 109in

In addition to the above off-the-shelf items, you are likely to need 2mm and 3mm mild sheet steel. The original construction was in 14 SWG (2mm) steel with many of the brackets made in 11 SWG (3mm). Avoid using galvanised steel: it can give off toxic fumes when welded and, unless the zinc coating is ground off, it gives a poor weld. Replacement chassis sections usually come powder coated or pre-galvanised: again this will need to be cleaned off round the weld points.

General Advice and Considerations

It is not uncommon for chassis to have had poor repairs that can cause poor body and/or suspension alignment. If an original chassis is to be repaired from fully stripped state, a chassis jig based on heavy-duty box section might be required. However, significant structural repairs can be achieved to a high standard using a combination of string lines, spirit levels, laser levels, a flat floor and a measuring tape. The main thing to consider is not to remove too much of the chassis in one go so as to maintain structural rigidity and reference/datum points.

Simple, single or multiple use jigs can be easily fabricated for fitting outriggers, ensuring that bolt holes end up in the correct places. Be aware that Land Rover chassis were hand built and, while they were assembled on a jig, there will be variable tolerances. Most vehicles will have been built from new with spacers to align the bodywork, a topic dealt with in detail in Chapter 20. Be as accurate as you can, but millimetre-perfect is not always possible.

As well as jigs to retain/check/regain alignment, a repair spit is also an invaluable tool when carrying out multiple repairs. This can be made simply from box section and pick up on bumper and tow bar mounts (after any rear crossmember and dumb irons have

A box-section chassis jig makes life significantly easier but is not essential for most repairs.

LEFT: *A rotisserie makes life significantly easier when carrying out multiple repair jobs on a bare chassis.*

Chassis Replacement and Restoration

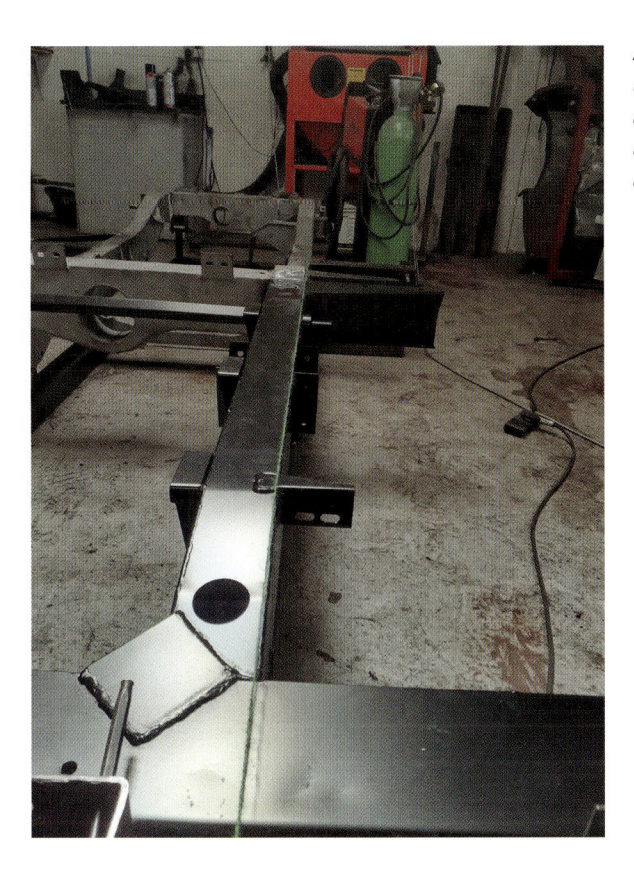

A string line can be used for a variety of alignment tasks, such as ensuring this half chassis is straight.

For best results, a stripped chassis should be sand-blasted to clean off all surface contaminants, reveal the extent of the corrosion and give a good surface for finished painting. Chemical dipping is another possibility for removing all internal coatings.

REAR CROSSMEMBER REPLACEMENT

While it is possible to fit a new rear crossmember with the body on, there is limited access to the top of the chassis rail, so very often this doesn't get welded or is welded poorly. To do the job to a high standard really requires the rear body to come off or alternatively remove the rear floor.

been carried out). This will also be invaluable for painting and rustproofing the chassis further down the line.

Flush welding and dressing can hide a repair, but to do so requires full penetration to ensure that flatting back does not compromise strength. Inserting a backing plate with plug welds is a good method to ensure a strong repair that can be flush finished. A good honest, neat visible weld is preferable to a hidden poor one.

Be aware that many chassis will have been filled with anti-corrosion wax and plastered in underseal, which will tend to contaminate the welding process.

Rear crossmember removed in sections to refit as per factory weld runs.

End rails dressed to receive the new crossmember. This side was in good condition.

- Keeping the rear body on has the advantage of acting like a jig where the new crossmember can be hung on the bolts on the back of the body and welded into place.
- Alternatively, a jig made up from simple box section can ensure alignment. Do be aware that previous repairs might not have been as accurate as you're planning to be, so always take multiple measurements.
- If corrosion is limited to the rear crossmember and the surrounding chassis rails are in good condition, a plain crossmember without extensions can be fitted. This gives the added advantage of ensuring that the factory weld lines are maintained, however, it is the most time-consuming method.
- Removing a complete crossmember to replace it as per factory fit takes multiple cuts and significant dressing of the chassis rails. Do not underestimate how long it can take to dress back old welds to ensure that the repair is invisible.
- If fitting a crossmember with extensions, the option with the spring hangers pre-attached makes life easier if there is significant corrosion further along the chassis rails. The extensions are designed to slide over the existing chassis rails. This can make for a strong repair, although at the expense of having a visible non-factory weld point. This is by no means a problem, it just comes down to personal approach and preference.

Chassis Replacement and Restoration

TOP LEFT: The spring hanger had rotted off on this side, a common occurrence.

MIDDLE LEFT: Spring hanger refitted after remedial reconstruction works to the chassis rail.

BOTTOM LEFT: Using a spirit level to ensure the new crossmember goes on straight and level.

ABOVE RIGHT: Original 75mm square strengthening gusset remade and fitted.

ABOVE LEFT: Fitting a rear quarter chassis/rear crossmember with extensions. These come designed to be slotted over the existing rails. Note this particular one was poorly made and had to be modified to fit properly.

ABOVE RIGHT: Rear quarter chassis fitted flush after some remedial work on the repair section.

Chassis Replacement and Restoration

Extensive rear crossmember repairs were carried out on the author's very original Series III, though replacement would have been easier.

- Another option is to trim the extension sections and flush-weld them using backing plates with plug and seam welds to give an invisible repair.
- Be aware that the rear wiring loom runs through the chassis. This should either be removed or pulled sufficiently forward (with a robust wire to pull it back) to avoid heat damage to the insulation.
- Repairing a rear crossmember is an option if the corrosion is limited. On this particular vehicle, which is owned by the author, the chassis was otherwise in very good condition and new metal could be let in so the repair was invisible. This is particularly important on a patina restoration or a recommission of a highly original vehicle. If you just want to carry out functional repairs, that's fine, just make sure the work is strong with good penetration back to good metal.

REPLACING A REAR HALF CHASSIS

Again there has to be a judgement call on the longevity of the rest of the chassis, but if it is otherwise sound, a rear half chassis represents a significant time and cost saving over a full replacement. When carried out correctly, it is possible to execute a repair that is strong, accurate and not immediately apparent.

- 88in half chassis extend from the rear crossmember to join the main rails behind the PTO crossmember (the one with the large, tubed hole in it) and includes the front body outriggers.
- Be aware that the new body outriggers seldom have the L-shaped attachment brackets, so these may need to come off your old outriggers or fabricated.
- Keeping the body on can help to align the rear half chassis replacement, although it is a cumbersome shape and weight to hold accurately in place during the replacement process.
- An alternative is to strip off the rear body and fabricate a box-section jig, which can be welded into place before making the brave final cuts. The rear axle, propshaft, rear brake line and exhaust sections have to be removed for this job.
- While a rear half chassis is designed to slide over the original rails with joggled ends, it is possible to execute a flush repair using internal gussets. In this instance, 200mm long plates were plug- and seam-welded inside the original chassis rails, the new half chassis slid over the top and seam- and plug-welded into place. While seeming simple, this takes significantly longer to execute than the traditional slide-over method and requires considerably more accuracy. The advantage is that the finished result is strong and pretty much invisible when dressed.

ABOVE LEFT: *A 109in rear half chassis complete with spring hangers.*

ABOVE RIGHT: *109in chassis jigged up ready for the relevant sections to be cut off.*

Chassis Replacement and Restoration

Complete rear section of chassis cut off.

RIGHT: *Rear section cut off and gusset plates puddle welded in (this is on an 88in chassis but it's the same technique).*

Using a G-clamp and a sash clamp to pull the chassis legs in tight for a perfectly straight finish.

LEFT: *New section slid over ready to be seam- and puddle-welded.*

- Whatever technique you use it is vital to maintain structural integrity and accuracy. You must prepare the weld joints thoroughly and ensure that you have full weld penetration. String lines are a simple but highly effective method for gauging accuracy. Measure multiple times during the rigging process. Use clamps and/or self-drilling screws to hold components into place. Tack weld in multiple places to ensure it doesn't move.
- When it comes to welding up, control how much heat goes into each run by alternating sides. Regularly check for any movement or distortion.

ABOVE LEFT: Join seam- and puddle-welded and ready for dressing.

ABOVE RIGHT: Rear section finished and ready for priming. This involves lots of work, but is worth it on a significant vehicle.

In-service fitment of an 88in rear half chassis using a box-section jig.

BULKHEAD OUTRIGGER REPLACEMENT

- Bulkhead outrigger replacement can be easily executed with the body on if carrying out running repairs, a recommission or a patina restoration. The advantage is that because the bulkhead remains in place, it acts as a jig to locate it accurately: simply use the bulkhead bolt to hold the outrigger in place during welding.
- If carrying out a repair with the body removed, accurate measuring and a jig will be required. This doesn't have to be overly complicated: simple box section tacked in place and accurate measurements to mounting points is usually adequate.
- Removing the old outrigger is straightforward using a grinder and slitting disc. It is common for the chassis rail behind the outrigger to have corroded through, so remedial work might be required to repair this.
- Replacement outriggers come with a backing plate designed to surface fit against the chassis rail. For a simple functional repair, this is perfectly acceptable.
- If, however, you wish to achieve a factory-fresh finish you have a couple of options. If the chassis rail is sound, you can cut the backing plate off and weld the outrigger directly onto the original rail.

ABOVE LEFT: Rusty outrigger – but the corrosion is reasonably isolated and not too deep.

ABOVE RIGHT: Chassis blasted and in the jig ready to remove the outrigger.

Chassis Replacement and Restoration

ABOVE LEFT: There was the usual rusty hole behind the outrigger, but corrosion was very isolated.

ABOVE RIGHT: New metal let in with a 1mm gap to allow for a good seam weld.

ABOVE LEFT: Welds dressed back ready to fit the outrigger.

ABOVE RIGHT: Outrigger comes with a backing plate, which can be cut off. Note also that the 109in bulkhead outrigger is deeper than the 88in type.

New outrigger fitted using the jig: note 'half welds' as used by the factory.

LEFT: A simple outrigger jig can be made using 2in box section to check the dimensions left to right.

Chassis Replacement and Restoration

- If the main rail has corroded, another option is to flush fit the outrigger complete with backing plate, cutting out the exact size of the backplate from the corroded rail.
- If fitting the outrigger to a stripped chassis, a simple jig combined with multiple measurements is invaluable.

DUMB IRONS

Dumb irons carry the stress load of the front suspension and potentially significant loads from recovery points. It is essential that they are in sound condition, but unfortunately they often suffer from corrosion. Land Rover uprated the strengthening gussets from approximately 1980, but these still suffer the same fate. Replacements are available for the earlier type used from 1958, but at the time of writing the later type was not readily available.

- The dumb iron can be fitted as an overlap sleeve or as a flush fitment for a factory finish. If doing the latter, adding backing plates on the joints to ensure a strong, full penetration weld is a wise idea.
- Be aware that some replacement dumb irons are more accurate than others. Ensure that the fitment positions the spring hanger in the correct place and that the bumper will sit level.
- A simple jig can be welded in place to align the position of the spring hanger bolt.
- If changing both dumb irons, ensure that you buy a matched set of replacements parts. A tube through both spring hangers will assist in aligning everything correctly.
- It is advisable to replace one at a time to ensure that you do not lose a datum line or reference point.
- Always take multiple measurements before and during the welding process. Tack the dumb iron in place and keep checking its accuracy as you seam-weld it in place. Alternate the welding seams to reduce the possibility of twisting.
- Be aware that the chassis number was originally stamped on the RHS dumb iron and it is advised to restamp the number back into the new component. This will remove any doubt over the identity of the vehicle should it need to be inspected.

ABOVE LEFT: *Typical corrosion inside a dumb iron – it looked OK from the outside.*

TOP RIGHT: *Using a simple jig to carry out an in-service dumb iron replacement.*

ABOVE RIGHT: *109in chassis in the jig with new dumb iron ready to fit.*

Chassis Replacement and Restoration

ABOVE LEFT: *All the rot has been cut out to the appropriate join point.*

ABOVE RIGHT: *New dumb iron mocked into place to check the fit.*

ABOVE LEFT: *Backing plates going in to carry out a flush repair.*

ABOVE RIGHT: *New dumb iron fitted and welds flatted back.*

PATCHING AND REPAIRS TO MAIN RAILS

- If patching a chassis, ensure you cut out any rusty metal or you will simply be trapping moisture against existing corrosion. Surface patches can be very strong but not as visually appealing as flush repairs.
- Flush repairs can be achieved as butt welds or with a backing plate, but you must ensure good weld penetration, especially if butt welding. A small gap between the sections to be welded aids good penetration and this can be easily achieved with a slitting disc.
- Series Land Rover chassis were mostly built as a box section with welds along the seams (note later Series III 109in were made from twin C-section pressings). If replac-

Using clamps to fit backing plates on a chassis rail repair.

Chassis Replacement and Restoration

ABOVE LEFT: Backing plates tacked in place.

ABOVE RIGHT: Clamping the repair section in place for seam welding.

ABOVE LEFT: Thinned bottom rail cut out, leaving a neat side edge to weld up to.

ABOVE RIGHT: New metal seam-welded in along the original weld lines.

ABOVE LEFT: Main rail drain hole reinstated.

ABOVE RIGHT: Tack welding a longer section of bottom rail in place. Each tack is used as a bend point to match the original profile.

Chassis Replacement and Restoration

Large side repair section tack-welded to a straight edge to hold it in place for flush-welding.

ing a top or bottom plate, it is usually best to cut back to the existing factory weld. Pre-cut sections of 75mm wide, 2mm steel sheet make life a lot easier: this is available from chassis parts suppliers or speak nicely to your local steel fabricators.

- Do not be afraid to cut out larger sections of chassis to remove corrosion, but do be aware of the dangers of twisting due to the weight of an assembled vehicle. If working on a bare chassis, larger areas can be cut out in one go, but it is vital to retain structural and geometric integrity.
- Tacking in place and alternating the location of short weld runs will reduce the likelihood of twisting. It is amazing how much a chassis will twist if too much localised heat is applied.

FINISHING

Sandblasting/Shotblasting

If carrying out a full chassis restoration, sandblasting is vital to ensure all the corrosion is removed and any weakened sections revealed. It also creates clean metal for welding repairs and a key for painting further down the line. Do be aware that once blasted the chassis will need to be kept dry or it will flash-rust very quickly.

Re-galvanising

The process of galvanising involves lowering steel into a bath of molten zinc, the zinc then forms a corrosion-resisting coating on the steel. It is essential to drill holes in box section to ensure the zinc flows in but doesn't form high-pressure pockets that can blow steel apart. Before galvanising, a chassis must be chemically dipped to remove any paint and other contaminants. The galvanisers will be able to advise the best method of preparation should you wish to go down this route. Some restorers are wary of galvanising repaired chassis and some galvanising companies refuse to dip them. Do your research and make a balanced decision: if it works well then it offers the best protection available, if it goes wrong, you could end up with a scrap chassis.

Painting

There is often great debate when it comes to painting a galvanised chassis. While galvanising is probably the best method of preserving steel, it can and does corrode. By nature it is slightly sacrificial and, on a vehicle used in arduous conditions, it will not guarantee the chassis remains rust-free. While a new bare galvanised chassis does look good, for extra protection and for the factory look it is advisable to paint a chassis. Paint does not stick well to new galvanising and it is advisable to use a 'mordant' solution to clean and dull it before using an appropriate etching primer. There are, however, products available that have been developed to go straight on to galvanising, acting as both etch primer and topcoat. These can be bought as a kit with comprehensive instructions and a suitable preparation degreaser. Correct preparation and application is vital to ensure the paint sticks.

Sand blasting is the most efficient way to remove paint and corrosion prior to and after significant repairs.

Chassis Replacement and Restoration

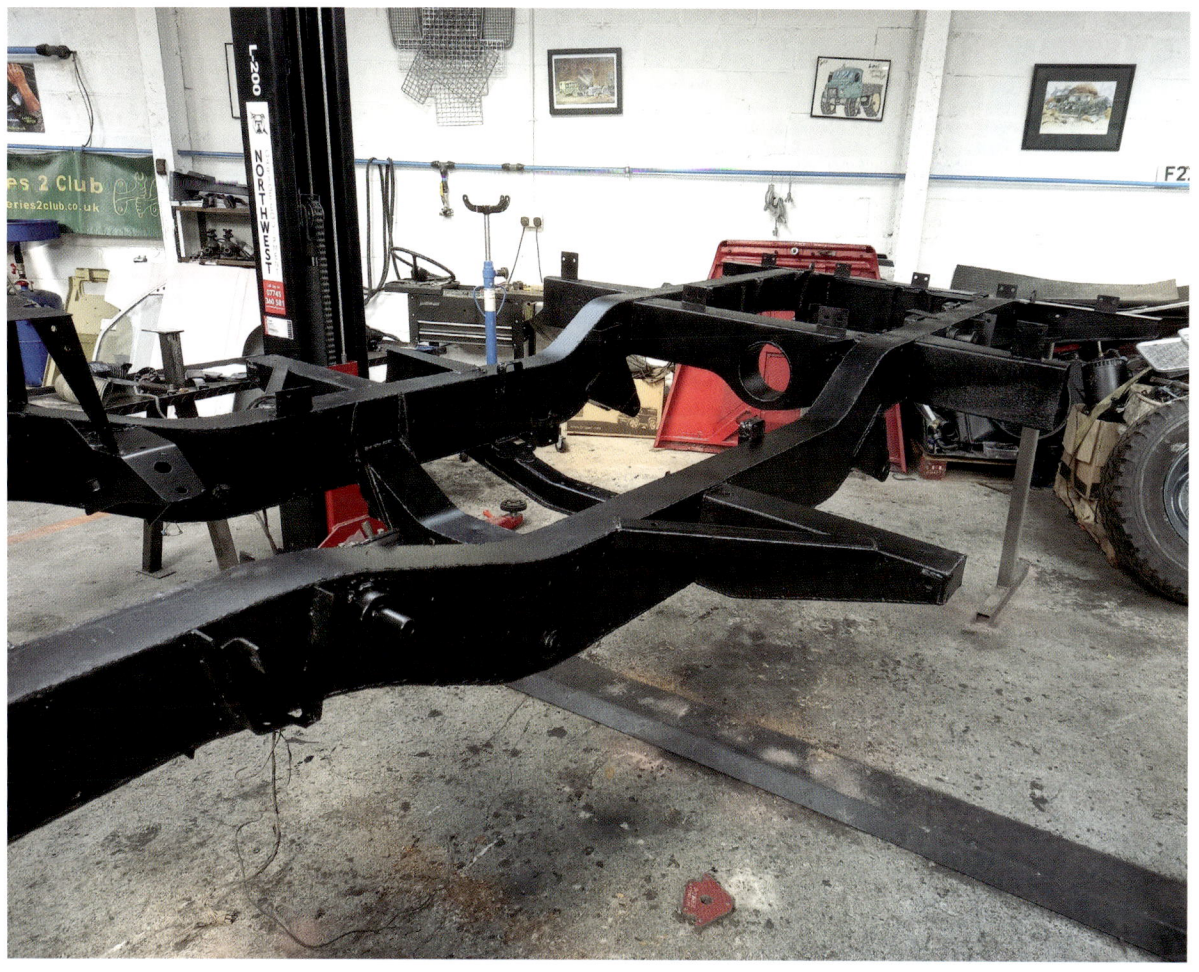

Fully restored Series III chassis finished in an etching paint and topcoat for longevity. The inside was also filled with cavity wax.

It is often assumed that Land Rover chassis were finished in matt black, but they were actually relatively glossy when new. A semi-gloss finish might be the closest match, although it does come down to personal taste and a resto-mod can look fantastic with a high gloss chassis finish. If going for a factory finish, note that if you examine an original chassis with original paint on it, you will see that paint runs are common, caused by the way the chassis was taken out of the dip tank: getting it 'perfect' might not actually be historically accurate. There is a broad range of products available from different manufacturers, some as a straight to metal primer and topcoat in one, some require a primer then a finish coat. Whatever you choose, thoroughly read and follow the manufacturer's instructions and safety notices.

Rustproofing

Whether galvanised or not, a chassis will always benefit from a thorough rustproofing inside and out. There is a wide range of products from different manufacturers, from thin cavity wax to thicker underbody sprays and undersealer. There are proprietary DIY hand pumps available for application, but a compressor-operated Schutz-type gun with appropriate nozzles and cavity tubes will tend to give better coverage and atomisation when applying to the inside of the chassis. If rustproofing a bare chassis, it is preferable to be able to rotate it on a spit to ensure complete coverage.

Old school techniques include using old gearbox oil sprayed on liberally. This has certainly worked on the author's own 1968 Series IIA. The chassis has never been repainted but was thoroughly sprayed with oil by its previous owner throughout its working life on a Lancashire farm. It retains much of its original paint and has required next to no welding. It is worth noting that Land Rovers do tend to leak engine and gearbox oil, so you will seldom find one with rust round those vital organs.

It is also worth noting that many Land Rovers will have had a very hard working life with minimal care and attention and yet have still survived to this day. Nowadays many classic Land Rovers will be living a retired life in relative luxury, often being regularly cleaned, and many covering small distances only during the summer months.

227

19
Bulkhead Restoration

Alongside the chassis, the condition of the bulkhead is of vital importance for the structural integrity of the whole vehicle. It supports and aligns not only the bodywork of the vehicle but also carries the steering, brakes, clutch and wiring systems. A Land Rover with a poor bulkhead is not only potentially dangerous, but it makes a significant impact on the integrity and value of the vehicle.

Bulkheads rust, in part due to the fact that it is an exposed steel component, but this is further exacerbated by the fact that the original construction method included multiple overlapped panels that create moisture traps. Bulkheads are time-consuming to repair to a high standard and poor historical repairs are all too common. Poor repairs can not only be unsightly and dangerous but also potentially detrimental to the alignment of the whole vehicle. The importance of the bulkhead in body alignment is dealt with in depth in Chapter 20 but, in short, a poor bulkhead will make a poor restoration.

NEW REPLACEMENT BULKHEADS

The cost of a new bulkhead is similar to the cost of a replacement chassis and the time involved in replacing one is similar to carrying out a complete body-off chassis swap. New bulkheads are available from a range of manufacturers. Some follow the original construction techniques and designs exactly, some improve them (for example with adjustable feet), simplify them (fewer overlapped joints) or rationalise them (such as providing a generic fit with fewer details). Some manufacturers galvanise their bulkheads for longevity, some manufacture them out of 'zintec' (zinc coated) sheet, others e-coat (electrophoretic paint) them. In addition, there are numerous specialists who will repair your original bulkhead to a high standard. Depending on the amount of work involved, this could work out almost as expensive as a new one, but will of course preserve the originality.

REPAIR SECTIONS

Repair sections for bulkheads have long been available, but in the last few years the quality and range of repair pieces has vastly improved. In the past, repair sections were pretty much limited to basic flat footwells and corner repair pieces. Historically, the relatively low value of the vehicle meant that it was not cost-effective for manufacturers to invest in developing a full range of more accurate parts. However, with the rise in values, rarity and the growing desire to restore vehicles accurately, the demand and will is there to produce authentic-looking parts that fit with minimal or no modification. Bulkheads that would otherwise have been scrapped and replaced with a better second-hand one in the past are now being repaired. In recent years both large and small companies have started to produce accurate footwells with the correct strengthening pressings and side panels, new 'feet' connecting to the outriggers, accurate door pillars,

ABOVE LEFT: *Be realistic! If your bulkhead looks like this, don't bother and order a new one.*

ABOVE RIGHT: *There are a few companies producing high-quality replacement bulkheads with all the right details.*

Bulkhead Restoration

Building a Jig

If you intend to undertake significant bulkhead repairs with it removed from the vehicle, you are very likely to need a jig. For this reason there are occasions when it is advantageous to leave it in place on the chassis after removing the surrounding components. Aligning door pillars and feet is particularly challenging without fixed points and datum lines. It is also vitally important to try to do one job at a time to retain structural integrity and fixed points. For example, you might choose to replace a foot and door pillar before removing the footwell. Obviously this will depend on what work is actually required: no two bulkheads corrode the same, although there is definitely a pattern of degradation. Footwells, attachment feet and top corners are the most common rot points.

If you do remove the bulkhead, a jig can be fabricated out of angle iron and box section. This will need to establish the bottom attachment points as an absolute minimum, but could also pick up on the lower windscreen attachment points as well as the forward depth of the footwells. The jig used in the repair photos in this manual is not the only method, but it does establish key data points. Coupled with a tape measure and a skilful pair of hands, it has been used to accurately restore many bulkheads. Do be aware that a jig needs to have a small amount of flexibility to accommodate small manufacturing tolerances. Remember the original units were assembled by hand and the repair sections are also hand made. Sometimes new and old parts need to be fettled to fit together.

A simple bulkhead jig can be made up using box section and angle iron. It must be able to set the position of the key fitting points and ensure that the bulkhead remains straight throughout the repair process.

A late Series IIA bulkhead restored from scrap by the author and ready for paint prep – it took four days in the workshop.

centre panels, full vent repair sections, drip channels, internal gussets and top rails.

A REALITY CHECK

Make no mistake, bulkheads are time-consuming to repair well. Most repair jobs require a significant strip-down of surrounding components such as wings, steering boxes, brakes, clutch, dash and wiring. Depending on the extent of the repairs, your own skill level and your time constraints, buying a new bulkhead or an already restored bulkhead might be the better option. Having said that, it's remarkable just what can be restored with patience and skill. Do not underestimate just how long it takes to drill out spot welds, clean up contact points, dress welds, ensure geometric accuracy and fettle new panels to fit.

Many seriously corroded bulkheads can be restored, but there has to be a point where you need to consider the time/cost/quality of the finished product. Bulkheads were assembled with a multitude of different sections spot-welded together. Ideally a complete component can be unpicked and replaced, however, if you have corrosion across multiple interlinked individual components, it is much harder to execute a good repair. The dash and interlinking parts on a Series II or IIA are a challenge, as are all bulkheads if the internal and external components in the top corners are severely corroded. While top rails are now available, the pressed sections round the vent panels are always a challenge to repair. There has to be a point when you need to balance the time/skill/money required to return a product you are happy with.

Sandblasting

If you are removing your bulkhead for a full restoration, sandblasting is ideal for removing paint, corrosion, giving good clean surfaces for welding and giving a good key for painting. Sometimes it can be advisable to give a bulkhead a second blast after repairs and before painting. A bulkhead should take about an hour for a professional company to blast and will be money well invested.

Bulkhead Restoration

FOOTWELLS

It would be very rare to find a Series Land Rover that had never had the footwells welded. They are in the firing line of road dirt and salt and are constantly damp due to the fact that no Land Rover is watertight. It was commonplace in the past to see repairs pop-riveted and bonded in place. While this can actually be done reasonably neatly, a properly executed repair must be welded in place. The footwells were originally spot-welded in place. If simply replacing a like for like panel, it is perfectly acceptable to replace spot welds with puddle welds or a series of penetrating tack welds of approximately 10mm. If a repair is carried out across a panel, however, it should technically be fully seam-welded, which can cause panels to warp. A section of flat copper plate is ideal to act as both a backing plate and a heat sink to execute a good repair without blowing through and warping the panel.

ABOVE LEFT: *Typical horrible previous repairs with nuts, bolts and screws – please don't do this.*

ABOVE RIGHT: *It can be a challenge to find all the old spot welds. Use a flap disc or a DA sander to get them to appear.*

Drilling out all the spot welds can take a lot of patience. A centre punch and a 10mm drill bit are fine or a special spot-weld drill can be useful if you only need to drill through one skin.

RIGHT: *Sometimes it is helpful to carry out a 'relief cut' to remove sections of the panel. A plasma cutter is ideal for this, although a slitting disc does the job fine.*

Bulkhead Restoration

ABOVE LEFT: It is essential to dress the edges of the old panels to ensure a good fit and a clean weld. Use a hammer and dolly to straighten any bent edges.

ABOVE RIGHT: Most footwells come as two sections: a toe board and a side panel. Fit the side panel to the door pillar and clamp in place before tack welding in place. Make sure they can be removed if necessary.

Offering a new toe board into place. It is common to have to trim the inner edge for the best fit. Clamp it in place and hold it in place with some tack welds.

RIGHT: Ensure that the bottom flange of the footwell is parallel to the bulkhead outrigger or frame of the jig. This is essential to ensure the floorplates and transmission tunnel fit correctly.

Bulkhead Restoration

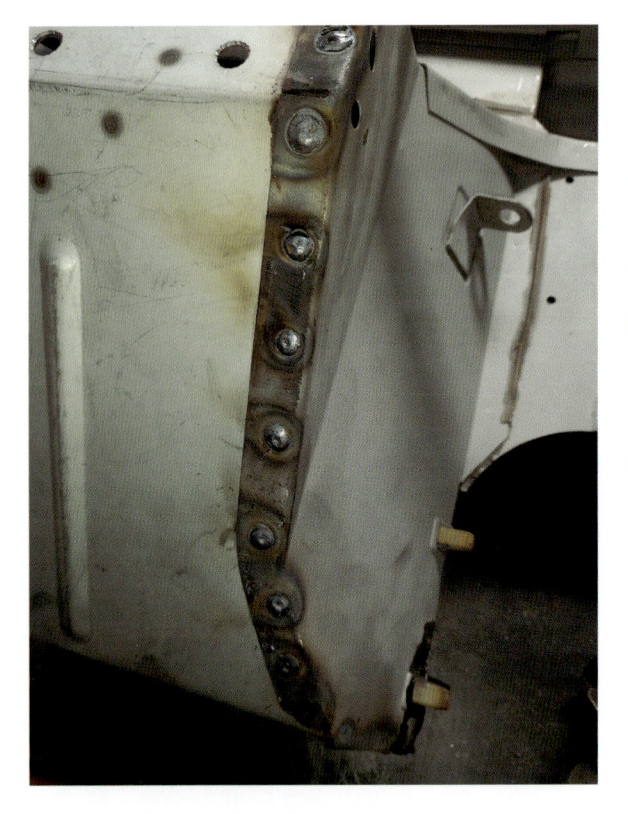

It's very likely you'll have to carry out other remedial work to surrounding panels once the main section of footwell is in place.

LEFT: *Once the position of the footwell has been checked and checked again, fill in all the drilled spot weld holes with plug welds. Use a clamp to hold the panels tight adjacent to each weld as the heat will tend to lift the metal apart.*

ABOVE LEFT: *Very often the bottom edge of the centre panel will have rusted through. Here a new section is being butt-welded into place with a copper plate behind to reduce blow-through and warping.*

ABOVE RIGHT: *If the top or side of the footwell is still in reasonable condition, the new panel can be joined in at the most appropriate place rather than having to unpick a lot of good metal.*

LEFT: *In this instance, sections of footwell were blended in along the upper return and down the lower section of the side panel. It was then fully seam-welded before flatting back to give an invisible repair.*

Bulkhead Restoration

ABOVE LEFT: A raw repaired bulkhead with new/repaired footwells will still need a lot of additional fettling work to make it look as good as new.

ABOVE RIGHT: And here it is: tiny amounts of filler, some seam sealant, some etch primer and topcoat and it's as good as new.

FEET AND PILLARS

Feet and pillars can be replaced without having to remove the bulkhead from the vehicle and the chassis and surrounding bodywork can be used as a jig as long as there is still some structural integrity. If both pillar and footwell need replacing on a vehicle, do one at a time. Often it is easier to replace a pillar/foot first, as this puts accuracy and rigidity back in before hacking too much out.

ABOVE LEFT: An all too common bodge fitting a bulkhead foot. This one was simply bolted in place through the hinge bolts: the photo was taken halfway through rectification.

ABOVE: The bulkhead foot is attached with multiple spot welds and it can take a while to find them all.

LEFT: All spot welds drilled out, other remedial works will be carried out when the structure is sound again.

Bulkhead Restoration

ABOVE LEFT: *Old foot knocked off. It's rare for them to come out this cleanly and it can take ages to remove stubborn sections.*

ABOVE RIGHT: *The new foot will usually be coated and this must be removed before it can be welded into place.*

ABOVE LEFT: *Clamp the foot into place aligning with the door hinge holes and the outrigger bolt/jig.*

ABOVE RIGHT: *Puddle-welded in place, this can then be flatted back to give a good finish.*

Bulkhead Restoration

Door pillar replacement is just a variation on the theme, but it is vital to maintain the geometric integrity of the bulkhead on the jig or vehicle before cutting out too much surrounding metal.

RIGHT: *Pillar and footwell tacked together. Check the alignment in multiple places before committing to fully welding.*

ABOVE LEFT: *Most pillars don't come with the door seal return lip. Here a strip of folded steel is being fitted to give the original look.*

ABOVE RIGHT: *Pillar and footwell finally welded up and multiple plug welds flatted back.*

TOP RAIL REPAIRS

Top repair sections are available from basic corner through to full vent panels. The vent panel area is particularly time-consuming to repair and the corners have multiple layers of steelwork that often corrode inside and out. A range of repair sections is available, but multiple sections requiring repair in this area may be the death knell for a bulkhead, or at least a significant factor in deciding whether to replace with a better one or a new replica. Another alternative is to source a used top rail from a better bulkhead and blend it in.

Bulkhead Restoration

ABOVE LEFT: The quick way to repair the top corners is to overlay a repair section – functional but not pretty.

ABOVE RIGHT: Top corner opened up showing the multiple layers of internal metalwork.

ABOVE LEFT: Sections of a front repair panel trimmed to fit for a flush finish.

ABOVE RIGHT: Multiple clamps may be required to hold repair sections in place while they are tacked in.

ABOVE LEFT: Corner repair section flatted back for an invisible repair.

ABOVE RIGHT: An unusual large hole behind the drip channel makes for a challenging repair.

Bulkhead Restoration

Drip channel drilled off with a spot-weld drill bit and new metal let in.

BELOW LEFT: *This Series III bulkhead needed the full works – pillars, feet, footwells and top corner repairs. Here it is being prepped for paint.*

PAINT/PROTECTION

There is great debate regarding galvanising a bulkhead. Some replacements come pre-galvanised, other companies shy away from the process as it can lead to warping and so fabricate the bulkhead using Zintec coated steel. Repaired bulkheads are particularly prone to warping, although some report that they come out fine if appropriately prepared and jigged. However, well-applied paint and cavity wax should offer good protection: the factory applied only a thin coat of primer and topcoat and many bulkheads have lasted decades of hard graft, not the occasional use that many of our classic Land Rovers get now. Ensure a good-quality etch primer is used and build up a few good layers of paint. Up-end the bulkhead and get a good dose of wax into pillars and top corner cavities.

Only later Series IIIs had any form of seam sealer between panels. If carrying out a full restoration with sandblasting and new paint, it may well be a sensible addition, even if it wasn't original. As well as reducing the likelihood of moisture creeping between unpainted layers of steel, it can also hide a slightly rough welded joint.

BELOW LEFT: *After a coat of etch primer and a primer filler, the decision was made to apply seam sealer to the joints to reduce moisture ingress. This was a factory process on late Series IIIs.*

BELOW RIGHT: *The Series III bulkhead shown in many of the photos finished in two-pack Marine Blue and ready to be fitted.*

BOTTOM LEFT: *With accurate measuring and a jig this bulkhead fitted straight back onto the chassis with no issues. Take your time, keep measuring and even a rough bulkhead will go back on again.*

BOTTOM RIGHT: *With the correct profile footwell repair sections painted up, you'd never know this bulkhead had been repaired.*

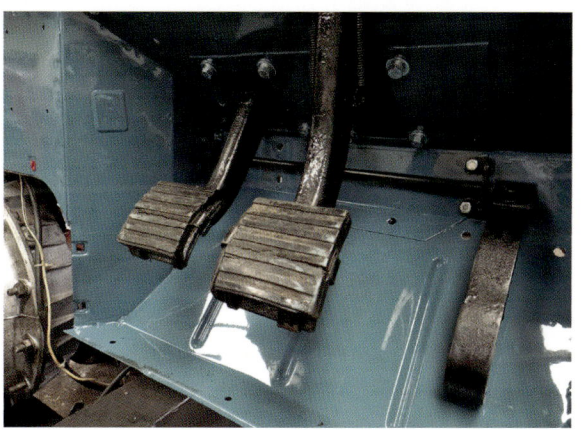

237

20 Bodywork Fitting, Repairs and Finish

Land Rover bodywork has to be the ultimate life-sized model kit. One of the joys of the Series Land Rover is that simple aluminium panels bolt together onto a steel chassis and bulkhead with basic fixings. The simplicity of the kit means it is easy to assemble – equally well, it is also easy to assemble badly. Poor body alignment is common and doors that require a hefty slam to close are often accepted as the norm. While the Land Rover was built as a basic working vehicle, this does not mean that it can't be assembled well with reasonable alignment and doors that close with a satisfying 'clunk'. It's fair to say that there were 'engineering tolerances' when the vehicles were new, but if you study period factory photos, none of them will show vehicles with droopy wings and poor panel gaps. With a systematic approach and patience, it is perfectly possible to match if not better the factory standard of body fitment. The old 1970s poor-quality mitigation joke, 'they all do that, Sir', need not apply and this chapter covers a range of tasks from repairs to body alignment tips.

CHASSIS AND BULKHEAD INTEGRITY

Obviously the chassis is the backbone of the vehicle and the fit of the bodywork is dependent on its geometric integrity. It is worth checking key dimensions on a repaired chassis (see Chapter 18) before fitting bodywork. If fitting a new chassis from one of the well-known manufacturers, it is unlikely that there would be significant inaccuracies. Obviously there could be mistakes in the build process, but these are uncommon. Having said that, small fixing holes might have to be opened up to achieve the best fit. Remember, these are predominantly hand-assembled items. However, many problems encountered when building a vehicle onto a new chassis are down to the inexperience of the assembler and bolting the bodywork up too tight in the wrong order.

Again, Chapter 19 above is dedicated to repairing a bulkhead. The whole bodywork depends on the bulkhead being geometrically accurate and, just as importantly, correctly fitted to the chassis. Even from new, bulkheads were usually fitted with spacer shims and washers: you can reasonably expect to adjust the bulkhead on various occasions throughout the bodywork assembly process. New bulkheads should be supplied as accurate units ready to fit and again problems are mostly down to the skill of the assembler. However, a thorough inspection and a dry build is worthwhile before committing to an expensive paint finish.

'No, sir, they don't all have droopy doors that need a slam to close.'

Chassis and bulkhead integrity are obviously essential for good body alignment, but a skilled hand and patience is also necessary.

Bodywork Fitting, Repairs and Finish

DRY BUILD

Just about every top restorer carries out a 'dry build'. A dry build is a trial assembly of the bodywork to confirm alignment and carry out any fettling jobs before committing the metalwork to any finishing process. You can reasonably expect to have to make slight adjustments, drill or enlarge fixing holes and, on occasion, carefully manhandle components together to judge best fit. Remember that a Land Rover will usually have had a hard working life. Panels do flex and bend as well as suffering obvious accidental damage, knocks and bruises. A dry build should be done before final painting, just in case remedial work is required.

BODYWORK ASSEMBLY ORDER

There are variations on a theme when it comes to the assembly order, but the most common mistake when assembling the bodywork is to fit the bulkhead and wings solidly to the chassis and then work backwards. While this can be successful, it is often far easier and more accurate to follow a systematic approach, mostly working from the back to the front.

The following order is obviously open to change and personal preference, but it is a tried and tested approach and can be modified for both an initial dry build and for final assembly.

- Fit the bulkhead loosely to the chassis with the long bolts through the outriggers. The bulkhead can then be dressed with the steering box, upright mounts and pedal boxes. Do not tighten any mounting bolts at this stage, but eye it in at 90 degrees to the top of the chassis rail.
- If possible, set the rolling chassis on level ground and, if necessary, level the vehicle up, checking with a spirit level. While being level is not 100 per cent essential, it is an additional aid when checking alignment.
- Place the rear body tub on the chassis and loosely bolt in place on the tabs on the rear crossmember. This is often considered a fixed point at this stage, but small adjustments are possible.
- Fix a string line all the way around the waistline/body swage from the bulkhead to the rear of the tub. The swage on the bulkhead door pillar will become an alignment datum point as this is a fixed height point (unless previously unnoticed remedial structural modifications are required to the chassis/bulkhead).
- Adjust the forward height of the rear body to match the string line using a trolley jack to raise/lower. Temporarily nip up the fixing bolts in the forward body mounting outriggers. Spacer plates may be required to take up any gaps between the tub mounting points and the outrigger tabs.
- Adjust the body on the rear crossmember tabs to achieve the best fit and nip up. The tub must also be adjusted for both up and down and side to side planes at this point.
- Note that there might be a small gap between the tub floor crossmembers and the corresponding chassis supports. Don't worry about this at this stage, as appropriate rubber packers can be fit-

Early on in a dry build ensuring the restored bulkhead is a good fit on the restored chassis.

ABOVE LEFT: *Trial fitment of the rear tub to ensure it lines up with the bulkhead swage line.*

ABOVE RIGHT: *Dry build confirms that a door gap of 880mm is achievable.*

Bodywork Fitting, Repairs and Finish

- ted if necessary. Remember that, with wear and tear, rear bodies do get stretched and misshapen and chassis mounting brackets can vary in height.
- The tailgate/rear door aperture should also be checked at this point. The sides should be parallel, but they often taper in or out at the top leading to a poor tailgate fitment. It can be adjusted by using a sash clamp to open or close it as necessary.
- With the rear body roughed in place and nipped up, you can now work forwards to the bulkhead to set the front door gap and finalise the bulkhead position.
- The door gap from tub to bulkhead should be set to approximately 875–880mm at bottom and top. Measure from where the body panel turns 90 degrees inwards to the seal lip (that is, the visible door aperture when the door is closed). Set the bottom door gap first.
- If necessary, an appropriate number of washers can be inserted between the outrigger and bottom mounting foot. To avoid having to remove the bolt numerous times, a washer can be cut to create a U- shape that can be dropped in from above.
- The top door gap is set by adjusting the angle of the bulkhead with a combination of setting the upright/steering box bracket within the slotted holes and an appropriate number of packers to the footwell.
- A ratchet strap or a sash clamp might be required to hold the bulkhead in the correct place while the fixings are nipped up.
- In some cases it might be necessary to slightly elongate the holes in the bulkhead/steering box upright to ensure a good fit.
- Once the door gap is correctly set, firmly nip up all the nuts and bolts in the rear tub and bulkhead while checking the alignment remains correct: it is common for it to change as the bolts tighten.
- Fit the door hinges. Series II and IIA models fit into captive threaded plates, Series III hinges have J-nuts, which hook in though the square hole in the pillar. Buy the best you can afford as some are prone to twisting, allowing the square nut to pop out. The standard thread size is 5/16th UNF although metric equivalent M8s are also available, so check the thread before fitting. Remember to fit the plastic shims/gaskets. Note that a small amount of grease allows adjustment without damaging the paint.

ABOVE LEFT: *The starting point of good body alignment with the bulkhead loosely bolted to the chassis.*

ABOVE RIGHT: *Rear of tub lined up with the tabs on the rear crossmember.*

LEFT: *Later Series IIIs had captive nuts on a plate to make it easier to bolt the rear of the tub.*

Bodywork Fitting, Repairs and Finish

ABOVE LEFT: *A string line tied tightly round the barrel swage line is essential to gauge alignment.*

ABOVE: *Using a block of wood on a trolley jack to adjust the tub height.*

LEFT: *Tub swage line perfectly aligned with the string and ready to tighten in place.*

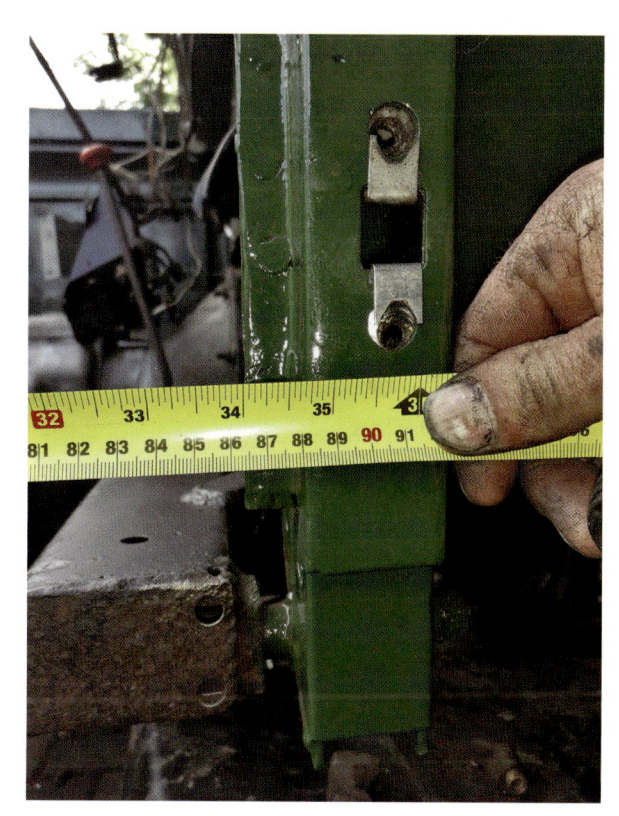

ABOVE LEFT: *Checking/setting the bottom door gap to 880mm.*

ABOVE RIGHT: *Setting/checking the top door gap to match the bottom.*

241

Bodywork Fitting, Repairs and Finish

Two different types of J-nuts: the later type on the right is easier to align, although it is only available in metric.

RIGHT: J-nuts in place and daubed with copper grease to assist hinge movement.

ABOVE LEFT: Hinge in place with a plastic seal/gasket behind.

ABOVE RIGHT: Rear of door adjusted to match the swage line and parallel to the rear tub.

- Hang the door on the hinge and adjust the door position to match the waist alignment and give a good balance of shut lines. Note that doors might not be perfectly square and the skin may taper out towards the bottom.
- Doors are often slightly twisted and this, coupled with different swage line profiles, can mean the door does not sit flat to the rear body side. The door may have to be carefully twisted to line up: this is common and just part of the process of assembling the bodywork.

Bodywork Fitting, Repairs and Finish

TOP LEFT: *Front of door adjusted to match the swage line and barrel side.*

MIDDLE LEFT: *Note that 88in (shown here) and 109in inner wings are different to match the profile of the chassis. A 109in wing will fit an 88in (with a gap), an 88in wing will need to be trimmed to fit an 109in.*

BOTTOM LEFT: *Wing height adjusted to match the bulkhead and door swage line and barrel side.*

ABOVE RIGHT: *Wing is slotted in place on the spire bolts.*

Wings should be horizontal and parallel to the bumper: space the front panel up slightly if necessary.

243

Bodywork Fitting, Repairs and Finish

At this stage, walk around and be critical – does it line up as well as it can? Sometimes a bit of compromise is required, but do your best.

ABOVE LEFT: Cappings fitted and still in line – you can space them up if necessary.

ABOVE RIGHT: Passenger side is usually slightly easier to align for some reason.

Bodywork Fitting, Repairs and Finish

Hard top trial-fitted to ensure that the screen angle matches the door top. Hard top sides might need to be spaced up with washers for the best fit.

- Once both sides have been fully roughed in, run the string line round again and check for accuracy. It is common for slight movement to occur at this stage, so check and check again. Be aware that on occasion you will need to find a compromise; after all every part of the vehicle is hand built within the limitations of time and budget.
- While there are likely to be numerous engine bay jobs to complete at this stage, if working on the final assembly it is advisable to carry out a trial fitment of the wings, front panel and bonnet.
- The wings attach to the bulkhead pillars on J-nuts and spire bolts. Note that these are *not* the same as floor screw fixings (floor screws are considerably lighter duty). A smear of grease on the attachment point allows for easy adjustment without damaging the paint. Carefully match the swage line of the wing to the bulkhead pillar. Fitting a wing is much easier with two people, especially if newly painted.
- Note that the front panel can be spaced up slightly to finalise the wing alignment. The bottom of the wings should be parallel to the bumper and the chassis rails. It is very common for wings to have been leaned on/forced in, and for the outer edge to be bent down and inner edge bent into the chassis dumb irons. Once the front panel has been fitted and wings bolted on, careful lifting at the corner can gently bring the wing back into alignment.
- Fit the hinges loosely to the bonnet and fit to the bulkhead. Carefully lower the bonnet down to the front panel. If working with newly painted panels, put clean cardboard on the wing top to protect them. The bonnet can then be adjusted to fit before tightening the bonnet hinges. The position of the top of the front panel may have to be adjusted to sit parallel with the leading edge and allow for the striker plate components to line up.
- It is common for the wing tops to have been bent down, leading to a large gap to the wing top. This seems to be exacerbated by the fact that some bonnet pressings seem to rise up, especially on the driver's side (often the case on late Series III with a deluxe bonnet). This can mean that the brake fluid reservoir is easily visible. This can be adjusted by lifting up the lower inner wing fixing to bulkhead upright and by careful fitment of the inner wing mud shield. However, it might have to be accepted as just one of those Land Rover quirks.
- Once the lower bodywork has been fully roughed in, the door sills, seat box, transmission tunnels and floors can be fitted.

REAR TUB (BODY) REPAIRS

Land Rover always referred to the load area as the rear body, but common nomenclature is to refer to it as the rear tub. Obviously these were different between 88in and 109in utilities, and of course the 109in Station Wagon. There were also small differences between different year models. The wheel arch shape of 109 models changed during Series IIA production with a more progressive curve on later models. Note also that the 6-cylinder had a rear-mounted fuel tank and filler, which was standardised for all 109in models in 1974. Note that the location of the number plate varies: in the UK the number plate was usually fitted to the offside until about 1979, when it moved to the near side to accommodate the legal requirement to have a rear fog lamp on the offside. Changes to the rear tub also included different light arrangements towards the end of Series III production. A 'top and bottom' light arrangement started to be introduced in 1983, matching that on the newly introduced coil spring One Ten model.

The most common damage to the rear body is corrosion to the aluminium panels where they touch against the steel mounting points on the chassis. A combination of dissimilar metals, salt and moisture is the perfect environment for aluminium to turn to powder. This is also common in the rear floor

Bodywork Fitting, Repairs and Finish

Good tip – a complete lower Land Rover body will just fit inside a rear tub for storage purposes.

New rear floor bonded in place and new galvanised floor crossmembers riveted in place.

where the aluminium touches the steel floor strengthening crossmembers.

The original construction of the rear body was a combination of rivets and spot welds. The usual 'approved' repair process is to replace the panels using pop rivets and bonding adhesive as it is challenging to execute a good weld on old aluminium. Specialist welding equipment and skills are required if a 'factory' finish aluminium repair is required. There are a number of DIY aluminium brazing rods on the market that can give mixed results. Often it comes down to good surface preparation and getting appropriate heat in quickly to minimise panel warping.

Rear Floor Panel

The simple method is to overlay the existing floor. This can be bought as a pre-cut sheet from one of the specialist suppliers or can be cut from a sheet of appropriate grade of aluminium. The original 'Birmabright' was an alloy of aluminium and magnesium: a modern equivalent is NS4 or 5251. A combination of a suitable bonding adhesive and countersink pop rivets can produce a very neat result for a DIY build.

Alternatively, a full floor panel section can be bought complete with top hat strengthening sections attached. The top hat strengthening strips are prone to corrosion where the body crossmembers touch it: this area is constantly dirty and damp with no corrosion protection. Again, the full floor can be fitted using bonding adhesive and pop rivets if specialist welding is not viable. Note that the original floor was fitted using a combination of rivets and spot welds. Rear floor crossmembers are very likely to have corroded and new galvanised ones are available.

FULL BODY SIDES

Full body sides are available and represent good value for money if there is considerable damage to the original panel. These were originally fitted with rivets and spot welds, although for the DIY restorer it is considerably easier to fit with rivets and a suitable polyurethane adhesive. Bonding technology has developed significantly in modern times. Countersink rivets can also be used and then hidden with a small skim of filler as necessary.

ABOVE LEFT: *Old repairs were poor, so the side has to come off this rear tub.*

ABOVE RIGHT: *Drilling out multiple side panel spot welds.*

Bodywork Fitting, Repairs and Finish

Whole side removed and dressed for a new panel.

LEFT: *Even more spot welds. The eagle-eyed will see that this is a Ninety tub, but it's constructed in the same way as a Series vehicle.*

Take time to rough the panel in before committing to any drilling, bonding or welding.

RIGHT: *Visible exterior rivet to match the factory assembly techniques: it holds the side in place while the adhesive goes off.*

For the 'rivet counter' approach, take note of the pattern of the original rivets and locate them in the same place. In addition, an appropriate round punch can be used to replicate the pattern of the original spot welds.

REAR SIDE PANELS

These are available from a variety of sources; some come in bare aluminium, some are powder coated. These can be fitted with rivets and an appropriate bonding adhesive.

Alternatively, if a neat DIY repair is acceptable for your build standard, the original panel can simply be over-plated using a suitable grade of aluminium. A folded return into the recess for the rear door seal is a neat solution to make the repair invisible. In addition,

Bodywork Fitting, Repairs and Finish

ABOVE LEFT: Typical tub rear panel with bimetallic corrosion on the lower edge from the steel crossmember tab.

ABOVE RIGHT: New rear panels are readily available. This one came in bare aluminium for welding in place, but most seem to have a coat of black primer.

An alternative to bonding the panel in place is to do a series of puddle welds with a MIG set up for aluminium.

RIGHT: Another option is to overplate a damaged rear panel with flat aluminium sheet with a return fold to the door aperture. This can be bonded and held in place with rivets in the capping holes while it goes off.

the panel can be bonded in position using temporary rivets in the body capping holes to hold it in place until the adhesive goes off. The rivets can then be drilled out before painting and then refitted with the body cappings.

FRONT PANEL REPAIRS

The bottom of the front panel is particularly prone to corrosion. A range of good repair sections is available from different suppliers, but go for the one that has all the correct radiused return on the lower lips – it doesn't cost a lot more to fit something 100 per cent correct.

Bodywork Fitting, Repairs and Finish

Typically rusty front panel with a good-quality repair section ready to be fitted.

RIGHT: Drilling out the spot welds to the radiator panels.

BELOW LEFT: Lower section being cut off. Do not cut through the backing section.

BELOW RIGHT: New section ready to be fitted.

Using clamps to hold the sections together for tacking in place.

LEFT: Using box section to assist in clamping the repair section on straight.

Bodywork Fitting, Repairs and Finish

Multiple clamps being used to ensure every arris lines up perfectly.

RIGHT: *Seam-welded on the back side, it can be flatted on the front side.*

The finished repair flatted back and ready for a tiny skim of filler and paint.

LEFT: *Reinstating a spot weld with a puddle weld on the front face.*

DOOR REPAIRS

Door Bottoms

Repairing the bottom of a door makes very little sense commercially, unless the intention is to undertake a patina restoration retaining the original body panels. New doors are available at a reasonable cost and the quality of products on the market has improved significantly. For a long time, many aftermarket doors were very prone to corrosion, in particular bimetallic corrosion between the steel frame and the aluminium skin.

Repairing a door is very satisfying and viable on a DIY basis. Repair sections are available either as a plain bottom profile section or with a return up the door frame, including the holes for the lower hinge.

Door Tops

Door tops rot and it is very rare to see any Series Land Rover with its original

Bodywork Fitting, Repairs and Finish

Typical rusty Series rear door bottom.

RIGHT: Cutting out along the old mitred joint. Use a chisel to stop the cutting disc from damaging the skin.

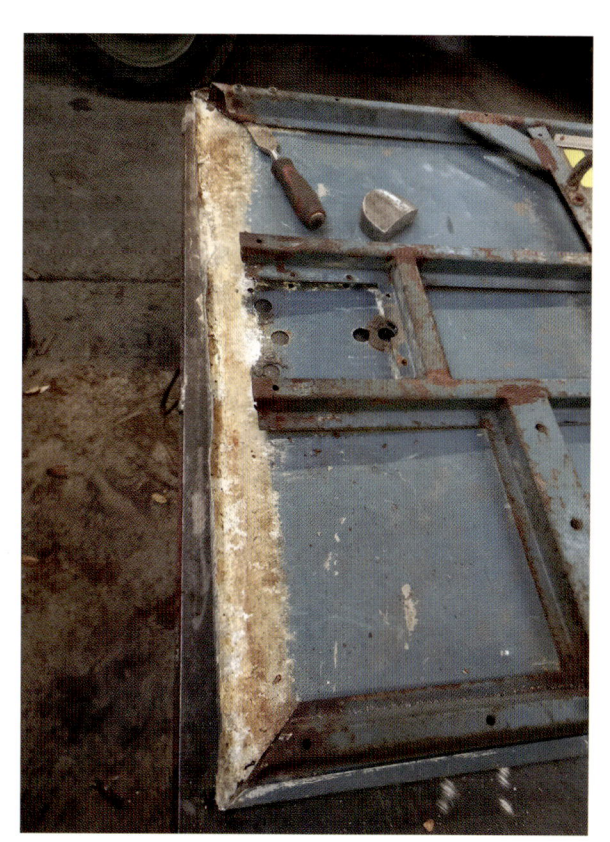

ABOVE LEFT: With the skin edge folded back, the offending rusty bottom is removed, revealing all the old bimetallic corrosion powder.

ABOVE RIGHT: Cleaned up and ready for a thin coat of etch primer.

door tops in reasonable condition. This is mostly due to the fact that water from the windows runs into the slider channel and into the door top before draining out through two small drain holes. The inside of the door top seldom dries out and is usually poorly painted, so it's inevitable that corrosion will set in.

It is sometimes possible to execute reasonable repairs to door tops if original to the vehicle and corrosion is limited. Otherwise, it is far more time-

Bodywork Fitting, Repairs and Finish

Using a combi-square to mark a 45-degree mitre cut in the repair section.

RIGHT: Door bottom repair section cut and primed prior to welding in place.

ABOVE LEFT: Polyurethane adhesive bonds the section in place prior to welding and creates a corrosion barrier.

ABOVE RIGHT: Repair section clamped in place and ready to be welded in the corners.

Bodywork Fitting, Repairs and Finish

and often cost-effective to replace them with new ones. Both glazed and unglazed options are available. The drawback with glazed ones is that they are only finished in primer and the glazing will have to be stripped off to paint them properly. It is always wise to add a healthy dose of paint and rustproofing inside the door top before fitting.

If wishing to keep the original patina/paint of the outer aluminium panels, it is possible to carefully remove the panels and fit them to a few frame.

ABOVE LEFT: *Sometimes corrosion creeps around the corners. Either buy the larger repair section with uprights or repair like this.*

ABOVE RIGHT: *Mitred joint welded and flatted back.*

ABOVE LEFT: *Folding the bottom panel lip back using grips and a thick metal plate to avoid damaging the skin.*

ABOVE RIGHT: *Sometimes localised repairs are all that are necessary in a door bottom.*

Bodywork Fitting, Repairs and Finish

ABOVE LEFT: *New steel in place making an invisible repair when painted.*

ABOVE RIGHT: *This door skin was removed from a rotten frame and transferred to a new one to preserve the original paint.*

While door tops are seldom worth repairing, the skins can be reused on an original patina vehicle.

PAINTING

Hand Painting

Many Land Rovers have been brush- or roller-painted over the years with varying results. Contrary to popular belief, it is possible to get a perfectly reasonable brush/roller finish on an everyday vehicle. However, there is also a growing trend to appreciate 'patina'. This is a debatable concept, but if a vehicle still has its original factory paint in reasonable condition it is often better to leave it. Original factory paint is relatively rare and, if sound, overpainting it badly will tend to devalue the vehicle. Obviously, it is down to the individual owner, but slightly age-worn factory paint is always going to be better than a poorly executed refresh.

The key to any good paint job is in the preparation. Old paint must be sanded back to a solid base and must be primed. Bare aluminium must be etch-primed to ensure good adhesion. This can then be followed by a primer filler to iron out any imperfections before flatting back. Finally a topcoat can be applied. A number of thin coats is usually better than one thick coat. There are a number of specialists who supply good-quality brush or sprayable coat enamel and have extensive information on coach painting to give a quality finish.

Spray Painting

DIY Advice

Land Rovers were spray painted at the factory and, contrary to popular belief, were shiny with a good-quality finish. The paint was applied very thinly over a wash coat of etch primer, which has a golden colour.

Most professional bodyshops use 2K (2-pack) paint that gives off harmful fumes and requires specialist breathing apparatus, so is not usually suitable for DIY use. However, a good home respray is possible with synthetic coach enamel and specialist suppliers usually have a good website with a range of tips and techniques. For small repairs, a rattle can is a viable alternative to an air-operated spray gun, although it would be very expensive and wasteful for a whole vehicle.

Professional Painting

It is actually very difficult to replicate the original factory finish, but a good professional bodyshop should be able to get reasonably close. Most of the time and expense of a professional respray is in the preparation. To keep costs down, a large proportion of the work can be done on a DIY basis.

It is always preferable to remove all old paint: this can be done with professional strength paint stripper, but is very time-consuming. All traces of any chemicals must be removed and panels usually need to be 'DAed' (dual action sanded) to give a good key. Given how long this task takes, it may be more effective to have the panels professionally dipped to remove all traces of old paint. An alternative would be to have the aluminium soda-blasted. Note that 'sand' blasting is too aggressive for aluminium and will usually leave a very harsh gritty surface and distort the panel.

Bodywork Fitting, Repairs and Finish

It's massively time-consuming removing all traces of old paint – it's much easier to have it professionally dipped.

LEFT: Using industrial strength paint stripper to remove layers of old paint.

A professional respray being carried out on the author's Series III. Note the bright white paint booth lights to show any imperfections.

LEFT: A very thin layer of body filler used on some shallow dents.

Bodywork Fitting, Repairs and Finish

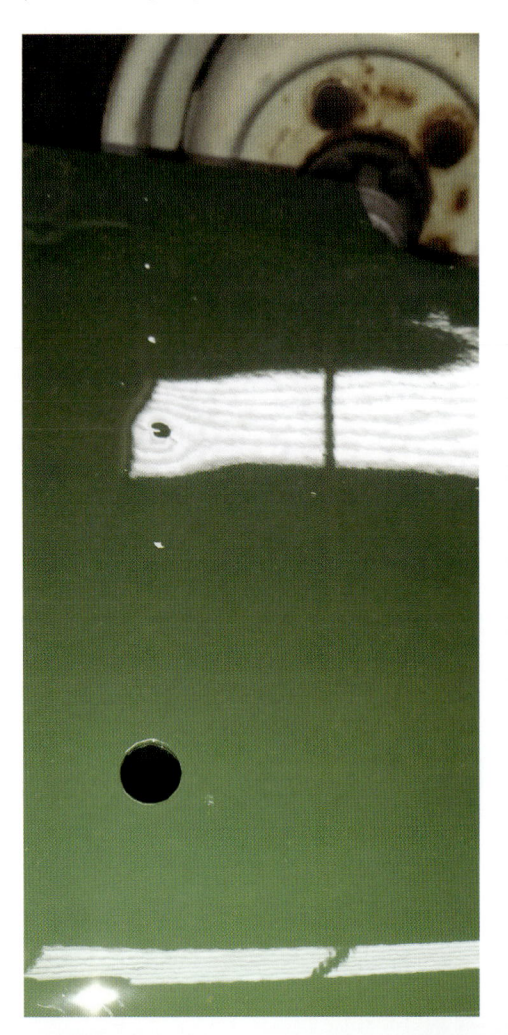

FAR LEFT: *Modern paint goes on thicker than the original, but it is good to keep the old spot welds visible.*

LEFT: *Land Rovers weren't painted under the wings, it was just overspray.*

BELOW LEFT: *It is technically not correct to fully paint under the bonnet, but it does look good against a galvanised frame.*

BELOW RIGHT: *Even the best bulkhead repairs need a skim of filler for a factory-fresh look.*

BOTTOM LEFT: *Bulkhead coated in etch primer and then undercoat. Here it's being flatted back ready for a topcoat.*

BOTTOM RIGHT: *Seam sealer on all joints to reduce moisture creep.*

Bodywork Fitting, Repairs and Finish

Bulkhead finished in 2K Slate Grey topcoat and looking better than new. Yes, it's a Ninety bulkhead but the process is the same.

BELOW: *The author's own Series III looking resplendent after countless hours of work aligning and finishing the bodywork.*

BODY CAPPINGS AND RIVETS

Galvanised cappings are one of the charming features on a Series Land Rover. In the past the tendency was to refresh them with silver paint, but times have changed and the trend is to have them re-galvanised. Experience tells us that if the cappings have little or no rust, there is no need to have them blasted before being re-galvanised. If the cappings are blasted before dipping, the finish of the galvanising is often rough, not the smooth, 'leaf' type effect of the originals. Obviously, significant rust will have to be blasted, but it is best to keep it to a minimum if the factory-look finish is important.

The cappings were originally fitted with a mixture of pop rivets and full-domed rivets, although due to cost savings pop rivets became more common. By the late 1970s Series IIIs only used pop rivets, and by the end of production even the number of them was paired down on the tub cappings.

It is worth noting that the original factory process was to paint the bodywork and then fit the cappings, so the rivets remained unpainted. This is actually a good way to tell if a vehicle has been resprayed in the past. Also note that the

ABOVE LEFT: *Fitting rear corner cappings. It's advisable to insert them all before squeezing up to ensure best alignment.*

ABOVE RIGHT: *An air riveter is ideal: easy to use and reduces the likelihood of slipping and damaging paint.*

257

Bodywork Fitting, Repairs and Finish

pop rivets used were 'blind', that is they have a closed back. Standard pop rivets are 'open' and the end of the mandrill sticks out the end, potentially allowing water to track through. Note that rivets used to fit door skins and bonnets were painted as the skins were fitted to the frames before painting.

Different people have different methods, but an air-operated rivet gun is quick and easy for pop rivets and minimises the potential for damage over mechanical options. For full rivets, a snap punch and an air hammer are ideal.

ABOVE LEFT: *Using a tapered punch to align the rivet holes.*

ABOVE RIGHT: *Multiple rivets loose-fitted in the body capping before squeezing up tight.*

ABOVE LEFT: *Unpainted rivets are correct in the body sides. The cappings were fitted after painting.*

ABOVE RIGHT: *Full-domed rivets were used on early vehicles: by the late 1970s they were all pop rivets.*

ABOVE LEFT: *Snap punch clamped in a small vice to counter-hold it when making full rivets.*

ABOVE RIGHT: *An air chisel with a concave bit is ideal for peining the back of the rivet.*

Bodywork Fitting, Repairs and Finish

ABOVE LEFT: *Assistant holding the snap punch on the domed side while the air chisel is used on the shank.*

ABOVE RIGHT: *On movable panels, the snap punch can be put in a bench vice.*

ABOVE LEFT: *Here a bonnet rivet is being lined up on the snap punch.*

ABOVE RIGHT: *At the top, the air chisel is rattled firmly and quickly.*

ABOVE LEFT: *A row of perfect domed rivets on the bonnet skin.*

ABOVE RIGHT: *A really neat finish on the peined side of the rivet given by a domed air chisel.*

21
Lighting

While lighting is clearly part of the electrical system, a separate section is included for a number of reasons. Land Rover lighting changed throughout Series Land Rover history, so if historical accuracy is important to your restoration, you will need to know what is correct. In recent times more companies have started to remanufacture some obsolete lighting units, such as the Lucas 700 headlight. In addition, lighting technology and legislation has changed over the years. This means that drivers have become accustomed to higher lights and higher speed driving. Halogen lights became the norm during the 1980s and in the last few years LED lighting has become commonplace. The filter down of technology to aftermarket lighting means that there are options to upgrade. There is also the resto-mod consideration where a combination of classic-looking components with a modern twist is becoming popular.

LIGHTS

Series II Models 1958–61

The original headlights on a Series II are in the front grille/slam panel and were standard Lucas 700 reflector units fitted with pre-focus bulbs. Full bowls were attached to the front panel and they were finished off with a chrome bezel.

Side and tail lights were Sparto 57101 with a built-in reflector, but there was also a period when a Lucas L581 alternative was fitted. When the model was launched in 1958, flashing direction indicators on front and rear were not a legal requirement. However, the design did include space for indicator lights to be added on the rear body cappings above the brake/tail lights. A Series II that hasn't been drilled for indicators is a pretty rare sight as indicators were usually fitted by the supplying dealer.

Sidelights were standard fitment to the front wings with a pressed aperture. Indicators, however, were fitted by simply cutting suitable apertures and fixing holes. The same front wing pressing continued to be used until 1969 with the arrival of the 'lights in the wing' model. The original design had the sidelights in the pressed recess

Lucas 700 light units with chrome bezel and pre-focus bulbs as fitted to Series II and early IIA models.

RIGHT: *Sparto 57101 lamps were fitted to Series II and early IIA models. Note the integral reflector and there is a clear aperture for a number plate light.*

Lighting

ABOVE LEFT: *Sparto sidelight and domed indicator on a Series II.*

ABOVE RIGHT: *While Lucas L488s were never officially fitted to Land Rovers, they look in keeping and give a classic look.*

in the wing, but with the indicators mounted adjacent and inboard. Military models had the indicators immediately below the sidelights. Indicator lights were often domed Lucas L594 or a Sparto equivalent. Note that Lucas 488 glass lenses have often been fitted to Series II and IIAs and do look good, but technically they were never factory fitment.

Series IIA Models 1961–71

This period saw a number of small changes to the lighting, culminating in the most visually obvious change to the headlights moving to the wings during 1969. Chrome bezel lights changed early on in Series IIA production to lights flush with the front panel, requiring a new front panel pressing. These lights have the advantage of being adjustable without having to remove any trim. Headlamp units changed to Lucas sealed beam units around 1963.

Side, indicator and tail lights changed a number of times throughout Series IIA production with both Sparto and Lucas equipment. It is hard to get a definitive timeline of what type was fitted when, so examining other original vehicles of a similar age to your own will help if you want it to be 'age correct'. The Technical Officer at the Series 2 Club will also be able to guide you.

During 1968 changes to lighting regulations in NADA (North America Dollar Area) and the Benelux countries required headlights to be closer to the extremities of the vehicle, so the lights were moved to the wings. New wing front pressings weren't available at this point, so the headlights were fitted flush to the original wing front, giving a very distinct 'bug eye' look. A special grille was also fitted to these vehicles. The rather amateur change was made more permanent-looking from 1969 with new wing fronts with the headlamps recessed and finished with a new aluminium bezel. With the new look front came a new 'Maltese Cross' wire grille.

Series III Models 1971–85

The same headlamp design from the last Series IIA continued throughout Series III production, fitted with Lucas sealed beam headlamp units. The original design of the headlamp bowls comprises a steel backing bowl with an inner sprung adjustor bowl. The sealed beam unit screws on to the inner bowl

ABOVE LEFT: *Lucas sealed beam unit fitted to the author's Series IIA. Note the differences with the Series II: no chrome bezel and exposed adjustor screws.*

ABOVE RIGHT: *Later type Sparto indicator and Lucas L581 tail light with reflector.*

261

Lighting

Fitting L488 lights means a separate number plate light and a reflector should be fitted to comply with lighting regulations.

tail light continued until about 1974, when it was replaced by a normal-sized tail lamp and with the addition of a separate number plate light and separate round reflectors. During the mid- to late 1970s Lucas indicator lenses had tighter rings in the moulding. It's not uncommon to see a standard ringed design sidelight on the same wing.

The rectangular rear fog lamp that arrived in 1979 had to be fitted to the offside of the vehicle. This in turn required the number plate to be moved to the nearside of the vehicle. Initially this was fitted with a large rubber buffer to protect it from the rear door swinging open, but was deleted from 1981.

Round reversing lights were standard fitment on Stage I models and County Station Wagons and an option on other models. County Station Wagons were also fitted with Lucas driving lights mounted on the front bumper.

From the early 1980s Wipac became the supplier of the side, indicator and tail lamps and the base of the light unit was made in moulded plastic. (Previous Lucas parts had a steel backing plate with a rubber cover.) For the last year of production, the position of the tail lights changed to a brake top/indicator bottom arrangement, matching that on the newly introduced One Ten.

with a chrome retaining ring and three grub screws. Modern plastic bowls are available with the significant advantage of being corrosion resistant, but more recently steel bowls have been remanufactured for the authentic look – having said that, you'd need to look under the wheel arch to tell the difference.

Side, tail and indicator lights were mostly supplied by Lucas, although at the end of production these were supplied by Wipac. The larger Lucas L581

The headlights were moved to the wings on late Series IIA and Series III models. Note Lucas branding on the sealed beam, indicator and sidelight lenses.

RIGHT: *Lucas L581 continued into early Series III production. This is a 1973 model.*

262

Lighting

A fog lamp became a legal requirement in 1980. Early models had a rubber buffer to protect it from the rear door. Note that the number plate was moved to the near side.

LEFT: *Lucas lights on a 1976 Series III. This type requires a separate number plate light.*

Late model Series IIIs had silver headlamp bezels.

LEFT: *Some very late Series III models had the top and bottom light positions introduced for the new One Ten. This is a 1984 model.*

Headlamp bezels were originally body-coloured but this changed with the arrival of the Stage 1. Sometimes black bezels were fitted to Stage I models, but towards the end of Series III production most standard models had silver bezels.

LIGHTING SWITCHGEAR

It is not uncommon for Land Rovers to have had their lighting switchgear modified over the years, often out of expediency as parts break and at a time when originality was less important. The following is a basic overview of the original switches.

Series II

Side and headlamps controlled by a combined rotary light/ignition switch

263

Lighting

Combined light and ignition switch was fitted to Series II and IIA to 1966.

RIGHT: Rotary direction indicator switch as fitted to late Series I and early Series II models.

on the dash panel. The headlamp high and dipped beams were controlled by a floor-mounted dipswitch. High beam indicator is a red light on the left-hand instrument clock.

Direction indicators were controlled by a rotary lever on an auxiliary panel on the dashboard.

Series IIA

Side and headlamps on a combined lights/ignition switch on the dashboard as per Series II until suffix D. Suffix D saw the introduction of the 'black dash' and key start, and the lights were moved to a separate toggle switch on the dashboard. The dip switch remained on the floor.

A self-cancelling indicator switch manufactured by Tex Magna was fitted to Series IIA models. These units are reasonably robust and can be easily dismantled for service and repairs. Spare rubber cancelling wheels, which are the common wear point, are available.

Series III

The Series III saw a significant modernisation of the dashboard with the introduction of left- and right-hand-drive binnacles, putting the clocks directly in front of the driver. The lights are controlled by a toggle switch on the binnacle with a high/low/indicator/horn stalk on the steering column. This also added the ability to flash the headlights, which were sealed beam units on all but County Station Wagon models.

The rear fog lamp, added from 1979, is controlled by an illuminated pull switch on the centre auxiliary dash. Again, these were fitted to a range of contemporary vehicles and are readily available.

Hazard lights were added from approximately 1980 and these are oper-

ABOVE LEFT: Series IIA black dash with separate light switch.

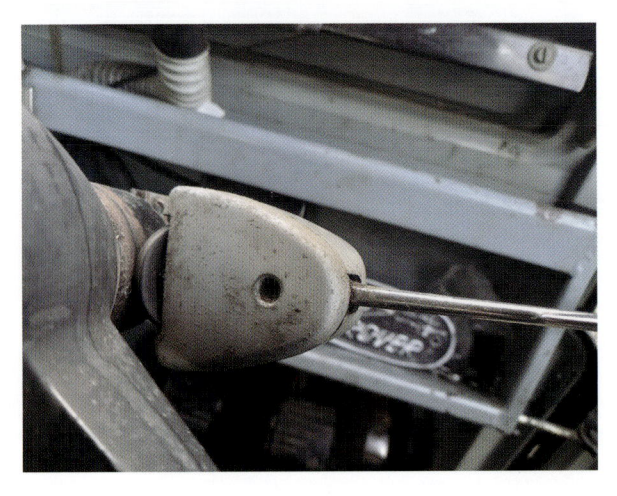

ABOVE RIGHT: Tex Magna indicator switch as fitted to Series IIA models.

Lighting

ABOVE LEFT: Main Series III switch gear stayed the same throughout production: toggle switch for lights and conversional indicator/dip/flash stalk.

ABOVE RIGHT: Centre dash was fitted from 1979 to house a fog light and hazard switch.

ated from a pull switch on the centre auxiliary dash. While this was built into the loom, a separate 'plug and play' auxiliary loom is available to retro-fit hazards to earlier Series III vehicles.

LIGHT AVAILABILITY AND UPGRADES

Supplies of original, new old stock parts are dwindling, but as interest in building historically accurate vehicles has grown and the value of Series vehicles has increased, it has become viable for specialist companies to retool to make excellent replicas of all the commonly fitted Series II and IIA lights. Glass Lucas L488 lights and lenses are readily available and, although not always historically correct for some vehicles, they look fantastic on a resto-mod vehicle. Generic Wipac side, tail and indicator lights are available individually or as a full vehicle set for very little money and represent very good value for money.

Lucas 700 headlamp units are now available and the Lucas Classic range is being added to as the interest and historical value in classic Land Rovers grows. Sealed beam units are more of a problem as old stocks dry up and getting hold of Lucas branded ones will mostly rely on getting lucky at autojumbles.

Halogen conversion bulbs are available for the 414 50/40W pre-focus bulbs as fitted to 700 headlamps. This will give the same external look as the originals but significantly improve your visibility. Halogen conversions for sealed beam units have long been available with a range of different designs. If wanting something that looks reasonably original, go for a curved rather than flat glass.

One of the significant limiting factors with headlamps is the fact that the wiring and switchgear is not designed to carry significant current. A headlamp upgrade can find the weak spot in an old switch or poor connection and overheat. The thin wires have a tendency to strangle the potential of a light upgrade. The solution is to fit a relay for both high and low beam circuits: the main feed can come directly from the battery in a larger gauge wire and the original high and low beam circuits can be used to switch the relays. The relays can be hidden behind the grille beside the termination of the bullet connections.

LED (light emitting diode) light units and bulbs have grown in popularity over recent years and have dropped significantly in price. They have the advantage of producing bright light with low power consumption. However, there are potential legality issues over them and any lighting upgrade should carry a CE mark. LED headlights can be bright but tend to have a distinct cut-off point in illumination area. The beam pattern can be poor and the light can potentially blind other drivers. If you do choose to fit LED lights, check the current rules regarding the legality and always fit the best you can afford. If you want a classic look, LEDs are probably not for you.

A neat relay system fitted to a Series IIA to minimise the current load on the old switch when running halogen headlamps.

22
Internal Trim, Fixings and Glazing

Land Rovers are of course predominantly utility vehicles and the seating, trim and internal fixings are pretty basic. Very little changed in terms of the basic Series II/IIA interior design between 1958 and 1971 other than the materials used and a number of small details and evolutions. The Series III saw the introduction of a vinyl dashboard, some plastic fixtures and fittings and finally optional cloth seating on County trim models. It is safe to say though that Series Land Rovers have never been known for their comfort levels. This chapter outlines a broad range of different original internal fixtures and fittings, and suggests common fixes and current aftermarket options.

SEATING

Basic: The basic seating arrangement was three individual front square seat squabs and backs. An adjustable seat base frame was an option, but most basic seats had fixed squabs. 'Elephant hide' grey vinyl material was used until 1967, then black vinyl to the end of Series III production. Elephant hide seats had horsehair stuffing over springs; later black seats had foam internals. The bases were made from a moulded compressed fibreboard. The seat backs had a steel frame that could be held in the upright position with leather straps to the rear body bulkhead or folded flat. The squabs either fit tightly in the adjustable seat frame or are held in place with leather straps and a pair of small L-brackets to stop forward movement. Loose seats were a common MOT 'fail', but as long as the leather straps were present for the non-adjustable type, that's simply how they were made.

Deluxe: The deluxe seat option had three individual front seats with pleated squabs and backs. An adjustable base frame allowed for fore and aft movement on the outer seats. Genuine original deluxe seats are remarkably comfortable and heavy duty with deep pleats, substantial side bolsters and a strong steel backing plate with additional padding at the top. As well as the compressed fibreboard base, original deluxe seats often had an additional metal cover on the base.

County: Cloth seats were introduced in 1982 for County Station Wagon models, but were also available as an option on other models. The front seats feature a self-supporting frame (that is, it doesn't need to lean back against the bulkhead) with a headrest and on adjustable runners. These are often referred to as 'Defender' seats in as much as the basic design became the standard seat for most coil spring models from 1983 until the end of production in 2015.

Station Wagon 88in: Three individual front seats and four individual fold-up rear seats in the rear. The rear seats actually shared the basic back design shape from the front seats of the Series I from 1953 to 1958. Two-man rear bench seats were an option for utility and 'export' side window models.

Station Wagon 109in: The twelve-seater had three individual front seats, three individual second row seats and two three-man bench seats in the rear. The ten-seater had three individual front seats, a second row forward-facing bench seat and two two-man bench seats in the rear. The ten-seater

ABOVE LEFT: Good-quality reproduction 'elephant hide' trim is now available as the value of restored vehicles makes it financially viable.

ABOVE RIGHT: Original 'patina' basic seats as fitted to later Series IIA and III models. There is a range of reproduction options to suit a range of budgets.

Internal Trim, Fixings and Glazing

ABOVE LEFT: *Original deluxe seats as fitted to later Series IIA and III models. Again a range of aftermarket options is available, but there is little to beat the comfort of the original ones.*

ABOVE RIGHT: *County or 'Defender' seats are a direct fit into a Series Land Rover.*

ABOVE LEFT: *Four individual flip-up seats were fitted to station wagon models.*

ABOVE RIGHT: *The 10-seater station wagon had a second row bench seat, the 12-seater had three individual seats and three-man bench seats in the back.*

option was rare in the UK due to tax reasons and is sometimes referred to an 'export estate'.

Vehicles with their original seats are pretty rare and over the years a range of companies have developed aftermarket options and improvements, from a simple copy of the original designs to high-back seats with built-in head restraints. A factory-approved period modification was the Bostrum sprung seat, which was available in the 1960s. In addition, owners have fitted seats from a variety of different vehicles over the years. Volvo 340 seats were popular in the 1980s and 1990s and a range of different seats from 'end of life vehicles' have been fitted since. More recently, the trend has been to go back to variations on the standard designs, although 'Defender' seats have become a common upgrade as they fit directly into existing fixings and have a low enough profile to ensure the driver does not sit too high.

Land Rover seats are never going to offer car-like comfort, but it is important to ensure driver and passenger are comfortable and safe. It is actually hard to beat the quality and comfort offered by the original deluxe seats, but most will have suffered significant wear and tear by now. Aftermarket seats are relatively inexpensive, offer remarkably good value and are a good way to breathe life into a shabby interior. In addition, as the relative value of the vehicle rises, we have seen a welcome rise in the quality of the aftermarket seating options. That trend is likely to continue as the interest in high-quality restorations increases.

SEAT BELTS

Seat belts became a legal fitment in 1965–6 and this coincided with a change to the 'swan neck' handbrake design to make it easier to reach. The original seat belts were only fitted to the outer front seats and were a very basic static Rover 'aviation' style affair in grey webbing with a 'lift to release' buckle. The Series III saw the introduction of black static seatbelts (usually made by Britax) with press-to-release buckles. Later in production a lap belt was fitted to the centre seat.

Only very late model Series IIIs saw the introduction of inertia reel seat belts. However, in-service upgrades are very common and, as long as they use existing mounting points or updated versions, can be considered an

Internal Trim, Fixings and Glazing

ABOVE LEFT: *Aviation-style seat belt as fitted to later Series IIA models.*

ABOVE RIGHT: *Britax static seat belts as fitted to most Series III models.*

ABOVE LEFT: *Static seat belts had a small storage hook, though they were probably seldom used.*

ABOVE RIGHT: *Inertia reel seat belts were fitted to late Series IIIs and make for a sensible upgrade on earlier vehicles.*

Inertia reel belts can be fitted using the top mounting bracket from a 90/110 model.

additional safety and convenience feature.

Land Rover used a number of different fitting arrangements over the years. Early seat belt models had buckle brackets that simply bolted to the tub, but by the end of Series III production, these had been beefed up with extra bracing to the chassis. The original over-the-shoulder mounting point was on the body tub bulkhead with an eye bolt. This is quite low for comfort and may not offer the best position in the event of a crash, so Land Rover moved the position higher on later models. A full-width brace bar with upper fixing points was used on late military soft-top models with an inertia reel bolted to heavy-duty spreader plates on the tub bulkhead. On hard-top variants, it is common to use the shoulder-mounting brackets as used on coil spring models.

There are a number of different options when it comes to mounting inertia reel belts and off-the-shelf kits usually have their own fitting instructions. Various companies have developed and improved seat belt anchor points, especially for soft tops and truck cabs.

Station Wagon second row and rear seats were never fitted with seat belts but it is common to use parts from coil spring models from the late 1980s

Internal Trim, Fixings and Glazing

onwards to update earlier models. Again, using original parts and fixings should make for the safest option. As with any modification, the insurance company should be informed should there be any changes to the original specification.

INTERNAL TRIM

Door Cards

These were standard on Station Wagon models and an option on other vehicles. The original front design consisted of three pieces: a lower trim of vinyl-covered hardboard held in place by spring clips and included a map pocket, a vinyl-covered padded armrest with aluminium backing and a door top trim made from vinyl-covered aluminium sheet. These are available from a range of aftermarket suppliers, although most do not have the map pocket. Second row Station Wagon doors had a two-piece design and the rear door was a simple one-piece board. Again, aftermarket replacements are readily available or, if desired, can be easily made with simple DIY skills. In addition, the original design also included door latch covers as well as cast metal handles to close the door.

Headlining

Station Wagons and the optional deluxe trim models were fitted with a headlining kit. This consists of felt bonded to the roof and a vinyl covering with a metal frame round the edge. The 88in consists of a front and rear section, the 109in has an additional middle section. Again, these are likely to have suffered over the years and droop down, as well as the fabric rotting and ripping. If originality is important, a new headlining to the original design can be made reusing the frame sections. This would be a simple job for a professional upholsterer and not beyond someone with reasonable DIY sewing machine skills. The sun visors have become very rare and quite desirable, often changing hands for disproportionate sums of money.

Various specialist trim companies have developed aftermarket options that, while not necessarily original, are often better than the original design. Good results can also be had from using closed cell insulation and/or covering with four-way stretch lining fabric, as used in camper van conversions.

Additional Roof Trim

The original Station Wagon trim also included vinyl-covered padding round the metal rim of the roof panel, a cover plate above the windscreen and vinyl-covered cards in the rear glass panels. The deluxe truck cab trim was a relatively complicated affair with various vinyl-covered cards.

Floor Matting

Matting was an option from the factory. Link mats were fitted to early models. Later it became an embossed rubber mat with a spring clip by the seat box heel board to hold it in place. Stocks of genuine old stock mats will mostly have dried up but a range of aftermarket options are available. Station wagons had ribbed rubber in the second row and rear load area. A common DIY option is to fit heavy-duty stable matting, which gives additional sound proofing and insulation qualities. This is usually supplied in 6 × 4ft

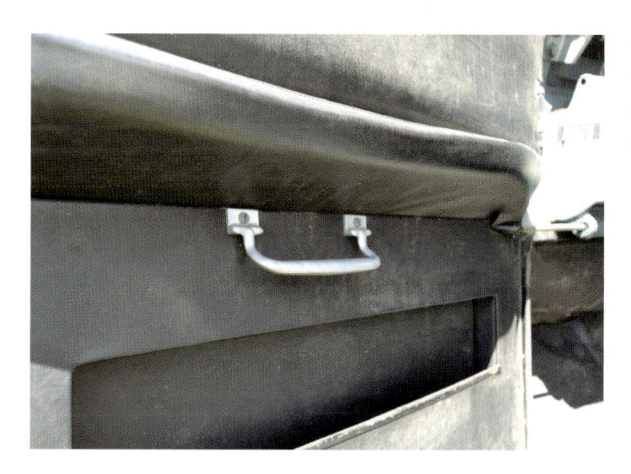

Original door trim with armrest and door pocket: aftermarket options are available.

ABOVE LEFT: *Most door trim will either look like this or will have been thrown out.*

ABOVE RIGHT: *It is a simple DIY job to recover the aluminium trim sections for a good home refresh.*

Internal Trim, Fixings and Glazing

ABOVE LEFT: Original type vinyl headlining on a frame is a challenging repair and may be best entrusted to a specialist upholsterer.

ABOVE RIGHT: Original rubber floor matting as fitted to later Series IIA and Series III models.

ABOVE LEFT: Original embossed PVC Hardura trim with a felt backing fitted to the author's Series III 6-cylinder.

ABOVE RIGHT: Hardura trim kits are available off the shelf. It can also be bought by the metre and cut to fit using the originals as a pattern, as shown here for the author's Series III.

mats that can be easily cut to shape with a Stanley knife.

Bulkhead and Footwell Trim

The original style bulkhead trim was made from Hardura, an embossed PVC vinyl with a felt backing. This was glued to the centre section of the bulkhead and sides of the footwells. In addition, Hardura-covered card was held in place in the top of the footwells with aluminium channel and clips. On the 109in Station Wagon, additional Hardura trim was fitted on the upright section of the second-row toe board. Hardura trim kits are available from a range of aftermarket suppliers and it can also be bought as a sheet material. Modern moulded matting and soundproofing kits have been available for a number of years and offer high performance, albeit at the expense of originality.

UPPER AND LOWER DASHBOARDS ON SERIES III MODELS

The Series III saw the introduction of more 'car-like' features such as the clocks and controls directly in front of the driver. It also saw the introduction of an upper and lower dash that combined crash protection and a fresh air heater. While this does offer a certain amount of comfort, it is also something of an Achilles heel. The lower dash has a pressed steel backing that is prone to rusting. The outer padded vinyl covering is also prone to wear and tear. The upper dash is exposed to UV light, often causing the vinyl to crack, revealing the foam below.

Lower Dash Removal and Repairs

The lower dash is simple to remove. It is held in with screws round the edge and a pair of 2BA bolts at the top, hidden under the parcel shelf insert. Note that the control wire for the lower vent flap will need to be removed from the heater control lever. Some basic restoration can be carried out on the lower dash. The vinyl covering can be removed – it is held on with spring clips round the edges. The steel backing can be repaired by welding in new material or a neat repair can be executed with glass fibre. The vinyl covering can be refitted with the original

Internal Trim, Fixings and Glazing

ABOVE LEFT: *The heater/lower dash is prone to corrosion, making the Series III heater totally ineffective.*

ABOVE RIGHT: *The all too common cracked dashboard top on a Series III. DIY repairs or finding a good used one are the only options.*

Series III lower dash attaches with screws round the perimeter and two 2BA bolts along the top behind the parcel shelf tray.

The top dash is attached along the top with large screws that are tight to access if the screen is still on.

clips and if necessary some appropriate adhesive.

Upper Dash Removal and Repairs

The dash top is held onto the bulkhead with screws along the front edge by the windscreen and by two 2BA fixings onto the vent panel cover plate. It is easier to remove the top with the windscreen folded down, but if this is not convenient it is possible to unscrew the fixings by the screen with a screwdriver bit held in self-grip pliers. It's worth noting that there were two different types of upper dash: those from about 1971 to 1974 had large vents and those from 1975 to 1984 had smaller vents. They are interchangeable as a complete upper unit. All are prone to cracking and good used ones are rare, with new old stock ones even rarer. They can be repaired with reasonable DIY skills. The foam backing can be repaired with expanding foam or the original foam can be stripped off, replaced with closed cell foam sheeting and then recovered in vinyl material. It is a simple profile with a large flat top and plastic end covers, so it is a fairly simple retrimming job with no compound curves to deal with. A retrim kit is available from online sellers with the option to add a colour detail stitching.

VENT FLAPS AND ASSOCIATED MECHANISMS

The opening vent flaps are one of the enduring charms of a Series Land Rover. While the general external look didn't change significantly, there were a number of different lever designs:

Series II and early IIA: The vent flaps were held on with separate bolt-on hinges and the operating mechanism was controlled by a Bakelite turn knob.

Later Series IIA: The vent flaps had integral hinges and were operated by a lever with lock stop positions. The lever knobs had a round profile and the down position closes the vent flaps.

Series III: The design was similar to the Series IIA, but the lever knob has a

271

Internal Trim, Fixings and Glazing

ABOVE LEFT: *The Bakelite vent screw knob as fitted to Series II and very early IIA models.*

ABOVE RIGHT: *Series IIA-type vent handles.*

Series III-type vent handles.

hooked profile and up is the closed position.

Flyscreens were an option on Series II/IIA models and standard on Series III models.

Removing and refitting vent flaps is reasonably straightforward, although the 2BA bolts are quite fiddly to access and the vent hinge pins are prone to seizing. Aftermarket hinge pins vary in quality and can cause rust staining, so if the old sherardised ones are in good reusable condition, it can pay to refit them. Stainless steel pins are also available: these provide a good upgrade at the expense of originality. No matter what is fitted, it is advisable to grease the pins before fitting.

VENT SEALS

Series II/IIA and III vent seals were originally bonded in place onto the bulkhead. If refitting the original design for your vehicle, use an appropriate adhesive: polyurethane sealant is ideal for this as it is sticky enough to hold the rubber in place but doesn't go off quickly like contact adhesive, so allows time to position it correctly. Close the vent flap while the glue is going off. Note that some aftermarket seals can be too 'plump' and may not allow the flap to close, so do a dry run before committing to sticking them in place.

Another option is to use later 'Defender' seals. These are made from EPDM closed cell foam rubber and have a self-adhesive strip. They are stuck to the vent flap, not the bulkhead, and offer a range of improvements over the original design. They are cheaper to buy, easier to fit and reduce the area of moisture trap round the bulkhead pressings. All this, however, is at the expense of originality and will be noticeable from outside the vehicle.

DOOR SEALS

Later 'Defender' EPDM vent seals are a cost-effective and easy alternative to the original rubber type.

Series II/IIA and III door seals remained pretty much the same basic design throughout most of production. The seals are made from a rubber profile with an internal metal strengthening strip. Each door seal consists of

Internal Trim, Fixings and Glazing

Soft rivets are available for the original type door seals from specialist suppliers, but seal kits tend to come with pop rivets.

Push-on 'Defender' Door Seal Option

The seal recess round the door aperture had a return lip to hold the rivet-on seal in place. However, bulkhead pillar repair sections typically do not have this return lip and can lead to poorly fitting seals with insufficient space to rivet the seals in place. Original specification door pillars are now becoming available; alternatively, an appropriate L-section can be welded into place. Another option is to cut off the return lip all round the aperture (a 1mm slitting disc is ideal for this) and to fit the push-on seal as fitted to the very last Series IIIs and to all coil spring Land Rovers. Again, this is a compromise to originality but it does make fitting significantly easier. It is also cheaper and indeed it offers a significantly better seal. These seals can simply be pushed and tapped into place with a soft-faced mallet, starting in a top corner and working round and down.

HEATER AND DEMISTER VENTS

A heater and demister system was an option on Series II/IIA models. It was standard fitment on most Series IIIs except some hot climate vehicles.

Series II/IIA Heater to 1968: This was a round Smiths heater with a matrix and an internal fan, and sat to the left-hand side of the centre bulkhead panel. It was plumbed into the engine cooling system and could be isolated by a turn tap valve on the rear of the cylinder head. The heater front featured a crinkle-painted cover with two opening doors that controlled warm air either into the cab or to an outlet that fed hot air to vents on the windscreen. With the arrival of the single wiper motor in 1967, the demister vents were screwed to the cover for the wiper drive mechanism.

In terms of restoration and maintenance, the matrix is prone to leaking, although new ones are available at a cost. Note that there are two different depths of matrix and, while they are interchangeable, appropriate length spring clips will be required. If the leak is small, a generic radiator leak stop might offer a temporary/mid-term fix. The fan motors are generally robust

individual short sections that were mostly riveted on with soft semi-tubular rivets. Very late model Series IIIs saw the introduction of a one-piece press-on seal, introduced for the incoming One Ten model launched in 1983.

Rivet-On Door Seals

Full seal kits are readily available and the sections will have pre-marked holes for the fixing rivets. As an easy expedient, pop rivets can be used to fit the seals, but if going for originality soft rivets are available, which can be easily fitted used rivet pliers. Be aware that some aftermarket seals can be very hard or not quite to the original specification and may cause problems when closing the door. In particular, the seal down the edge of the bulkhead can ride and bunch up. A good new seal can make the door slightly harder to shut and the door catch might require some adjustment, but it should not require significant force to close the door. Genuine, OEM or G-branded seals should cause no problems. When a new door seal set has been fitted, it is advisable to leave the doors tightly closed for a few days to help the rubber to gain a 'memory'.

Good-quality individual door seals are relatively expensive and a budget alternative is to buy a roll of generic door seal material. This does not have the metal insert but appropriate strips of metal can be inserted. These seals can be either glued or riveted in place.

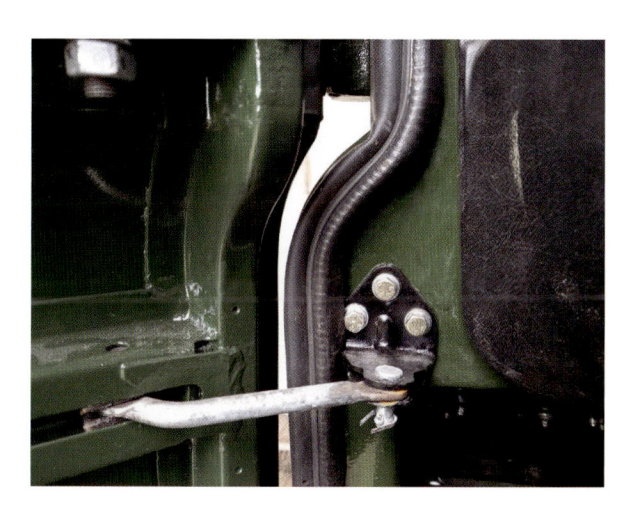

Push-on 'Defender' seals were fitted to the very last Series IIIs but offer a cost-effective and functional alternative, at the expense of originality.

273

Internal Trim, Fixings and Glazing

ABOVE LEFT: *Round Smiths heater was an option from 1958 to 1968. Parts are available, although the matrix is a slightly different design.*

ABOVE RIGHT: *The all too common rusty Series III heater snail. New ones are rare and expensive.*

and are easy to remove. The covers can be easily restored and finished in the correct crinkle coat paint and the knobs, which often break, are available as a remanufactured part.

Series IIA Heater 1969–71: This saw the introduction of the square Smiths heater. Due to the limited time in production, parts are harder to track down.

Series III Heater: The Series III heater consists of a matrix in a box secured to the engine side of the bulkhead and a separate blower fan that draws fresh air from outside. Air blows through the matrix to exit into the lower dashboard in the vehicle cab. From there, the warm air either exits through vents in the lower dashboard or is directed up to the demister vents in the top dash. The air direction is controlled by a sliding lever on the side of the driver's binnacle, which operates a piano wire to open and close flaps within the lower dash box. The temperature is controlled by another lever and wire, which operates a valve on the cooling system at the front of the engine.

There are multiple common problems with the Series III system. Leaking matrix, rusty heater 'snail', rusty matrix box and all too common holes in the lower dash. In addition, because very few people adjust the direction lever off the demist setting, the piano wire either seizes or breaks with the flaps stuck in the half-open position. The flap foam sealing pads are prone to breaking up as well. The demister vent hoses have very poor sealing rubbers as they come out of the lower dash and these are prone to perishing. The control cable to the heater valve on the engine is also prone to seizing, as is the valve itself. Finally, the snail fan itself isn't exactly efficient.

Despite the seemingly catastrophic list of endemic problems, it is possible to have a relatively efficient heater in a Series III.

New genuine fan snails are hard to come by, although there are some aftermarket replacements available. If a good replacement cannot be found, a reasonable repair can be executed with fibreglass.

Fitting a new matrix is a straightforward job and simply a case of removing the box from the vehicle and undoing the casing screws. When the matrix box is refitted, the condition of the foam seal to the bulkhead should be considered and replaced as necessary, either with the genuine part or some generic neoprene foam or suitable sealant.

The lower dash is not too challenging to remove and any holes can be either repaired or replaced with a better one. At the time of writing there were no aftermarket replacements available, but this may change over time as more and more classic parts are being remanufactured. The top cover can be removed from the lower dash to give access to the internal flaps. The piano wire control attaches with a solderless nipple and can be replaced.

BONNET/SLAM PANEL CLOSURE TRIM STRIP

The original canvas strip is one of those little features that is often overlooked but finishes off a good-quality restoration. These were held in place with bifurcated rivets and come as part of a kit with the strip. Modern replacements

Using a soldering iron to make a neat hole in the bonnet rest strip for the bifurcated rivets.

274

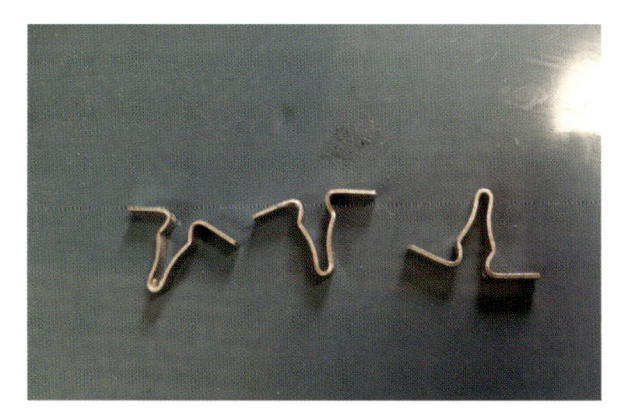

Internal Trim, Fixings and Glazing

DOOR TOP SEALS

The seal between the door top and bottom is supplied as universal left- and right-hand side. Some do not have cut-outs for the door top bolts, but these can be easily and neatly stamped out with a hole punch. The seal is pop-riveted to the door top: the original fixings included washers to spread the force and avoid pulling through the rubber. The correct orientation of the seal is with the lip on the inside pointing up. This means the rivets sit within the recessed channel and water from the windows runs out through the drainage holes. Once the door top is bolted onto the door bottom, the ends of the rubber can be trimmed round the shape of the galvanised capping.

GLAZING

Windscreen

Series II/IIA and III windscreens are all the same. The screen was bedded in the screen frame with a sticky flexible glazing strip and held in place with aluminium retaining strips. New glazing strip can be bought on a roll. Note that old screens tend to get scratched and give poor visibility at night. New screens are readily available and are inexpensive. Heated screens are also available and offer a significant improvement when it comes to demisting with the aforementioned terrible heater.

Side Windows/Door Top Windows

The door top glazing channel is particularly prone to corrosion due to the fact that the felt seldom dries out. Plastic channel is available, but has the disadvantage of being more prone to rattling.

Full door top glazing and fitting kits are readily available and represent good value for money with all the seals, nuts, screws, glazing strip, window channel and spacer strips cut to size. This is a straightforward job but it can be fiddly drilling holes and getting the screws lined up. A known alternative is to stick the channel in place with small blobs of polyurethane sealant. This has the advantage of being easier and quicker to fit, but will be harder to remove in the future.

This is the later type bifurcated fixing as fitted to Series IIIs, and comes as part of the strip kit.

Yes, this is the correct orientation for the door top seal – lip in and up – and has been checked with numerous original vehicles.

The windscreen should be bedded in on a flexible glazing compound strip bought on a roll.

A door top fitting kit represents very good value for money with all the appropriate spacers, the window channel cut to size, fixings, glazing strip and rubber seal.

tend to be made out of nylon and the required holes can be easily made with a hot soldering iron. The bifurcated rivets simply push into place. To tidy up the end of the strip, it can be tucked into the gap between the front panel and wing before fully tightening the fixing bolts. Note that many Series III models had a sprung type clip in place of the bifurcated rivets.

275

Internal Trim, Fixings and Glazing

Bedding the fixed door top glass in with the flexible glazing strip included in the kit.

BELOW LEFT: Fitting the front glass and retaining strip with the correct small slotted screws.

BELOW RIGHT: The fiddly job includes drilling and fitting the countersunk channel screws. Some people choose to use polyurethane sealant.

Window channel can also be bought in long lengths and can be easily cut to length with a thin slitting disc.

Rear Hard Top Windows

The rear windows are held in place with a glazing rubber and expansion strip. When refitting, it helps to smear washing up liquid on the rubbers. The expansion strip is best fitted with the correct fitting tool but can be fitted with a wide-blade screwdriver. Note that the original design was with the expansion strip on the outside; later coil spring models, however, had the strip on the inside to improve security.

23
Vehicle Details and Rivet Counting

This restoration manual is written to cover a range of different skills, budgets and finish levels. It is perfectly acceptable to build a Land Rover that is solid, reliable and functional without restoring to concourse or rivet counter levels. However, it is also important that the manual considers some of the finer details that can give an extra level of satisfaction to a proud owner. To some, historical accuracy is very important and if there is a desire to create a vehicle that is close to original factory specification having reference material is vital. Unrestored vehicles are an invaluable source of information when it comes to getting a vehicle 'just so' and little details can show the craftsmanship of the builder of a resto-mod vehicle. With this growing desire for accuracy, more and more correct specification parts and ancillary detail features are being remanufactured.

PLATES AND DECALS

The number of plates and decals increased through the Series IIA and Series III era. In many ways, the evolution of the Land Rover was in direct response to complying with increased worldwide motoring legislation. As well as functional information and warnings for owners, many decals were simply applied to confirm compliance. The following examples cannot be an exhaustive guide to every model and change, but they do give an insight into the factory finish. They also add to the history of the Land Rover, cataloguing the changes in law, technology and the global markets the vehicles were being sold into. Many of these plates and decals have been remanufactured recently and add to the authenticity of the build.

Chassis/VIN Plates

These are also dealt with in detail in Chapter 3. The location varied throughout production as outlined below, although the change points are approximate and military vehicles vary again. The chassis plate on Series III models also outlines the vehicle weight and towing capacity. Replacement chassis plates are available from a range of suppliers, but if ordered through a Land Rover club some offer a number stamping service with proof of ownership.

Tyre Wear Warning Plates: These were separate small plates fitted just below the chassis plate on Series II and IIA models. On Series III models it was a larger plate that combined information on use of the 4WD system.

Negative Earth Plates: Negative earth electrics were introduced to Series IIA models about 1967 and additional warnings were required as the now conventional system replaced positive earth. The warning plates were fitted to the top face of the front grille panel, either with flathead screws or small rivets.

Alternator Warning Plate: Alternators became an option about 1968, initially with an external control box, then later a built-in diode pack. The alternator converts AC to DC and there is a danger that a surge from arc welding could damage the control unit. Clearly Land Rover understood back then that the chassis were likely to rust.

ABOVE LEFT: *Series II and early IIA chassis plate.*

ABOVE RIGHT: *Series IIA chassis plate.*

Vehicle Details and Rivet Counting

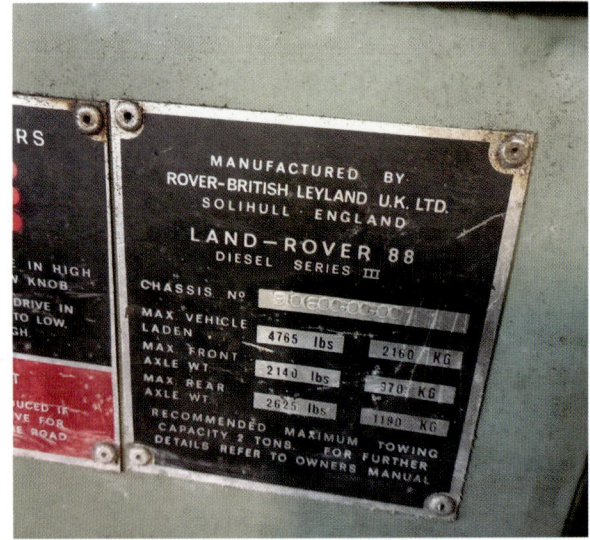

ABOVE LEFT: Late Series IIA chassis plate.

ABOVE RIGHT: Early type Series III chassis plate.

ABOVE LEFT: Late 1970s chassis plate.

ABOVE RIGHT: VIN plate fitted from 1980.

ABOVE LEFT: Series III transfer gear and tyres information.

ABOVE RIGHT: Negative Earth plate on the front panel on a late Series IIA.

Vehicle Details and Rivet Counting

These plates were fitted to the top face of the grille panel on very late Series IIA and Series III models.

Seat Belt Compliance Decals

With worldwide changes in motoring legislation, seat belts became a mandatory fitment at the factory. This change also brought in the 'swan neck' handbrake to make it easier to reach. The compliance decals state the mounting points complied with the relevant laws. Suffice to say that crash testing was not that rigorous back in those days. These decals are now being remanufactured and for full authenticity they should probably be fitted slightly squint! On the Series IIA it was fitted to the left-hand end of the parcel shelf on the bulkhead or on the seat box by the lower seat belt mounting. On the Series III it could also be fitted to the wiper motor cover.

European Compliance Decals

There were a host of E mark compliance decals fitted to the engine side of the bulkhead on late model Series IIIs. Again, many of these are available for the rivet counter restoration.

Freewheeling Hubs and Overdrive Decals

Fairey Overdrive and freewheeling hubs were a factory-approved optional extra introduced in the mid-1970s. These were often fitted by the supplying dealer and an information decal was included in the kit. This was usually fitted to the dashboard top or wiper drive assembly cover. An oval sticker 'Overdrive by Fairey' was often fitted to the rear tub side panel.

Heater Decals

Smiths heater decals were fitted to the square Series IIA heater and to the matrix box and blower fan on the Series III. Decals were also fitted on Series III heater control levers. Early models (about 1971–73) had symbols, later models had words. Again, all these are now available for the discerning rivet counter.

Engine Bay Decals

There were various information decals on the oil filler, oil bath air filter, brake and clutch reservoir. On a late Series III, you'll often find a Unipart compliance warning label and a coolant/antifreeze label.

ABOVE LEFT: *Alternator warning plate on a Series III.*

ABOVE RIGHT: *Original seat belt compliance label as fitted to later Series IIA and Series III models.*

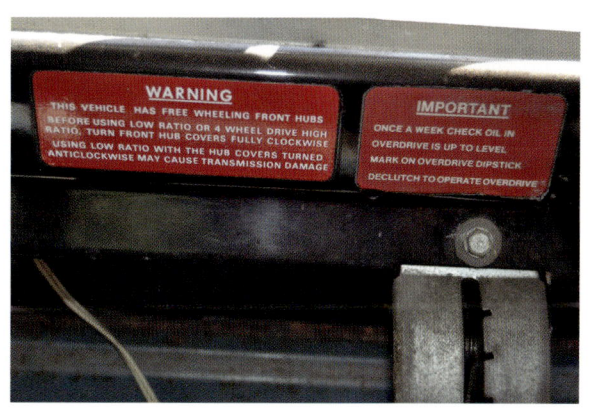

ABOVE LEFT: *Perfect reproduction E11 compliance stickers fitted to the bulkhead on the author's Series III.*

ABOVE RIGHT: *Fairey freewheeling hub and overdrive warning labels came with the factory-approved kit from the mid-1970s.*

Vehicle Details and Rivet Counting

Reproduction early style AC air cleaner label.

LEFT: Heater control information on an early Series III.

Reproduction information sticker fitted to the oil bath air filter.

RIGHT: Reproduction Girling warning label on a combined brake and clutch reservoir.

Vehicle Details and Rivet Counting

ABOVE LEFT: *Reproduction Unipart warning label as fitted to late model Series IIIs.*

ABOVE RIGHT: *Reproduction Unipart antifreeze label on the top of a late Series III radiator.*

Series III Screen Washer Decals

Washer bottles were made by Trico until 1976, then by Lucas/Unipart. Motors often had Lucas decals, while bottles often had Unipart decals.

GRILLE AND TUB BADGES

A range of different grille and tub badges were fitted to Series II/IIA and III Land Rovers over the years. This is an overview of the common types.

Land Rover Birmingham Oval: Fitted to grille and rear of vehicles from 1958 to 1959. These were a carry-over from the Series I and are quite rare. Few people want to part with them, but you can get lucky at autojumbles if the seller is unaware of the scarcity.

Land Rover Solihull Warwickshire: Fitted to the grille and rear of vehicles from 1960 to 1971 and rear of vehicles to 1984. These are the most common type available and can be picked up cheaply.

Rover Diesel Badge: A round plastic badge fitted to the bottom of the grille on Series II and IIA models. These tend to fade and suffer UV damage over time; remanufactured ones are available.

Plastic Land Rover Oval: Fitted to some (though not all) late model Series IIIs as well as Hi-Cap models. This design also continued into the first year of One Ten production. If you're lucky you might find a new old stock one.

Series III Plastic Grille: The most visually recognisable feature on a Series III is the ABS plastic grille with the Land Rover logo at the top. There have been various aftermarket versions available over the years, some accurate, while some had blanked mesh sections in the middle. More recently aftermarket options no longer have the Land Rover logo. It is therefore advisable to find

Original Lucas washer motor with decal: reproduction decals are available.

ABOVE LEFT: *Early type 'Birmingham' Series II badge as fitted to 1958–9 models.*

ABOVE RIGHT: *The more common 'Solihull' badge as fitted to most Series II, IIA and III models.*

Vehicle Details and Rivet Counting

ABOVE LEFT: *Rover diesel badge as fitted to most Series IIA diesel models.*

ABOVE RIGHT: *Plastic tub badge as fitted to some of the last Series IIIs and to early One Tens.*

ABOVE LEFT: *A genuine Series III grille. Modern replacements tend not to have the Land Rover moulding and sometimes have a 'filled in' mesh in the middle.*

ABOVE RIGHT: *Series III grilles were originally fitted with spring clips to reduce rattles: most get lost or rust off.*

the best genuine used one you can and restore it as necessary. Many people are not aware that they were actually held in place by anti-rattle spring clips as well as screws.

FACTORY PROCESS MARKINGS

During the original factory build, various process markings were made to show that a particular task had been completed. On Series III vehicles, the most common are yellow, red or orange paint daubs on diff pans, marking that it had been filled with oil. In addition, yellow paint is often found on the swivel

ABOVE LEFT: *Chalk process markings were often scrawled on body panels.*

ABOVE RIGHT: *Series IIIs usually had factory process paint on the oil fill points, such as diffs and swivels.*

Vehicle Details and Rivet Counting

Factory fleet number on the author's Stage 1 Prototype front axle.

and differential fill points. Chalk marks are also common on inner wings and under the rear floor. These little details are a nice addition to a concourse or authentic patina restoration, as well as being a functional feature to remind a restorer to carry out final quality control checks. Be aware that these markings were not applied with any form of finesse as to the finished look: they were daubed on at speed on a fast-moving production line. If you are lucky enough to own an ex-factory engineering vehicle, the vehicle fleet number was often written in yellow paint on the axles. The usual format was wheelbase/fleet number, for example 109/38.

NUMBER PLATES

When the Series II was launched in 1958, the standard number plate design was white or silver letters on a black background. These were either pressed aluminium with raised letters or plastic/aluminium letters held onto an aluminium backing plate. About 1967 white front and yellow rear reflective number plates started to be introduced and by 1973 became the standard format. Mostly the plates were plastic letters on an aluminium backing, covered in reflective material, although pressed aluminium plates were also common in the mid- to late 1970s. Plastic laminated plates became available in the early 1980s, so could just have been fitted to late Series IIIs.

A number plate can make a significant difference to the general look of a vehicle, so getting it right is important. The older styles of plate can be made up by specialist suppliers: pressed black and silver, pressed yellow and white, and most types of raised letter options as well as pre-2001 laminated plates. Do be aware that the size of the number plate font changed in 2001, so a generic aftermarket pressed number plate may not have the correct size letters. There are a number of specialist plate suppliers that can also match original dealership names and logos.

Original raised letter plates can also be restored. The letters are held in place with starlock clips and these corrode, causing the letters to fall off. The reflective backing can also fade and flake off. 5mm starlock clips are readily available and old number plate letters can be found at autojumbles and online. Reflective sheet can be bought to replace the original, but be aware that technically it should have the appropriate BS markings for the reflective

Black and silver plates could be fitted up to 1973.

ABOVE LEFT: *White and yellow plates with plastic letters became commonplace from 1967 onwards.*

ABOVE RIGHT: *Note that number plate font size changed in 2001 and many suppliers default to the new smaller size.*

Vehicle Details and Rivet Counting

New plastic letter plates can be bought from specialists or old ones can be restored.

LEFT: *Plastic letter starlock clips rust and cause letters to fall off.*

grade. Having said that, not all aftermarket 'show' plates have the appropriate BS markings either.

Number Plate Position

In the UK the rear number plate was square and from 1958 to 1979 was mounted on the offside quarter panel. In 1979 a requirement for a rear fog lamp on the offside meant that the number plate was moved to the nearside quarter panel.

Front number plates varied, but from 1958 to 1969 were usually square and mounted on the offside front wing until the introduction of the 'Maltese Cross' grille and lights in the wings in 1969. After that it was oblong and often mounted on a plinth plate on top of the bumper. Because the plate would have been fitted by the supplying dealership, this did vary and sometimes it was fitted directly to the bumper, either centrally or offset to allow for access to the cranking handle hole or a winch.

BODY FIXING BOLTS

The majority of Series II/IIA and III models' bodies were held together with 1/4 and 5/16th UNF (Unified Fine) nuts and bolts. The company used a range of different suppliers, the common ones being Wiley and GKN. Towards the end of Series III production the company was gradually moving towards metrification with M6 and M8 replacing 1/4 and 5/16th, although a number of fixings remained UNF, such as the riv-nut fixings in the bulkhead.

UNF bolts can usually be identified by the radial tensile strengthening markings on the head. Body bolts commonly have three radial markings to denote High Tensile. Metric bolts can usually be identified by a numerical tensile grading: body bolts are marked 8.8 to denote High Tensile. Note that this is only a basic identification guide and the only way to confirm the thread is measuring with a pitch gauge.

The majority of body fixings were sherardised, a form of zinc coating that gives a dull grey finish. Later models moved on to the now common BZP (bright zinc plated). Very late model

ABOVE LEFT: *Sherardised GKN 5/16th UNF bolt as fitted to 1970s Series IIIs. Note the radial tensile markings.*

ABOVE RIGHT: *The more common, modern M8 equivalent finished in BZP with 8.8 tensile marking.*

Series IIIs tended to have yellow passivated fixings, which look somewhat out of place on a classic vehicle. We often forget that these vehicles were once shiny and new.

BZP fixings are widely available from a range of sources and some specialists can supply sherardised fixings. Yellow passivated fixings are available, although significantly less common than BZP. Bolts and body mounting brackets can be electro-plated yellow by specialist plating companies.

PERIOD DOCUMENTATION AND LITERATURE

Beyond the vehicle itself, period documents and literature add an extra tangible element to the classic Land Rover ownership experience. A Parts Manual, Workshop Manual and Operation Manual should be considered essential reading. Beyond that, historical documents relating to the vehicle itself are great to have. Old MOT certificates, tax discs and any service records and bills not only add interest but provenance, desirability and, potentially, financial value. It's worth considering yourself as a custodian of the vehicle and each owner adds a bit to the history file.

Many old school garages fitted service record stickers to the driver's door jamb as a visual reminder of the last and next service. Replacements can be bought and they not only look period correct but still provide a good aide-memoire, even in the digital age.

Period dealer or garage stickers are always a nice touch, as are tax disc holders and period breakdown badges and warranty stickers, such as AA, RAC and Leyland's own Supercover warranty scheme.

RESTORATION FILE/ CELEBRATION ALBUM

Taking photos of your restoration as it progresses is not only fun but invaluable when it comes to looking back at how far you've come. We all get restoration blues and sometimes we need a reminder of just how much we've achieved. Not only that, but it can also be very useful when it comes to working out what goes where and identifying all those parts you no longer recognise. In the digital age, photos are easy to take and store, but there is something very satisfying about a physical photo. Choosing the best of your digital photos and getting a restoration photo book made up is a lovely way to celebrate the completion as well as being a coffee-table item to show off your hard work.

The last original tax disc still fitted to the author's 6-cylinder Series III before it was parked in a barn for more than two decades. Reproduction ones are available.

LEFT: *The original build sheet from the author's Series III is a delightful historical document.*

The original Series III handbook in the author's 1984 Series III adds charm and period authenticity.

Index

axles
　case types
　　front axles 144
　　rear axles 144–146
　differential pinion seal replacement
　　148–149
　problems and assessment 146–148
　rear halfshaft change 149
　remove and replace
　　front differential 151
　　rear differential 149–151
　steering swivels
　　adjustment 154–155
　　replace 155–158
　wheel bearings
　　adjustment 151
　　replacement 151–153
　　stub axle land or distance piece
　　　153–154

bodywork
　assembly order
　　common mistakes 239
　　personal preferences 239–245
　cappings and rivets 257–258
　chassis and bulkhead integrity 238
　door repairs 250–253
　dry build 239
　front panel repairs 248
　full body sides 246–247
　hand painting 254
　rear side panels 247–248
　rear tub repairs 245–246
　spray painting 254
braking system
　bleeding brakes 200–201
　brake adjustment 195
　brake drums and shoes, removal of
　　189–192
　brake pipes 195–196
　brake upgrades 201–202
　fitting shoes 193–194
　flexi pipes 198
　master cylinder replacement
　　198–200

　parking brake 189
　parking brake system 201
　refitting/replacing drums 195
　service brake 189
　wheel cylinders replacement
　　192–193
Bulkhead restoration
　feet and pillars 233
　footwells 230
　new bulkheads 228
　paint/protection 237
　reality check 229
　repair sections 228–229
　sandblasting 229
　top rail repairs 235

chassis replacement and restoration
　advice and considerations 216–217
　body removal 214
　bulkhead outrigger replacement
　　221–223
　cutting equipment 215
　dumb irons 223
　galvanising process 226
　options 213
　painting 226–227
　patching and flush repairs 224–226
　rear crossmember replacement
　　217–219
　rear half chassis replacement
　　219–220
　repair sections and materials
　　215–216
　rustproofing 227
　sandblasting/shotblasting 226
　welding equipment 215
clutch systems
　bleeding techniques 108–109
　clutch booster system 109
　clutch change 104–106
　evolution 100–101
　problems
　　clutch judder 102
　　clutch slip 102
　　failure to release 103–104

　　noisy clutch 104
　　remote servo 109
　　replace master and slave cylinder
　　　106–108
cooling system 92
　evolution
　　Series II 92
　　Series III 93–94
　　Series II/IIA 92–93
　maintenance
　　check for leaks 98
　　coolant hoses and hose clips
　　　97–98
　　coolant vs water 95
　　fan belts 95
　　flushing 95–96
　　Otterstat switch 99
　　pre-use/post-lay-up checks 95
　　temperature gauge and sender
　　　98–99
　　thermostat replacement 96–97
　　water pump replacement 96
　problems 94

diesel system
　exhaust and inlet manifolds 81
　exhaust systems 82–84
　　engine conversions 84
　fuel lift pump and filter 78
　fuel tanks 81–82
　glow plugs 81
　injection pump and injectors 78,
　　80–81
　　fitting and timing 79–80
　problems 78–79

electrical wire connections 211
electronic ignition 90
engine
　block reassembly process
　　camshaft fitting 62
　　crank fitting 59–60
　　diesel skew gear 64
　　distributor and skew gear fitting
　　　62–64

Index

piston fitting 60–61
conversions
  2.5-litre naturally aspirated diesel (12J code) 68
  2.5-litre petrol 67–68
  2.5-litre turbo diesel (19J Code) 68
  200Tdi Discovery/Defender 68–69
  300Tdi engine 69
  post-1981 2286cc petrol and diesel engines 67
  Rover V8 69–70
history and evolution 40–41
number prefix codes 70
removal and refitting 51
viability 35–36
exchange/repair gearbox 114
exhaust systems diesel system 82–84
export estate 267

gearbox
  assembly 123–128
  components inspection of
    bearings 119
    bushes 119
    gears 119
    shafts 118–119
  engineering changes 111
  exchange or repair 114
  factory-fit overdrive option 128–129
  fitting bearings
    front layshaft bearing 121–122
    front mainshaft bearing 120
    rear layshaft bearing 121
    rear mainshaft bearing 120
  high range transfer box 129
  identification numbers 110–111
  mainshaft assembly 122–123
  problems 112–113
  removing and refitting process 114–115
  Roamer/Roverdrive units 129
  stripping 115–118
  synchro and non-synchro 110
  Toro/Bearmach overdrive 129
  transmission modifications 128

identity and historical vehicle status 16
ignition system
  components
    coils 87–89
    condenser 86–87
    distributor 85–86
    distributor caps 87
    HT leads 87
    points 86
    rotor arm 87
    spark plugs 87
  electronic ignition 90
  high and low tension circuits 85
  problems 90–91
  timing
    dynamic timing 90
    principles of 89
    static timing and distributor orientation 89–90
internal trim
  bulkhead and footwell 270
  door cards 269
  floor matting 269–270
  headlining 269
  roof panel 269

Land Rover 109 V8 14
lighting
  availability and upgrades 265
  Series IIA models 1961–71 261
  Series III models 1971–85 261–263
  Series II models 1958–61 260–261
  switchgear 263–265

On the Rock method 48 51

petrol systems
  air cleaner box and intake hose 77–78
  carburettors 71
    issues 73
    replace and set up 73–74
    strip and rebuild 74–76
  fixed fuel lines 78
  fuel pumps and filters 71–72
    issues 72–73
  inlet and exhaust manifolds 76
  problems 72–73
  rubber fuel lines 78
propshafts
  orientation 161
  problems 158
  removing and refitting 159
  rubber gaiters 161
  universal joints 159–161

Rule of Nine technique 48, 49, 51

seat belts 267–269
seating 266–267

Series I history of 12
Series II IIA and III
  body fixing bolts
    BZP fixings 284–285
    UNF bolts 284
  canvas strip 274–275
  common engine problems
    2052cc and 2286cc diesel 41–42
    2286cc petrol 41
  door seals 272–273
  door top seals 275
  engine block reassembly process
    camshaft fitting 62
    crank fitting 59–60
    diesel skew gear 64
    distributor and skew gear fitting 62–64
    piston fitting 60–61
  engine components, assessment and preparation of
    block 56–58
    crank 58
    piston and con rod 58–59
  engine conversions
    2.5-litre naturally aspirated diesel (12J code) 68
    2.5-litre petrol 67–68
    2.5-litre turbo diesel (19J Code) 68
    200Tdi Discovery/Defender 68–69
    300Tdi engine 69
    post-1981 2286cc petrol and diesel engines 67
    Rover V8 69–70
  engine history and evolution 40–41
  engine number prefix codes 70
  engine removal and refitting 51
  factory process markings 282–283
  full engine strip-down
    camshaft removal 53–55
    crank and piston removal 55–56
    engine stand vs working on the floor 51–52
    front of engine block 52
    preamble to 52
    rear of engine block 52–53
  glazing 275–276
  grille and tub badges 281–282
  heater and demister system 273–274
  history of 13–15
  in-service engine assessment and repairs
    compression test 42

Index

Series II IIA and III *continued*
   cylinder head and bore
      inspection 45–47
   cylinder head and gasket removal
      44
   cylinder head gasket failure
      symptoms 43–44
   cylinder head refitting 47–48
   removing lapping and refitting
      valves 47
   setting valve clearances 48–49
   number plates 283–284
   period documents and literature
      285
   plates and decals 277–281
   restoration
      concourse standard 7–8
      file/celebration album 285
      functional rebuild/everyday
         restoration 10
      patina restoration 9–10
      resto/retro mod 8–9
   Series IIA identification
      bodywork and visual features
         20–22
      chassis details 17–19
      chassis number 16–17
      chassis number codes 28
      datable ancillary components
         25–26
      key component serial numbers
         24–25
      number plates 26–28
      original engine options 23–24
      vehicle history 28
   Series II identification
      bodywork and visual features 20
      chassis details 17–19
      chassis number 16–17
      chassis number codes 28
      datable ancillary components
         25–26
      key component serial numbers
         24–25
      number plates 26–28
      original engine options 23–24
      vehicle history 28
   Series III identification
      bodywork and visual features
         22–23
      chassis details 19
      chassis number 16–17
      chassis number codes 29
      datable ancillary components
         25–26
      key component serial numbers
         24–25
      number plates 26–28
      original engine options 23–24
      replacement chassis 19–20
      vehicle history 28
   timing chain fitting 64–66
steering
   ball joints 163–166
   conversions 171–172
   relay 166–167
   safety assessment 162–163
   setup 170 172
   steering box 167–170
   swivel assemblies 172
   wheel evolution 163
support networks 10
suspension
   changing spring/chassis bushes
      184–185
   chassis inspection 182
   damper inspection 182
   dampers/shock absorbers 187–188
   leaf spring inspection 181–183
   parabolic springs 183–184
   remove and refit springs 185–186
   reviving old springs 184
   ride on- and off-road 180
   U-bolt mountings 182–183
   walk round inspection 180–181

tax exemption rules 16
transfer box
   4WD selection problems 133–135
   bottom cover leaks 133
   cleanliness 138–140
   drive options 130
   evolution 130
   fixings 131
   front output seal replacement
      131–132
   large intermediate shaft 130
   problems 130–131
   rear output seal 132–133
   reassembly 140–143
   refitting 143
   removal 135
   small intermediate shaft 130
   split and strip 135–138
tyres
   classic tyre options 177–178
   DoT markings 179
   fitting and balancing 179
   modern tyre options 178
   safety and local legislation 178–179

upper and lower dashboards, Series III
   models 270–271

vent flaps and pins 271–272
vent seals 272
viability
   axles and steering 36–37
   body and paintwork 38–39
   brakes 37–38
   bulkhead repairs
      footwells and door pillars 34
      new bulkheads 34–35
      professional repairs 34–35
      top corners and vent panels 34
   chassis assessment
      chassis rails 33
      dumb irons 32
      outriggers 33
      rear crossmember 32
      replacement chassis 33–34
   engine assessment 35–36
   gearbox assessment 36
   interiors 39
   reality check 30–32
   suspension 37
   wiring assessment 37

wheels
   88in wheels 173
   109in wheels 173–174
   aftermarket options 174
   colours 176–177
   date stamping 177
   Discovery 1 steel wheels 176
   divided/split rims 174
   forward control/1-Ton wheels 174
   painting vs powder coating 177
   problems 177
   Rostyle wheels 174–176
   tube vs tubeless wheels 174
   wolf wheels 176
wiring
   charging systems 210–211
   colour identification system
      dash light circuits 204
      gauge circuits 204
      lighting circuit wires 204
      power distribution 204
      wiper motor wires 205
   dashboard 208
   electrical connections 211
   faults 212
   fuse boxes 209
   ignition switch 209–210
   looms 205–208